ARCHBISHOP, CHANCELLOR, KINGMAKER

ARCHBISHOP, CHANCELLOR, KINGMAKER

A Life of Thomas Arundel

CHRIS GIVEN-WILSON

YALE UNIVERSITY PRESS
NEW HAVEN AND LONDON

For information about this and other Yale University Press publications, please contact:
U.S. Office: sales.press@yale.edu yalebooks.com
Europe Office: sales@yaleup.co.uk yalebooks.co.uk

Set in Adobe Garamond Pro by IDSUK (DataConnection) Ltd

Printed and bound in the UK using 100% renewable electricity at CPI Group (UK) Ltd

Library of Congress Control Number: 2025942014
A catalogue record for this book is available from the British Library.
Authorized Representative in the EU: Easy Access System Europe, Mustamäe tee 50, 10621 Tallinn, Estonia, gpsr.requests@easproject.com

ISBN 978-0-300-28640-3

10 9 8 7 6 5 4 3 2 1

Contents

Illustrations

Plates

Genealogical Tables

Note on Money

From Anglo-Saxon times until February 1971, English money was reckoned in pounds (£, for *libra*), shillings (*s.*, for *solidus*) and pennies (*d.*, for *denarius*). There were twelve pence in a shilling and twenty shillings in a pound – thus 240*d.* in £1. The actual coins in circulation were silver pennies and shillings. Gold coins valued at one pound ('sovereigns') were first minted in 1489. Marks, reckoned at two-thirds of a pound (13*s.* 4*d.*), were also used as a money of account. To avoid confusion, I have generally changed contemporary valuations in marks into their equivalent value in pounds, shillings and pence, except when quoting original sources.

Preface

In December 2005, a BBC poll sought nominations for the ten most infamous British villains of the previous millennium, one from each century. Several of the names that emerged as 'winners' are unsurprising: for the twentieth century, Oswald Mosley; for the nineteenth, Jack the Ripper; for the thirteenth, King John. Also included were two archbishops of Canterbury: for the twelfth century, St Thomas Becket, who 'divided England in a way that even many churchmen who shared some of his views thought unnecessary and self-indulgent'; and for the fifteenth century (ahead of, for example, Richard III), Thomas Arundel, the subject of this book, who 'used his authority to persecute the Lollards, a group promoting lay priesthood and translations of the Bible'.[1]

Thomas Cranmer, the first Protestant archbishop of Canterbury (1533–55), would not have demurred. In 1540, as the epochal religious reforms of the 1530s reached their climax, Cranmer oversaw the demolition and removal of the free-standing chantry chapel which Arundel had endowed to enclose his tomb-chest in the nave of Canterbury cathedral 130 years earlier. Nothing was left but 'a bare gravestone levelled with the floor'.[2] England's early Protestants such as Cranmer, John Foxe and John Bale loathed Arundel. They believed that he had introduced to England the practice of burning heretics. To the modern mind, a heretic-burning medieval archbishop might well evoke Oscar Wilde's epithet on fox-hunting – 'the unspeakable in pursuit of the uneatable' – but to imagine that, had we lived in different times, we would have upheld the values of our own times, is really just another form of what E. P. Thompson called 'the enormous condescension of posterity'.[3]

It would be equally simplistic to blame vindictive Protestant historiography for the difficulties involved in presenting medieval Catholic prelates in an attractive light. Pilloried and satirized by both lay and clerical contemporaries as proud, worldly, venal and reactionary (to which the modern age has added the charge of incorrigible patriarchy), they are widely seen as culpable for the hypocrisy and intolerance of a Church which wielded power far in excess of its desire to exercise it for the benefit of society at large. Easier to commend nowadays are those, especially those within the Church, who fought against the tide, trying to reform the Church and return it to the ideals of poverty, simplicity, charity and humility advocated by Jesus: men such as St Francis of Assisi and women such as St Catherine of Siena – or perhaps even Lollards.

That Arundel arouses strong feelings is not surprising. Born in 1353, he became bishop of Ely at the age of twenty, below the canonical age, and went on to hold successively the archbishoprics of York (1388–96) and Canterbury (1396–1414) during a time of turmoil for Christianity, notably the Great Schism of the Western Church (1378–1417) and the Lollard movement, the first serious outbreak of heresy in England for a millennium. From his first robust intervention in secular politics, in the parliament of October 1385, he never shied away from confrontation. Between 1386 and 1414, he also held office as chancellor of England – in effect, the king's chief minister – on five separate occasions, totalling over twelve years. Exiled and deprived of his archbishopric in 1397 for his opposition to King Richard II, he returned two years later to orchestrate the revolution whereby he and Henry of Bolingbroke overthrew the king. Bolingbroke became King Henry IV and Arundel was restored to Canterbury. Three more times he served Henry as chancellor. The only other archbishop of Canterbury since 1066 to have served simultaneously as chancellor for more than twelve months was Hubert Walter (1199–1205).[4] Thomas Becket famously, and a number of others less dramatically, resigned as chancellor when elected archbishop. There was no tradition in medieval England of the head of the Church also acting as head of the royal administration. Rather, Arundel was the precursor of the great archiepiscopal chancellors of the early Tudor period: John Morton (1487–1500), William Warham (1504–15) and Thomas Wolsey (archbishop of York and chancellor 1515–28).[5]

The best account of Arundel's life prior to his exile is Margaret Aston's *Thomas Arundel: A Study of Church Life in the Reign of Richard II* (1967), but she only told his story as far as September 1397, whereas, as she pointed out, the years from 1399 to 1414 were 'the most outstanding and influential of his whole life, and brought the full impact of his person and position to bear upon the secular and ecclesiastical events of his time'.[6] Aston's meticulous research makes it unnecessary to go back in detail over the first forty-four years of Arundel's life, but they are sketched out in the Introduction, relying largely on her work. This book is therefore a biography of Arundel from 1397 until his death in 1414. Aston also provided a more nuanced and generally more favourable picture of Arundel than the popular image – but it is, of course, never easy to dislodge a popular image.

I am grateful to the following for their help at various stages during the writing of this book: Cressida Williams, Library and Archives Manager at Canterbury cathedral; the ever-helpful staff at Lambeth Palace Library, the British Library and St Andrews University Library; Heather McCallum for her enthusiasm and the many others at Yale University Press who helped to bring this book to fruition; and the anonymous readers to whom Yale University Press sent the typescript and who provided such useful comments. This book is dedicated to my daughters, Rachel and Hannah, and my grandchildren, Roxana, Neko, Luna and Cody, for the joy they bring to my life.

Introduction
1353–97

Late on a summer afternoon in 1413, while staying at Lambeth palace, the archbishop of Canterbury received a visit from the mystic and visionary Margery Kempe, which she later recounted in her autobiography. Margery was eccentric. She wept copiously in public, gesticulating and crying out for God's forgiveness, claiming to hear heavenly melodies or to be conversing with Jesus or his mother Mary. She preached, which was forbidden to women by the Catholic Church. Onlookers mocked her and told her to shut up, or accused her of being a heretic, so she was probably accustomed to the welcome she received at Lambeth. As she passed through the hall of the palace, a number of the archbishop's esquires and yeomen 'swore great oaths and spoke reckless words' to her, but she 'boldly reproached them that unless they ceased their swearing, they would be damned'. Moving on, she was accosted by a woman in a fur coat who 'cursed her most abominably', telling her that if she could, she would 'bring a faggot to burn you' (as a heretic), for 'it is a pity that you are alive'.

Eventually Margery found her way through to the palace garden, where the archbishop awaited her. She had come to ask him to grant her two privileges: to be allowed to choose her own confessor, and to receive communion every Sunday. Both were highly unusual, especially for a woman of her social status (she was the daughter of a merchant from King's Lynn in Norfolk). The Church decreed that lay people need only confess their sins and take communion once a year, but Margery often confessed twice a day. Nevertheless, after listening to her, the archbishop granted her wishes 'most benignly', even refusing to allow his clerks to take the customary fee for writing out a letter authorizing her privileges. Then they sat together in the garden, the two of them, and she told him about her way of life, and 'the grace that God worked in her mind and in her soul', and asked him whether he 'found any fault in either her contemplation or her weeping'. He told her that he did not, and that 'he approved her manner of living, and was right glad that our merciful lord Jesus Christ showed such grace in our times'. When she rebuked him for allowing members of his household to swear, he listened 'benignly and meekly', allowing her to have her say. They continued talking 'until stars appeared in the firmament', and when, eventually, their conversation ended, she left him 'well comforted and strengthened in her soul'.[1]

The archbishop was Thomas Arundel (henceforth, and throughout this book, simply 'Arundel'). He was sixty years old in 1413 and had been a bishop for forty years, archbishop of Canterbury for sixteen and chancellor of England intermittently for nearly three decades. His social status was also very different from Margery's. Born between March and August 1353, he was the third and youngest son of Richard Fitzalan, tenth earl of Arundel (1330–76) and his second wife, Eleanor, the daughter of the earl of Lancaster. Four of his siblings survived into adulthood: Richard (b. 1346), who succeeded his father as the eleventh earl; Joan (b. *c.* 1347), who became countess of Hereford and Arundel's lifelong friend and confidante; John (b. *c.* 1349), who became marshal of England; and Alice (b. *c.* 1350), who became countess of Kent.[2] This was a family with broad and powerful connections, one of the four or five greatest in the country. Arundel and his siblings never lacked money, for their father was the richest lord in fourteenth-century England. At his death in 1376, he left over £60,000 in cash alone, more than half of it in chests in the High Tower of Arundel castle. The sources of his wealth were entrepreneurial management of his great estates in Sussex and the

Welsh March, capital investment with foreign and English merchants, and the profits of influence and credit, for he held high governmental positions and regularly loaned large sums to lords, to mercantile syndicates and to King Edward III. His returns were not just further financial profit but also influence and favours for himself and his family.[3]

Thomas was an uncommon name in the Arundel family. Perhaps the tenth earl named his third son after the boy's maternal great-uncle, Earl Thomas of Lancaster, who was executed for treason by King Edward II in 1322 but had come to be popularly venerated as a martyr. Perhaps he was named, as were many children in medieval England, after England's most celebrated saint, Thomas Becket, murdered in his cathedral in 1170. Either way, it seems that from the time of his boyhood his father planned a career in the Church for his youngest son, and it was with this in mind that in 1369–70, aged sixteen, Arundel was sent to Oxford, where he studied for his B.A. at Oriel College. Oriel was doubtless delighted, for to mark his gratitude Earl Richard built a new college chapel, the construction of which his son supervised. Simultaneously, Arundel acquired a number of ecclesiastical livings, the most significant of which was the archdeaconry of Taunton (Somerset). In 1372, he was also granted a pension of £67 a year from Canterbury cathedral, an indication of his growing repute and, no doubt, of the value of his father's good will.[4] All this paled, however, by comparison with his provision by Pope Gregory XI to the well-endowed bishopric of Ely in August 1373, at the age of twenty. 'No one so young has been appointed to a see', commented the pope, but he had agreed at the request of Arundel's father, 'whose example in defending ecclesiastical liberties the pope exhorts him to follow'. Earl Richard had visited Avignon several times as Edward III's ambassador. Crucially, he also secured the king's support for his son's provision, even though Edward III had initially proposed his confessor, John Woderove, for the see.[5] Money surely changed hands at some point to secure Arundel's promotion.

Although his provision to Ely turned out to mark the beginning of one of the most illustrious episcopal careers in the medieval English

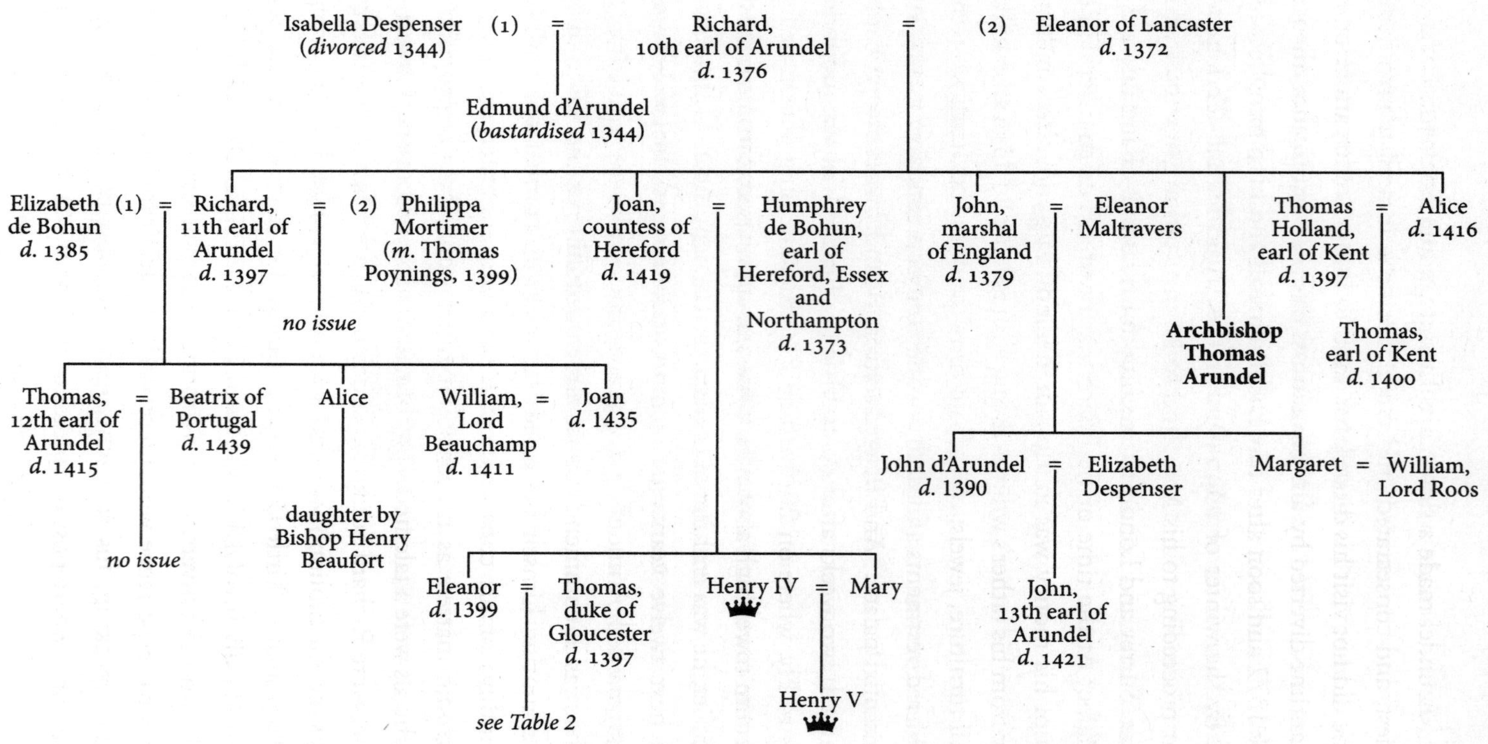

Table 1. The descendants of Richard, tenth earl of Arundel, *c.* 1340 to 1430.

Church, Arundel made a slow start. Despite being ordained as deacon and priest, and consecrated as bishop, all on the same day, on 9 April 1374, he did not visit his diocese for another two years, his attention in the meantime diverted by family matters. His mother, Eleanor, died in January 1372 and soon after this Earl Richard appears to have become infirm. By the winter of 1373–4, therefore, Arundel had left Oxford without proceeding to his M.A. and spent much of the next two years in Sussex, Surrey and London attending to his father's estates and business affairs.[6] At the time of Earl Richard's death on 24 January 1376, £2,000 of his money was in Arundel's hands. Arundel also benefited directly from his father's will, receiving a legacy of £1,333 in cash and a hoard of furniture, jewels, chalices, crosses, candlesticks, coffers, ewers, embroidered vestments and hangings – enough, perhaps, to furnish his first episcopal palace.[7] And it was to his episcopal duties that Arundel now turned: two weeks after his father's death he left Sussex and made his way to Ely, where on 20 April 1376, under the magnificent octagonal lantern tower high above the cathedral crossing, constructed thirty years earlier, he was enthroned as bishop.

The next twelve years, until he was promoted to be archbishop of York, marked Arundel's episcopal apprenticeship. From 1376 to 1386 he was a commendably attentive bishop, touring his diocese and acquainting himself with the responsibilities of his officials and the workings of his consistory (diocesan) court in such perennially troublesome matters as matrimonial and testamentary disputes. His chief officials were a talented, loyal and learned group, the most notable of whom were Richard Scrope, Henry Bowet (both future archbishops of York) and the bibliophile John Newton.[8] His preferred residence was Downham manor (Little Downham), three miles north of Ely.[9] He was also periodically involved in the ever-delicate relationship between the Church and the universities of Cambridge (which was in his diocese) and Oxford, experience which would later stand him in good stead.[10] Generally speaking, his rule at Ely was characterized by a desire to vindicate or – where possible – extend the rights of the Church, and a tendency to secure compliance in principle while showing a willingness to compromise in practice.[11]

Arundel enjoyed a 'lordly, peripatetic, hospitable' lifestyle, as befitted the bishop of one of England's wealthier sees, and he was generous to his servants.[12] His episcopal household of around eighty servants and between forty and seventy horses cost him an average of about £1,000 a year. He and it moved regularly along well-trodden paths, or sometimes fenland waterways, between his manors at Downham, Holborn, Hatfield, Fen Ditton and Ely, often entertaining guests when they stopped for more than a night or two. Among those who dined with him in November and December 1383, when he was based firstly at Holborn (London), for the parliament, and then at Hatfield, were his brother Richard (eleventh earl of Arundel); his sister Joan; John Buckingham, bishop of Lincoln; Thomas of Woodstock, earl of Buckingham; John Waltham, master of the rolls of chancery; and Lords Lovell and Beaumont. John Lovell was a particular friend, the only lay lord to dine in Arundel's household more than once during these months and the recipient of a number of gifts including a fur gown worth £2; he remained a lifelong friend.[13]

An Ely chronicler remembered Arundel as a generous benefactor and a bishop who consolidated (*corroboravit*) the temporalities of the see and ruled rigorously (*strenuissime*), overcoming the Church's enemies. He also spent considerable sums on building or refurbishing work at several of his manors, especially Holborn (or 'Ely Palace'), the bishops' traditional London residence, where he rebuilt the gatehouse, and at Ely itself, where he was praised for constructing 'beautiful and sumptuous buildings' and presenting the cathedral with a number of rich vestments and ornaments, including a golden reliquary 'full of relics of saints' worth £200, which he had purchased from the Black Prince, who had received it from the 'king of Spain'.[14] No details survive of his rebuilding work at Ely, but it was focused on the bishop's palace rather than the cathedral.

Arundel also actively patronized a clutch of Cambridge-educated lawyers who worked in the Ely consistory court. As well as Richard

Scrope and John Newton, they included Walter Hilton, who, following a legal career, briefly retired to live as a hermit before spending the last ten years of his life (1386–96) as an Augustinian canon at Thurgarton priory (Nottinghamshire). Hilton was one of the most influential spiritual authors of his day, compiling several treatises on prayer, meditation and the 'mixed life' – that is, the balance to be struck between engagement with the world and reclusive contemplation. These are the themes of his best-known works, such as his *Letter on Reading, Intention, Prayer and Meditation*, his *Scale of Perfection* (which survives in sixty-two manuscripts) and his *Epistle on the Mixed Life*.[15] One of the fundamental questions with which Hilton and his admirers grappled was the latitude which might be allowed to recluses, mystics and other lay folk who, like Margery Kempe, wanted to pursue their own spiritual paths without ecclesiastical supervision – paths which might exclude strict adherence to Catholic worship yet which many devout laity found attractive. What, in other words, was the best way to provide the kind of broad and humane pastoral guidance which preserved the devotional inspiration of intense spiritual experiences while not allowing matters to slip beyond the Church's purview, let alone veer towards heterodoxy?

It was in part the immense popularity of the writings of the hermit Richard Rolle of Hampole (d. 1349) which made this necessary. Rolle, a prolific author whose works survive in over four hundred fourteenth- and fifteenth-century manuscripts, had extolled the solitary life as the only true way to experience the reality of God's 'warmth' (*fervor*) and thereby to come to know Him better. It was this way of living, he claimed, which allowed him to hear angelic choirs, to enjoy deep mystical encounters and, inspired by the Holy Spirit, to acquire an inner understanding of the Scriptures. After his death, his hermitage at Hampole (Yorkshire) became a place of veneration and pilgrimage, and, although he was never canonized, miracles were reported to have occurred there.[16]

Yet, although Rolle's rejection of institutionalized religious worship was implicit rather than explicit, neither Hilton nor Arundel could fail to perceive the danger to the Church of the widespread adoption of such practices. The challenge, naturally, was to ensure that reductionist or unrealistic expectations did not lead to the repudiation of ecclesiastical authority. Processions, mystery plays, images, saints' cults old and new, even new forms of administration of the sacraments could help to achieve this by intensifying – even popularizing – traditional forms of worship, but it was never an easy balance to strike. Hilton and others warned in their works against striving to achieve the kind of experiences which Rolle had described, and of the necessity to attend to their social and communal responsibilities as well as their souls: in other words, the mixed life. And if Hilton was the outstanding spiritual thinker within this circle, there were many others who followed where he led, such as the Carmelite friars Thomas Fishlake (who translated the *Scale of Perfection* into Latin) and John Pole, as well as Scrope and Newton.

When Arundel was promoted to York in 1388, several of his clerks at Ely followed him. Here they continued the work initiated by Archbishop Thoresby (1353–73), which had focused on improving the education, conduct and pastoral care of the priesthood through close supervision of the religious life of his diocese.[17] Thoresby's successor at York, Alexander Nevill (1373–88), did little to advance this, and by the time Arundel succeeded him there were new challenges to face. Lollardy (the 'English heresy') was first identified around 1380–1 as a significant problem among a group of Oxford scholars who espoused the thinking of the university's premier logician, John Wyclif.[18] Wyclif himself left Oxford in late 1381, spending the remaining three years of his life at Lutterworth (Leicestershire), but his principal academic followers – Philip Repingdon, Nicholas Hereford and John Aston – continued actively to promulgate his views at the university, prompting William Courtenay (archbishop of Canterbury 1381–96) to summon a synod to the London Blackfriars in May 1382 to devise measures to suppress them. Although fundamentally an intellectual rejection of certain elements of Catholic dogma, Lollardy was also seen by some as the consequence of the uncontrolled spread of the kind of individualized religious experience popularized by Rolle and his followers. Arundel encountered little heresy while at Ely and was not one of the nine bishops whom Courtenay summoned to Blackfriars, but following another upsurge of Lollard agitation at the time of the 1388 parliament, when he was chancellor, the council introduced stricter measures to identify and suppress heresy. Later, as primate, he would come to be almost obsessively preoccupied with heterodoxy.[19]

Arundel's promotion to York in April 1388 was primarily in recognition of the prominent role which he had by now assumed in the government of the kingdom. As one of the twenty-one bishops of England and Wales, he had been summoned to every parliament since the dramatic Good Parliament of April 1376, an assembly which cannot have failed to impress upon him both the fragility of power and the potential for the combined resolve of commons and lords to hold the government to account.[20] Following the accession of the ten-year-old King Richard II in June 1377, Arundel's name began to figure more prominently in the parliamentary record: every meeting from October 1377 to February 1383 saw him nominated as a trier (scrutineer) of petitions, and in November 1381 he was one of eighteen lords spiritual and temporal appointed to a commission for 'the amendment of the government' in the wake of the Great Revolt.[21] Commissions of reform had also been appointed in the April 1379 and January 1380 parliaments, and would be again in 1385, but once parliament ended the king and his ministers ignored them.[22] Here too was a lesson for a young bishop: that it took more than a royal promise to hold a king to his word.

There was, of course, much more to politics than parliaments, and as an aristocrat as well as a bishop Arundel found it harder than most of his episcopal colleagues to avoid it. It is sometimes thought that the fourteenth century witnessed an increase in the number of aristocratic bishops, but this was not the case. Just fifteen of the eighty-five bishops who held sees under Edward III were of noble birth, almost exactly the same proportion as under Henry III a century earlier.[23] What did change was, firstly, the distinction of the families which provided members of the episcopacy in the later fourteenth century and, secondly, the status of the sees they held. Arundel, William Courtenay (his predecessor at Canterbury), Alexander Nevill (his predecessor at York), Henry Beaufort of Lincoln, Edmund Stafford of Exeter, and Thomas Percy and Henry Despenser (both of Norwich) all came from families which either held an earldom or would do so before the century was out. Equally great men had held sees before – Henry of Blois, for example, the younger brother of King Stephen, was bishop of Winchester from 1129 to 1171 – but never in such numbers. This naturally increased the chances of the rivalries or alliances of England's great aristocratic families resonating in the ecclesiastical arena. Henry Despenser, for example, was descended from Hugh Despenser the younger (d. 1326), whose daughter Isabella had been the tenth earl of Arundel's first wife; when Earl Richard divorced Isabella in 1344 he also retrospectively bastardized and thus disinherited the son she had borne him, Edmund. Not surprisingly, Edmund did not accept this, and following Earl Richard's death in 1376 he agitated for his disinheritance to be reversed.[24] As his uncle, Bishop Despenser felt honour-bound to take up Edmund's case – even planning to take it to Rome, until the king forbade him in no uncertain terms to do so.[25]

Yet if Earl Richard's divorce from Isabella Despenser in 1344 soured relations between the Fitzalans and the Despensers, his remarriage in the same year to Eleanor of Lancaster laid the groundwork for an alliance of far greater significance between the Fitzalan and Lancastrian families. John of Gaunt, Richard II's uncle and duke of Lancaster from 1362 to 1399, was by some way the most powerful man in England after the king, and at least during the first few years of his nephew's reign he could count on the support of the Fitzalans. In 1381, the two families colluded in the abduction of the twelve-year-old Mary, joint heiress to the great de Bohun patrimony, from the custody of the nuns into whose care Gaunt's brother, the earl of Buckingham, had consigned her. Buckingham had hoped that she would remain unmarried and that the entire de Bohun inheritance would thus pass to his own wife, Eleanor (Mary's sister). But he underestimated the girls' vigorous and independent-minded mother, Countess Joan of Hereford (Arundel's sister), who spirited Mary away to Arundel castle, where she was quickly betrothed to Gaunt's son Henry (the future Henry IV). They married at Joan's manor of Rochford (Essex) a few weeks later. According to the chronicler Jean Froissart, Buckingham 'never after loved the duke of Lancaster as he had done hitherto'.[26]

So much was at stake in the affairs of these great families, and so tangled were the ties of blood, marriage or common cause that coupled or uncoupled them, that few alliances stood the test of time and, once ruptured, it took cool heads to repair them. Unfortunately, not all the Arundel siblings were blessed with cool heads. Arundel's two older brothers, Earl Richard and Sir John, were violent and impetuous men, imbued to the core with the militaristic ethos of a warrior nobility and ever eager to undertake martial enterprises. The high point of John's career was his appointment in 1377 as marshal of England, but two years later he was drowned in a storm off the Irish coast – a disaster for which he, as commander of the fleet, was widely held responsible.[27] Earl Richard would live for another eighteen years, displaying throughout a surly determination to play the ultimately tragic role of Richard II's nemesis. Their first open clash came at the Salisbury parliament of April 1384, when an intemperate speech by the earl appearing to blame the king for all the realm's ills led to Richard II, 'white with passion', shouting at the earl, 'You lie in your teeth! You can go to the Devil!'[28] Words soon turned to blows: on 25 January 1386, during an argument (probably) about the squandering of financial resources, the king punched Earl Richard to the ground.[29]

Although more circumspect than his brothers, Arundel's first significant intervention in affairs of state made it clear where his sympathies lay. This came in the parliament of October 1385, but it was rooted in Bishop Despenser's disastrous 'Flemish Crusade' two years earlier, following which Despenser was impeached in parliament and deprived of his temporalities (the major portion of his episcopal income). Prominent among Despenser's accusers was Michael de la Pole, Richard II's chancellor, whom Earl Richard and Arundel regarded as the epitome of all that reeked about the government and the royal court. At this stage, Arundel's loyalties must have been divided, for he had been a member of the joint committee of lords and commons which, in February 1383, had recommended approval of Despenser's campaign rather than John of Gaunt's plan to lead a campaign to Iberia – a harbinger of the eventual fracturing of the Lancaster–Arundel axis. As a bishop, moreover, it was neither in his interests nor to his liking to see great ecclesiastics punished so severely, regardless of any lingering animosity between his family and Despenser's. Indeed, he apparently tried to protect Despenser from the king's wrath.[30]

The seizure of Despenser's temporalities posed a threat to ecclesiastical liberties, which Arundel always held dear. Two years later, the parliament of October 1385 witnessed an escalation of this threat when some of the lay lords and commons proposed the confiscation of all ecclesiastical temporalities so that they could be used to help finance the war. Thanks to the vigorous resistance of Archbishop Courtenay, this scheme was scotched, but it provided the opening for Arundel to plead for Despenser's temporalities to be restored to him.[31] According to the St Albans chronicler Thomas Walsingham, chancellor de la Pole – newly promoted to the earldom of Suffolk – rounded on Arundel:

> What is this, lord bishop, that you are asking? Surely you do not regard it as a trivial matter for the king to give up the temporalities of Norwich now, which provide him with a revenue of more than a thousand pounds annually? The king has no need of counsellors like you; he does not need such men as friends who want to rob him of so much money.

But Arundel was not a man to buckle: 'What do you mean, Sir Michael?' he retorted:

> I am not asking the king for what belongs to him, but what belongs to someone else, which he has no just right to withhold, for this situation has pertained because he is under the influence of your iniquitous counsel and that of men like you. If you are so concerned about the king's losses, why did you accept from him so eagerly an annual income of a thousand marks [£666] when he made you earl of Suffolk?

According to Walsingham, de la Pole reacted 'as if struck by a javelin [and] did not dare to offer any further opposition in this matter'. Despenser's temporalities were restored on 24 October.[32]

It would not be long before Arundel was obliged to live up to his words, for exactly one year later, on 24 October 1386, he replaced de la Pole as chancellor of England. The intervening twelve months had seen the government lurch from bankruptcy to panic to humiliation. Exchequer debt, already dangerously high, spiralled out of control as the flow of cash dried up. The royal household, increasingly obliged to borrow or anticipate revenue in order to cover its daily costs, defaulted on its creditors; merchant syndicates became ever more reluctant to advance loans. Compounding the crisis, England faced its first serious invasion scare for 170 years when, in the spring of 1386, a French fleet gathered at Sluys (Flanders), preparing to cross the Channel. By August, London and the south-eastern counties were in a state of consternation: magnate retinues were summoned, local militias assembled, defences hastily erected.[33] John of Gaunt, pursuing his claim to the throne of Castile, had left England in early July and would not return for three years. Perhaps this emboldened the French; it also left the field open for other English magnates such as Gaunt's brother Thomas, duke of Gloucester (formerly earl of Buckingham), to assume a more active political role.

In the event, contrary winds prevented the French from invading, but not before parliament had met at Westminster on 1 October 1386 and been presented by chancellor de la Pole with a statement that the government would need to raise the unprecedented sum of £155,000 – equivalent to four tenths and fifteenths[34] – to meet its mounting obligations. The outraged lords and commons demanded 'with one assent' that he be dismissed forthwith 'because they had matters to resolve with Michael de la Pole which they could not pursue while he held the office of chancellor'.[35] What they meant was that he should be impeached. The king, who saw challenges to his regal authority as bordering on treason, retired in high dudgeon to his manor of Eltham (Kent). When the members told him that no further progress could be made without his attendance, he invited them to send forty members of the commons to him. What he got was a delegation led by Arundel and the duke of Gloucester.

Their conversation with the king, or at least the substance of it, has been preserved. It was 'anciently established', they declared, that if a king, through his own 'irresponsible resolution', absented himself from parliament for more than forty days, the members were at liberty to return to their homes. Richard replied that if his subjects continued to resist him, he would 'seek the support of our cousin [the king] of France against our enemies', for it was 'better to submit ourselves to him than to our own subjects'. This, they told him, was most unwise: the king of France was his foremost enemy and generations of Englishmen had died fighting the French, to say nothing of the taxation raised to prosecute the war, much of which had been squandered by his incompetent ministers. Finally – just in case Richard was still inclined to resist – Arundel and Gloucester came to the nub of the matter: there was an 'ancient law', they told him, that if a king refused to abide by the laws of the land or the counsel of his nobles, but instead followed his 'intemperate will', it would be lawful, by common assent, to depose him and replace him with another member of the royal family, 'as had happened recently'. The reference was, of course, to the deposition of Edward II sixty years previously: and unless Richard was prepared to dismiss his current ministers, 'there would be little or nothing they could do to save you'.[36]

This brought the king to his senses: de la Pole was dismissed on 23 October, impeached and sentenced to imprisonment. Arundel became chancellor, and by the time parliament ended five weeks later a commission of government comprising fourteen lords spiritual and temporal had been established to govern the country for the next twelve months.[37] The nineteen-year-old king had been sidelined and power had been transferred to a magnate committee and their nominated ministers, chief of whom was Chancellor Arundel.

Apart from his aristocratic connections and a readiness to speak his mind, it is not easy to see why at least some of his contemporaries believed that the thirty-three-year-old Arundel had the experience or qualities to run the chancery. He may have been appointed to (ineffective) parliamentary commissions and attended a few meetings of the king's council, but he had never held public office, let alone run a government department. Probably more important, especially to the clerics, was that he had a reputation as a defender of ecclesiastical liberties, both in his diocese and at national level. He also had a reputation for integrity, at least in reformist circles.[38] And although his term as chancellor was marred by royalist sabotage and factionalism culminating in a brief period of civil war, Arundel came through it with his reputation intact. He would return as chancellor four more times during the following twenty-five years.

His first chancellorship covered the thirty angry months between November 1386 and May 1389.[39] Despite the formal swearing-in of the commissioners on 19 November 1386, Richard adopted obstructionist tactics designed to make it as difficult as possible for them to do their job. De la Pole, after the briefest spell in custody, was back at court in time for Christmas. Between February and November 1387, the king and his household spent no more than three or four weeks in the vicinity of London, instead touring the Midlands and North-West, avoiding the commissioners' scrutiny and recruiting support in the shires for Richard's planned revenge. The nature and scale of the latter became clear in August 1387 when, summoning the royal justices, he obliged them to answer his infamous 'Questions to the Judges', the implication of which was that those who had been instrumental in the establishment of the commission or the impeachment of de la Pole deserved to be executed as traitors.

When news of this reached the commissioners, the more radical among them, led by the duke of Gloucester and Arundel's brother Earl Richard, reacted with a decisiveness born of genuine fear. The commissioners had never been united in their opposition to Richard, and the Questions to the Judges definitively sundered whatever unity of purpose they had had. Gloucester and Earl Richard, soon joined by the earls of Warwick, Derby and Nottingham, challenged Richard directly by bringing an appeal of treason (as a result of which they are known to history as the Appellants) against five of his leading supporters: Robert de Vere, duke of Ireland; Michael de la Pole; Alexander Nevill; Nicholas Brembre, mayor of London; and the chief justice, Robert Tresilian.

Initially the king tried to raise the Londoners against them, but the citizens refused; a fraught period of negotiations, in which Arundel played a leading part, eventually left Richard with no option but to accept that the appeal would be heard in a parliament to be held in the new year. But the king was merely playing for time. De Vere was dispatched to Chester, where he raised an army of royalist retainers and marched south, but he was intercepted at Radcot Bridge (Oxfordshire) where, on 20 December 1387, his makeshift force was routed by the Appellant retinues. De Vere escaped and fled abroad, as did de la Pole and Nevill. None of them would ever be seen in England again. Meanwhile, the victorious Appellants marched to London, where they purged the royal household, dismissed and arrested dozens of the king's officers and courtiers, and took control of the royal administration. With the parliament promised by Richard due to meet at Westminster on 3 February, England held its breath.

The 'Merciless' Parliament of 3 February to 4 June 1388 – the longest parliament held in England to date – fully deserved its name. It began with the five Appellants, dressed in identical livery gowns of gold-threaded brocade, their arms linked to signify unbreakable resolve, processing ceremonially into the White Chamber of Westminster palace and formally reiterating their appeal of treason to the enthroned Richard. Although the three principal culprits had fled, Brembre and Tresilian were not so lucky. Both were tried, convicted and subjected to the full horrors of a traitor's death, 'drenching the streets with their flesh, in the accustomed manner for traitors', as the Appellants' apologist Thomas Favent exulted.

By the time the parliament ended, despite increasing distaste among the lords and widespread unease about the legal basis of their convictions, another six of the king's supporters, including his former tutor, Sir Simon Burley, had also been executed; some thirty knights, clerks and other royalists had been dismissed from court; and two bishops (Nevill and the king's confessor, Thomas Rushook) had been convicted of treason and exiled.[40] Also exiled were the six justices who had agreed to the Questions to the Judges, spared the scaffold only after their plea of coercion was accepted. Not for sixty years, since the blood-soaked climax to Edward II's misrule, had England witnessed such an orgy of quasi-judicial aristocratic barbarity. Numbed and humiliated, overridden or silenced if he attempted to intervene, Richard was reduced to the role of impotent onlooker as, one by one, his friends went to their fates. And, although he learned to bide his time, he never forgot.

Since canon law dictated that clergy should absent themselves from trials involving the death penalty, Arundel and the other prelates were spared the difficult choices facing all but the most implacable of the king's opponents. There were certainly times when Arundel might have intervened: the Westminster chronicler accused him of failing to uphold Tresilian's right of sanctuary in the abbey (where he was found hiding).[41] But in general the role either assumed by or assigned to Arundel, especially during the critical months leading up to the Merciless Parliament, was that of mediator between Richard and the Appellants. Evidently trusted by both sides, he acted as the king's spokesman to the lords while ensuring, sometimes with brutal clarity, that Richard understood how narrow was his range of options. It was during this time of crisis that Arundel acquired that reputation for plain speaking and powerful oratory which he would retain for the rest of his life. It was he, for example, who was chosen to try to persuade the querulous London guilds to shelve their differences. As chancellor, he also made a 'most wise and eloquent' opening speech to parliament, and announced to the lords and commons the decision to exile rather than execute the justices.[42]

It was this burgeoning stature within the English hierarchy which was recognized when Arundel replaced the exiled Nevill as archbishop of York.[43] At the same time he continued to serve as chancellor.[44] At his initial appointment in October 1386, what many had expected from him was not just effective supervision of the royal administration but also reform. Given the circumstances attending his two-and-a-half-year tenure of the office, it was clear that meaningful reform would be difficult to implement, yet reforms there were, the most keenly anticipated of which were the dispersal of the miasma of cronyism clinging to the royal administration and the restoration of confidence in crown finance. The former was certainly achieved, if not without bloodshed. The latter took time, with reform measures concentrated during the earlier and later periods of Arundel's tenure, either side of the crisis months from October 1387 to June 1388. Along with the treasurer, John Gilbert, bishop of Hereford, Arundel and the commissioners managed to stabilize – though certainly not wholly resolve – the cash flow to departments such as the royal household, partly by reducing superfluous expenditure.[45] There were also administrative reforms – or at any rate consequences – such as the restriction of the king's ability to override chancery warrants by using his signet (his personal seal, which he wore as a ring), and the amalgamation of the records of the chancery and privy seal in the Tower of London, a measure designed to coordinate the work of the two departments.[46] The fact that Arundel enjoyed good personal relations and a common sense of purpose with both Gilbert and the privy seal keeper, John Waltham, must have helped to facilitate this.

At some point in 1388–9 Arundel issued a set of twenty-five ordinances for the roughly one hundred and twenty clerks who staffed the royal chancery.[47] In the main, these codified and clarified existing practice rather than introducing novel measures – and, following the irregularities and confusion of the mid-1380s, clarification was badly needed. The parliamentary commons certainly believed that there was much about the chancery's working practices that needed to be regularized. Among the charges laid against de la Pole in 1386 was the allegation that he had sealed letters patent dealing with 'murders, treason, felonies, erasures of rolls and sales of laws' without proper warrant. He had also granted to the king's favourite, Sir Simon Burley, franchises at Dover castle which were 'to the disinheritance of the crown and the subversion of . . . the courts of the king and of his laws'. De la Pole's reply was that he had a warrant for the grant, but the commons declined to accept this and said it should be annulled. Three weeks after Arundel became chancellor, therefore, he cancelled the grant, declaring that the warrant for it had been issued 'irregularly' under the king's signet.[48] It is not surprising, then, that a principal issue addressed by Arundel's ordinances was the authority required for issuing warrants. There is not a single instance throughout the first two years of his chancellorship of the signet being accepted as an adequate warrant for the great seal.[49]

Arundel also confirmed – or perhaps reinstated – the traditional distinctions between the three different grades (or 'forms') of chancery clerks and the arrangements for them to be able to live and work together, simultaneously insisting that they should all remain unmarried, thereby keeping clerical influence in the chancery immune from the creeping secular influence manifesting itself in the treasury.[50] What these ordinances reveal is Arundel's characteristic concern for reform through the elucidation and redefinition of existing procedure, his preference for the reaffirmation and tightening up of good practice rather than a taste for novelty.[51] In addition, the bureaucratic independence of the chancery was stressed: although it was unquestionably the chief organ of the *royal* administration, the king had no formal role in its running and the clerks were prohibited from touting for business in the royal or noble households. What was expected was public service, reinforced by traditions of continuity, and as much freedom from political control as was possible.

Yet freedom from political control was always relative, for it was, in normal circumstances, the king who appointed his ministers. For eleven months following the end of the Merciless Parliament, while Richard licked his wounds, the Appellants and the ministers appointed in 1386 remained in control of the government, but on 3 May 1389 Richard surprised them by declaring at a council meeting that he was twenty-two, quite old enough to govern, and demanding the resignation of his chancellor, treasurer and privy seal keeper.[52] They were certainly not disgraced, and within just over two years all three were reappointed, but Richard's coup marked the launch of his bid to reassert his kingly authority.[53]

Release from government office presented Arundel with an opportunity to make his mark in his archdiocese, which he had barely even visited thus far but where he spent much of the next two and a half years.[54] Around him he gathered the clerks who had served him so well at Ely, several of whom received lucrative appointments at York: John Newton became his vicar-general; Richard Scrope, his official; Henry Bowet, his archdeacon's official; Thomas Dalby, archdeacon of Richmond; William Noion, archiepiscopal treasurer; and Thomas Haxey, cathedral treasurer.[55] Their immediate task was to repair the damage inflicted on diocesan finances and relationships under Nevill. Buildings and manors had been dilapidated through neglect or exploitation, while long-running disputes with the chapters of York, Ripon and above all Beverley (where the canons had in effect been on strike for eight years) required resolution. Mediation, compromise and a steady hand were needed – just the sort of qualities in which Arundel excelled and which, combined with his continuing influence in high places, enabled him to achieve much in his diocese before, in September 1391, he was called to preside over the royal administration again.[56]

Yet, even when surrounded by his own faithful clerks, and despite his newly enhanced political stature in the kingdom, Arundel by no means had everything his own way at York. As the only holder of the see between 1316 and 1424 who was not a native of the northern province, as well as being an absentee for some six of his eight years, he may well have been resented as an outsider. His relations with his cathedral canons were sometimes bumpy. Twice, in 1390 and again in 1396, he tried to impose his jurisdictional authority on the dean and chapter by increasing the number of canons residentiary (thereby shrinking the financial benefits of the privileged few – just four in this case) and even intruding himself as a prebendary, but, despite enlisting papal support, he was rebuffed on both occasions. His insistence on his right of visitation – so often the spark for conflict – also aroused resentment, not just at the cathedral but also at St Mary's abbey, York, and at Carlisle cathedral.[57] He even made a half-hearted attempt to have himself declared, *ex officio* as archbishop, to be the founder and patron of Meaux abbey in Holderness, but was seen off by the demonstrably superior claim of the duke of Gloucester, lord of Holderness. At Beverley, he was more persistent and more successful, undertaking a thorough overhaul of the minster's constitutional arrangements – in reality, as so often with Arundel, largely a restatement of existing practice rather than an attempt to redefine fundamental principles – and here his settlement endured.

In summary, his primacy at York was characteristic of the man: insistent on his prerogatives, he did not shrink from advancing his claims, but did so tactfully if possible and in practice was willing to compromise. York's contemporary historian – doubtless influenced by Arundel's customary munificence to the cathedral, which included rich vestments, silver-gilt plate and cruets, and a gold ornament containing two pieces of the crown of thorns – branded his rule there as admirable (*laudabiliter*).[58]

Despite his dismissal as chancellor in May 1389, there is no indication that Arundel's reputation suffered either in England or abroad. One well-placed source stated that Boniface IX 'summoned him to the cardinalate' (*vocavit ad cardinalatum*) in 1390, but if he was offered a red hat he must have declined it, as did several of his English contemporaries. However, he certainly became a papal legate, either now or a year or two later,[59] and on 27 September 1391 was reappointed as chancellor, this time at Richard's behest. Thus it was, inescapably, affairs of state which mainly preoccupied Arundel for the next five years, and he lost no time in revealing his priorities. If the crown's financial embarrassment had to some extent abated since 1386, there was still much to do to achieve solvency. Imaginative thinking was required, and it seems to have been Arundel who provided it.

In the parliament that met on 3 November 1391, six weeks after his return as chancellor, a statute was passed restricting the growing practice whereby churches and religious houses were employing 'subtle schemes, plots and devices' (principally enfeoffments-to-use, or trusts) to evade the financial consequences of the 1279 Statute of Mortmain, thereby depriving lords and the crown of the financial benefits of their feudal lordship. Henceforward, those who had made such arrangements without purchasing licences to do so were obliged to purchase them from the king before the end of September 1392, failing which the lands in question would be forfeited to the crown.[60] The monks were furious. Henry Knighton called the new statute 'execrable' and 'profane' (*execrabile, prophanum*). The chronicler of Meaux complained bitterly that the fines payable for such licences were raised to twenty times the level at which they had previously been set, attributing this swingeing increase to Arundel personally, despite the fact that he was 'a churchman endowed with pontifical dignity'. For the royal exchequer, however, it provided a welcome windfall: according to the Westminster chronicler, the effect of the statute was that 'ministers, namely the chancellor and the treasurer, had by Michaelmas [1392] accumulated untold sums of money to fill the treasury to overflowing'. Doubtless this was an exaggeration, but there is no mistaking the upturn in crown income during the early 1390s.[61] For Arundel, it was an early test of what would become one of the defining questions of his career: to what extent should he prioritize the needs of the State over those of the Church?

Arundel continued during his second chancellorship to visit his diocese when he could.[62] One contemporary even claimed that he was instrumental in the king's decision in May 1392 to move the chancery, common bench and various exchequer offices from London to York, because he 'wished these offices to belong to his own city'. In fact, the main motive for the move was the king's wish to punish the Londoners for refusing to loan him £10,000. Arundel played his part in this chastisement, addressing the citizens 'with marked severity' for their poor city governance when they appeared before Richard at Nottingham on 25 June. After five months, once the Londoners had submitted, the departments of state returned to the capital. Yet Arundel's evident attachment to his northern see found more enduring expression in the grant of a royal charter in May 1396, whereby York received the privilege of internal civic self-government.[63]

For the king to reappoint a man so recently an outspoken enemy of the court was a sensible move, adding credibility to his restoration of authority.[64] Yet to act as the pope's legate while simultaneously serving as the king's chief minister required flexibility.[65] When the perennial topic of papal provisions – essentially a stand-off about who should benefit from the massive reserves of patronage held by the English Church – returned with a vengeance in the parliament of January 1390, leading to the Second Statute of Provisors, Archbishops Courtenay and Arundel protested that they could not agree to anything which derogated from the pope's rights and insisted that their objections be enrolled on the parliamentary record.[66] Three years later, however, the two archbishops appeared quite willing to go along with the Third Statute of Praemunire, which undoubtedly restricted papal rights in England. The clue to such apparent inconstancy may be the fact that, although passed in 1393, the act seems to have been largely ignored for the next forty years.

Of much greater effect in the medium term was the introduction in 1393 of a moderation (*soufferance*) of the Statute of Provisors which allowed the king to negotiate exemptions from its penalties in certain cases. This was of cardinal importance to kings: whereas lesser lay patrons were principally concerned to be able to provide priests or chaplains to benefices to which they held rights of advowson (presentation, very often a hereditary right), and university scholars needed what were in effect sinecures to allow them to study, the main concern of kings was to be able to reward their clerks and administrators with cathedral or college canonries or prebends. The problem was that these more valuable prizes also caught the papal eye. The introduction of a *soufferance* in the king's favour in the 1393 parliament was thus not, for a papal legate, an easy compromise. Yet neither Courtenay nor Arundel appears to have objected to it, and so advantageous to both Richard II and Henry IV did it prove that it continued to be renewed from parliament to parliament, although the commons – the most vociferous opponents of papal provisions – always kept a close eye on it.[67] Provisions would continue to test Arundel's ability to finesse Anglo-papal relations for many years to come.[68]

These different standpoints were not, of course, adopted in a vacuum. In January 1390, Richard was still a wounded king, tentatively feeling his way back to power, hesitant to ruffle feathers.[69] By 1393, he was in a much stronger position: truces with France and Scotland had helped to restore the crown's solvency and obviated the king's need to approach every parliament cap in hand; he had embarked on a programme of retaining knights and esquires up and down the country; he had largely avoided quarrelling with his magnates; and the commons had been mollified with legislation on issues such as livery and maintenance. Yet there was one magnate who showed no desire to be placated. Arundel's brother Earl Richard had withdrawn from government after 1389, but by January 1394 he was no longer able to contain his contempt for the king and launched a sneering attack in parliament accusing him of over-familiarity with his uncle John of Gaunt and of favouring Gaunt's personal ambitions abroad to the detriment of England's interests.[70]

Six months later their mutual loathing once again erupted in violence. When the funeral of Richard II's queen, Anne of Bohemia, was held in Westminster abbey on 3 August 1394, Earl Richard not only arrived late, missing the procession of the cortège from St Paul's, but compounded his discourtesy by asking to leave early since he had pressing matters to attend to. Furious, the grieving king seized a baton and 'struck the earl violently upon the head with such force that he collapsed and his blood flowed profusely over the pavement'. The funeral was halted while the church was cleansed and Earl Richard was sent to the Tower. Walsingham said that the king would have liked to kill him, but better counsel prevailed and after a week the earl was released, several magnates having agreed to stand surety for him on pain of the enormous sum of £40,000.[71]

Foremost among those who stood surety for Earl Richard was his brother. The incident was doubly embarrassing for Arundel, since he officiated at the queen's funeral.[72] Nor was the earl always straightforward with his brother. At times, he sought to capitalize on Arundel's influence as chancellor – as when he wrote asking Arundel to help him secure a respite from a royal summons – but at other times he went behind his brother's back, as in 1395 when he told one of his officials to secure a Welsh benefice for one David Carpenter 'without the knowledge of our brother', since he knew that it was by rights in the chancellor's gift.[73] There was at any rate no indication in the mid-1390s that the king regarded Arundel as complicit in Earl Richard's follies. Seven weeks after Anne's funeral, Arundel accompanied Richard to Ireland on his flagship, *La Chaumbre*. A few weeks later, the king entrusted him with a cache of personal documents – copies of the king's will and of the papal pronouncements on the marital affairs of Richard's mother – which he would hardly have committed to someone whose discretion he doubted.[74] However, Arundel was little involved in Richard's big 1396 project: his truce with France and his marriage to Isabella, daughter of the French king Charles VI.

Archbishop Courtenay's life was now ebbing away and he died on 31 July 1396. He was a patient, conservative and forbearing man who mixed firmness with moderation in dealing with the king, with the monks of Canterbury, even with those of heterodox persuasions. Despite the challenges he faced, he generally managed to hold the line against state encroachment on the Church's liberties and remained on good terms with most of his diocesans. Arundel probably learned a lot from him. They also appear to have got along well and shared much in common apart from aristocratic birth and high ecclesiastical office.[75] In one important respect, however, they were quite different. As far as he could, Courtenay kept out of politics, especially after the crisis of 1386–8. Arundel was innately political. Richard II was well aware of this, and of Arundel's political sympathies, but there is no indication that he tried to block Arundel's elevation to the primacy – indeed, his succession to Courtenay seems almost to have been a foregone conclusion. Still only forty-three years old, but with eight years as an archbishop, seven as chancellor and no significant embarrassments behind him, Arundel's pre-eminence among the English hierarchy was unchallenged. The dean and chapter of Canterbury cathedral supported his candidacy; Richard II agreed; Pope Boniface IX complied; and on 25 September 1396 he was provided to the see.

Inauspiciously, this day also marked the crushing defeat of a Christian crusading army at Nicopolis (modern Bulgaria), a disaster which set back for fifty years western European efforts to slow the advance into Christendom of the Ottoman Turks (although Mongol intervention and fratricidal squabbling meant that it was thirty years before the Ottoman conquest of the Balkans resumed in earnest). However, definitive news of Nicopolis did not reach England for three months, allowing Arundel's primacy to begin on a positive note. Five weeks after his provision, he solemnized the marriage of the king and Isabella in the church of St Nicholas at Calais.[76] Although he resigned the chancellorship on 15 November, there is nothing to suggest that this was as a consequence of royal displeasure: episcopal chancellors promoted to Canterbury often resigned, since combining the two positions was regarded as too onerous.[77] Within another year, however, Arundel would be not just a dethroned archbishop but also a convicted traitor and an exile.

Part One
THE PUBLIC LIFE
1397–1414

1

Exile
1397–9

The celebratory spirit of late 1396 continued into the new year. On 7 January 1397, Arundel crowned Queen Isabella in Westminster abbey; four days later he received his archiepiscopal temporalities, and when the first parliament of the year met on 22 January, he took his place at the head of the lords spiritual.[1] Yet barely had the session opened when the mood darkened. Richard II, it transpired, had pledged more to Charles VI when the two kings had met three months earlier than he had been willing to divulge – in particular, that he would help Charles to raise an Anglo-French army to invade Italy to curb the expansionist ambitions of the duke of Milan. It was a scheme as reckless as Henry III's calamitous 'Sicilian Venture' a century and a half earlier, especially since news had now arrived of the Nicopolis disaster. The commons' reaction was polite but firm: although the decision was for the king to make, they for their part would not 'be a party, nor suffer loss' because of it. In other words, no taxes would be granted for such a scheme.[2] Although the king tried to change their minds, he soon realized that it was futile, and parliament heard no more of it.[3]

Yet what followed suggests that this defeat rankled. It also provided the first real test of Arundel's mettle as primate. On Friday 2 February, 'after he had eaten', the king summoned the lords to inform them that he had heard that the commons were proposing certain matters which were 'contrary to his regality and estate and his royal liberty'. The matters in question were set out in a bill containing four points. It was the fourth that gave the king 'great grief and affront'. This was a complaint that the king's household was needlessly extravagant, especially because of the 'multitude of bishops . . . and many ladies and their attendants' who had taken up residence there at his expense. The royal household, Richard declared, was his business and his alone. Who was it, he asked, that had put this bill forward? The speaker of the commons, Sir John Bushy, did his work quickly: the offender's name, he told the king the next day, was the clerk Thomas Haxey. Despite a grovelling apology from the commons, Richard was not mollified. Haxey was imprisoned at Windsor and two days later the lords were induced to declare that anyone who encouraged the commons to tell the king how to manage his person or his household was to be regarded as a traitor. On 7 February, Haxey was condemned to death for treason. No sooner had he been condemned, however, than Arundel, to whose custody he had been committed, stepped forward 'with great humility' and begged the king to pardon him, which Richard, 'of his royal pity and his special grace', promptly agreed to do. Three months later, Haxey was discharged and restored to his livings.[4]

This curious affair has aroused much speculation.[5] Was Haxey a stooge, or was he the front man for disaffected lords such as Earl Richard or perhaps even Arundel (whose treasurer Haxey had been at York), or for a coterie of royal clerks disappointed by the king's preference for appointing friends and personal servants such as his confessor and physician to the episcopacy? Might he even have been put up to it by Richard himself in order to make a point about the tolerable limits of criticism? Haxey's record suggests that he was ambitious and had a wide circle of contacts among the leading clerks in the royal administration. That he was representing the views of others besides himself is entirely plausible – his petition also complained about papal taxation of the clergy, although the king seems to have ignored this – but this does not mean that he was simply acting as a stooge. In fact, it is difficult to see either the king or the Arundel brothers as Haxey's puppeteer, but in a sense the ruction played into both the king's and the archbishop's hands: Richard's, by presenting him with the opportunity to draw a line between what he would and would not countenance; Arundel's, not only because it showed that he would continue to extend his protection to a man who, despite a reckless miscalculation, had served him faithfully for many years, but also because it gave him the opportunity to demonstrate leadership of the Church in the face of royal indignation.

Nor was this the only such opportunity afforded him during the January 1397 parliament. Like William Courtenay in the early 1390s, he led the lords spiritual in protesting that the renewal of the 'moderation' of the Statute of Provisors should not prejudice their allegiance to the papacy or the liberties of the Church. He also joined with the prior and chapter of Canterbury in successfully petitioning the king to overrule Courtenay's executors and allow the cathedral to retain the keeping of the lordship of Tonbridge (Kent).[6] It must have been with satisfaction on both sides, therefore, that, once parliament ended, Arundel made his way to Canterbury, there, in the presence of the chapter, to be ceremonially enthroned as archbishop on 18 February.

In itself, the Haxey affair was a storm that threatened more damage than it caused. More disturbing was what it signified in terms of the king's increasingly erratic behaviour. For the moment, however, Arundel's mind was focused on another matter: heresy. Following the Blackfriars synod of 1382, the authorities hoped that Wyclif's followers at Oxford had been silenced. Far from it: the university would continue to arouse suspicion in orthodox circles throughout the reigns of Richard II and Henry IV.[7] Equally worrying was the spread of Wycliffite and anti-clerical views among artisans, poor priests, and lords and knights with connections at court and in parliament. In 1388, during and after the Merciless Parliament, several suspects were interrogated about their beliefs, and commissions were issued ordering the seizure of heterodox books and the suppression of heretical preachers. Simultaneously, the royal council was given new powers to investigate suspect books and preachers; since Arundel was chancellor at the time, he must have played a part in these proceedings.[8] Four years later he sat on a tribunal to investigate a Cistercian, Henry Crump, for heresy.

Yet it is not until 1395, after audacious Lollards posted their Twelve Conclusions on the doors of St Paul's cathedral and Westminster abbey while parliament was in session, that positive evidence survives of Arundel's intervention, when several theologians at Merton college were disciplined and a committee set up to examine Wyclif's works. It was probably this intrusion into academic freedom which led the university authorities to seek the notorious papal bull dated 12 June 1395 by which Boniface IX granted the university exemption from ecclesiastical visitation. To Arundel, this was no more than a cloak for heterodox speculation, and once he became archbishop he set out to overturn it.

By the time that the Canterbury convocation met on 26 February 1397, he had prepared his ground.[9] Convocations were in effect the clergy's parliaments. There were two: Canterbury, which represented the eighteen southern and Welsh dioceses, was much the bigger and more influential, and it usually met at the same time as parliament; York, which represented the three northern dioceses, met at more variable times. All bishops, abbots, priors, archdeacons, representatives from each chapter and deans were meant to attend, and Arundel was a stickler for attendance. In 1397, he knew that the Oxford doctors and masters were divided: while the university chancellor, Dr Thomas Hendyman, and several of his colleagues appeared at St Paul's on 27 February to defend the bull, also present were several doctors of civil and canon law who had come to protest against the 'grievances, excesses and defects' of Hendyman, whose power within the university was allegedly becoming ever harder to challenge. Several of these were men whose careers were to a greater or lesser degree dependent upon archiepiscopal favour, and it was they who were called to speak first.[10] Boniface's bull, they claimed, was simply a 'private schedule', perhaps even a forgery, intended to prevent them from appealing against Hendyman's 'oppressions'. As a result, it was becoming impossible to observe the statutes and customs of the university, and the bull – if bull it was – should be overruled without delay.

Arundel made a show of consulting with his episcopal colleagues and lawyers, but the outcome was a foregone conclusion: with Michael Cergeaux, the archbishop's chancellor and a doctor of both laws, acting as their spokesman, the doctors, bachelors and scholars, on behalf of 'the whole university', formally renounced 'this absurd privilege of exemption', a decision which Arundel naturally endorsed. Outflanked and humiliated, Hendyman resigned his office and 'departed from the said council with insulting words' (*a prefato concilio cum verbis contumeliosis recessit*), pursued by an archiepiscopal messenger ordering him to reappear the following day to hear judgment.

Nor was Arundel done. Having seen off the papal bull, his attention now turned to a schedule of heretical or erroneous opinions expressed by Wyclif in his *Trialogus*, a disquisition on divine power, knowledge and the sacraments fit to be ranked alongside the most excoriating contemporary satires against the Catholic Church. Wyclif, declared Arundel, had been 'born in an evil hour' (*in mala hora natus*).[11] Eighteen suspect articles, apparently still being taught at Oxford, were read out, among them the denial of transubstantiation, always regarded by Arundel as a line in the sand between orthodoxy and heresy. A discussion on the following day (28 February) provided the ammunition for a more substantial treatise refuting the *Trialogus*, written, at Arundel's request, during Lent 1397 at the duchess of Norfolk's Framlingham castle (Suffolk). The author was William Woodford, lector at St Paul's, the duchess's confessor and one of Wyclif's most vehement detractors.

But Hendyman and his allies did not give up. A few weeks later, they wrote to Arundel begging him not to be angry with them and asserting that the bull of exemption had been validly secured and acknowledged by Archbishop Courtenay. Arundel's response was to enlist the king's support, and Richard duly wrote to the university on 30 March ordering that the bull be publicly renounced in the presence of a royal emissary. Two months later he wrote again, insisting that the right of visitation of the university 'belonged, ought to belong and in future will always belong' to the archbishop of Canterbury *pro tempore*.[12] Yet if Arundel had unquestionably won the first round against his alma mater, the 1397 convocation was in fact merely an early salvo in a battle that would last as long as he retained the primacy.[13]

During the spring and early summer of 1397, Arundel mainly divided his time between Canterbury and Lambeth, attending to diocesan and provincial affairs, including a preliminary visitation of his Canterbury diocese.[14] In April he appropriated a number of livings to Prior Chillenden and his Canterbury chapter, hoping to reinvigorate the rebuilding of the cathedral's nave initiated some fifteen years earlier by Archbishop Sudbury.[15] If he felt disquieted by Richard II's heavy-handed reaction to Haxey's bill, there is nothing to indicate the fact, although one incident, if true, would doubtless have irritated the king. As an 'assiduous investigator of things that had been left by his forbears', Richard was rummaging around among some chests in the Tower one day when he discovered an eagle-shaped ampulla containing the miraculous holy oil which the Blessed Virgin Mary had allegedly given to Thomas Becket more than two centuries earlier. An accompanying scroll stated that the first English king to be anointed with it would be a great conqueror, defeat the pagans in the Holy Land and expand his dominions. When Richard heard this, he asked Arundel to use this oil to anoint him for a second time, but the archbishop, 'a man of profound judgment', refused: one anointing, he declared, was enough for any king. Richard eventually accepted this, although he henceforth always carried the ampulla with him.[16] This undated conversation must have occurred in 1397, following Arundel's consecration but before the September parliament.

By this time, signs of waxing royal autocracy were gathering pace. Especially disturbing to several of the magnates was the king's willingness, expressed in the January parliament, to reconsider territorial settlements dating back to the mid- or even early fourteenth century, such as the rival claims of the earl of Salisbury and the earl of March to the honour of Denbigh in north Wales, or the claims of the earl of Nottingham and the earl of Warwick to the lordship of Gower (West Glamorgan).[17] It was also clear that the long-standing antipathy between Richard and the three leading Appellants, the duke of Gloucester and the earls of Arundel and Warwick, was far from buried. When the king summoned Gloucester and Earl Richard to a council at Westminster in February, they refused to come, making the king 'extremely angry'.[18] In July 1397 he lost patience. His plan was to invite the three leading Appellants to a banquet at Westminster and arrest them. Only Warwick was unwary enough to turn up, whereupon he was promptly imprisoned in the Tower. Gloucester claimed ill health, while Earl Richard, 'to whom the king's malice was better-known', simply immured himself behind the imposing walls of his castle at Reigate (Surrey).[19] The king tried a different ploy: summoning the archbishop to his presence, he told him to bring his brother to him. 'If he comes, will you do him harm?' asked Arundel. Richard swore upon the host – blessed by Arundel – that he would not. Despite his misgivings, Earl Richard eventually agreed to come to Westminster, where he was handed over to the earl of Nottingham, who 'took him into another chamber and closed the door'.[20] Arundel waited all day to see his brother again before returning 'downcast' to Lambeth, while the king raised an armed force and rode through the night to Pleshey castle (Essex), where he surprised Gloucester at daybreak and arrested him too. Earl Richard was dispatched to Carisbrooke castle (Isle of Wight), Gloucester to Calais.

According to Thomas Walsingham, when news of the arrests became public, there was 'general dismay' and prayers and processions were held for the lords.[21] There was certainly widespread speculation as to the king's plans, which only became clear when, on 5 August at Nottingham castle, eight of his leading courtier nobles, appearing before him in the great hall, presented a bill appealing the duke of Gloucester and the earls of Arundel and Warwick of treason, based on what they had done a decade earlier. Parliament was due to meet on

17 September. As the day approached, the mood in London turned menacing. With Westminster Hall being rebuilt, Richard had a marquee erected in the palace yard with an elevated throne at one end. Then, summoning his notorious Cheshire bodyguard and ordering his noble allies to gather their retinues, he 'rode fearsomely (*terribiliter*) through the heart of London with a hundred thousand armed men', before ordering his archers to surround the marquee, bows at the ready.[22] Parliament's purpose, it was clear, was the consummation of Richard's vengeance.

Despite his involvement in the events of 1386–8, the archbishop remained at liberty through July and August, spending most of his time at Lambeth before taking his accustomed place at the head of the lords spiritual in parliament, seated next to the king.[23] Hardly had the session opened, however, when it became clear that his earlier transgressions had not been overlooked. As in January, it was the royal councillor John Bushy whom the commons elected (or, as Walsingham claimed, the king appointed) as speaker, and to whom it thus fell to introduce the appeal of treason on Tuesday 18 September. The principal charge against the Appellants was that, 'with the assistance of Thomas Arundel, then chancellor of England', they had committed treason by coercing the king to agree to the 1386 commission of government, in order to achieve which they had sent 'a great person, a peer of the land' – which must mean Arundel – to threaten the king with deposition if he did not agree to it. It was also claimed that it was at Arundel's request, as chancellor, that a special pardon had been granted by the king to Earl Richard in 1394, whereas he should, 'by virtue of his office', have opposed it.

When Bushy proposed that the pardon be revoked, Arundel tried to save his brother by arguing that the king's person was so exalted that to revoke his own acts was in effect to deny his kingship, since 'he who removes from the king the opportunity for showing mercy removes the foundation of royal authority'. However, no one was in the mood for sophistry, and when Arundel also tried to block the appointment of a proctor for the lords spiritual – thereby implicating them by proxy in passing sentences of blood – Bushy rounded on him directly, accusing him of being as much of a traitor as his brother. When the archbishop rose from his seat to respond – striving, as the poet John Gower put it, 'not against the law, but to divert the king from his wrath' – Richard silenced him, saying he wished to consult with his advisers.[24] Bushy advised against this, on the grounds that Arundel was 'so clever and so superior to us in intelligence that we are afraid that he will deceive and harm us by his ingenuity', but the king prevaricated, telling Arundel, 'You may leave in safety, father.' Two days later, when the archbishop tried to return to parliament to answer the charges against him, he was forbidden to enter.[25] Thus he was not present on Friday 21 September when his brother was brought into parliament to stand trial for treason.

Earl Richard's defence was predictably suicidal. 'Where are the faithful commons?' he demanded of Bushy. 'I know you and your crew well enough, and why you have gathered here – not to act in good faith, but to shed my blood. The faithful commons of the realm are not here, while you, I know, have always been false.' 'Then why did you need a pardon in the first place?' asked John of Gaunt. 'To silence the tongues of my enemies,' replied Earl Richard, 'of whom you are one. And I tell you this for sure, that when it comes to treason, you need a pardon more than I do.' When Gaunt's son, the former Appellant (and future king) Henry, earl of Derby, reminded him that when they had first banded together in 1387 Earl Richard had suggested seizing the king, he retorted, 'You, earl of Derby, you are lying through your teeth.' But the king had heard enough: 'Pass sentence on him', he declared, and Gaunt, as steward, did so. Earl Richard was to be drawn, hanged, beheaded and quartered, his lands forfeited, his heirs disinherited, although, in recognition of his high birth, Richard II commuted the death sentence to beheading only. And so – in a scene described with awe by the chroniclers – he was led away through the city to Tower Hill, distributing alms to the poor, foretelling doom to his enemies, making his last confession, a great crowd of mourners following, and all the while 'his countenance no more changing colour than if he were on his way to a banquet'. And it was on Tower Hill that he was decapitated, whereupon his headless corpse was reported to have risen to its feet 'for as long as it might take to recite the Lord's Prayer', before falling to the ground. It might have been the catalyst for a martyr cult to rival those of Simon de Montfort or Thomas of Lancaster, but more sober counsel – or, perhaps, recollection of Earl Richard's political follies – prevailed.[26]

When parliament reconvened on Monday 24 September, it was announced that the duke of Gloucester could not appear to stand trial because he was dead. In fact, he had been murdered on the king's orders – suffocated with a feather-bed in the back room of a Calais hostel – and although it took two years before the truth came out, it is hard to imagine that anyone believed his death at such an opportune moment to be coincidental. Nevertheless, he was posthumously convicted of treason, partly for his conduct in 1386–8 and partly on the basis of a confession obtained two weeks earlier at Calais. His lands were forfeited, his heirs disinherited and, since he was the son of Edward III, it was declared that none of his descendants should be permitted to bear the royal arms. It was presumably the fact that he was the king's uncle that induced Richard II to do away with him in secret rather than stage a public trial.

The next day, 25 September, came the archbishop's turn, although, since he was still barred from appearing in his own defence, he was tried *in absentia*. Apparently, the only charge on which he was convicted was his role in setting up the commission of government eleven years earlier, for which he had submitted himself to the king's grace. Nevertheless, he was condemned to banishment and forfeiture of his temporalities, along with any lands which he held by descent or purchase and all his goods and chattels, since the king realized that 'he would never have peace with this archbishop of Canterbury'. He was to leave the realm within six weeks, by 9 November.[27] Three days later, Warwick was similarly banished (to the Isle of Man), following which, with vengeance served, several of the king's leading allies were promoted to dukedoms and earldoms, acts were passed consolidating parliament's judgments and on 29 September Richard declared the session adjourned until 27 January 1398, when it would resume at Shrewsbury.

Shortly after this, Arundel met the king one more time before going into exile. The gist of their conversation was reported by a Canterbury chronicler as follows:

> The archbishop declared that he did not wish to depart: this was where he had been born, and this was where he wanted to die. The king and the duke of Lancaster [Gaunt] went into the chamber where he was sitting, downcast, with some other earls, and the king said to him: 'Do not be sad, and do not refuse to depart, because I assure you that in a short time you will be recalled, and that for as long as we two are both alive nobody except you will be archbishop of Canterbury.' The archbishop said to him: 'Before I depart, there are things I want to say to you', whereupon he delivered a lengthy sermon concerning the extravagance which reigned among those about him, and the rapacity and arrogance of the court, through which they corrupted the whole realm.[28]

No doubt this riled the king for, although he continued publicly to recognize Arundel's primacy until at least the end of November, he immediately made plans to replace him.[29]

Arundel, meanwhile, was preparing for his passage abroad. He was still at Lambeth on 14 October, drawing up an ordinance for the administration of his diocese during his absence. On 19 October he received licence from the king to take twenty servants (*familiaribus*) abroad with him, any of whom were allowed 'to pass to and fro at will in the transaction of his business'. By 24 October he was gone, sailing from Dover.[30] Previous archbishops of Canterbury had endured periods of exile – Anselm, Becket, Langton, Winchelsea – but none of them had actually been banished. In each case, they had left England because a crisis in Church–State relations made their dealings with the king too difficult, and negotiations for their return continued during their absence. Arundel's case was different not just because he was banished, but because he was condemned for his political opposition to the king, not as archbishop but as chancellor. The odds on his return were longer, and it cannot have failed to occur to him, as the great white teeth of Dover receded from his view, that he might never see the land of his birth again.

Arundel probably sailed to Bruges, for within a few weeks he had reached Ghent, whose civic officers were thanked by the king in a letter dated 23 November for receiving him kindly, since 'although the said archbishop, owing to his crimes and according to law, has been exiled, the king does not want his person or his belongings to be molested'.[31] Meanwhile, however – before the end of September – Richard had written to Pope Boniface IX asking him to translate Arundel to St Andrews (a purely titular appointment, since Scotland recognized the Avignon papacy) and to provide the king's treasurer and former secretary Roger Walden to Canterbury.[32] As winter approached, therefore, Arundel made for Rome. According to a Canterbury chronicler, the king arranged for bandits to waylay him and he 'barely escaped with his life'.[33] Once in Rome, he was greeted warmly by Boniface and the cardinals, but when Richard heard that he had tried to persuade the pope to restore him to Canterbury, he wrote furiously accusing Arundel of being the author of all the 'damnable treasons, conspiracies and machinations' of his reign and warning Boniface not to be taken in by his 'blandishments or cunning' or present him with any excuse to return to England. Instead, Richard wanted him to be translated to somewhere 'remote and distant from us'.[34] Despite Boniface's alleged reluctance to deprive Arundel of his see, sympathy was, in the circumstances, all that he could realistically offer. By the time the new year began, the 'late archbishop' had left the Curia and made his way to Florence.

It was at or near Florence – 'this earthly paradise', as he described it in a letter dated 8 January 1398 to the prior and convent of Canterbury

– that Arundel spent the majority of his exile. His letter, written in his own hand (*manu propria*), says little about his activities but a good deal about his predicament.[35] Quoting extensively from Augustine and the Bible, he proclaimed his enduring affection for 'his sons and brothers in Christ' at Canterbury and thanked them for their prayers for his safety, of which he had been informed by one of the monks, William London, who had travelled to Italy to be with him and apparently remained with him throughout his exile.[36] Despite his straitened circumstances, much of Arundel's letter has a positive tone. He had found favour with the pope such as he had never thought or hoped to find and remained patient and strong in adversity. Urging the monks too to be patient, he declared his 'persecution' to be either God's punishment for his sins or a test of his fortitude; yet, 'although I have been displaced, I am neither despondent nor beaten', and he still hoped for either divine or royal mercy, for in this ever-mutable world, 'although it is hard to rise, it is very easy to fall'. 'As for my own affairs,' he declared, 'I have hopes that things will turn out far better than my enemies believe they will, for a true brotherhood [the Canterbury community] cannot be rent apart, just as a head and limbs cannot be separated.' In conclusion, he begged the monks, for their own safety, to 'store these things in your bosom', promising similar discretion on his own part, before signing off as 'Arundel, minister and archbishop of the church of Canterbury, although unworthy'. He can hardly have been already planning his return, but he was watching as well as waiting.

Arundel's depiction of Florence as an 'earthly paradise' had much to do with the friendship he struck up with Coluccio Salutati, the celebrated humanist and chancellor of the republic since 1375, who enabled him, in a limited way, to exercise the spiritual functions commensurate with a churchman of his standing, such as inspecting religious houses.[37] The shared experience of recent sorrows and the therapeutic exchange of intellectual interests probably cemented their friendship. Salutati was grieving the loss of his wife, Piera (d. 1396); Arundel was grieving not just his brother but also his homeland and sense of purpose. As an expert on Dante's *Divina Commedia*, Salutati doubtless reminded his guest of Dante's implacable sense of divine justice: that the wheel of fortune turned, and his time would come again.[38] A number of later letters from Salutati to Arundel indicate that they discussed and agreed to share books, and through him Arundel must also have met the dazzling band of humanist scholars in Florence, of whom the chancellor was the acknowledged leader, which included Leonardo Bruni and Poggio Bracciolini.

Salutati's fascination with Roman history and poetry, derived in large part from Petrarch, and his interest in personal and political morality, stimulated by reading Cicero, was by this time finding expression in a treatise on tyranny, *De Tyranno*, which he published in the following year. The central question which *De Tyranno* addressed was whether Dante had been justified in placing Brutus and Cassius in the deepest circle of Hell for murdering Caesar. His answer was that Dante was indeed justified. However, that did not mean that Salutati condemned regicide in all cases, for a lawfully chosen king retained his legitimacy only as long as his rule was not 'vitiated by pride, or [he] rules unjustly or does not respect rights or laws'. In this case, he became a tyrant, 'and he who destroys a tyrant in a lawful way is to be loaded with honours' – a conclusion which would surely have interested Arundel.[39]

The two men certainly discussed English politics. In the first of his three surviving letters to Arundel, dated 30 August 1399, in the thick of the revolution which overthrew Richard II, Salutati wrote that he had heard that Arundel had returned to England, 'concerning which I both hope and fear: I fear the malice of enemies, and I hope that the Lord will come to your aid. You must take care to ensure that the malice of evil men does not prevail'. On 4 April 1401 he wrote again, expressing his delight that Arundel had been restored to his see and his hope that, whatever new and terrible things might happen, the archbishop would find it in his heart to be merciful, since that was less likely to lead to blood feuds – 'as the deposed and dead king [Richard II] may serve to you as an example'. In particular, he begged Arundel to act considerately towards Antonio de Mannini, his 'friend and neighbour', despite the fact that Mannini had formerly acted as Roger Walden's agent in Rome, for he had been sent there on Richard II's orders.[40]

Also striking, even allowing for the flamboyant courtesies of medieval letters, is the affection Salutati expresses: 'Remember me', he wrote simply in August 1399; then in April 1401, quoting the Roman poet Terence: 'You are always with me . . . day and night you love me, you crave me', before signing off to 'my father and lord, to be honoured with all reverence'; and, despite his age and declining powers – Salutati was over seventy by now – he declared in his third letter, written in January 1403, 'I cannot erase you from my memory . . . Farewell my lord, to be worshipped with reverence by all who serve'.

At some point during 1402, Arundel sent his servant Nicholas Lucefrus to Florence to make a copy of Salutati's treatise *De Nobilitate Legum et Medicinae*, and although Lucefrus was unable to do this, Salutati expressed a high opinion of him and offered to make a copy and send it to Arundel. In return, he begged Arundel to send him a copy of St Augustine's *De Musica*, which Arundel had probably acquired in Italy. When the convent of Santa Maria degli Angeli fell into debt, he also wondered whether the reinstated archbishop might contribute to its recovery, for 'we are all brothers in Christ'. However, it is Salutati's first letter which has most to tell us about Arundel. Written at the very moment when the Bianchi, the charismatic pacifist movement which swept central Italy between July and September 1399, were holding their spectacular daily processions in Florence, it provides a vivid account of the fervour which gripped many of the citizens at the time:

> All our city is in whites, like the city of Nineveh; all are converted to the Lord with such devotion that they are all dressed in sackcloth; they sing hymns, they visit the holy places and all strive together with a remarkable conversion to penitence; they abstain from meat

> and fast; no one, however noble or great, fails to visit holy places or to go barefoot about the city or weep with humility and devotion for his sins . . . everyone is reconciled to his brother or neighbour and lifelong enemies have become bosom friends . . . numerous miracles have occurred: blind people see again; the lame walk; the deaf hear . . . and in four places within [the city's] jurisdiction images of the crucifixion have sweated blood, to tell you more about which I am enclosing a copy of a letter sent to my magnificent lords describing this.

Peace and reconciliation were the central messages of the Bianchi, and the fact that they also advocated devotional processions to ward off the plague meant that they were initially welcomed almost everywhere, with bishops (including the bishop of Florence) offering to lead their processions and whole cities coming almost to a standstill until their nine days of ceremony were completed – the epitome of that 'explosive enthusiasm' so characteristic of medieval Italian religious life.[41] There was nothing to threaten the Church in what the Bianchi were doing: 'they were orthodox in their beliefs, traditional in their devotion, and orderly in their behaviour'. Yet if many churchmen (even Pope Boniface) were keen to capitalize on the religious fervour they excited, civic authorities were wary of popular disturbance, and after their initial round of processions the Bianchi were prohibited from entering towns or their subject territories, whereupon enthusiasm soon declined.[42]

Although accounts of the Bianchi doubtless grew in the telling, there is no mistaking the excitement in Salutati's letter for what his city was witnessing, which makes Arundel's reaction to the news, which he probably received around the beginning of October 1399, all the more interesting. For in the parliamentary session which began on 14 October – the first of the new reign, the day after Henry IV's coronation – the king announced that he had been 'reliably informed' that a 'new sect in white clothing, pretending to great sanctity' had arisen overseas, and that since the English might easily allow their souls to be imperilled by such novelties, leading even to the 'overthrow of the realm', the Bianchi were to be forbidden from entering the kingdom on pain of forfeiture for anyone who encouraged them to come.[43]

This announcement was not based on a common petition; it was an unsolicited royal decree, and although there must have been other Englishmen who had heard of the Bianchi by this time, the only person who possessed both the knowledge and the authority to move the king to act must surely have been his newly reinstated archbishop of Canterbury. In other words, far from sharing Salutati's zeal, Arundel's instinct was not just caution but proscription. Even Walsingham, always suspicious of religious novelty, expressed admiration for the Bianchi: 'Common people throughout the whole of Italy without distinction were moved to fresh devotion' by them, he wrote: 'in every place to which they went they brought peace among those in dispute', and the pope blessed them 'every day'.[44] No doubt Arundel was mindful of the fractious state of the kingdom following Richard's overthrow, but even so it is a telling demonstration of his ingrained conservatism, a more prohibitive version of his desire to channel the spiritual fervour of a Richard Rolle or a Walter Hilton into forms of practical devotion which would not threaten the unity or orthodoxy of the English Church. He certainly did not disapprove of devotional processions per se: four years later, he commended the way that, when Italians saw a priest carrying the Eucharist through city streets in order to perform the last rites, someone would light a candle in honour of the host and a crowd would gather to lead the priest to the dying person's house.[45] Yet it was not the fervour of the zealot which provided the wellspring of Arundel's faith. For him, it was primarily a construction of approved historical practice and the power of self-discipline. In this case, he need not have worried, for by the time the Bianchi were forbidden to enter England they had already in effect evaporated, having never spread beyond Italy.

How long Arundel remained in Florence is unclear. He may have visited Rome again in early 1399.[46] What probably persuaded him to leave Italy was news of the death on 3 February 1399 of John of Gaunt, which he must have heard about by mid-March. It was at any rate in the spring of 1399 that he re-crossed the Alps and made his way via Cologne to Utrecht, where reports from England would take but a few days to arrive.

2

Kingmaker
1399

It is not necessary to accept the entirety, perhaps not even the majority, of the aspersions cast on Richard II's reputation following the revolution of 1399 in order to understand why Thomas Walsingham believed that, during the last two years of his reign, the king 'began to tyrannize the people'.[1] Rather than his appetite for revenge being sated by the condemnations and forfeitures of September 1397, it seems only to have been whetted, and when an opportunity presented itself at the postponed Shrewsbury session of parliament to claim the greatest prize of all, the vast inheritance of the house of Lancaster, and simultaneously bring down the remaining two Appellants, he saw his chance.

It was the celebrated quarrel between Thomas Mowbray and Gaunt's heir, Henry of Bolingbroke, now respectively dukes of Norfolk and Hereford, which gave the king his excuse. Accusations of treason were traded and eventually it was decided that the only way to save both men's honour was to arrange a duel, to be fought at Coventry in September 1398.[2] Meanwhile, Richard busied himself with measures to ensure the financial and political security of his regime, demanding 'great loans' from his subjects; fines from those who had shown their support for the Appellants in 1387–8; and 'blank charters' (*cartes blanches*) from the seventeen counties closest to London, admitting their former treason and submitting themselves and their possessions to the king's pleasure. Compliant sheriffs were retained in office, the judicial benches were packed with supporters and letters sent out of the kingdom were censored.[3] Meanwhile, the cost of the king's household doubled, from £19,000 to £38,000 a year.[4] Especially resented was the violent conduct of Richard's bodyguard of Cheshire archers, numbering at least a thousand and perhaps double that, who accompanied him everywhere, believing that for as long as they sported Richard's livery of the white hart they need obey no law but the king's. Even a chronicler favourable to Richard acknowledged that the behaviour of his Cheshire bodyguard meant that he was 'held in fatal odium by his ordinary subjects'.[5]

Arriving at Coventry on 16 September 1398, Norfolk and Hereford presented themselves to the king, greeted the impressive crowd that had gathered and took their places at either end of the lists, but hardly had the herald bidden them do battle when Richard threw down his baton to halt the contest and ordered them to return to their pavilions while he retired with his counsellors to consider his next move. Two hours later, Bushy emerged to proclaim the king's decision: although Richard was at pains to stress that neither man had forfeited his honour – a point of cardinal importance – he had decided to exile Henry for ten years and Mowbray for the term of his life. This was greeted with astonishment that such harsh sentences should be passed on men against whom nothing had been proven. Mowbray was ordered to spend his exile in Germany, Hungary or Bohemia, or to undertake a pilgrimage to Jerusalem. No such limits were placed on Henry's movements, but both he and Mowbray were strictly enjoined not to engage in any kind of communication either with each other or with Arundel, since, said the Canterbury chronicler, the king 'feared [the archbishop's] wisdom and counsel'.[6]

By mid-October, both men had left the kingdom: Henry made for Paris, Mowbray for the Holy Land. However, Richard had made one important concession to both exiles: that if any lands should fall by inheritance to either of them during the period of their exile, their attorneys would be allowed to petition for livery to be granted to them *in absentia*.[7] It can hardly have been anticipated that the moment of reckoning would arrive so soon. John of Gaunt died on 3 February 1399, and on 18 March Richard announced his decision: unable to resist the lure of such weighty acquisitions to the royal treasury, he extended Henry's term of exile from ten years to life and sequestrated both his and Mowbray's inheritances.[8]

No wonder, then, that, when Arundel heard of Gaunt's death, he moved closer. By early June 1399 at the latest he and Henry were both in Paris.[9] It was around this time that, according to Walsingham, Arundel had a vision. One night, sensing that the door to his bedroom was opening, he found himself gazing at an apparition of John of Gaunt prostrating himself three times and begging him, 'Have mercy on me who am enduring torments and pardon me for acting so unjustly towards you and yours, for I now repent of this and am myself tormented by the thought of what I did.' Moved to tears, Arundel replied, 'May Almighty God forgive you, pardon your sins, and bring you to a place of rest and peace. Whatever I can do by praying to God and giving alms for your deliverance, I will do with feelings of deep love.' Whereupon 'Gaunt' bowed deeply, knelt and departed, 'and after this the archbishop saw him no more'.

Walsingham's purpose in recounting this is clear. Relations between the houses of Lancaster and Fitzalan had been strained since the mid-1380s. The last time Arundel had seen Gaunt and Henry was in September 1397, when Henry had provided one of the most damning pieces of evidence upon which Earl Richard was convicted, and when Gaunt had pronounced sentence of death on him. What Walsingham was trying to explain was Arundel's and Henry's readiness to rinse away the bad blood between their families. There were, of course, compelling pragmatic reasons why they should do so, at least in the short term: the restoration of each man to what he regarded as rightfully his. Yet how – or from whom – had the St Albans chronicler heard this story? Walsingham certainly embroidered or slanted stories, but he did not generally invent them. And it goes without saying that the only living witness to Arundel's vision must have been the archbishop himself. In other words, Arundel must have wanted his account of his vision to be known, presumably to signal at least a degree of posthumous redemption for the progenitor of the dynasty which he now enthroned, or to provide a justification for doing so, or both. And in order to do this, he felt obliged to present his reconciliation with Henry not just as remarkable but, more compellingly, as providential.[10]

For the next six months – from their return to England, through the almost bloodless campaign culminating in Richard's capture, the negotiations leading to his forced abdication, the stage management of Henry's usurpation, the brittle splendour of his coronation, and the tricky balance of conciliation and retribution which characterized his first parliament – Arundel was constantly at Henry's side, his comrade in arms, principal and indispensable adviser, spokesman, henchman, cheerleader and kingmaker.[11] They left together from Boulogne and landed around 1 July at Ravenspur (Spurn Head) on the Humber. They rode together at the head of an ever-growing army through the heart of England to Bristol, where on 29 July they presided over the beheadings of three of Richard's most heartily detested councillors, William Lescrope, John Bushy and Henry Green. Soon after this, Henry appointed Arundel as his stop-gap chancellor, a post he held for just two weeks, until they returned to London together. Following Richard's return from Ireland, they tracked his flight northwards – Richard shuffling with at most a few dozen followers along the Welsh coast, Arundel and Henry processing with many thousands along the Anglo-Welsh border to Chester – before hunting the king down at Conway castle, whereupon it was Arundel, together with the earl of Northumberland, whom Henry sent to induce Richard to leave the castle to meet him.[12] And, once Richard had been lured out and led to Flint, it was Arundel and Henry who jointly presented the (minimal) range of options open to him before escorting him to London where, on 29 September, in the Tower, Henry obliged him to read out his bill of abdication.

The next day, at Westminster, Arundel delivered a sermon to an extraordinary assembly of lords, prelates and 'common people', declaring that England had 'for a long time been led, ruled and governed by children', as a result of which it had been brought to the brink of disaster, from which 'Almighty God through his great grace and mercy sent a wise and prudent man' to deliver them. Although primarily intended to highlight Richard's 'childlike' failings, this statement also served by implication as a rejection of any claim to the throne that might be advanced on behalf of the seven-year-old Edmund Mortimer, the heir to the earldom of March. The assembly duly gave its assent to Richard's deposition and Henry's accession, and Arundel and the archbishop of York 'sat him down on the throne as king', whereupon Arundel gave another, longer sermon elaborating on his earlier theme. Quoting liberally from 1 Kings (1 Samuel), Isaiah, Ecclesiasticus and St Paul to the Corinthians, he portrayed Richard as a child, deceitful, wilful and gullible, whereas Henry was a man, someone who thought before he spoke, acted rationally and kept his word – a man, moreover, who had declared, 'I came not to do my will but that of He who sent me, namely, God.'[13] Not just the wheel of fortune, then, but divine justice.

None of this was achieved without a liberal dose of deception, of which Arundel, Henry and probably many others were equally guilty. At least three independent sources claimed that at some point Henry had sworn on the gospels (or the host) that it was not his intention to seize the throne. After all, it was not he but Edmund Mortimer, the great-grandson of Lionel of Clarence, who was the primogenitary heir to Richard. Edmund's claim was simply ignored, as it continued to be in official sources throughout Henry's reign, although chroniclers and dissidents had no trouble remembering it. It is hard to believe that Arundel, who must have witnessed these oaths, did not see Henry's usurpation as the most likely outcome. Several sources also asserted that Richard only agreed to leave Conway castle after being given assurances that he would be allowed to remain as king. It certainly stretches credulity to accept the bland assurances of the official *Record and Process of Richard II's Deposition*, of which Arundel was probably the principal drafter: namely, that, 'while still at liberty' in the castle, Richard 'had promised Lord Thomas archbishop of Canterbury and the earl of Northumberland that he was willing to yield up and renounce his crowns . . . on account of his own inability and insufficiency, which he himself admitted there'; or that he subsequently, 'willingly and, so it seemed, with a cheerful expression' (*hilari vultu*), read out his deed of abdication. Indeed, there are plenty of sources which flatly contradict these claims, even from a chronicler as favourable to Henry and Arundel as Adam Usk.[14]

Amid this welter of discordant narratives, the directness of the Canterbury chronicler – a man who was deeply attached to Arundel but knew a lie when he saw one – is refreshing. When Henry and Arundel met Richard at Flint, he wrote, they straightaway informed him that 'in a short time he would cease to reign', following which Arundel continued:

> You are a fine-looking man, but you are the falsest of men. You promised me, and swore upon the body of Christ, that you would not harm my brother. Yet after I brought him into your presence, I never saw him again. You falsely promised me that you would recall me from exile, but you appointed another archbishop and tried to have me killed. You did not rule your kingdom but despoiled it, imposing great tolls, extorting taxes annually, not for the benefit of the kingdom, which you never cared about, but to satisfy your own greed and flaunt your vainglory. You followed the counsels of your low-born sycophants, who constantly demanded gifts from you, and you promoted them. Those who offered good counsel, the great lords, your kinsmen, you unlawfully put to death, because they wanted to curb your extravagance, as they are entitled by the statutes of the realm to do and indeed ought to do when the kingdom is in danger, and like a tyrant you also commanded that their progeny be destroyed; but your statutes will not endure. You lived a life of debauchery, and by your foul example you besmirched your court and the kingdom.

It was the third time (after 1386 and 1397) that Arundel had harangued Richard II to his face, yet not until Henry called out 'Enough!' (*sufficit*) did he stop.[15] It must have been a sweet moment indeed for Arundel when, on 19 August, the captive king was obliged to send out a list of parliamentary summonses, the first name on which was 'Thomas, archbishop of Canterbury'. In Arundel's mind, he had never ceased to be primate.[16]

Yet if Arundel found it hard to forgive Richard, he showed no desire to humiliate the man who had usurped his see. By most accounts, Roger Walden was not an unpleasant man. Usk, a great admirer of Arundel who also worked under Walden as archbishop for two years, described him as 'modest, pious and courteous, practical and sensible in conversation', though 'better versed in the matters and ways of the world than in church affairs or learning'. John Prophet, clerk of the king's council in the 1390s, said that Walden neither revelled in his triumphs nor grumbled about his misfortunes. Even Arundel himself declared Walden to be an honest man. Only the waspish Walsingham dissented, calling him 'utterly incompetent and uneducated', given to 'dishonesty and deceit', and declaring 'God knows how' he had been made archbishop. It was true that he was not university-educated, but he had served in the royal administration since 1371, and from 1392 to 1397 he acted firstly as the king's secretary and then as treasurer of England. As the son of a butcher from Saffron Walden (Essex), it can only have been talent that took him so far.[17] Nevertheless, he was an unlikely choice as archbishop, for he had no experience of ecclesiastical administration, and when Richard's regime crumbled in the summer of 1399 he was an obvious target. Arrested by a London mob in August, he was held in custody until Arundel and Henry arrived in the capital. The hangings and badges displaying his arms in the archiepiscopal palace were pulled down and 'stuffed ignominiously under benches', and the jewels and furnishings which he attempted to remove – six cartloads, it was said, worth £4,000 – were impounded. His mother's house at St Bartholomew's was ransacked.[18]

Wisely, Walden lost no time in seeking forgiveness. On 1 September 1399, the day Arundel and Henry entered London with the captive Richard, he visited (or was taken to) them at the bishop of London's palace to hand over the cross of Canterbury and ask that his life be spared. Arundel supported him and Henry willingly agreed. Nor was Walden imprisoned, although he had to compensate Arundel for the issues of the archbishopric during the past two years and he was removed from his crown offices.[19] Yet he was soon back in favour, and in 1404–5 was restored to the episcopacy as bishop of London.[20] Arundel had no wish to persecute Walden or any other bishop (however close to Richard II) who was willing to acknowledge him as primate. These were, after all, the men he had to work with, and with one or two exceptions they too recognized that his restoration was a fait accompli, even though it was not until 19 October that the confirmatory papal bull arrived.[21] Apart from the restoration of his temporalities two days later, no further formalities were required: no re-consecration, no second enthronement, no request for annates. His register simply continued from where it had left off two years earlier, noting that this was now the fourth year of his archiepiscopacy.[22] Walden's 'intrusion' had never been. Arundel was simply back at his post.

Given the risk which Arundel and Henry took in returning to England unbidden, the overthrow of the Ricardian regime must have seemed to them to have been almost too easy. They were right. If they hoped to use the parliament which met on 6 October as a forum for reconciliation and forgiveness, for many among the lords and commons it was a chance to exact revenge. First and foremost, naturally, was the question of what to do with Richard. It was Arundel, Henry's effective master of ceremonies throughout the session, who on 23 October put this question in confidence to the members.[23] The commons asked that the former king be brought into parliament, but the earl of Northumberland told them that Henry had no intention of putting his predecessor on trial. By 27 October, it had been agreed to condemn Richard to perpetual imprisonment.[24] Much more was probably said in camera.

The trials of the former king's chief supporters, on the other hand – furious, theatrical exchanges which in some cases came close to lynching – the chroniclers reported at length.[25] Since these were potentially life and death questions, the clerics took no part, although once the lords temporal had opted for mercy, they agreed with the verdict. This was that the six guilty earls and dukes should lose the titles and lands which they had been granted in 1397–8, that they be forbidden in future from retaining supporters by distributing livery badges and that, if they attempted to restore Richard to the throne, they would *ipso facto* be guilty of treason. And thus, said Gower, 'their petty fame vanished'. This led to some grumbling that Henry, Northumberland and Arundel had 'preserved the lives of men whom the common people thought evil and who deserved to die'.[26]

Yet the grumblers would not have long to wait, for barely had the parliament ended (on 19 November) than the demoted lords began plotting to restore Richard. Chief among them were the earls of Huntingdon, Kent and Salisbury, Thomas, Lord Despenser, and Ralph, Lord Lumley.[27] Their plan – the 'Epiphany Rising' – was to seize Henry and Arundel at Windsor, where the king had arranged a day of masques and jousts on 6 January. Through either carelessness or ill luck their conspiracy was discovered, and by Sunday 4 January 1400, when they rendezvoused at Kingston-upon-Thames (Surrey), the king was already hastening back to London, summoning his retainers and issuing orders for the plotters to be arrested. Arundel, meanwhile, had spent Christmas at Canterbury and was on his way to Windsor when, as he explained in a letter to his chapter,

> we were making our way from our manor of Croydon to join our lord the king and, having arranged to spend the night in the town of Kingston-upon-Thames . . . as we were approaching the town, quite unaware of any form of deceit, we were by divine mercy forewarned of a secret and abominable ambush which had been laid by people who thirsted after our blood

whereupon he turned about and took refuge in Reigate castle. The 'divine mercy' was in fact a messenger dispatched just in time by Henry.

Informed by a member of the archbishop's household that their prey had evaded them, the conspirators dispersed. Kent, Salisbury and Lumley were arrested at Cirencester and lynched by the townspeople; Despenser suffered the same fate at Bristol; Huntingdon was captured in Essex, handed over to Arundel's sister Joan and beheaded at Pleshey castle. On 12 January, with the danger over, the king presided over the trials at Oxford castle of another ninety men accused of being in on the plot, twenty-seven of whom were executed.[28] Four days later, safely back in London, Arundel delivered a sermon on the theme 'I bring you tidings of great joy' (Luke 2:10), before leading a procession through the streets of the city chanting the Te Deum to give thanks for the king's deliverance.[29] Within another month, Richard II was dead, very probably on Henry's orders.[30] With the rubble of Richard's 'tyranny' swept away, the new king and his archbishop could now turn to the task of building their new order.

3

The Episcopate
1399–1401

Of the twenty-one bishops who held English or Welsh sees in 1399, only four – Henry Despenser of Norwich, William Wykeham of Winchester, Ralph Erghum of Bath and Wells, and Arundel – had been members of the episcopal bench since before 1377. The other seventeen had been appointed during Richard II's reign and thus, in varying degrees, with royal support or at least acquiescence.[1] Indeed, eleven of them had been promoted between 1394 and 1398, the years of Richard's burgeoning autocracy, and for five of these – Thomas Merks of Carlisle, John Burghill of Coventry and Lichfield, Tideman Winchcombe of Worcester (Richard's physician and reputedly a magician), Guy Mone of St David's and Robert Rede of Chichester – royal patronage had been decisive in securing their elevation.[2]

For the most part, those bishops whose personal allegiance to the former king was beyond doubt simply retired to their dioceses after 1399, shunning involvement in politics: this was the case, for example, with John Fordham of Ely,[3] Richard Medford of Salisbury (both of whom had been dismissed from court by the Appellants in 1388) and Thomas Peverell of Llandaff.[4] Several of them were elderly by now: Medford and Burghill were around seventy in 1399, Fordham at least sixty. Wykeham was seventy-five, Robert Braybrooke of London sixty-three. The latter two had both served as chancellor of England in their time, but those days were gone and, although they occasionally attended council meetings during Henry IV's early years, they no longer carried weight nationally. The same was true of William Bottlesham of Rochester, provided by the pope in 1389 contrary to Richard II's wishes, and Ralph Erghum of Bath and Wells, who was in any case a former chancellor of John of Gaunt and one of the Lancastrian faithful.[5] Both were in their sixties. William Strickland, who would replace Merks at Carlisle in late 1399, was of similar age, but distance from Westminster as much as anything else blunted any political aspirations he might have entertained.[6] Henry Despenser, also about sixty, is a more interesting case, to be discussed later.

That left the bishops whose talents could not be ignored and who, regardless of age, seemed willing enough to serve the new king, the new archbishop or both. Much the youngest was Henry Beaufort, one of John of Gaunt's legitimated bastards and thus Henry IV's half-brother, for whom the rich see of Lincoln had been secured in February 1398 by the unscrupulous (and almost unprecedented) removal of the aged and ailing John Buckingham, who had held the see for thirty-five years.[7] Beaufort was twenty-four and would remain a bishop (and, from 1426, cardinal) for almost fifty years, dying in 1447 after a lifetime devoted almost entirely to national and international politics at the highest level and hardly at all to the English Church. His allegiance to the Lancastrian regime was not in doubt and in February 1403 he became chancellor of England.[8] The most distinguished of a clutch of more conventional prelates prepared to serve the new king was Walter Skirlaw, a doctor of canon law who had been entrusted with more embassies than any other diplomat during Richard II's reign, as well as being keeper of the privy seal from 1382 to 1386. Elevated to the episcopacy in 1385, he was translated in 1388, at the behest of the Appellants – who, recognizing his talents, chose to ignore his close association with the court – to the rich and coveted see of Durham. Deeply involved in 1399–1401 in the delicate negotiations for the return of Queen Isabella to France, Skirlaw retired thereafter to enjoy a princely lifestyle in his great northern castles until his death in 1406.[9]

His neighbour here was Richard Scrope, promoted in March 1398 to the archbishopric of York, a diocese he knew well not just from birth (coming from the Yorkshire baronial family, the Scropes of Masham), but also from having served as Arundel's archiepiscopal official during the 1390s. The close bond between Scrope and Arundel would be dramatically demonstrated in June 1405.[10] Another aristocrat and a man valued for his administrative talents was Edmund Stafford of Exeter. Although he had served as Richard II's chancellor for the last three years of the reign (apparently on Arundel's recommendation), he was specifically exempted by Thomas Walsingham from the cronyism believed by the chronicler to be endemic in the royal administration in the late 1390s. Stafford remained on Henry IV's council and was chancellor again from March 1401 to February 1403. Competence, not courtly influence, was the key to his advancement.[11]

Henry and Arundel also received welcome support from a group of bishops holding sees in Wales or on the Anglo-Welsh border. John Trevor, an Oxford doctor of laws and a worldly diplomat who spent many years in Rome and was provided by Pope Boniface to St Asaph in 1394, deserted Richard II with alacrity in 1399 and held the testing posts of chamberlain and lieutenant of Chester and Flint until 1404.[12] Another doctor of laws and habitué of Rome – and thus probably, like Trevor, more of a papal than a royal choice – was Richard Young of Bangor, one of the outstanding diplomats of his age, who would spend much of Henry's reign on embassies to Denmark, France, Flanders, Scotland, the Empire and the Curia.[13] John Trefnant of Hereford, another lawyer and diplomat, was not just acquiescent in Richard's deposition but actively involved in promoting it, being one of the proctors (along with Richard Scrope) who presented the king's 'willing abdication' to the meeting of the estates on 30 September 1399. Shortly thereafter, he was sent by the new king to Pope Boniface IX to explain the reasons for it.[14]

From these three, Henry and Arundel probably did not expect any trouble. The post-1399 career of Guy Mone, bishop of St Davids, would have been more difficult to predict. A protégé and trusted financial administrator of Richard II, he was a royal councillor and receiver of the king's chamber during the 1390s, keeper of the privy seal in 1396–7 and treasurer of England in 1398. His provision to St Davids, undoubtedly at the king's behest, was dated 30 August 1397, but he was not consecrated until 11 November, after Arundel had gone into exile. However, there is no sign that he demurred in accepting the new regime,[15] making his profession of obedience to Arundel on 9 October 1401 in the archbishop's oratory at Lambeth and resuming public office as treasurer of England in October 1402.[16] By this time, with the Welsh rebellion making it impossible to remain in his diocese, he had taken up residence at his manor of Charlton (Kent), where he remained for most of the next five years, and he appears to have struck up an unlikely friendship with Arundel. When he made his will in August 1407, a few days before his death, among his very few personal bequests were a gold cup worth £40 and another £40 in cash to his 'father and lord' – Arundel.[17]

More remarkable still was the will of Roger Walden, who, despite his demotion in 1399, was still a consecrated bishop. Arundel appeared more than willing to try to find an English see for him. When Rochester became vacant in 1404, both the king and the archbishop supported Walden's candidacy, but the pope translated Richard Young from Bangor. Walden's eventual elevation to the bishopric of London was a more convoluted story,[18] but when he drew up his will on 31 December 1405, it was to Arundel that he ascribed his good fortune, asking to be buried either in St Paul's or in the chapel which he had recently constructed in St Bartholomew's conventual church in Smithfield, 'according to the choice and decision of my father and lord, the most reverend in Christ, Thomas archbishop of Canterbury, who raised me up from lying under the feet of men and the dust to the heights of the church of London'.[19] He died eleven days later, forgiving and forgiven.

The elevation or translation of a bishop required negotiation and compromise, often taking months or even years. Four parties were, to a greater or lesser degree, involved: the cathedral chapter, the pope, the king and the primate. During the thirteenth century, the practice of 'free and canonical' capitular election enshrined in King John's charter of 1214 was generally respected,[20] but from the early fourteenth century it gradually gave way to papal provision. Papal provision meant the direct appointment of all bishops by the pope, which from the mid-fourteenth century until the Reformation become the *sine qua non* for every canonically valid promotion to a see. That, at any rate, was the theory. In practice it was the king – his leverage bolstered by successive Statutes of Provisors and then by the Great Schism – whose backing was usually crucial, even if a royal nominee still had to secure papal provision.[21] It was also the king who bestowed the temporalities on the successful candidate (and might, very occasionally, refuse to do so). Moreover, capitular election might still be decisive (especially in monastic sees), but the chapter in question must be prepared to risk royal or papal wrath – or both. Officially, the archbishop's role in this process was formal: he 'admitted' the chosen candidate, received his profession of obedience, released the spiritualities of the see to him and enthroned him (although in practice enthronement was usually delegated to his archdeacon or a suffragan). However, that certainly did not preclude him from lobbying any of the other parties on behalf of his preferred candidate: Arundel did so on many occasions.

One of the reasons why promotion to the episcopacy was so coveted was that bishops were appointed for life. They were not expected to retire, and they could not be demoted. They could be translated to remote or unobtainable sees – as were Alexander Nevill and Thomas Rushook in 1388, Arundel himself in 1397 and Merks in 1399 – but in fact this was rare, a consequence of the unusually acrimonious nature of Ricardian politics.[22] In the vast majority of cases, it was a question of dead men's shoes – an indeterminate wait followed by an undignified scramble.

Not always, however: the first bishop to die after 1399 was William Bottlesham, bishop of Rochester, who, although well enough to deliver the opening sermon to convocation in October 1399, died on 26 February 1400.[23] Arundel lost no time in replacing him, a relatively simple process since Rochester was unique among English sees in being under the direct patronage of the archbishop rather than the king, which meant that it was the archbishop who issued the *congé d'élire* (permission to elect) and who held the temporalities as well as spiritualities of the see during vacancies.[24] In 1400, at any rate, the process was trouble-free, and by the second week of April Arundel had secured Rochester for one of his lifelong protégés, John Bottlesham (probably, though not provably, a relative of his predecessor).[25] Bottlesham was a Cambridge graduate, doctor of laws and former master of Peterhouse, who had followed Arundel from Ely to York, and in October 1399 had become the archbishop's chancellor. Four years later, he referred in his will to Arundel as 'my most special lord, in whose authority I have special trust', and asked him to be the 'upholder, father and protector' of his executors.[26]

While Rochester was being settled, the see of Bath and Wells also fell vacant, when Ralph Erghum died. If Rochester had been about as untroubled a process as an episcopal promotion could be, Bath and Wells was anything but.[27] Among those who coveted it was Henry IV's keeper of the privy seal, Richard Clifford. Clifford had enjoyed a politically agile career: bedded into Richard II's household from at least 1380, he was one of the clerks whom the Appellants dismissed from court in 1388, but once the king recovered his authority he was soon brought back. A pluralist on a heroic scale, he entertained generously, amassed canonries, archdeaconries and deaneries worth at least as much as most bishoprics and seemed almost to bounce from one promotion to the next.[28] But what he really coveted was his own see. In 1395 he was almost successful, being nominated by both king and chapter for Salisbury but denied by Pope Boniface's provision of Richard Medford.[29] This seems only to have stiffened his resolve: by 1397–8, having now risen to the keepership of the privy seal and been appointed as archdeacon of Canterbury, he was suspected of scheming to have the aged Erghum removed from Bath and Wells.

True or not, once Erghum died on 10 April 1400, it took Clifford less than five weeks to secure a papal bull of provision. Unfortunately for him, both chapters (monastic Bath and secular Wells), at the instigation of the king and Arundel, elected Henry Bowet, who was in Guyenne at the time and did not react as quickly to Erghum's death. It was not that either the king or the archbishop wished to deny Clifford. Although no theologian, he was widely acknowledged as an administrator of exceptional competence, and alone among Richard II's senior ministers who had been kept on by Henry, as keeper of the privy seal. Bowet, however – who had studied law at Cambridge and Bologna, held a doctorate in laws and had spent almost a decade in Rome – had what the king saw as even more compelling credentials: Arundel's former official at Ely, he subsequently devoted himself to the service of John of Gaunt and was close enough to Henry to have gone into exile with him in 1398. A further badge of honour was his conviction for treason in 1398.[30]

Usually in such cases one side was persuaded to back down, but not this time. By September 1400, the archbishop was referring to Bowet as bishop-elect of Bath and Wells,[31] but the pope was unmoved. Light is thrown on the affair by a letter written to Arundel in November 1400 by Francis Marinis, a member of the Florentine *compagnia* of the Albertini, the pope's bankers, informing him that, when a certain William Creek returned from Rome recently, he had not brought with him a bull providing Bowet or anyone else to Bath and Wells, although he claimed to have brought a letter from Boniface telling the king to write back with more definite instructions. However, neither Marinis nor anyone else had seen the letter and he for one did not trust Creek, since what he said was usually 'all lies' (*toutz sount mesongez*). If anything had happened to undermine Clifford's provision, Marinis was sure that his colleagues would have informed him, because it was a matter that greatly concerned the Albertini. He thus urged Arundel to beg the king to accept Clifford's provision.[32] That the Albertini should throw their considerable weight behind Clifford was understandable for, as later became apparent, Clifford had sealed an obligation for £666 to them in return for securing his provision – nominally for their expenses, but in effect a bribe – and had also promised to pay them £1,333 for the first fruits (or annates) of the see in the event that he was successful.[33] Doubtless Boniface would also have received a proportion of the Albertini's 'expenses': thus he too had some incentive to support Clifford.

By the time parliament met in January 1401, the situation was becoming embarrassing. Generally speaking, the commons recognized that episcopal appointments were a matter for greater persons than they, but on this occasion, uniquely, they submitted a petition on the last full day of the parliament (9 March) on Clifford's behalf, pointing out that it was papal provision which had denied him Salisbury six years earlier but that he was now being denied Bath and Wells *despite* papal provision. Politely, but firmly, Henry disagreed: although well aware of Clifford's excellent record of service, he explained that Bowet had also done him good service, even putting his life in peril on his behalf, and moreover had been elected by the chapters 'in accordance with the custom of the kingdom' – which, practically speaking, was stretching a point. Parliament was not satisfied, and the lords spiritual and temporal now added their voices in favour of Clifford, while the commons suggested rather optimistically that the king might be able to 'make provision for both Richard Clifford and Henry Bowet'. Henry said he would love to, if only he could 'grant one thing to two people'.[34] A month later, he gave Bowet custody of the temporalities of Bath and Wells, making it clear that he had no intention of stepping back. This was normally the last step before consecration, only taken once a new bishop had been elected and provided. But it was still Clifford who had the bull of provision.[35]

How long the impasse might have continued is difficult to know, had not Tideman Winchcombe of Worcester obliged by dying on 13 June 1401, whereupon all parties moved quickly to resolve the situation. Clifford, supported by the pope, king and archbishop, was elected to Worcester within two weeks and Bowet simultaneously confirmed at Bath and Wells.[36] Anxious to bring the fifteen-month vacancy to an end, Arundel accepted Bowet's profession of obedience by proxy – the first recorded occasion in the history of Canterbury administration when this was allowed.[37] Clifford, meanwhile, was trying to wriggle out of his promise to pay the Albertini £666 for his ineffective provision to Bath and Wells and, although Arundel and others asked the king to help him, Henry refused to comply, claiming that he had seen Clifford's promissory letter himself 'sealed by the said bishop'. Yet in September 1406 the Albertini were still claiming that they had not been fully paid.[38] Within another year, in the episcopal reshuffle following the death of Richard Scrope, both men would be elevated further, Clifford to London and Bowet to the archbishopric of York, which they retained until their deaths in 1421 and 1423 respectively.

Many years later, Thomas Gascoigne, royal chaplain and chancellor of Oxford university, recalled an anecdote which provides a footnote to this story. One day, Henry IV asked Bowet why it was that modern bishops were not translated (from their graves, bodily, with a view to canonization) on account of their famous miracles, as they had been in the past. Bowet said nothing, but a clerk who overheard the question volunteered the following reasons: firstly, because God used to show who should become a bishop by working miracles through them, but now it was kings and others on earth who chose the bishops that pleased them; secondly, because kings used to implore holy men to become bishops, to which they only consented for the sake of saving souls; and thirdly, bishops of old had no desire to be translated from one see to another in order to obtain larger revenues, but now they did and, having been translated during their lives, did not deserve to be translated again after death. 'Why, you, my lord', said the clerk to the king, 'know of one man who gave two thousand marks [£1,333] to an earthly lord (*domino terreno*) to be translated from his bishopric to an archbishopric.' Henry apparently found this amusing, but not Bowet, to whom it referred.[39]

4

Visitations
1400–1

While the struggle for Bath and Wells rumbled on, Arundel made an energetic start to one of the most time-consuming pastoral duties incumbent on any archbishop: metropolitan visitations. Established canonically and practically in England from the mid-thirteenth century,[1] visitations proclaimed a high ideal for the Church. Their purpose was both to allow an archbishop to show himself to his clergy and to ensure as far as possible that, throughout his province, the approved beliefs, practices and responsibilities of the Catholic Church were being upheld and performed. In each diocese that the archbishop visited, the suffragan bishop and his ministers, heads of religious houses, archdeacons, deans and even, in theory, four parishioners from each parish were interviewed and invited to present any grievances, negligence or abuse which required correction. Enquiries were made, *inter alia*, about such matters as appropriations of churches, titles to benefices, payment of pensions and tithes, standards of clerical education, immorality and suspicion of heresy. To remedy any defects, all jurisdictions subordinate to the metropolitan's – episcopal, abbatial, decanal – were suspended for the duration of the visitation and any fees accruing to them diverted (as 'procurations') to the archbishop. This meant that it was the archbishop or his officials who, *pro tempore*, held ordinations, filled vacant benefices, proved wills and resolved disputes. When bishops in turn undertook visitations of their dioceses, they delved deeper into parish life, checking the physical condition and prescribed equipment (furniture, mass-books, candles) of each church and the operation of local ecclesiastical courts. The expectation was that a bishop should visit his diocese every three years, and at times this was realized. Undertaking visitations is above all what is meant when modern historians characterize bishops or archbishops in medieval England as 'conscientious'.[2] Parishioners might also welcome them as an opportunity to register complaints about their priest or about neighbours.

Yet along with acceptance of the practice of metropolitan visitation there was also a tradition of resistance to what some bishops saw as unnecessary or even malicious interference. It is easy to assume that the main reason for this was the financial loss incurred by diocesan officials, and sometimes this was true. But not always: at Oxford university, for example, it was the perceived threat to academic privilege; in other cases, cherished claims of exemption from visitation, either particular (by a monastery) or general (for example, by the friars) were put forward, partly in order to preserve claims for the future (in effect, 'use it or lose it', a widely accepted principle in medieval times). The uneasy balance between metropolitan and suffragan jurisdiction was always likely to throw up anomalies. Not infrequently, an archbishop was met at the entrance to a cathedral or religious house with an initial refusal to submit to visitation which, after formal recording of the objection and a discussion over refreshments, soon evaporated.

But at times resistance was more serious. When Archbishop Courtenay visited Exeter diocese in the spring of 1384, Bishop Brantingham appeared at first to welcome him, but a week later issued an inhibition against any of his subjects obeying the archbishop's instructions, accompanied by a letter setting out precisely which episcopal functions Courtenay might exercise during his visitation and which he might not – the latter naturally including many which he claimed. For three months, to the accompaniment of inhibitory mandates, summonses, threats of excommunication and petty violence (a group of archiepiscopal officials was assaulted and one of them made to eat the wax from his seal), Courtenay and Brantingham each made a show of running the diocese while feigning ignorance of the other. Eventually, on 2 July, the bishop submitted and acknowledged the metropolitan's claims. After this, most of Courtenay's visitations passed off without serious incident, although at Salisbury in 1390 Bishop Waltham, having appealed to the pope for protection, failed to appear before him, whereupon the archbishop excommunicated him and his supporters. Fortunately, the dean of Salisbury brokered an agreement and, once Waltham had submitted, the excommunication was lifted and the visitation went ahead. To mollify Waltham, some of his officials were included among the commissaries who carried out the visitation.[3]

There was a requirement, or at least a tradition, that, before visiting any other diocese, the primate should visit his own. Arundel took this seriously and had undertaken a preliminary visitation of Canterbury diocese as early as March 1397, which he completed during the first few months of 1400, basing himself at his archiepiscopal manors – or 'palaces' – at Maidstone, Otford and Charing.[4] Canterbury diocese was relatively compact, and a visitation did not require a great deal of travelling. He also spent some time in neighbouring Rochester while installing John Bottlesham as bishop.[5] Easter, which fell on 20 April in 1400, found him back at Canterbury, after which he spent about a month, from late May to late June, visiting Chichester diocese, his ancestral home and a county with a good number of archiepiscopal estates, staying mainly at his manors of Mayfield and Slindon.[6] The remaining summer months, while Henry IV undertook campaigns to Scotland and Wales, Arundel spent largely in his diocese, preparing his next round of visitations.[7]

By early October 1400, he was ready to venture further afield. Visitation was also a useful way to keep an eye on bishops who were politically suspect, which may be why Arundel began by visiting Coventry and Lichfield diocese, for if any bishop was likely to prove difficult, it was John Burghill. Burghill was Richard II's last confessor and the only bishop to have attended the former king's funeral in March. Arriving at Shrewsbury on 15 October, Arundel met up with Henry, just back from a punitive circuit around Snowdonia in response to the Welsh uprising in September. King and archbishop must have welcomed the chance to confer, but Burghill was rather less hospitable.[8] While Arundel perambulated his diocese, he remained brooding at Eccleshall castle.[9] If this disappointed Arundel, he had little to fear, for Burghill had no desire to risk his life in pursuit of heroism. When required to respond to royal or archiepiscopal queries he could be disarmingly polite,[10] but otherwise he kept his distance: not once after 1399 did he attend parliament (not even in 1404, when it was held at Coventry), instead remaining resolutely in his diocese until his death in 1414, a disgruntled but unthreatening phantasm. Yet he appears to have been a generous and conscientious diocesan and, although the archbishop's clerks evidently enjoyed telling scurrilous jokes about him, Arundel was content to let him be.[11]

Following his brief meeting with the king on 15 October,[12] Arundel began his visitation of Burghill's large and rambling diocese. In practice, an archbishop tended to focus personally on visiting the cathedrals and major religious houses of the diocese, leaving the scores of officials who accompanied him to go around the lesser communities and parishes. Arundel was no exception: the metropolitan visitation of Coventry and Lichfield lasted six months (18 October 1400 to 16 April 1401), during which twenty-eight religious houses, thirty-one deaneries, five archdeaconries, four royal chapels and two cathedrals were visited. Many recommendations for improvement were made, even at venerable monastic houses such as St Werburgh's at Chester and royal chapels such as Wolverhampton, and several resignations followed, including Thomas Southam as abbot of Burton (Staffordshire) and Matilda de Bottourd as abbess of Polesworth (Warwickshire). However, Arundel was only present in person for the first three weeks, until 8 November,[13] when he received an urgent message advising him to return to the capital in order to 'deal with the wolves and foxes who were infecting the English Church with their pestiferous teaching and depraved heresy' – that is, the Lollards.[14]

It was a harbinger of things to come: as the great matters of Church and State began to press in on him, the archbishop would find it increasingly difficult to focus on his more routine responsibilities. Even so, he managed until the autumn of 1403 to avoid spending more than about four months of each year in London, roughly half of which was at meetings of parliament and convocation. His preference was to conduct his business elsewhere – at Canterbury, at his favoured Saltwood castle, or on visitations.[15]

By September 1401, after a spring and summer of burgeoning political crisis, Arundel was ready to resume his round of visitations, beginning with his old diocese, Ely, where, between 15 September and 11 October, he and his commissaries visited ten monasteries, eight deaneries, one hospital, Cambridge university and five of its colleges (apparently without opposition), and Ely cathedral.[16] When he arrived at Ely on 19 September, he was 'honourably received' by Bishop Fordham, but what he found was a chapter in turmoil.[17] Prior William Walpole, who had only held office for four years, was said to have committed numerous 'indiscretions', although the only one mentioned was that his election in 1397 was uncanonical; given two days to consider his position (*ista in mente revolvens*), he agreed on 22 September that he was unfit to preside over the church, and duly, 'of his own free will, without force or threat', resigned.[18] Whereupon, with the archbishop looking on, a new prior, William Powcher, was immediately – 'as if at the instigation (*instinctu*) of the Holy Spirit' – elected, carried to the high altar and acclaimed. The proceedings were rounded off by Arundel reading a collect of St Etheldreda, the reputed founder of the cathedral, presumably from the *Liber Eliensis*. Yet he had no desire to punish the disgraced prior further: before leaving Ely, he directed that Walpole should be provided for life with £20 a year of manorial income, £10 a year for clothing, a chaplain of his choice and lodging in the priory with food and drink for himself and his servants. Sometime later, on hearing that these terms were not being fulfilled, Arundel wrote twice to the chapter ordering them to maintain Walpole 'as befitted his former status'.[19]

Walpole's resignation was evidently negotiated relatively easily; more problematic was the settlement of the long-running dispute between Bishop Fordham and his archdeacon, John Welborne. These two had been at loggerheads for years over their respective powers, causing judicial delays, additional work and expense, and 'intractable questions' (*questiones intricabiles*). In May 1401, Arundel had commissioned one of his officials, John Barnet, to sort out the issues between the two, but without success.[20] It was a problem with which Arundel was all too familiar: he too had encountered difficulties with his archdeacons while bishop of Ely.[21] The main issues were the claims of successive archdeacons to decide matrimonial disputes, prove wills and exercise judicial functions within the Isle of Ely, traditionally regarded as jurisdictionally separate from the diocese as a whole.

As bishop of Ely, Arundel had taken a fairly lenient line with his archdeacons, but now, bolstered by his authority as metropolitan, he was more robust. Ordering both men to swear to submit to his arbitration, he imposed a composition, dated 8 November 1401 at Canterbury, which, although weighted in favour of the bishop, also made concessions to Welborne. In essence, it committed all ecclesiastical jurisdiction in the city, the Isle of Ely and nine named parishes to the bishop, but left the rest of the diocese to the archdeacon. Crucially, however, Welborne's jurisdiction over testamentary and matrimonial disputes (usually the most profitable cases) was severely restricted, while the appointment of his officials was to be overseen and their number limited. By way of compensation, the bishop agreed to grant the appropriation of the living of Haddenham (Cambridgeshire) to the archdeacon – a valuable acquisition, although it cannot have made up for more than a portion of the revenues Welborne would lose.[22]

Eighteen months later, Arundel issued a further set of financial reforms at Ely.[23] The gist of these was the insistence that income from the monastic estates was to be collected by the stewards and bailiffs of the manors and given by them to two monk-treasurers who would be responsible for their disbursement to members of the community. They were to render accounts twice a year. Similar measures had been tried at Ely before, but had fallen into disuse. His hope was that strict adherence to this system would ensure better attendance at services, since it would obviate the need for monks to leave the monastic precincts to collect their rents. All revenues were to be passed to one chief cook and one cellarer, who would be responsible for preparing all the community's food and drink in one kitchen, instead of having separate kitchens for the prior's hospice, the refectory, the guests' hospice and the infirmary. Only the sacristy (with its special needs for cathedral services) and the almonry would retain their own kitchens. Further injunctions sought to regulate the entertainment of guests under one hosteller rather than several; the 'honest', rather than 'customary', distribution of bread and ale to the monks; and a prohibition on the granting of excess food, clothes or the monks' standard six-monthly clothing allowances to relatives or friends. Leftover food was to be distributed solely to the poor, via the almonry.

These early visitations provide a good indication of the kind of inter-clerical rivalries and corrupt or inefficient practices which it fell to a primate to try to resolve, and of Arundel's way of dealing with them: firmness without vindictiveness, and distinct demarcation lines between responsibilities. His financial reforms mirror his views at the provincial or national level – for example, the management of York archdiocese during his frequent absences, or the measures he had introduced as chancellor a decade earlier.[24] He believed in centralization under a relatively small number of officials: men whom he trusted but who were also subject to regular audits to ensure that they did not betray that trust; he also believed in a reversion to first principles, as long as they were effective, rather than showy innovations; and he was ever eager to eliminate corruption and unnecessary expense.

On 23 September 1401, he left Ely to visit Bishop Henry Despenser and his chapter at Norwich. Despenser, like Arundel, was an aristocrat and had been a bishop for nearly thirty years. Unlike Arundel, he never sought political or administrative office in the crown's service, preferring to reside in his diocese, where he sedulously nurtured a succession of feuds with his prior and chapter, with the townsmen of Norwich and Lynn, and with local nobles such as Sir Thomas Erpingham.[25] Fame and infamy clung to Despenser in equal measure: widely praised for his vigorous response to the East Anglian rebels in 1381, he was almost universally condemned for his inept handling of the Flemish Crusade two years later.[26] However, his courage was not in doubt: even as Henry Bolingbroke carried all before him in the summer of 1399, Despenser was one of the few men who tried to rally support for Richard II, for which he was taken into custody.[27] Once parliament met on 6 October, he was released to take his seat among the lords spiritual and, in November, to return to his diocese, but instructed to remain there unless summoned by either the archbishop or the king.[28] His role in the Epiphany Rising, if any, is unclear but, given that his nephew Thomas (the demoted earl of Gloucester) was one of the conspirators, it is not surprising that suspicion fell on him. In a letter to another nephew, he swore 'by the faith I owe to God and to Holy Church' that he knew nothing about it and had only left his manor of South Elmham (Suffolk) once since mid-December, to attend a servant's funeral.[29] He was still arrested and, on 5 February 1400, handed over to Arundel, under whose care he remained at Canterbury for the next eleven months.

Although quarrelsome and at times obtuse, Despenser did not lack friends.[30] Henry IV's sister Philippa, queen of Portugal, writing to Arundel in the autumn of 1399 to ask him to try to repair the rupture between the king and the bishop, extolled the kindness he had shown her in the past; Thomas, Lord la Warre, likewise reminded the archbishop of Despenser's 'great kindness and consideration to me through all my great troubles'; and a letter the bishop wrote to his niece after her husband's death in 1400 reveals real sensitivity.[31] Shared aristocratic birth and episcopal longevity – much of the time in neighbouring dioceses – might also have created a bond between him and Arundel. At any rate, despite his adherence to Richard II, or the earlier disagreements between the Despensers and the Fitzalans, Arundel tried to help him.

Friction between the bishops and chapter of Norwich had deep roots, and ten years of almost continuous residence in his diocese by Despenser from 1385 to 1395 had evidently proved too great a strain. Foremost amid a complex web of grievances were the jurisdiction of the prior and convent in their estates, rights of appointment to cathedral offices, and the discipline of the community and its dependent monastic cells. Following an appeal by the monks to Pope Boniface in 1394–5, one of the first tasks assigned to Arundel when he became archbishop had been to try to effect a reconciliation between them and the bishop, but before anything could be resolved he was exiled and the case was passed to Roger Walden, who in March 1398 (with Richard II's backing) imposed a settlement almost entirely in favour of the bishop. Following Arundel's restoration, the monks again appealed to Rome, and thus the case stood when, in the spring of 1400, with Despenser now resident at Canterbury, Boniface IX again tried to enforce a settlement. What followed was an ultimately humiliating exercise in papal bombast. Declaring the 'pretended sentence' of 1398 to have been 'iniquitous', the pope imposed silence on both parties, forbade Arundel from conducting a visitation of Norwich on the grounds – tellingly – that he was too favourably disposed to the bishop and committed the case to an arbitrator of his own choosing, who produced a more even-handed judgment.[32] Despenser, now back in his diocese after being pardoned in the parliament of January 1401,[33] simply ignored this, as did Arundel, who, papal prohibition notwithstanding, arrived at Norwich on 24 September 1401 and spent five days there.

Welcomed by Despenser, the prior, chapter and 'whole citizenry', the archbishop was escorted in solemn procession to the cathedral before retiring to the Carmelite friary, where, tactfully, he stayed at his own expense. By the time he left, he had managed, 'by good mediation' and 'an outpouring of divine grace' (*divina gratia exuberante*), to persuade them to 'put aside the malice' which they bore towards each other and restore 'peace to the church and unity and concord to the father and the sons, to the praise and exultation of citizens and subjects'. Yet, although his composition earned praise for its clarity in defining the spheres of their respective jurisdictions, it differed only in minor details from the royal judgment of 1398: that is to say, it largely favoured Despenser. This was probably predictable. An archbishop generally had little option but to uphold his suffragans' authority within their dioceses for, if he lost the support of his bishops (as Thomas Becket had done), his task became almost impossible. Nevertheless, Arundel succeeded in imposing a truce – largely, it seems, because the monks decided that nothing more was to be gained from pursuing their grievances and compounded with the bishop in return for the enjoyment of their former (limited) privileges. Pope Boniface in turn had no alternative but to swallow his pride and confirm the judgment, which he did in December 1402.[34] And it lasted, more or less, for as long as Despenser lived – that is to say, for the next four years – following which Arundel would once again be obliged to intervene at Norwich.[35]

Moving westwards, Arundel made two more visits. The first was to Walsingham priory, the site of England's most famous Marian shrine, where he found another prior accused of 'many and various defects' and ordered him to resign – although to avoid future difficulties he took the deposed prior into his own obedience, exempting him from the jurisdiction of the bishop or new prior. As at Ely, he instructed the convent to make sure that their former prior was given £27 a year for life to support himself and his servants.[36] Secondly, Arundel visited the great and ancient Benedictine monastery of Bury St Edmunds. This was not a visitation, simply a visit, but because the surviving account of it comes not from the archiepiscopal records but from a monk of Bury who compiled an internal memorandum a few days later, it is instructive as to how even the possibility of visitation was viewed by those on the receiving end. According to this memorandum, when the prior of Bury heard on the afternoon of 30 September that Arundel was staying twelve miles away at Mildenhall, he went to meet him there, bringing gifts of bread, wine, beer, mutton, rabbits, chickens, and oats and hay for the horses. Taken by surprise, the archbishop's officials were unsure whether they ought to accept these without his assent, but when Arundel saw the gifts he accepted them 'most enthusiastically and gratefully, showing a cheerful and kindly face to all'.[37] What the prior really wanted to know was whether the archbishop had any intention of trying to visit Bury, for the 400-year-old abbey had time-honoured papal and royal exemptions from visitation.[38] He was doubtless relieved to hear that, on this occasion, the archbishop thought it unlikely that he would do so.

The next day, however – 'moved by I know not what spirit' (*nescio quo spiritu ductus*), as the memorandum put it – Arundel changed his mind, so that when, on the morning of 1 October, his officials arrived in Bury with his baggage train seeking accommodation for the night, 'we were troubled and greatly astonished' (*turbati fuimus et multum attoniti*). Abbot William Cratfield hastily convened a conventual meeting to decide how their ancient papal and royal exemptions might be upheld without causing offence to a man who 'apart from the king, was greater and more powerful than anyone else in the kingdom of England'. Some thought a solemn procession would of necessity have to be arranged for him, but others argued that if this was done 'we would in some way be placed in subjection and would then be no different from others who were obedient and subject to him elsewhere in the kingdom', for no such procession had been offered to any archbishop of Canterbury in modern times (*moderna tempora*).

Eventually it was agreed that the abbot, sacrist and cellarer, accompanied by the sixteen-year-old Thomas, Lord Mowbray, heir to the earldom of Nottingham, should ride out to meet him, thereby showing a carefully calibrated degree of respect while avoiding the need for a formal procession. This proved to be a shrewd move, for once Arundel appeared the community's fears soon melted away in the face of his easy and unthreatening manner. Nevertheless, the community remained vigilant, leading him through the town to the cathedral but carefully not opening the great west doors or ringing bells as was done for formal processions, then entering the church via the cemetery, and so up to the high altar and St Edmund the Martyr's shrine – where Arundel took particular delight in examining the jewels – and into the 'palace'. Here he was offered wine before attending vespers, flanked by the abbot and Lord Mowbray.

After spending the night in lodgings in the town (having declined the abbot's offer to stay in the monastery), the archbishop rose 'very early', attended five masses in the reliquary chapel, one of which he celebrated, and was taken to see St Edmund's shirt, where he made an offering. Then, following a tour of the monastic buildings, he returned at eleven o'clock to the palace, where he and his officials enjoyed a 'cheerful and convivial' meal with the abbot, the earl of Suffolk and their servants.[39] According to the monk, Arundel's clerks and esquires declared that 'they had not seen their lord happier or jollier while eating with any other lord that whole year'. Eventually, after a farewell drink with the abbot, the archbishop rode away towards Newmarket, accompanied for four miles by the abbot, the earl of Suffolk, Lord Mowbray, the prior, the sacrist, the cellarer and a great crowd of others. 'I have written all these things down', concluded the monk, 'so that our successors should learn and understand how to conduct themselves towards archbishops of Canterbury in the event of them similarly wishing to come to our monastery.'[40] It was an object lesson in tactfulness on both sides, something of a rarity in the Trollopian world of medieval clerical politics.

Soon after this, Arundel returned to Canterbury, leaving his commissaries to continue the visitation. And, as it turned out, his East Anglian tour of September–October 1401 marked the end of the initial round of visitations on which he had embarked eighteen months earlier. It would be another ten years before he conducted a visitation in person, although he continued to visit individual houses when alerted to serious problems, imposing condign punishments. The most notable was to Glastonbury abbey, one of England's oldest and most celebrated monasteries, in

September 1408, which resulted in the resignation of the prior, Thomas Coffyn, the transfer of six 'delinquent' monks to other Benedictine monasteries, the imprisonment of others and the renunciation of various privileges.[41] Metropolitan visitations also continued to be conducted by his officials, often in conjunction with *sede vacante* administration, partly in the hope of forestalling episcopal objections. Winchester was visited following Bishop Wykeham's death in 1404, Norwich in 1406 and again in 1411–12, and Salisbury following the death of Bishop Medford in 1407.[42] Individual houses, or just individuals, causing concern were also visited by Arundel's officials, such as Amesbury convent (Wiltshire) in 1401, or the archdeacon of Exeter, William Pylton, who was obliged to resign in February 1410.[43] It was not that Arundel grew indifferent to the myriad of complaints about communities, individuals or discreditable practices that were constantly brought to his attention. He was simply overwhelmed by the accumulating political and ecclesiastical crises engulfing the Lancastrian Church and State.

5

William Sawtre: A Candle Lit
1401

On 7 August 1407, towards the end of a lengthy interrogation of the inveterate Lollard William Thorpe, Arundel exclaimed to him, 'Know this for sure, you wretch (*losel*): that it was God, as I know well, who summoned me back to this land in order to destroy the false sect of which you are a member. And, by God, I shall pursue you as far as Acle, until there is not one trace of you left in this land!'[1] He was not exaggerating. Lollardy, to his mind, posed the first existential threat for more than a millennium to the integrity of the faith in England, the charge with which God had entrusted him. Even before his exile, he had made a vigorous start to his campaign to extirpate heresy from England, and by Easter 1400 he was ready to renew the offensive.

Documentation relating to the Lollards' beliefs is plentiful, but evidence of their detection is much harder to come by, for it was usually only after heterodoxy was already suspected that it appeared in the records. Most heretics were probably identified through their preaching, for sermons were at the heart of the Lollard mission to lift the veil of misinterpretation from the eyes of the faithful. William Ramsbury, an early Lollard preacher in the diocese of Salisbury, declared that 'it would be much more meritorious for priests to travel through the country with a Bible under their arm and preach to the people than to recite matins or celebrate masses or other holy offices'. Preaching, moreover, must be grounded in the Scriptures, not in the kind of 'fables, poetry or chronicles' with which friars habitually larded their sermons.[2] One way in which the authorities sought to bring heterodox opinions to light was thus to restrict those who were permitted to preach, through a system of licensing: while Lollards claimed that authority to preach came directly from God, through spiritual inspiration or divine calling, the Church maintained that it should be restricted to those whom it licensed to do so, and ever since the Blackfriars council of 1382 it had sought to draw the temporal powers into the task of muzzling the unlicensed. How exactly a licensing system should be enforced was, of course, not an easy question – although it was one which Arundel, when bishop of Ely, had interpreted unambiguously, placing the responsibility on 'each and every one of our subjects, ecclesiastical and secular of both sexes' to prevent the unlicensed from preaching in 'churches, chapels, oratories, cemeteries, cities, villages or other places, whether sacred or profane'.[3]

On 12 May 1400, therefore, doubtless at Arundel's bidding, the king ordered sheriffs throughout England to issue a proclamation forbidding any chaplain, regular or secular, under pain of imprisonment and forfeiture, from preaching either publicly or covertly in any place whatsoever, 'until by the diocesan admitted [licensed] to do so', since it had 'newly come to the king's ears' that some chaplains 'in their sermons do sow divers errors, heresies and other nefarious innovations repugnant to the Catholic faith and to the sanctions of the fathers'.[4] A month later, probably as a result of this proclamation, John Beket of Pattiswick (Essex) was brought before Arundel at Slindon (Sussex) to be interrogated about certain 'detestable heresies and errors' which, through 'blind ignorance' he had promulgated. These included: (1) that a priest in mortal sin could not consecrate the host or baptize; (2) that kings and secular lords in mortal sin need not be obeyed; (3) that sexual intercourse outside marriage was not necessarily a sin; (4) that children could eat meat on the Sabbath without incurring sin; (5) that it was wrong to worship sacred images, including the crucifix; and (6) that there should be no impediment to priests marrying, or to men or women of religion returning to secular life, and that their teaching and preaching were more pleasing to God than the teaching and preaching of the whole Church. Beket either was or was pretending to be a friar, and friars often claimed exemption from licensing regulations, citing a papal mandate to preach throughout Christendom.[5] Either way, his views were indisputably unorthodox and since he refused to recant he was excommunicated. On 10 June, however, having 'regained his senses', he agreed to abjure his earlier opinions, which he did publicly in Arundel's presence, whereupon his excommunication was lifted.[6]

On 12 January 1401, as the second convocation of the reign approached, the net was widened when Arundel appointed a different John Beket and the otherwise unknown John Pedmersch to search out each and every person (*omnes et singulos*) who 'asserted, taught and publicly preached damnable and reprehensible opinions and conclusions in contempt of the Creator and of their souls and those of other faithful Christians', and to summon them before the archbishop. To enable them to conduct their search, the king took them under his protection for a year.[7] It was probably as a result of this sweep of the nooks and shadows of heterodoxy that William Sawtre or Chatrys was apprehended.[8]

It may have been while Henry Despenser was staying with him at Canterbury in 1400 that Arundel first heard Sawtre's name. On 30 April 1399, while serving as parish chaplain at St Margaret's church in (King's) Lynn, he was interrogated by Despenser on suspicion of preaching heretical opinions in Lynn and at nearby Tilney. That at least some of the conclusions which he advocated were heretical, there is no doubt. They included: (1) that he would rather worship a king or a truly contrite man than a crucifix; (2) that money spent on pilgrimages was wasted and should instead be given to the poor; (3) that it was more important for priests to preach or teach than to conduct canonical services; and (4) that after the consecration of the host at mass, real bread remained on the altar (in other words, he believed in consubstantiation rather than transubstantiation).[9] Invited by Despenser to retract his views, he initially refused but eventually submitted, publicly abjuring his beliefs in Lynn on 25 May 1399, and five days later promising the bishop and his lawyers that he would never again 'preach, affirm, nor hold' them.[10] By early 1400, however, having left Norfolk and become a parish chaplain at St Benet Sherehog in London, he had resumed preaching and was consorting with other Lollard suspects. He may also have been involved in the Epiphany Rising, for on 6 February 1400 he was pardoned for unspecified 'treasons and felonies with which he was lately charged'.[11] Yet it was probably only a matter of time before Sawtre once again came to the authorities' notice.

Convocation was summoned to meet at St Paul's on 26 January 1401. Before that, however, on 20 January, came the opening of Henry IV's second parliament at Westminster. Much had changed in the fourteen months since the last parliament, and little if any of it reflected well on the king. He had antagonized the French, led a fruitless two-week campaign into Scotland and faced rebellion in Wales. Already regarded by his enemies as a usurper, he was now decried by some as a regicide to boot, while the financial incompetence of his ministers was plunging the government into insolvency. Furthermore, the Lollards were growing bolder. These, then, were the three issues uppermost in the minds of those who gathered at St Paul's and Westminster in January 1401: Wales, ministerial control of finances and heresy. The first two were primarily matters for parliament, not convocation, to address, and address them it did, passing a slew of racist laws against the Welsh (which only inflamed nationalist sentiment) and forcing the king to replace his chancellor, the three chief officers of his household and, three months later, his treasurer of England. All this naturally took time, and after six weeks of ill-tempered negotiation it might be thought surprising that parliament still had time to address the question of heresy.[12]

Yet it is clear not only that it did but that for many of those present it was just as pressing an issue as Wales or crown finance. From the first day to the last, accounts of the session are shot through with the language of reformism and reaction. 'At the time of this parliament', wrote Adam Usk, 'certain of these Lollards, assembling in London from every part of the kingdom, intended utterly to destroy the clergy, who were at that time meeting in convocation there. But my lord of Canterbury [Arundel], forewarned of their evil schemes, had prepared suitable counter-measures.'[13] Rarely was Usk guilty of understatement, but others shared his apprehension. It was customary during the opening speech of parliament, whether given by a cleric or a layman, to reassure members that the king was committed to the protection of the Church in England. However, on this occasion, when the chief justice Sir William Thirning rose to speak on 21 January, he added the words – uniquely in the history of medieval parliaments – that the Church which Henry promised to sustain was that which had been 'approved by the holy fathers and doctors of Holy Church and by holy Scripture'. Heterodox deviations, in other words, would not be tolerated.

Also uniquely, the speaker of the commons, the loquacious and sanctimonious Sir Arnold Savage – once a knight of Richard II's chamber, now firmly Lancastrian – declared that the three estates of the realm (king, lords and commons) 'might be best represented by a Trinity'. Towards the end of the session, he remarked that 'the business of parliament truly resembled a mass': the archbishop of Canterbury, he explained, had 'commenced the office, read the epistle and expounded the gospel'; the king had continued it, 'declaring many times before all his lieges that it was his wish that the faith of Holy Church be sustained and governed as it had been in the time of his noble progenitors, and as is affirmed by Holy Church and by the holy doctors and by holy Scripture' (thereby echoing Thirning's words); and the commons had brought it to an end by saying '*Ite, missa est*' and '*Deo gratias*', the proper conclusion to the Catholic mass. In this parliament, Savage went on, the commons had particular reason to be grateful, for 'when the faith of Holy Church had been on the point of annihilation by evil doctrine . . . our lord the king had given and ordained a good and just remedy for this, resulting in the destruction of this doctrine and of its sect'.[14] To talk of the 'destruction' of Lollardy in 1401 was wishful thinking, but such sacramentalist language was evidently designed to create the impression that, if nothing were done soon to curb the spread of heresy, it would be too late.

Where parliament led, convocation needed no second bidding to follow. Assembling on 29 January in St Paul's chapter house, the clergy were told by Arundel that their primary task was to enquire into the 'errors and heresies' of those who held clandestine meetings, preached heterodoxy or even questioned the sacrament of the altar, thereby undermining the faith of 'the simple'.[15] No sooner had he finished than a powerful royal delegation arrived, led by the earl of Northumberland, who assured the clergy that the king was as concerned as they were about the alarming spread of heresy and would fully support them in ensuring that delinquents were punished. Yet, in order to 'defend and save' the realm, the king needed money, and the clergy must be willing to grant a subsidy. The gist of this quid pro quo had doubtless already been agreed between Arundel and Henry; no more need be said for the moment and, once the delegates had departed, the archbishop 'almost immediately' (*quasi incontinenti*) announced a two-week prorogation. This may have been when Sawtre was apprehended. Thomas Walsingham said he was arrested during the parliament, and there is no indication that Arundel had questioned him before convocation reconvened.[16] It was the record of his examination by Bishop Despenser nearly two years earlier which provided the basis for his interrogation when, on Saturday 12 February, he was brought into St Paul's to stand trial.[17]

Here was a man, Arundel began, a 'self-styled chaplain' (*capellanum praetensum*), who had already abjured his 'heretical and erroneous conclusions', but had since then openly and secretly preached and taught the same or similar conclusions. Robert Hallum, the archbishop's chancellor, read out the eight articles of his 1399 abjuration and Sawtre was invited to respond. He asked for a copy of the schedule and time to prepare his defence, both of which were allowed to him. Next Friday, 18 February, he was brought in again and his written response read out by Hallum. Much of this was well reasoned, unprovocative and revealed impressive understanding of the Scriptures and of orthodox doctrine.[18] Sawtre covered all the articles on which he had originally been examined: his views on the adoration of the cross, his scepticism about the status of angels, the value of pilgrimages and the canonical hours, and the meaning of transubstantiation. His response to the last was as follows:

> I say that after the pronouncement of the sacramental words of the body of Christ, bread remains, the bread which we break, both bread and the body of Christ; it does not cease to be simply bread, but continues to be holy, true, and the bread of life. I also believe this to be the true body of Christ following the pronouncement of the sacramental words.

This attempt to square the circle between Catholic doctrine and what Sawtre evidently could not in conscience deny was never likely to satisfy his interrogators. For Arundel, and doubtless for many in St Paul's that day, acceptance of the Eucharistic sacrament of the mass – the belief that, once consecrated, the host ceased utterly to be bread and was transubstantiated (transformed in substance) into the body of Christ – was the acid test of orthodoxy. Leaving aside Sawtre's first seven answers, therefore, Arundel continued to interrogate him on this question alone. Did Sawtre mean that he now rejected the doctrines on which he had been examined by Bishop Despenser? Sawtre said he did not. So, did he still believe that 'material bread' remained on the altar after pronouncement of the sacramental words? Sawtre did not know, but he knew that it was 'true bread, because it was the bread of life, which came down from heaven'. When pressed on the point, he would not give a definitive answer. Changing tack, Arundel asked him if the words pronounced by the priest transformed 'the nature of bread' into the body of Christ. Sawtre 'did not know what that meant'.

Arundel now suspended the trial and advised Sawtre to think carefully overnight about his responses, but when the interrogation resumed at eight o'clock the next day, 19 February, Sawtre was more evasive.

Once again, he was asked whether the words of the priest could 'transubstantiate the bread into the true body of Christ'? He 'did not understand this'. Asked if he thought that the priest's words meant the 'round and white' host ceased to be simple bread, Sawtre grew impatient and replied, 'as if mockingly' (*quasi deridendo*), that he did not know. This was enough for Arundel – indeed it would have been hard for him to find many more ways of framing the same question – but he gave the defendant one last chance: was he willing, on the question of transubstantiation, 'to stand by the determination of the Church' that consecrated bread ceased thereby to be bread? Sawtre could only reply that 'he was willing to stand by the determination of the Church insofar as it was not contrary to divine will'.

Three hours had passed without discernible progress and, with convocation's agreement, Arundel told his chancellor to pronounce sentence and declare Sawtre to be an unrepentant heretic who deserved to be punished 'as a heretic'. Hallum did so. Sawtre's response, according to Usk, was a forceful (*magno impetu*) outburst against the archbishop: 'I, who am sent from God, say to you that you and all your clergy, and the king too, will shortly succumb to an evil death, and that a people's foreign tongue will soon conquer and rule over this kingdom; and that these things are on the very threshold of coming to pass.'[19] Another source states that he appealed to the king and 'all the parliament' to be allowed a public hearing before them, for 'I, William Sawtre, protest that I do not wish to defend these or any conclusions in a false way (*falso sensu*), without sufficient deliberation, under the constraint of violent persecution and imprisonment.'[20] Arundel prorogued convocation until 23 February.

Whatever Sawtre believed to be the punishment awaiting him, he must have decided by now that he could not betray his conscience. Yet what form that punishment might take was by no means clear. Petitions against heresy were submitted during this parliament by both clergy and commons. That of the clergy can hardly have been drafted before

12 February, for convocation had not had time to discuss it; it was probably not drawn up until after Sawtre's conviction on 19 February. Its targets were the usual ones: heretical preaching, conventicles, books and schools; the danger to souls and incitement to sedition; and the necessity for the secular authorities to devise 'grave penalties' to deal with them. What this meant was that a suspect should be arrested by the bishop and held in prison 'until he or they shall canonically purge themselves . . . or shall abjure this wicked sect'. Any who refused or who subsequently relapsed were, after conviction in the presence of the king's secular officials, to be handed over to the lay authorities, who should then 'do that which is incumbent on them in this matter'. It was not the clergy's petition but the king's response to it which introduced the possibility that, if imprisonment or monetary fines failed to persuade culprits to abjure, 'they shall cause these persons to be publicly burned in a high place . . . and may punishment of this sort strike fear into the hearts of others'. The much briefer petition of the commons merely asked that, when any man or woman was imprisoned for Lollardy, 'let them have such punishment as they deserve . . . to make them adhere to the Christian faith'.[21] It was the petition of the clergy and the royal response to it which provided the text for the subsequent statute.[22]

There was thus no certainty as to the fate awaiting Sawtre when, on 23 February, he appeared once more in convocation. Due formalities were observed: the record of his recantation to Despenser in May 1399 was read out. Arundel asked him if he understood the process against him. He did. Did he wish to object to anything in the process? He did not. When Arundel reminded him that he had expressed the view that the host remained 'material bread' after consecration, which was manifestly heretical and which he had previously abjured, he replied, 'as if smiling or mocking' (*quasi ridendo sive deridendo*) that he 'denied and did not understand the question' (*praemissa negavit et ignoravit*). However, he admitted publicly teaching such views since his abjuration and knew no reason why he should not be declared a heretic. Convocation was once more prorogued. When it met again on Saturday 26 February,[23]

Sawtre was solemnly degraded and stripped of the vestments of each of the seven holy orders, from priest down to doorkeeper ('ostiary'), his tonsure was shaved off and a striped cap (*capitum stragulatum*) was placed on his head as a mark of his laity. Having thus been deprived of every scrap of clerical status, he was handed over to the marshal and constable of England, both present in person to receive him.

According to Walsingham, Sawtre remarked 'arrogantly' to the archbishop before he was taken away, 'Your malice is now complete. What further harm can you do me?' The answer was none, for the Church was done with him; he was a layman now, subject to the mercies of lay power. Walsingham adds that Arundel turned to the marshal and said 'Take him, so that he may be punished according to your law.' According to the archiepiscopal record, Arundel 'asked the said court [of the constable and marshal] as far as possible to treat the said William, thus remitted to them, favourably (*favorabiliter*)', but this was merely the conventional distancing of the clergy from responsibility for what was to be done.[24] Later the same day, the king wrote to the sheriffs of London ordering them to burn Sawtre 'in an open and public place . . . as is customarily done in such cases, according to divine, human and canonical law'.[25] No mention was made of any new statute or petitions.

Capital sentences were usually carried out immediately, but on this occasion, while Sawtre languished in prison, attention turned to a more notorious Lollard, John Purvey, who was brought into convocation on 28 February. Purvey, later described as the 'librarian of the Lollards', had probably studied under Wyclif at Oxford and had been his companion and amanuensis in his later years. He is thought to have helped to translate the first Wycliffite Bible into English.[26] How long he had been in custody is unclear: little had been heard of him for over a decade and, as it turned out, little would ever be heard of him again. He was immediately confronted with a list of his heretical opinions, which included: (1) the denial of transubstantiation; (2) scepticism about confessional absolution; (3) the belief that only God, not prelates, made priests; (4) that every human being was predestined, or not, to salvation; (5) that immoral priests forfeited their sacerdotal authority; (6) that the pope had no power to excommunicate; and (7) that there was no scriptural justification for clerical celibacy. At first he prevaricated, and it may be that the decision to commit Sawtre to the flames was taken in part to pressurize him. It was at any rate on 2 March, during Purvey's trial, that Sawtre was taken to Smithfield and, on the wide open space just outside the city wall where, twenty years earlier, Wat Tyler had confronted the fourteen-year-old Richard II, 'bound, standing upright, to a post set in a barrel with blazing wood all around, and thus reduced to ashes'.[27] A century and a half later, the Protestant martyr Hugh Latimer's last words to his fellow martyr Nicholas Ridley, as the flames leapt around them, were reported as: 'Be of good comfort, Master Ridley, and play the man; we shall this day light such a candle by God's grace in England as I trust shall never be put out.'[28] In fact, it was William Sawtre, England's Protestant protomartyr, who lit that candle.

Any remaining doubts about what awaited Purvey were now dispelled. Three days later, on 5 March, he abjured all his heretical opinions before Arundel and the bishops in convocation, and on the following day, Sunday 6 March, was taken to St Paul's Cross where he confessed to a great crowd, 'gathered as if for a sermon', that he had been in error, declaring that anyone who held such views in future deserved to be burned in 'perpetual fire'.[29] Six months later, he was admitted as rector of West Hythe (Kent), hard by Saltwood castle, where Arundel could keep an eye on him, but within two years he was gone, and his subsequent whereabouts are unknown until January 1414, when he was imprisoned for his part in the Lollard Rising.[30] He died four months later, apparently of natural causes.

Other heretics abjured alongside Purvey in March 1401, but their names are not known.[31] It only remained for convocation to grant the subsidy requested by the king – a generous one and a half clerical tenths – and, on 11 March, for Arundel to declare the session adjourned.[32]

Meanwhile, on 10 March, parliament was also adjourned, but not before passing the statute commonly known as *De Heretico Comburendo* ('For Burning a Heretic'). The fact that this was not passed until eight days *after* Sawtre's death has often been noted, the reason less frequently: it was simply unnecessary. Homegrown heresy may have come late to England, but it was certainly not unheard of before Wyclif, and heretics had been burned in England in the thirteenth and fourteenth centuries, if only occasionally. When the early Leicester Lollard William Swinderby was examined in Lincoln cathedral in 1382, he clearly expected to be burned if convicted; Bishop Despenser of Norwich swore in 1388–9 that any Lollard who dared to preach in his diocese would be either 'consigned to the flames' (*ignibus traderetur*) or beheaded.[33] As the king's writ to the sheriffs on 26 February pointed out, burning was the 'customary' and canonically approved punishment for relapsed or obdurate heretics.

Thus *De Heretico Comburendo* certainly did not (nor did it claim to) introduce the penalty of burning for heresy to England. What it did was to add statutory authority to what was already widely recognized as the appropriate punishment, thereby providing the last piece of the jigsaw in a twenty-year campaign by the English Church to recruit the secular authorities to practical as well as theoretical engagement in the prosecution of heterodoxy.[34] It appealed to different people for different reasons: to many churchmen, obviously, but also to many of the commons, who, as noted above, expressed deep concern about the 'wicked sect' which threatened the Christian faith, and to the king, for (as the statute pointed out) heresy was popularly associated with sedition, and the early years of the new reign were nervous ones. Henry IV would also have known that bringing the full force of the law to bear on heretics would not harm his chances of persuading both clergy and commons to open their purses. Although he doubtless shared Arundel's antipathy to out-and-out heretics, Henry had many other concerns to juggle and had said nothing about heresy during the 1399 parliament – although, as noted above, he and Arundel did express concern about the Bianchi.[35]

Yet if Arundel would surely have appreciated the reinforcement of his armoury of deterrents, there is nothing to suggest that he took pleasure in implementing this draconian sanction. Sawtre had been given every chance to redeem himself. When he became evasive or impertinent, he was offered alternative paths to conformity. Arundel's approach to heresy was that of the physician, not the surgeon: a heretic burned was a soul lost; a repentant heretic was a soul saved. Six weeks after the passing of *De Heretico Comburendo*, the Lollard John Seynon of Donington (Leicestershire) appeared in Canterbury cathedral publicly to renounce his beliefs that: (1) the true body and blood of Christ were not present in the sacrament of the altar after consecration, which could not transform the original 'nature of bread', and thus that the raising of the host at mass was a purely memorial act of Christ's Passion; and (2) the crucifix was idolatrous and those who made the sign of the cross committed idolatry. Crucially, Seynon also vouchsafed (*asseruit*) that the decree passed in 'the last convocation and parliament against the heretic recently burned in London' was not the reason why he had recanted; rather, it was 'from certain knowledge and my own free will [that] I condemn, revoke, abjure and anathematize all such heresy and error'. Whether or not Arundel believed this, it was not from fear of burning that he wanted heretics to conform, but because they understood the error of their ways. Having recanted, Seynon was absolved and released.[36] Another soul saved: that was what the Church was for. During the next few years, the archbishop continued to investigate reported cases of heresy, interrogate suspects and demand recantations – in Bristol, in East Anglia, in London, in Lincolnshire, in Calais – but for the moment there were no further burnings.[37]

6

Liberties and Franchises
1399–1402

On 6 October 1399, a week before Henry IV was crowned, parliament had met for just one day to appoint triers and receivers of petitions, elect a speaker and hear Arundel's opening sermon, before being prorogued until the day after the coronation. His theme was from 1 Maccabees, 'It behoves us to ordain for the kingdom', and, unlike his sermon to the estates on 30 September, it was brisk and business-like, establishing ground rules for the future rather than harping on past failings, emphasizing that Henry intended to rule under the laws of the land and respect others' rights: 'it was especially the king's will', he added, 'that Holy Church should have and enjoy all her liberties and franchises'.[1]

The 'liberties and franchises of Holy Church' meant something closer to what might now be termed privileges and immunities. But what exactly were they, and what justified the benefits they conferred? Were privilege and immunity sanctioned by divine law and thus inherent in the clerical order, as canon law asserted? Or were they, like the liberties and franchises of lords or boroughs, revocable acts of royal grace granted by rulers on condition that they were not abused? In sum, were they an entitlement or a concession? The answer depended on the respondent.[2] Churchmen spoke of their 'grievances' (*gravamina*), of being 'oppressed' (*gravata*), of the canonically sanctioned *privilegium canonis* (protection from lay violence) and *privilegium fori* (immunity from secular courts). Laymen might cite Roman law, which placed clerics broadly under temporal jurisdiction.

That secular authorities would uphold Catholic beliefs and practices could usually be taken for granted, but other liberties were not so straightforward, for there was a great deal at stake. In theory, the clergy claimed the right to decide presentations to benefices, to be exempt from secular taxation, for their persons and property (especially churches) to be protected from violence, and to be tried only in their own courts. Although sometimes alleged to have existed from time immemorial, in practice it was from the mid-eleventh century, with the growth of papal government and the explosion of monastic foundations, that clerical liberties had been widely acknowledged, often after decades of struggle. The problem of separate jurisdictions, for example – often characterized as 'benefit of clergy' or 'criminous clerks' – was the most celebrated issue in the dispute between Henry II and Becket in the 1160s. During the thirteenth century, however, the tide began to turn, and by Arundel's time clerical liberties had been much diluted. Presentations to English benefices were in effect shared between clerics and laymen, with the balance tilting towards the latter, especially after the passing of the Statutes of Provisors and Praemunire; clerical taxation, although usually conceded (in convocation), assessed and paid separately from lay taxation, had nevertheless become normalized; the *privilegium canonis* was still generally recognized, at least in theory, but the *privilegium fori* was confined to criminal law and excluded cases of treason.

The problem was that, whatever distinctions might be recognized in theory – clerical and secular, temporal and eternal, body and soul – the Church was so enmeshed in the world through property-holding, secular office-holding, financial transaction, the exercise of lordship and much else besides, that it was almost impossible in practice to maintain the fiction that they inhabited separate earthly spaces.[3] Against this, however, could be set the stranglehold which the Catholic Church had over medieval belief and imagination. What could be more important than saving one's soul?

The 'liberties and franchises of Holy Church' was thus a phrase fertile with ambiguity, and barely were the words out of Arundel's mouth before he was obliged to face his first challenge of the new reign – the election by the commons of the Gloucestershire knight Sir John Cheyne as their speaker. Politically, Cheyne's credentials for the role were impeccable. A former retainer of the murdered duke of Gloucester, he had been about the royal court for a quarter of a century and was one of the crown's foremost diplomats. He had also regularly been elected to parliament before falling out with Richard II and suffering imprisonment during the king's purge of the Appellants' supporters in 1397–8. Yet to Arundel his election as speaker was anathema, for Cheyne was known to hold strong views about ecclesiastical reform and was associated with several of those whom Walsingham and Knighton dubbed the Lollard knights.[4]

When convocation gathered on 7 October, therefore, the archbishop announced to the clergy that there were among the parliamentary knights a number of men who were 'decidedly hostile' to the Church, and 'in particular', he went on, 'he feared the sentiments and opinions of Sir John Cheyne', who, 'if he were to learn of any activity among the clergy for which they could be blamed, would not be silent, but would publish it abroad as much as he could to secure the dishonour of the clerics'. He thus advised them to conduct themselves with circumspection. He must have communicated these fears to Henry for, when parliament reconvened on 14 October, the proceedings began with Cheyne taking his oath of office but then promptly asking to be excused – because, he claimed, he was too debilitated by his time in prison to carry out his duties in a satisfactory manner. The indecent haste with which Henry ordered the commons to elect a different speaker makes it clear that behind this charade lay royal pressure acceding to archiepiscopal pressure – not least because Cheyne continued to enjoy embarrassingly good health for another decade, serving for six years on Henry IV's council and undertaking some of the most arduous diplomatic missions of the reign: to the Empire, to Paris and to Rome.

Whatever the prelates thought of Cheyne, there is no suggestion that Henry's regard for him was diminished.[5] Nevertheless, this was a significant, albeit minor, success for Arundel, and an early indication of his determination to defend the Church.

The overriding reason for a meeting of convocation at the outset of the reign was to marshal clerical support for Henry's usurpation and his archbishop's authority. In both respects, it was successful. Before convocation met, Arundel issued injunctions to all the bishops to attend in the habit of their order (rather than in their more ostentatious ceremonial vestments). Although this occasioned some grumbling, no one challenged it, because, as Walsingham wrote, 'the whole world seemed to be giving the archbishop its support'. The best way to counter critics, after all, was to make it clear that the Church acknowledged its faults and was serious in its desire for self-reform.[6] Following an opening sermon in which the bishop of Rochester – so often the archiepiscopal mouthpiece – 'inveighed vehemently' against the holding of pluralities and told clerics that they must reside in their benefices,[7] Arundel repeated these exhortations: the clergy, he said, must 'behave in such a way and order their lives that the laity could not criticize them in any way', and he instructed five of his canon lawyers to draw up a list of articles detailing the matters 'by which they and the Church were oppressed (*gravata*)'. He must at least have been relieved to receive an assurance from the king's messengers to convocation (the earls of Westmorland and Northumberland, and Sir Thomas Erpingham) that Henry would not ask for clerical taxation on this occasion, albeit tempered by the rider that when he asked them to open their purses he expected all clergy to contribute.[8]

Taking their lead from Arundel, who was largely occupied with Henry's coronation during the next few days, the five canon lawyers drew up a list of sixty-three grievances.[9] These fall into four groups, evidently separately compiled. The first group (nos 1–26) dealt principally with abuses identified as requiring internal reform, such as forging documents, taking excessive fees for proving wills, charging for making presentations or exchanging benefices, the imposition of unwarranted fees on lesser clergy, clerical immorality, the wearing of appropriate ecclesiastical dress, unruly behaviour by students, failure to provide hospitality and the misappropriation of funds in charitable institutions such as hospitals. If these were familiar grievances, it was still important to demonstrate the Church's willingness to put its house in order. There was also a request for serial adulterers and other 'more serious' sinners to suffer corporal punishment. The next group of articles (nos 27–9) consisted of a suggestion that, as the 'spiritual patron of all English knighthood', St George's day be declared a feast day throughout England (no. 27); a request from the masters and scholars of Oxford that they be allowed to seek provisions from the pope despite the Statute of Provisors (no. 28);[10] and a declaration that, 'since the laity are utterly hostile to the clergy',[11] no opportunity should be given to them to get their hands on clerical possessions, for 'they plan, under the influence of Lollards, so it is said, to make, publish and introduce in this present parliament new statutes or constitutions against the prelates and other men of the Church, which are not in truth constitutions but distractions, or rather they should rightly be called destructions' (no. 29, in the form of a petition to Arundel).

By the time that convocation reconvened on 17 October, two further groups of articles had been compiled.[12] The third group (nos 30–43) considered abuses in the ecclesiastical courts in which the clergy were obliged to plead their cases (especially the archbishop's Court of Arches[13]), which were alleged to charge excessive notarial fees, to delegate cases to ignorant or corrupt commissaries, to refuse or make it difficult to hear litigants, and above all to issue inappropriate writs of inhibition (prohibition) preventing lower courts from hearing cases. It is unclear whether these complaints were aimed specifically at Arundel's predecessor, Walden, or should be seen within the longer-term history of complaints by bishops and their officials about the interference of the Court of Arches in diocesan matters.

The final group, nos 44–63, was directed squarely at the laity, especially the king's courts, and was evidently intended to be the clerical *gravamina* presented to parliament. Beginning (*imprimis*) with the customary request to the king to confirm the Church's liberties (no. 44), they enumerated long-standing issues such as the seizure of episcopal temporalities and clerical possessions; disregard for the boundaries between royal and ecclesiastical jurisdictions; the deleterious effect on the latter of prohibitions and other royal writs; inappropriately conceded exemptions; wrongful arrest and imprisonment of clergy; the misuse of chantry endowments and the profits of alien priories; benefit of clergy (in all cases except treason, which they acknowledged was not covered by *privilegium fori*); and the abuses committed by local crown officers when visiting parishes or religious houses, including misuse of purveyance and taking excessive advantage of clerical hospitality. The issuing of writs of prohibition by royal courts was a particular bone of contention, especially when such writs led to the summary ousting of rightful incumbents to benefices.

These were just the sort of recurrent grievances which lay at the heart of the clergy's insistence on its liberties. However, they do not seem to have been presented to parliament, perhaps because there was no time to do so, since, once the articles had been read out on 17 October, convocation was dismissed.[14] Not until the urgent political questions confronting the new regime – the fates of the former king and his chief supporters, the consolidation of Henry's authority, and the pacification of the kingdom – had been settled did clerical liberties again came to the fore.

What caused them to do so was the Epiphany Rising, for a number of prominent clerics had or were suspected of having joined the conspiracy, including three current or former bishops (Thomas Merks of Carlisle, Henry Despenser and Roger Walden), the abbot of Westminster (William Colchester) and two chaplains of the former king's household, Richard Maudeleyn and William Ferriby. Walden and Colchester were imprisoned but acquitted by the end of February. Despenser, as already noted, was committed to Arundel's tutelage for a year. Maudeleyn, archdeacon of Lincoln and a virtuoso pluralist, had been high in the former king's favour and was one of that small, fugitive band who remained with him until the moment of his capture at Conway.[15] Following the failure of the rising, he and Ferriby fled north, perhaps hoping to reach Scotland, but were caught, brought to London, condemned as traitors and executed on 29 January.[16] Although sentence was passed in a lay court, Arundel does not appear to have taken issue with it.

Bishops, however, were a different matter. The arrest or trial of a bishop by secular authorities was a matter which Arundel always took seriously. When Robert Rede, bishop of Chichester, was detained by a group of laymen in London, the archbishop wrote to Bishop Braybrooke of London with impressive indignation, quoting the Clementine decretal *Si quis suadente diabolo* ('If any person, seduced by the devil'),[17] ordering him, his chapter, all the rectors and vicars in the capital, and 'anyone who preaches at St Paul's Cross', to impose sentences of major excommunication on any person involved in the deed.[18]

The reason for Rede's arrest is unclear, but that is certainly not the case with Thomas Merks. A former Westminster monk, Merks was a scholar of repute and the author of a treatise on the *ars dictaminis* (letter-writing); like Maudeleyn, he had been with King Richard at Conway. Deprived of his temporalities on 19 September 1399, he was translated a month later to the unattainable see of Salmas (in modern Iran). On 29 October he was brought into parliament, where he too was questioned about his role in Gloucester's murder, of which many suspected him. Rising to defend himself, he was initially told by Henry – quite correctly – that he should appear before an ecclesiastical court, but he insisted on exculpating himself and proceeded to deliver what Walsingham called a 'fine speech', vehemently asserting his innocence and protesting at the time he had spent in prison. Henry told him he was only being held in custody for his own protection; if he wished, he could go free, but he would be well advised to retire to St Albans abbey for the moment, 'until the world was more favourable to him and the animosity of the common people had abated'.[19]

This he did, but not with the desired effect, for there is little doubt that Merks was implicated in the Epiphany Rising. Arrested on

10 January and sent to the Tower, he was told by the exasperated king that those who were guilty of treason would be dealt with according to the law of the land, clerical immunity notwithstanding. Tried before a lay jury on 4 February, Merks was condemned to death for treason (*lese maiestatis*). It was the first time since the Norman Conquest that a bishop (for Merks was still a bishop, albeit of an unattainable see) had been sentenced to death in England, and Arundel knew he must take a stand. Summoning a meeting of the prelates, he 'explained dejectedly to them how the temporal powers did not shrink from violating the liberties of the English Church, particularly with regard to the arrest, imprisonment and trial of bishops', and reminded them of the case, half a century earlier, of Thomas de Lisle, bishop of Ely. Lisle had been arraigned before secular judges in Westminster Hall but rescued by the intervention of Archbishop Islip (1349–66), who 'took him by the right hand and led him away, saying, "You are my subject. This place where you are standing is prohibited to you, and this man before whom you stand may not judge you. Come with me."' 'Behold, the Liberty of the Church!' gushed Adam Usk, who attended this meeting, where he claimed extravagantly that 'more crimes have been committed against prelates in England than in the whole of Christendom'.[20]

Yet Henry was determined to make an example of Merks and on 15 March wrote to the pope insisting that he be degraded and handed over 'plainly and summarily' to secular justice, failing which, 'if there exists anything in our royal power, we demand that it be executed'.[21] Eventually, probably as a consequence of Arundel's pleas, the king was persuaded to relent. Released from the Tower on 23 June 1400, Merks was committed to the custody of his close friend Abbot Colchester of Westminster (a test for another suspect) and on 28 November received a full pardon, although only as an act of special royal grace.[22] He was finally released on 26 January 1401, in time to attend the next convocation. Although never restored to the English episcopacy, he resumed his Oxford career and was treated with humanity, even generosity, by

Henry and Arundel, acquiring several benefices and perhaps attending the Council of Pisa, shortly after which he died.[23]

Henry IV may have taken a selective approach to clerical liberties, but he was not in theory opposed to the fundamental duality of Church and State. What infuriated him was churchmen who equated clerical immunity with legal impunity – and, as lay criticism of the regime grew, so did clerical opposition. Despite the taxes voted in 1401, the crown was bankrupt; piracy in the Channel and the North Sea led to a catastrophic decline in overseas trade; full-scale war between England and France seemed imminent; and by 1402 Glyn Dwr's rebellion had spread from its heartland in Snowdonia to central and south Wales. Everywhere Henry looked, England's imperial pretensions were being scorned, allies defecting, enemies circling. The loss of Ireland and Guyenne – which the English crown had ruled for more than two hundred years – became a real possibility; in England, anger at the government's financial incompetence was leading to a breakdown of law and order.[24] Even his friends were warning the king that things could not go on as they were. In May 1401, his confidant and future confessor, Philip Repingdon, had written to him 'borne down by grief' at the state of the realm, declaring that unless Henry showed himself able to 'fulfil faithfully the duties demanded of royal majesty', and to 'remedy the miseries of the people', he would suffer the same fate as Richard II.[25]

This letter is an example of the loyal criticism which kings were wont to receive from high churchmen and confessors, especially those in whom they trusted, which was certainly true of Repingdon, Henry's 'very special clerk'.[26] A few months later, however, a rumour – patently not 'loyal criticism' – began to spread that Richard II was still alive and on the point of returning to England to reclaim his crown. This fable probably originated at a hostile Scottish court, where King Robert III and the earl of Douglas enjoyed taunting the man whom they referred to as 'Henry of Lancaster'.[27] In the spring of 1402, it reached a peak.

Orders sent out by Henry IV to the sheriffs in early May – initially to try to prevent the story spreading southwards; then, when this failed, to clamp down on 'gatherings in taverns and other congregations' – were ineffective.[28] Itinerant Franciscan and Dominican friars promoted the rumours through preaching, and it was not just the marginalized or the desperate who believed them, or claimed to. By the end of the month, following sightings of 'Richard' in several parts of the country, it was being reported that the former king would make his triumphant return at Oxford on 24 June. Exasperated, Henry had some twenty men, mainly friars, arrested, charged with treason, interrogated (at least two by the king in person) and tried in King's Bench. According to a Franciscan chronicler, the jury originally selected to hear their case, composed of citizens of London and Holborn, refused to act, so new jurors had to be brought in and induced by threats to find them guilty. During the week beginning 9 June 1402, the rumour-mongers were drawn through London, hanged and beheaded at Tyburn.[29] They were not all friars, but at least twelve of them were – the largest number of clerics condemned to death in England at one time.[30]

Although Arundel had no sympathy with the rumour-mongers, he could hardly ignore such disregard for the principle of clerical immunity from secular justice. Yet the indictments against the friars had been drafted with care, accusing them not just of spreading seditious rumours – a grey area in terms of treason – but also of plotting to kill the king and his magnates, overthrow the common law and replace English with a foreign language.[31] This, undeniably, would have been treason, which, as convocation acknowledged in 1399, fell outside the scope of clerical immunity. Nevertheless, Arundel was bound to react, for it must have seemed as if the very principle of royal protection of the clergy was in danger of being lost by default.[32] And when parliament and convocation met in the autumn of 1402, react he did. Convocation did not meet until 21 October, by which time parliament had already been in session for three weeks, mainly discussing the situation in Wales and the Scottish marches, the collapse of law and order and, inevitably, the king's need for money, which eventually led to the grant of a fifteenth and tenth, although 'with great difficulty'.[33] Once convocation met, however, it was ecclesiastical affairs that leapt to the top of the agenda.

Records of the 1402 convocation mention only three items:[34] firstly, the grant to the king of one and a half clerical tenths; secondly, the examination (much briefer than in 1401) of three suspected Lollards;[35] thirdly, but clearly front and centre, the 'Petition of the Prelates and Clergy presented to the King in Parliament', which also appears on the parliament roll, together with the king's response.[36] Citing the statute commonly known as *Pro Clero* ('For the Clergy'), passed fifty years earlier, the petition noted that Edward III's decree had stated that clerics of any order or status who were convicted before secular justices 'for any treasons or felonies concerning any person other than the king or his royal majesty' were to be handed over to the ecclesiastical courts for punishment and thus 'freely enjoy the privileges of Holy Church'. Yet, the petition continued, several clerics had recently been put to death by secular justices for just such crimes, despite claiming benefit of clergy, 'which is a great offence to God and a manifest and notorious violation of ecclesiastical liberty', as well as being contrary to the statute of treason. Although this petition referred mainly to the hanging of the friars, there had been a number of other alleged violations of *Pro Clero*. Henry was asked to put a stop to these 'outrageous attacks' and to confirm his grandfather's statute. He had, after all, promised parliament in 1399 that no charges of treason would be brought in the realm except in accordance with Edward III's statute.[37]

But what sort of treason did *not* concern the king's person or majesty? The parliament which passed *Pro Clero*, that of 1352, had also passed the more famous Statute of Treasons, the primary aim of which was to curb the increase during the 1340s in the number of cases where royal justices were applying the penalties of treason (which included forfeiture to the king) in cases 'unknown to the commonalty as treason'. The upshot, at the time, was to produce a relatively narrow definition of treason by restricting it to crimes relating directly to the king, his family and his majesty – in effect, the origin of the distinction between high treason and petty treason, which was equated with felony. *Pro Clero* was a logical but rather sloppy attempt to apply the same principle to benefit of clergy – 'the first reason for which Saint Thomas died', as the prelates put it.[38]

That is why the indictments drawn up against the friars hanged in June 1402 included allegations of plotting to kill the king and overthrowing the common law, thereby classifying them as high treason. Not that Henry was desperate to secure the forfeiture of the (presumably meagre) chattels of a dozen mendicant friars, but he did want to make it clear that the kind of rumours they were accused of spreading required rigorous discouragement. His response to Arundel's petition was thus to reaffirm *Pro Clero* and any other such concessions to clerics 'for the preservation of their liberties and immunities', but, in return, the archbishop had to guarantee that in future a clerk convicted of 'treason which does not affect the king or his royal majesty' should not simply be released after purgation of his crime. This had happened commonly in the past, through a simple test of literacy, oath-taking and/or penance, leading to the not uncommon view that clerical immunity made a mockery of equality before the law. Instead, he should suffer some more condign form of punishment, such as a lengthy term of imprisonment.[39]

Arundel therefore agreed to draw up a constitution specifying the steps to be taken, which was to be presented for approval to the next parliament – although, if the king were to conclude that this 'does not provide a suitable remedy in this matter', then 'another remedy will be discussed and provided, in such a way as shall become evident'. In other words, it was up to the archbishop to make good on his promise. Whether this was done, however, is unclear. Records of the October 1403 convocation note nothing apart from a grant to the king of half a clerical tenth.[40] By the time the next parliament met in January 1404, more pressing matters had pushed such concerns to the margins. Yet

Arundel's efforts may not have been in vain, for Henry appears to have taken a softer line with clerical delinquents over the next three years.[41] Not until June 1405 would the issue of clerical immunity return, although, when it did, it provided the sternest test yet of the relationship between the king and his archbishop.

7

Clerical Wealth: The Shepherd and the Wolf 1403–4

Henry's attempts to stamp out rumours of Richard II's survival did not work. Rebels such as Sir Edmund Mortimer (who defected to the Welsh in 1402) and Henry Percy the Younger ('Hotspur') continued to proclaim their belief that he was alive and would be returning shortly to reclaim his throne. Needless to say, the former king failed to materialize, but that did not prevent thousands from joining Hotspur, and, had Henry lost the battle which followed at Shrewsbury on 21 July 1403, the Lancastrian regime would probably have fallen, and Arundel with it. Fortunately for them, it was a royalist victory (but only just). Hotspur was killed; his uncle Thomas Percy, who had joined him, was executed; and, although Hotspur's father, the earl of Northumberland, had avoided the battle and survived, Percy power was broken.[1] But the Lancastrian regime was not just failing: it was also bankrupt. The fight to defend clerical privilege may have been shelved for the moment, but what followed was a fight to defend the clergy's financial autonomy.[2]

The first real skirmish came six weeks after Shrewsbury, in early September 1403, when the king summoned a great council to meet at Worcester. He was on his way to Wales, hoping to repair the damage inflicted by Glyn Dwr and his men, and he needed money.[3] Present at the council were Arundel, Richard Clifford the diocesan and 'other bishops', and various royal knights and esquires who, in Walsingham's estimation, worshipped not Mars or Pallas Athene (the gods of war and wisdom), but Dione (the mother of Aphrodite, the goddess of love) and Laverna (the goddess of thieves).[4] Henry opened the council by admonishing the clergy for 'resting peacefully in their homes' while he risked life and limb to defeat the rebels. Arundel reminded him that the clergy, too, were enduring such hardships that they could 'barely sustain themselves in a decent manner'. Unimpressed, several knights urged Henry to deprive the bishops of 'their horses and gold' there and then and send them back home on foot. Arundel retorted furiously that before they despoiled his bishops of anything they would themselves suffer some 'harsh blows' – presumably spiritual rather than physical. Before matters degenerated further, the king calmed the meeting by begging the prelates to see their way to granting him a loan.

By the time convocation met at St Paul's a month later, Arundel had evidently concluded that, unless the clergy agreed to some kind of grant, they were in danger of losing much more. Appealing to their sense of self-preservation, therefore, as well as their national pride, he told them that, without the means to pursue his enemies, the king would become a laughing stock. If, on the other hand, they could advance funds to him now, Henry would 'be a good master to us and a protector of the Church'. There were several bishops, he went on, who could easily reduce their expenditure in the short term, although he recognized (or so, at least, claimed the monk-chronicler Thomas Walsingham) that this was not so easy for abbots, who had a large community to sustain. The upshot was the grant of a half tenth (about £8,000) and, until it was collected, a promise to advance as much as possible in the form of a loan. Arundel himself loaned £100, apparently about a fifth of the rather meagre total which could be raised at short notice. The abbot of St Albans loaned £67, reluctantly.[5]

The January 1404 parliament brought little relief, refusing to grant anything other than a nominal five per cent levy on landed and movable incomes, which proved difficult to assess and apparently yielded no more than about £9,000.[6] Once again, then, eyes turned towards the clergy and, under Arundel's leadership, they responded. The Canterbury and York convocations, meeting in April and June 1404 respectively, each granted another whole tenth to the king, plus a contribution from benefices which were normally exempt.[7] In return, the prelates demanded that the Church's liberties be confirmed and its goods exempted from purveyance, and that the grants be paid in instalments, the second of which would not reach the exchequer until May 1405. York was especially resistant, demanding written assurances from the king.[8] In total, this tax would have raised some £16,000, hopelessly inadequate for the crown's needs. With spiralling expenses, massive debts and the collapse of government credit during the spring and summer of 1404, another parliament in the autumn was unavoidable.[9]

It was against this backdrop of ever greater fiscal disarray that a proposal for a long-term remedy came to the fore: clerical disendowment. This most radical of solutions had had its advocates since the early days of the Christian Church. Its underlying rationale was that the holding of temporal possessions (boundless acres, soaring cathedrals, rich plate and vestments, secular offices) was a distraction from the saving of souls. Only when the Church was stripped of its earthly wealth and power could this be remedied. This view was shared by some clerics (such as the Spiritual Franciscans) and by many conscientious laymen. One persistent trope was that the root of Church corruption was the Donation of Constantine, by which the first Christian emperor, Constantine (d. 337), was said to have transferred temporal authority over Rome and the Western Roman Empire to Pope Sylvester I. In fact, this document was an eighth-century forgery, although this was not conclusively proven until the mid-fifteenth century.

'Oh, Constantine, how much evil was born / Not from your conversion, but from that donation / Which the first rich pope received from you!' wrote Dante at the beginning of the fourteenth century. By addressing the long-dead Constantine directly, Dante was extending the point: it was really the fault of emperors, kings and secular lords that the Church had been corrupted, because it was they who had granted the lands and offices. By resuming their grants, they would not just be relieving the Church of its burden of sin but also remedying the mistakes of their forefathers. Commenting in the 1380s on a passage in Ranulf Higden's *Polychronicon*, John Trevisa cited St Jerome (d. 420) as having lamented that 'ever since Holy Church increased in possessions, it has decreased in virtue'; the remedy was for secular lords to confiscate superfluous clerical possessions and give them to those in need. Those who did nothing became themselves the perpetrators of evil, 'whatever covetous priests might say'; indeed, it would be a greater 'act of charity' (*almesse*) to deprive them of 'the superfluity of their possessions' than it had been to grant them in the first place.[10]

By this time, Wyclif's views on the subject of clerical 'possessioners' were circulating widely. In his *De Civili Dominio* (1377), he too had castigated the clergy for their addiction to temporal wealth and office and had urged the secular powers to see clerical disendowment as an act of charity (*elemosina*). This was one of his twenty-four 'heresies and errors' condemned at the Blackfriars council in 1382.[11] Yet Wyclif's strictures found a ready audience, and not just among his academic acolytes. The fact that discussion of Lollard beliefs has focused on the theological and doctrinal questions which featured in heresy trials – images, pilgrimages, confession, the Eucharist – is understandable, but it has obscured the thrust and vitality of Lollard social policy, which was directed primarily at the Church's failing response to poverty. To the Lollards, charity was 'an obsession', 'the essence of Christian society'.[12] When they spoke freely, in their sermons, their treatises, their statements of belief, this was the subject to which they continually returned. 'When you give a banquet, invite the poor, the crippled, the lame, the blind, and you will be blessed' (Luke 14:13).

There were many among the orthodox, too, who were profoundly disturbed by the Church's response to poverty: Philip Repingdon, for example, the serious-minded and outspoken bishop of Lincoln who expressed misgivings about the Church's holding of temporalities and, most unusually, resigned his see in 1419. Five years later, when he drew up his will, he asked to be buried naked, in a sack, in open ground near the cathedral, 'there to be food for worms', and that every farthing of his worldly goods be distributed to the poor. Repingdon was, of course, an ex-Lollard, one of Wyclif's most prominent and distinguished early followers at Oxford. But a bishop could hardly argue for clerical disendowment.[13]

Agitation for disendowment in the late fourteenth and early fifteenth centuries was further fuelled by the changing tone of the debate about poverty and charity, responding in part to the Ordinances and Statutes of Labourers passed in the decades following the Black Death of 1348–9. Denouncing the 'malice of labourers' and their 'idle and vicious' lifestyles, this legislation accentuated the distinction between the 'deserving' and 'undeserving' poor: the former being the genuinely indigent, the latter being those who indulged in 'voluntary poverty', who would only work for 'excessive' wages or who were simply malingerers. (For Lollards, this included the friars, who chose to beg despite being capable of working.) Allied to this was the scourge of vagrancy, against which several acts were passed.[14]

Increasingly, the poor and the vagrant were seen as agents of disruption: not just a drain on society's resources but also a source of fear. Those who sought to relieve their plight came to be suspected of subversion – a view encouraged by the demand of the 1381 rebels that the clergy's goods, lands and tenements should be 'taken from them and divided among the commons'.[15] Simultaneously, institutional poor relief became increasingly impersonal: 'the poor were no longer lodged, fed and cared for but rather, they were appended to funerary and commemorative occasions, almost external to the act, just as the clergy was hired and the bells rung'.[16] Lollards rejected such mechanistic forms of relief: charity should be selective, targeted at those who needed it. It was this conviction that led to their demand that tithes, the principal portion of most parish priests' income, should be paid directly to the poor rather than to the Church. This too, of course, was quite unacceptable to the Catholic hierarchy. Tithes, they argued (not without reason), were the life blood of the parochial system.[17]

Yet, if it was undeniably true that confiscating Church lands would unlock a massive reserve of wealth, to press for this in order to alleviate the plight of the poor was optimistic. In order to convince a sufficient number of those with the power to implement such a policy, advocates of charity would need to find a more politically tempting rationale. And this they did. In the famous sermon which he delivered on Ascension Day 1382, Wyclif's fellow Oxford academic Nicholas Hereford argued that, if the king would only confiscate the excess wealth of the monks and friars, there would be no need for him to impose taxes on the commons of the realm.[18] Here was a much more enticing argument.

This is not to suggest that the lords and knights who presented parliamentary proposals for disendowment did not share the Lollards' philanthropic concerns; there is plenty of evidence that they did. However, it is not coincidental that those moments when the campaign for disendowment gathered enough momentum to present a serious threat to the Church tended to coincide with moments of acute financial stress. This was certainly the case in 1371, a time of urgent necessity for the war in France and apparently the first occasion that the idea was mooted in parliament, when the clergy's reluctance to grant a tax led two Austin friars to propose that a proportion of monastic temporalities be surrendered for the 'common needs' of the realm. After all, they pointed out, kings had often seized the temporalities of individual bishops; it was secular lords who had endowed the Church 'for the service of God and the poor', and if those conditions were not being fulfilled, they were entitled to resume them, since 'the necessity of all the people overrides the necessity of any individual'.[19] After the resumption of Anglo-French hostilities and the outbreak of the Schism in 1377–8, the 'alien priories' also provided a target, although in the end only a small number of French monks appear to have been expelled.[20] The exigencies of war were again at the heart of the debate in October 1385, the next time the subject was raised in parliament, when a group of lords and commons proposed the confiscation of ecclesiastical temporalities.[21] Neither of these proposals was mentioned in the official record of parliament, an indication of their sensitivity.[22]

With the suspension of the French war and the improvement in crown finances during the 1390s, disendowment receded from parliament's view, and it might have been hoped that the clergy's relative liberality in early 1404 (compared to the laity's niggardliness) would moderate any further demands on the Church from the parliament which met at Coventry in October. Not so. As usual with talk of disendowment, the official record maintains a discreet silence and it is Walsingham who provides the details.[23] It began, he said, when a group of parliamentary knights 'less knowledgeable than heathens', led by Arundel's bugbear John Cheyne (now a royal councillor), proposed that the English Church's temporalities be taken into the king's hands in their entirety for one year to relieve the crisis.[24] Walsingham said that Arundel was so distressed that he sought solace by reading a passage from the *Life of St Edmund of Abingdon*, his thirteenth-century archiepiscopal predecessor, before returning to the fray, 'no longer fearing any threats or death itself', in defence of his Church's liberties.[25] Inspired by his resolve, his fellow archbishop, Richard Scrope of York, threatened the knights with excommunication. Crucially, they won over some lay lords to their cause, of whom the most effective (*efficacissimus*) was the king's cousin Edward, duke of York.[26]

Buoyed by this powerful support, Arundel went on the offensive. In 1402, when the profits from the alien priories had been resumed (taken back) into the king's hands, the archbishop declared that the intention had been that they should be used to augment the royal coffers and relieve the poor, but instead they had been squandered on lords and knights: 'While you grow proud and enrich yourselves on these things, the king is in need and suffers penury.' And if the temporalities of the Church were seized, the same would happen. This may well have been a dig at Cheyne, who had recently been granted additional alien priory lands.[27] Scrope and, apparently, the bishop of Rochester backed Arundel up, threatening to excommunicate those who subverted the Church.[28]

Terrified at this prospect – or so says Walsingham – the knights backed off and sought forgiveness from the archbishop, thanking him for having saved them from committing such a sin; whereupon the king followed suit, praising Arundel's constancy and declaring that while he reigned no one was going to defraud the Church of its resources.[29]

Yet there was clearly a quid pro quo, for when the Canterbury convocation met on 24 November 1404 it granted, in addition to the tenth and a half already paid within the past year, a further one and a half tenths to be paid during the following six months. The York convocation, which met in December, also granted a tenth, although payment of this was to be spread over a year.[30] For the moment, then, Arundel had seen off the disendowment lobby, and since the commons, with uncommon generosity, granted two whole tenths and fifteenths – meaning Henry could anticipate receiving close to £100,000 in lay and clerical subsidies through the course of 1405 – there was a chance that the pressure might abate. But the price was high. The clerical tenths and additional grants promised by the two convocations between October 1403 and December 1404 (three tenths from Canterbury and two from York, combined in each case with the lowering or abolition of the taxable minimum for previously exempt benefices) amounted to an unprecedented outpouring of clerical wealth in such a short space of time.[31] It would take no more than a few months for the toll of such relentless pressure to become clear.

And what of Arundel's part in this? It is noteworthy that, whereas the northern province under Scrope had been careful to stretch out the timeframe over which the taxes it granted were to be raised – an effective way of forestalling further demands, for no new tax was meant to be granted until the previous one had been collected in full – the southern province did not. Had Arundel done all he could to defend the Church? A letter he wrote to the king on 6 December 1404 adds weight to this suspicion. Henry had pressed for an additional subsidy from stipendiary (unbeneficed, often poor) chaplains. Arundel promised the king, 'as witness God and the truth', that he had done everything in his power to try to persuade the clergy to grant this, but according to convocation's proctors (the bishop of Lincoln and the earl of Somerset) the clergy had 'unanimously, utterly and expressly refused' and nothing would be gained by trying again. Instead, he suggested that the bishops be encouraged to put pressure directly on (*inducerunt*) the chaplains; if the king would send him a mandate to do this, he could rest assured that he would find Arundel 'ready to help him in all things' (*habebitis me paratum in omnibus*).[32] Henry had much for which to thank his archbishop; to the clergy, however, their archbishop's willingness to do the king's bidding may have been coming to resemble the alliance of the shepherd and the wolf.

8

Archbishop Scrope: Thy Son's Coat, or No? 1404–5

On 20 March 1404, the last day of the parliament which had met at Westminster on 14 January, the king was asked by the commons publicly to nominate the members of his council, 'so that good and just government and remedy can be made for the many complaints, grievances and wrongs put to the king our lord in this parliament'. First on the list of twenty-two names put forward was Arundel's. He would remain a privy councillor for the next three years,[1] following which he would serve for a further three years as chancellor of England and thus *ex officio* head of the council. In a sense, this was acknowledgement of the fact that, despite not being a nominated councillor since December 1399, he had in practice remained Henry's most trusted adviser and had already, during the past year, begun to attend more meetings of the council than he had during the first three years of the reign.[2] In parliaments, he had habitually acted as the king's spokesman.[3] Nevertheless, the formalization of his conciliar role was consequential. It marked the end of the breathing space allowed to him during the previous few years to focus on archiepiscopal duties such as visitation. Politically, it bound him more closely to the framing and implementation of public policy, which meant, on the one hand, that he would find it harder to champion clerical liberties versus the demands of the State – hence, arguably, his willingness later in the year to try to extend the clerical tax base – but, on the other hand, that he might be able to use his position to induce the council to adopt stronger measures against Lollardy. Above all, it allowed him to demonstrate his commitment to the Lancastrian regime, which, surprising as it might seem, had recently come into question.

This curious and upsetting episode occurred near the beginning of the parliament, when the commons enquired as to the extent of the earl of Northumberland's involvement in his son's treason. Arrested under safe conduct at York on 11 August 1403, the earl had been imprisoned for five months awaiting trial. On 28 January, before Northumberland was brought in, the speaker of the commons, the ever forthright Sir Arnold Savage, suggested to the king that he might 'command all the lords who were present in Parliament to make known their wills concerning the king and the realm'.[4] Arundel, sensing Savage's real meaning, 'asked him very angrily why he said this', to which Savage responded charily that 'it was more honourable to make clear their wills at this point than to be found disloyal afterwards'.

A week later, on Monday 4 February, Northumberland was led in to reveal what he knew, which appeared to be disarmingly little, though his interrogation did not lack its moments of drama. For Arundel, the crucial exchange occurred two days later, when he and Edward, duke of York, were 'slandered by certain malevolent persons' who claimed that they and a number of others 'had been in agreement, collusion and conspiracy with Sir Henry Percy [Hotspur] and Sir Thomas Percy in the armed uprising which was made by them against our said lord the king' (at Shrewsbury). Northumberland was asked to reveal 'everything he knew about the matter'. He replied that 'he had never known anything about the said duke and archbishop or any of the others aforesaid which would be derogatory to the honourable estate of the king or to his royal majesty, but that they are good and loyal lieges to him'. Two weeks later, at the commons' request, Henry confirmed this exoneration of York and Arundel, adding that he did not wish that either of them 'should ever be in any way harassed, molested or harmed by him or by his heirs at any time to come for the aforesaid reason'. As for Northumberland, parliament agreed that he had not committed treason but merely trespass, for which he should pay a fine at the king's pleasure, which was promptly remitted. The whole episode has the appearance of being stage-managed.

Doubtless Arundel hoped that was that, and up to a point it was, but clearly there were whisperers at work against him, even among the king's councillors.[5] After all, it was the Percys who had dominated the council for three years before Shrewsbury, and since the new council nominated in March 1404 saw several members reappointed, these were the men with whom he now had to work. Arnold Savage, for example, who had been a councillor since 1402, and John Cheyne, a councillor since the spring of 1403, both returned. Both were well known for speaking their mind.[6] The declared aim of the conciliar reshuffle in March 1404 was to give the council a more 'substantial' (aristocratic or experienced) complexion following the demise of the Percys. Arundel certainly fitted that profile, and his voice would carry considerable weight, but this was not a council he could overmaster, especially when it came to the most pressing issue of the moment: how and from whom to raise the money which the crown so badly needed. The archbishop had clearly made enemies. Among them were members of the royal household (*familiares regii*),[7] presumably including some of the lords, knights and other laymen most actively involved in the wars which had dominated the reign thus far: those, perhaps, who had urged the king to send the bishops home on foot at the Worcester council, or who, like Cheyne, would support the call for clerical disendowment at the October parliament. This was a broadly based council, representing a range of often opposing interests at a time of great danger and discord. Henry's regime was vulnerable, and treason was in the air.

At the Coventry parliament of October 1404, said John Strecche, the chronicler of nearby Kenilworth priory, 'many people secretly plotted many things against the king'.[8] The following year would prove him right. On 13 February 1405, Edmund and Roger Mortimer – the thirteen- and eleven-year-old sons of the late earl of March, whose claim to the throne meant that they had been kept in close confinement since the start of the reign – were abducted from their lodgings at Windsor castle, apparently with the intention of leading them to their uncle (Sir Edmund Mortimer) and Glyn Dwr in Wales. They only got as far as Cheltenham before being recaptured and returned to custody. A meeting of the council on 17 February was told that the person behind the plot was Constance, Lady Despenser, the sister of Edward, duke of York. She admitted her involvement but said that it was not she but Duke Edward who had been the 'principal instigator' of the plot. She also accused him of having planned to climb over the wall at Eltham palace two months earlier, when the king was spending Christmas there, with the intention of assassinating him. This was too improbable to be believed, but York did admit to foreknowledge of the kidnapping, and he and his sister spent about a year in custody before being pardoned and released.[9]

Suspicion of complicity in the abduction also fell on a number of other lords, including Arundel, perhaps because of his earlier association with Duke Edward. He may have felt indebted to the duke for his support against the disendowment lobby, and the insinuations against the two of them in the aftermath of Shrewsbury probably helped to bring them together, but the duke was a dangerous friend. First cousin to both Richard II and Henry IV, he had been one of the most unpopular cronies of the former king and one of those behind the appeal of treason which led to the execution of Arundel's brother, Earl Richard, in 1397. Two years later, in the parliament of 1399, he was stripped of his dukedom of Aumale after being accused of complicity in Richard II's murder of the duke of Gloucester and seizure of the Lancastrian inheritance. Three months later, he was suspected of involvement in the Epiphany Rising. Nevertheless, although the doubts about his loyalty never went away, he was allowed to succeed to the dukedom of York when his father died in 1402, and he served continuously on the council until 1410.[10]

As to Arundel, what exactly he was suspected of doing, or knowing, is not clear, but the whispers against him provided Walsingham with the opportunity for a characteristically theatrical account of his exculpation. 'Aware of the bitterness with which the royal familiars (*familiares regii*) regarded him', he wrote, '[Arundel] rose to his feet in the council and, on bended knee, asked the king to invite anyone who wished to accuse him, whereupon he would clear himself by any means appropriate to an archbishop.' Henry expressed his delight at this, swearing 'by half his kingdom' that there was nothing that would please him more, whereupon Arundel insisted that not once had he shared 'anything sinister whatsoever' with anyone about the king: all he had done was to speak privately to Henry about matters relating to the king's honour, 'even if you have often taken my warnings hard'. The king graciously accepted this, and Arundel 'regained Henry's affection'.[11]

Stagy as Walsingham's account is, it conveys the impression of a candid, at times reproving, relationship between king and archbishop, the frankness of which may have been thought by some of the king's familiars to be inappropriate, or may even have aroused envy. To Arundel, and doubtless to Henry too, this was presumably no more than the sort of 'loyal criticism' Philip Repingdon had expressed in 1401, and many others before him. 'I am your spiritual father', Arundel is alleged to have said to Henry a few months later, 'and the second person in the kingdom after you, and there is no one whose advice you should take more readily than mine, if it is good.'[12] Yet loyal criticism had its limits. For prelates to offer the kind of advice which sought to lead a sinful or intransigent king back towards the path of righteousness and harmony in the realm was one thing. Indeed, it might strengthen royal power, revealing the king as a man who ruled under God's law, taking counsel in accordance with the irenic or mediatory model exemplified by the Old Testament prophets. This was the kind of advice which admired thirteenth-century bishops such as Stephen Langton and Robert Grosseteste had offered Henry III, as it was widely accepted that they were entitled to do. But when they moved from offering counsel to outright opposition, like the bishops who supported Simon de Montfort during the Barons' War of 1258–65, that was quite another thing.[13] And in May 1405, when a spate of uprisings and protest movements broke out simultaneously in Yorkshire, the king made it clear where he thought the dividing line lay.

There were at least two and probably three initially disconnected movements in Yorkshire.[14] The first was an attempt by the earl of Northumberland, supported by Thomas, Lord Bardolf, to reassert his authority in the north by capturing his hated rival, the earl of Westmorland – leading, perhaps, to the overthrow of the Lancastrian dynasty. Secondly, there was a general rising, centred on Cleveland, of prominent gentry (several of whom were Percy retainers), clamouring for redress of the 'troubles and failings' in the kingdom. Prompt action by Westmorland and the king's son John quickly snuffed these two out: Northumberland fled to Berwick, while the leaders of the Cleveland rising were arrested at Topcliffe, near Thirsk. Thirdly, an assembly met at York of citizens and clergy of the city and its hinterland, allegedly 9,000 strong, inspired by the preaching of Archbishop Scrope and led by him and Thomas Mowbray, the eighteen-year-old heir to the earldom of Nottingham.[15] Whether this should rightly be termed an armed uprising or a nonviolent protest movement depends (and depended) on one's point of view. Scrope almost certainly considered himself to be offering loyal criticism to the king. The manifesto which he circulated in York and its vicinity stressed his desire to act as a mediator between Henry and those who resented his impositions or decisions: not just great lords such as Mowbray who felt themselves excluded from power, but priests, merchants and townsmen beggared by the king's ceaseless demands for taxation or his violations of clerical liberties. Northern clerics were especially aggrieved, for unlike members of the much bigger southern convocation they often did not meet at the same time as parliament and thus had no opportunity to present their grievances in the form of legitimate parliamentary *gravamina*.

What Scrope appears to have advocated was a process of reconciliatory dialogue with the king based on a functioning and truly representative parliament, the upholding of clerical liberties and the peaceful resolution of aristocratic grudges.[16] This was, after all, a king who had promised to respect parliamentary and ecclesiastical liberties and who, so far, had shown himself willing to tolerate criticism offered via the customary channels. Henry saw things very differently. Tricked into surrender and separated from their supporters by the duplicity of Westmorland and Prince John, Scrope and Mowbray were already being held at Pontefract by the time that the king, seething at having to abandon his latest campaign against Glyn Dwr, arrived there on 3 June. Three days later, bringing the captives with him, he came to York, where the citizens, who had gathered outside the walls to plead for mercy, were fiercely upbraided and sent back into the city to await Henry's pleasure. Arundel, meanwhile, on being informed of his fellow archbishop's arrest, rode 'all day and night' to York to try to assuage the king's wrath, arriving early on the morning of Monday 8 June, the feast day of the twelfth-century archbishop and saint William of York, whose tomb was the cathedral's most venerated shrine.[17] On seeing Arundel, one day of the king's knights (unnamed) apparently told him that, if Scrope was allowed to live, all the king's followers would desert him.

Yet Arundel did at least secure an audience with the king, during which he advised Henry to submit Scrope for correction either to parliament or to the pope, warning him of the dire consequences which would follow if he executed an archbishop. For Arundel, this was personal as well as political: Scrope had been a colleague of his since his days at Ely, had followed him to York in the 1390s and had become an archbishop barely a year after Arundel became primate. Henry was unmoved, however, telling Arundel he must be tired after his journey and advising him to lie down before joining him for breakfast. It was while Arundel was breakfasting, according to one report, that the trial of Scrope and Mowbray was held; another said that Arundel was allowed to attend the trial but that the king told him not to say anything, for the prisoners would not be spared. Yet he was not the only dissenter. Sir William Gascoigne, chief justice of the King's Bench, refused to take part in the trial, claiming that the king's hastily convened tribunal had no power to try them.[18] Especially galling to Arundel, perhaps, was the fact that the members of the tribunal included his nephew Earl Thomas, who had returned to England with him and Henry six years earlier. Yet the king was beyond quibbling, and both Scrope and Mowbray were shortly condemned as traitors and immediately (to forestall any further objections) led out to a field of freshly sown barley just beyond the city walls, where they were beheaded beneath a windmill. The citizenry of York was ordered to assemble to witness their fate.[19]

Never before had England seen the judicial execution of a bishop, let alone an archbishop, and such withering disregard for clerical liberties had the potential to provoke a collision between Church and State on the scale of Innocent III's excommunication of King John two hundred years earlier or even the Henry II–Becket dispute. According to Walsingham, Arundel was so distressed that he 'grew weary of his life' and contracted a tertian fever which made him delirious for several days.[20] Yet Arundel's support over the past year for the king's demands for taxation might also have left him feeling a degree of contrition, even shame, for his friend's death. His justification would presumably have been that this was a compromise forced upon him in order to fend off the much greater threat of clerical disendowment. But did Scrope believe that? The trigger for his disquiet was probably the council which the king held at Worcester (planning to proceed into Wales) during the first week of May 1405, at which the archbishops were once again ordered to persuade their convocations to grant taxation, and this time to ensure that stipendiary chaplains and vicars were obliged to pay. It must have been almost immediately following Scrope's return to York, probably on Sunday 20 May, that he preached the sermon in York minster which sparked the protests there.[21]

As for Henry, it was believed by some that he soon afterwards contracted leprosy as divine punishment for Scrope's death.[22] That was certainly not true (he never had leprosy) but it is an indication of the widespread horror at the king's ferocity: not just the beheadings at York, but also the execution of some three dozen 'traitors', mainly local gentry, who had either held out for Northumberland and Bardolf or led the protesters in Cleveland – and all this, it should be emphasized, despite the fact that not a single life appears to have been lost on the royalist side as a result of any of the Yorkshire risings. But the king and his war captains were sick of sedition, especially priestly sedition, and were determined to make an example of Scrope.

Scrope's execution was probably Henry's greatest mistake. Venerated as a martyr to the cause of English liberties, his tomb in York minster became the focus of a miracle-working cult which rapidly achieved such popularity that order after order had to be sent to the wardens and clergy of the cathedral to erect screens around it, forbid pilgrims to visit and suppress rumours of cures and visions said to have taken place there.[23] In the following year, when the king tried to persuade parliament posthumously to condemn Scrope and Mowbray as traitors by eliding their actions with those of Northumberland, Bardolf and the Cleveland gentry, the lords declined to do so and the matter was dropped.[24] The crucial question was how the pope would react – and not just the pope, but also Arundel, so egregiously betrayed by the circumstances of his fellow archbishop's execution.

For the moment, Henry had more pressing matters to deal with, marching north to drive Northumberland and Bardolf into Scotland and bring the remaining dissidents to heel, before once again making his way to Wales. Meanwhile, Arundel spent the rest of the summer in his diocese and at Lambeth, attending to archiepiscopal and conciliar affairs.[25] At Worcester, where the king spent the last ten days of August, he summoned another great council – to judge by the preparations made for it, a weightier assembly than that held there two years earlier.[26] As ever, it was the king's need for money which dominated proceedings, and, despite their liberality during the previous eighteen months, the clergy were squeezed yet again. 'Many bishops' as well as the archbishop had been summoned. When they hesitated before responding to Henry's fervent (*avide*) plea for help, the knights in attendance told the king that he should simply seize their horses and whatever money they had brought to cover their expenses. Arundel's response was characteristically robust: 'By St James, you will not take anything from me unless you purchase it by violence.' Once again, Henry calmed the meeting, simply begging the archbishop to help him.

Walsingham's description of this meeting is so similar to his account of the Worcester council two years earlier as to invite suspicion of narrative confusion, were it not for the survival of a letter from the king to Arundel a few days later underlining his desperate need. There was a French army in Wales, he wrote, another in Gascony (both true); if he lacked the funds to pay his soldiers, both were likely to be overrun. Praying the archbishop to urge his bishops and archdeacons 'by all possible means' to advance the remaining half of the tenths granted at the last convocation, he asked Arundel to deliver the money to his treasury within three weeks.[27] The pressure on Arundel was growing: in late October, his sister Joan wrote to a friend at court, perhaps Sir Hugh Waterton, complaining that evil words (*male bouche*) were being spoken to the king about her and her brother, 'may God pardon and correct them'.[28]

Pope Innocent VII, meanwhile, had problems of his own to worry about, for on 7 August 1405 his nephew Ludovico Migliorati, head of the papal militia, seized and murdered eleven disaffected Roman citizens, whose corpses he threw into the street. The ensuing riot, in which some thirty members of the papal entourage were lynched, forced Innocent and the Curia (including the chronicler Adam Usk, then in Rome) to decamp to Viterbo, a hundred kilometres north of Rome, where they remained until March 1406.[29] It is not surprising, therefore, that it was not until the spring of 1406 that Innocent's response to the events of June 1405 reached England; when it did, it included a bull excommunicating all those who had been involved in Scrope's death – although without naming them.[30]

Arundel's orders were to publish it in England, which would have been deeply injurious to Henry's reputation both at home and abroad, but he temporized. He had already, in December 1405, joined the dean of York and the royal chancellor, Thomas Langley, in sending a strongly worded letter to the cathedral chapter 'ardently requiring' them to stop encouraging pilgrims to visit Scrope's tomb and to cease advertising the 'so-called miracles' (*miracula praetensa*) alleged to be occurring there, at least until they had been investigated.[31] Having already indicated that the security of the Lancastrian dynasty trumped the honouring of Scrope's memory, his reaction to Innocent's bull was unsurprising. According to a chronicler, the primate 'had no wish to act alone in this', and he declined to publish it. This was not a risk-free strategy: when Archbishop Langton chose to ignore a papal bull excommunicating the barons who rebelled against King John in 1215, Innocent III suspended him from office and he left England for three years.[32] But the schismatic papacy of the early fifteenth century was a diminished force, and Henry and Arundel knew it.

The king's reaction was to double down: sending the pope the coat of mail (*loricam*) said to have been worn by Scrope when he was taken captive, he included a message referencing the story of Joseph's bloodied robe: 'Father, see whether this be thy son's coat, or no?' (Genesis 37:31–3). What he meant, as the chronicler helpfully explained, was 'This is not an appropriate tunic for any spiritual son to be wearing when confronting the king, especially not an archbishop.' Had Scrope not been killed, Henry added, the risings could not have been quelled. This, as another chronicler pointed out, was not true, and the pope evidently agreed. His reply (extending the quotation) was 'Whether or not it was my son's tunic, he was in such danger that he was entitled to wear it, because I know well that an evil wild beast devoured him.' Had Innocent VII not died on 6 November 1406, there is no telling how long the stand-off might have continued, but, fortuitously for the English king, there followed 'such discord and schism in the Roman Church' that the matter fell into abeyance.[33]

9

Bishops Old and New
1404–7

Throughout the political traumas of 1404–6, Arundel and Henry were also engaged in almost constant correspondence with the papacy about promotions to the episcopacy, conversations which both shaped and were shaped by these events. The average life expectancy of a medieval English bishop from first consecration until death was eighteen years.[1] On average, therefore, with twenty-one sees in England and Wales, at least one bishop might be expected to die each year, but for three years after June 1401 none did so. In 1404, the floodgates opened: between April and October, Trefnant of Hereford, Bottlesham of Rochester, Braybrooke of London and Wykeham of Winchester all died. This was the king's chance to re-stock the episcopate with his supporters. His half-brother Henry Beaufort was translated to the wealthy see of Winchester and replaced at Lincoln by the king's confessor, Philip Repingdon; Hereford went to the king's former confessor, Robert Mascall.

There is nothing to indicate that Arundel influenced these appointments, or that he tried to, but Rochester and London were a different matter. When his friend John Bottlesham died in April, the archbishop, expecting to be able to exploit his unique position at Rochester, proposed another friend, Thomas Chillenden, prior of Christ Church Canterbury. Chillenden declined, preferring to remain with his community,[2] whereupon king and archbishop jointly nominated Roger Walden, but instead Boniface translated Richard Young, bishop of Bangor, a lawyer and diplomat of great distinction who had spent many years at the Curia and who had visited almost every part of western Europe except his diocese. This was hardly his fault: he was only provided to Bangor in 1399, whereupon Glyn Dwr's revolt promptly made it inaccessible to him. Nevertheless, Henry and Arundel both tried to block Young at Rochester, and the impasse was still unresolved when, on 28 August 1404, Robert Braybrooke's death opened up another avenue. Initially, Arundel tried to secure London for his archdeacon and right-hand man at Canterbury, Robert Hallum,[3] but he soon backed down, telling the pope that he had been unaware that the king was proposing Thomas Langley – an embarrassingly lame excuse. However, he did express to the pope the wish that Hallum might be favoured when another opportunity arose. In October, Langley was duly elected by the St Paul's chapter, but, unfortunately for him, Boniface IX died in the same month and on 10 December 1404 the newly elected Innocent VII provided Roger Walden to London. Impasse loomed, with neither king nor pope prepared to back down.[4]

Although frustrated in his initial choice for London, Arundel probably had no objection to the provision of the now fully rehabilitated Walden. The case of Richard Young, however, saw him at his most unreasonable. Piqued that he had been overridden even at Rochester, the one English see which a primate regarded as effectively in his gift, he reproached the pope for not informing him of the translation and declared that he had no intention of releasing the spiritualities or temporalities of the see until Young made his profession in person – for, he declared, he was loath to be thought of as in any way unworthy or negligent of his obligations, 'but I am always ready to uphold the ancient custom of the church of Canterbury in all matters, to the tiniest jot'.[5] Not unreasonably, Young had asked to make his profession by proxy (as Bowet did in 1401), since barely had he been provided to Rochester than he was sent on diplomatic business to France and Flanders, whereupon he was arrested and imprisoned for several months by the duke of Burgundy.[6] Yet not until March 1407 did Arundel release the Rochester temporalities and spiritualities. Young never fully forgave the archbishop for his petulance; after Arundel's death, he sued his executors for wrongly withholding his revenues.[7]

The archbishop's insistence on the exercise of his primatial authority 'to the tiniest jot' was to some extent innate but may also have been learned from his predecessor, for Courtenay had been a fierce defender of the rights of his office as well as of his Church. Yet Arundel seems also to have felt the need to assert himself in the role, perhaps because of his underwhelming academic qualifications compared to many of his bishops and officials as well as his predecessor. (Courtenay was a doctor and professor of laws and a former chancellor of Oxford university.[8]) At times, there was a whiff of the headmaster's study about the way Arundel addressed his bishops. When John Trevor took it upon himself to be inducted 'or rather intruded' and even installed as bishop of St Asaph (*se fecit induci quin verius intrudi, et de facto contra justiciam installari*), Arundel informed him that 'since time immemorial' bishops of the province had been inducted and enthroned in the corporal possession of their sees by the archbishop or his representative, and only after this might they personally exercise any episcopal function or even enter their cathedral. To usurp the archbishop's rights in this regard was to incur the penalties imposed on those who 'rashly contravene the holy canons and constitutions on this subject against intruders and ecclesiastical dignities'.[9] This was hardly Trevor's fault: he had been provided to St Asaph as long ago as 1395, while in Rome (where he was consecrated), but the subsequent death of Courtenay, exile of Arundel, intrusion of Walden, revolution of 1399 and Welsh rebellion from 1400 had caused too much disruption to arrange an enthronement in such a distant see.[10] Bishop Medford of Salisbury received a similarly sharp rebuke when he failed to correct a number of abuses identified at least a decade earlier during Courtenay's visitation.[11]

Nor was it just the elderly or politically suspect whom Arundel admonished, as can be seen from his letter to Henry Beaufort in the autumn of 1404 telling him that, according to information he had received, 'numerous serious defects in the manors, houses, granges, closes and other things belonging to the bishopric of Lincoln have been left uncorrected', especially since rumours of Beaufort's imminent translation to Winchester had begun to circulate. These were now giving rise to scandal and needed to be corrected so that Arundel 'like a stepfather . . . can continue to pursue with good will Saint Swithun and the bishopric of Winchester'.[12] Was this a thinly veiled warning that, if Beaufort did not take his responsibilities more seriously, Arundel might oppose his translation? A few months earlier, he had even sequestered the fruits, rents and profits of Beaufort's predecessor at Winchester, William of Wykeham, when he failed to attend the convocation of April 1404, although the sentence was soon relaxed and the revenues restored. Wykeham was eighty and ailing by April 1404 (two years earlier, he had been allowed to appoint proxies for parliament because he was infirm), and by October he was dead.[13] But for Arundel, attendance at convocation was not optional – Adam Usk said that 'none of the clergy of his province was for any reason excused or spared from attending, provided that he was fit to work'. That said, at a time when Arundel badly needed all the support he could muster from the episcopate, this was a strange, indeed rash, way to treat either the king's half-brother or England's longest-serving bishop.[14]

Archbishop Scrope's execution, followed by the death of four more bishops in 1406–7, heralded a further round of episcopal promotions and translations. Initially, Henry wanted Thomas Langley to have York, and the chapter obliged by electing him, but Pope Innocent, in no mood to humour the English king, provided Robert Hallum instead, almost certainly at the suggestion of Arundel but clearly not that of the king, who refused to recognize him. Henry did, however, give some ground by finally, within six weeks of Scrope's death, recognizing the pope's provision of Walden to London.[15] When Walden promptly died, in January 1406, followed by Skirlaw of Durham in March, Despenser of Norwich in August and Medford of Salisbury in May 1407 – the passing of an episcopal generation – further avenues opened up. Langley, who had long coveted Durham in preference to York, was quickly elected and provided there without controversy. Despite the fact that the king favoured Bowet, he appears to have been quite content with this as long as he still had his way with York, for which he now proposed Bowet. Arundel was persuaded to do the same, which meant that once again Hallum was left high and dry, despite his papal provision and despite having travelled to Rome in 1406 to try to persuade the pope not to backtrack. Since London had already been earmarked for Nicholas Bubwith, very much the king's man, his chances of securing a see were receding.

Despenser's death on 23 August 1406 should have opened a window of opportunity, but the Norwich chapter, hoping that by choosing one of their own they might avoid the strife of the past decade, quickly elected their prior of twenty-five years, Alexander Tottington, and the still defiant pope duly provided him.[16] The king was furious, imprisoned Tottington in Windsor castle and informed Arundel that under no circumstances would he deliver the temporalities of the see to 'this prior of Norwich', against whom he intended to invoke the Statute of Provisors. Arundel shared Henry's concern but, faced with both canonical election and papal provision, their options were limited.[17] Only after Medford died in May 1407 was the situation resolved. Initially, the king persuaded the Salisbury chapter to elect Bubwith, but when the new pope, Gregory XII, finally agreed to recognize Bowet's translation to York, Bubwith was moved yet again – his third see in fifteen months – to replace him at Bath and Wells, while Richard Clifford went from Worcester to more prestigious London. This left Salisbury vacant again, and now at last, having agreed to give up his claim to York, Hallum got his see.[18]

Viewed from a distance of six hundred years, the undignified episcopal jockeying of 1405–7 resembles a revolving-door pantomime more than a high-stakes exercise in international diplomacy. The upshot, however, was that by the autumn of 1407, with one or two politically insignificant exceptions, the king had got what he wanted – a reliably Lancastrian episcopate. Langley had served John of Gaunt during the 1380s and 1390s, acted as an executor of his will and was (until 1407) Henry's chancellor. Bubwith, like Clifford, was an administrator of exceptional competence, a former secretary to the king and now his privy seal keeper; after Arundel became chancellor, he would become treasurer.[19] For those whose loyalty the king valued most highly, able servants as well as personal friends, he had fought tenaciously – in Bowet's case, not just once but twice. Only at Norwich, where he eventually (in October 1407) agreed to recognize Tottington, was he frustrated.

As for Arundel, he cannot have been entirely satisfied, but nor would he have been entirely dissatisfied. His friend and deputy at Canterbury, the learned and self-assured Hallum, had eventually got what he deserved, and he was perfectly able and willing to work with the others who had emerged as winners.[20] There was, moreover, an added bonus for the archbishop and the king, for these promotions formed part of an unofficial Anglo-papal concordat worked out at the Curia, central to which was Pope Gregory's agreement to revoke the sentence of excommunication promulgated by his predecessor against Scrope's killers.[21] It was Henry Chichele – lawyer, diplomat, councillor, friend of Prince Henry and rising star of the English Church – who was chiefly responsible for brokering this deal, having spent the best part of a year in Rome (with none other than John Cheyne).[22] His reward was papal provision to the Welsh see of St Davids after Guy Mone's death in August 1407.[23] This was thin gruel for a man of Chichele's talents, but he did not have too long to wait. In 1414, he would replace Arundel at Canterbury and rule the English Church for almost thirty years.

Since no more English bishops died until April 1413, the provisions of 1406–7 mark the end of the convoluted story of episcopal appointments in England during Henry IV's reign. It is a picture complicated partly by the widespread practice of translation (in effect, promotion within the hierarchy), which became increasingly common from about

1360, and partly by the factional politics of the time. But it also helps to reveal the views of the parties involved – pope, chapter, king and archbishop – about the sort of person who should hold a bishopric. For Henry and Arundel, the first consideration was always that they should be loyal to the regime; if this could not be guaranteed, as for example with a number of those appointed during Richard II's reign, then they should at least not act on their inclinations. For the northern bishoprics – York, Durham and Carlisle – endemic border lawlessness had fostered a tradition of appointing militarily competent bishops,[24] which might help to account for Henry's insistence on the promotion of Bowet to York after the fall of Northumberland, when a power vacuum threatened in the north. However, neither Langley of Durham nor William Strickland of Carlisle was noted for his soldierly qualities.[25]

A letter written during the vacancy at Norwich in 1406–7, probably either to or from Arundel, raised a different issue:

> It is to be noted that in the diocese of the church of Norwich there are various sects, among them those who are called Lollards, who are greatly attached to various heresies, and unless they have [as bishop] a theologian who is expert in preaching (*virum theologum in sermonibus expertum*) who would extirpate their practices and heresies, it could easily spread to the extent that they cannot be restored to the way of truth.

Such a man, the writer went on, was Richard Dereham, master in theology, chancellor of Cambridge university, royal chaplain, diplomat, archdeacon of Norfolk and a more suitable bishop than Tottington. The king also supported Dereham's candidacy, but it was not to be.[26] Yet the Norwich chapter soon had reason to regret their choice. Like Despenser before him, Tottington quarrelled ceaselessly with his monks and was described in 1411 by a friar preacher as being 'ignorant and unworthy to rule his church', as a result of which heresies and errors now abounded in his diocese 'with the authorization of the bishop'.[27]

That he had 'authorized' heresy is improbable, but he was not a theologian nor even a graduate.

On the other hand, bishops who were also theologians were fewer on the ground than they had been in the thirteenth century, when scholars held several of the most prized sees. By the late fourteenth century, scholars tended to be relegated to the less sought-after bishoprics such as Rochester, Carlisle or Chichester. Not that fourteenth-century bishops were unlearned: two-thirds of Edward III's bishops had university degrees, a much higher proportion than under Henry III. However, only a quarter of them held degrees in theology, nearly all from Oxford. Soon after Richard Clifford secured the see of Worcester in August 1401, he wrote to the Dominican friar John Montague to come and be his adviser on all matters theological.[28]

Tottington was also, of course, both a Norfolk local and a monk. Two hundred years earlier, Archbishop Langton had deplored the fact that, when left to themselves, monastic chapters tended to elect a monk, believing that men of eminence and learning should become bishops.[29] There is nothing to suggest that Arundel objected per se to monks becoming bishops: he had recommended Thomas Chillenden, his prior at Canterbury, for Rochester, and he evidently thought highly of Philip Repingdon, an Augustinian canon (a monastic order) as bishop of Lincoln.[30] No one could question either Chillenden's or Repingdon's intellectual eminence. What he did object to was monastic cathedral chapters (of which there were nine in England) trying to pre-empt the rights of king, pope or archbishop by promoting internal candidates. When the Winchester chapter elected their prior in 1404, or the Durham chapter did so in 1407, they were quickly slapped down.[31] The episcopacy was too important to be left to the parochial preferences of monastic chapters, or indeed to local men. Unlike in Italy, where many dioceses were much smaller, few medieval English bishops were locals, although this did not stop many from being conscientious diocesans.[32] Nor were any English bishops of the fourteenth and fifteenth centuries canonized (as four of their thirteenth-century predecessors had been).[33]

As the clerk who jested with the king about Henry Bowet's promotion to an archbishopric pointed out, this was not an age of saint-bishops.[34]

What it *was* was the age of lawyer-bishops. From 1333 to 1396, Canterbury was almost always held by a lawyer. Between 1399 and 1443, the number of trained lawyers who became bishops rose from about a quarter to two-fifths. Many others had worked as papal notaries or auditors, or had held high office in the royal administration.[35] To some extent, this reflected the general acceptance of canon law in England by this time. That Arundel must have had a reasonable grasp of canon law cannot be doubted, but he would not have known its intricacies and byways to the same extent as the legal experts with whom he surrounded himself at Ely, York and Canterbury. Kings also favoured lawyers, both in the Westminster offices and as ambassadors. To be a bishop gave a royal chancellor or treasurer the necessary stature (Langley was only the second clerical chancellor in sixty years not to hold a see when he took over the chancery in March 1405, and this was soon remedied).[36] English embassies abroad, although nominally led by great magnates, invariably included at least one high-ranking clerical lawyer, often a bishop, whose task it was to ensure that the relevant precedents were cited and the protocols or treaties they negotiated and drafted were legally watertight. In order to carry conviction with the pope, the king of France or the Holy Roman Emperor, these men too should ideally be bishops.

Hallum, Bowet, Young and Chichele were among the most distinguished legal minds of their generation. The rise of the lawyer-bishop might have given rise to the fear that too many legally trained and (mostly) royally appointed bishops would have been tempted to blur the boundary between the powers of Church and State, but that does not seem to have happened.[37] And there was always room for others: men like Langley and Bubwith, for example, who were not lawyers and did not hold degrees but had simply proved themselves as outstanding administrators.[38]

Like most medieval kings, Henry IV knew what sort of men he wanted as bishops and usually got them. Yet his wishes were always contestable. Cathedral chapters, hoping to avoid the disputes which often bedevilled relations between them and external nominees, preferred the devil they knew to the one they didn't. Popes wanted men who would uphold papal prerogatives in England and the liberties of the Church. They, too, had a weakness for those whom they knew, which is why so many ambitious English clerks – of whom there was no shortage – spent years working at the Curia. It was in the hope of promotion that Adam Usk went to Rome in 1402, after the Welsh rebellion dashed his hopes at home. Initially he was successful, being appointed within a month as papal chaplain and auditor of the apostolic palace, but when he tried in 1404–5 to get Boniface IX to provide him successively to the sees of Hereford, St David's and Bangor, the king's wrath knew no bounds and he was outlawed and deprived of all his English livings.[39] Arundel also did his best for those whom he favoured, although in the end he usually fell in line. As a rule, then, as long as Henry was prepared to outface the pope and be both patient and ruthless, he usually got his way. But not always.

10

Arundel, the King and the Commons 1406

The threat of excommunication hanging over the king in 1406 seems to have had little effect on his ability to govern, despite it apparently being common knowledge.[1] It was certainly not discussed during the parliament which met at Westminster on 1 March 1406 and was finally dissolved on 22 December. In fact, the parliament was only in session for four months, punctuated by prorogations of a month in April, sixteen weeks in the summer and (probably) a further month in the autumn.[2] The reasons for this varied – Easter and the king's health in the spring, the wars in Wales and Guyenne which prolonged the customary summer recess, a French threat to Calais in October – but underlying them was the impasse over the measures needed to reform the government and achieve financial stability. Henry would not dissolve parliament until taxation had been granted, but the commons (or at least some of them) refused to grant taxation unless promised meaningful reform. The vacillations and volte-faces which dragged out the 1406 assembly marked the consummation of five years of parliamentary pressure bumping up against the king's prerogative, and the upshot was a succession of events and decisions which would reshape Henry's relationship with both his council and his archbishop.

Following a tetchy first session (1 March–3 April) during which the young and talented speaker of the commons, Sir John Tiptoft, had to apologize to the king for the fact that some members of the commons had spoken about him 'other than they should have',[3] the second session eventually began on 30 April, but without the king. Two days earlier, Henry had suffered a prolapsed rectum, leaving him unable to ride a horse and barely to walk. It would take several months for him to recover fully.[4] Thus, although he was able to attend intermittently during the second session – perhaps half a dozen days in total – for the most part it was Arundel who was left to manage the assembly and relay messages between different sides. This meant, *inter alia*, that he acted as spokesman for the council.[5] There were, as ever, numerous issues that needed to be addressed: the security of English shipping and Calais, the ongoing problem of aliens, the 'outrageous' expenses of the royal household (described by Tiptoft as being 'full of rascals', although he himself was a knight of the king's chamber), the Welsh rebellion, the growing French threat in Guyenne and much else besides. But it was the composition and powers of the privy council which emerged as the central question. Hitherto, the council had comprised a relatively large body (sometimes over twenty) of nominated but not always remunerated councillors, including – in addition to lords, bishops and the king's chief ministers – several knights, clerks, esquires and even London merchants, some of whom attended infrequently if at all. The commons had already indicated, in 1401 and 1404, that what they wanted to see was a smaller, more 'substantial' and more professional council capable of providing the king with independent advice and exercising greater control over financial affairs.

And this was, in the end, what was achieved, but only after much wrangling. On 22 May, seventeen councillors were nominated,[6] but on 27 November the composition was revised. In fact, both lists consisted largely of men who had already been councillors for several years, including knights such as Hugh Waterton, Arnold Savage, John Pelham and John Cheyne. Only at the very end of the parliament, in mid-December, was real change effected: the body now nominated was slimmed down to thirteen men, all of whom were either lords, bishops or ministers. The latter included not just the chancellor, treasurer and keeper of the privy seal – always the core of the late medieval council

– but also the three chief officers of the royal household: the chamberlain, Richard, Lord Grey; the steward, John Stanley; and Tiptoft, who on 8 December was appointed as treasurer of the household. Gone were the knights, esquires and clerks of the early years of the reign, many of them long-standing friends of the king. This was indeed a more substantial and professional body of councillors, each of whom was to be paid an attendance fee of either £200 or £133 a year.[7]

Three further developments were equally significant. Most importantly, Prince Henry, the heir to the throne, now began attending the council.[8] Aged twenty, he had hitherto been largely occupied with the rebellion in Wales, and although he continued to spend a good deal of time there for the next year or so, he now came more frequently to Westminster and, when he did, attended council. This was in part due to the king's declining health. Secondly, it must also have been agreed in December that Arundel would replace Thomas Langley as chancellor (although the latter was too competent not to remain a councillor). Although the archbishop was said to be reluctant to return to the chancery, this was in keeping with the increasingly prominent role he had played in policy-making during the past three years. Yet, according to Walsingham, there were some 'who cared about his honour' (*honorem eius diligencium*) who did not want him to become chancellor.[9] These were probably members of the clergy who feared that he would be too overburdened or too divided in his loyalties to focus on his ecclesiastical responsibilities. But if he was reluctant, which is plausible, it may well have been Henry who insisted on his acceptance – a point which is explicable by the third major development of December 1406. This was a protocol known as the Thirty-One Articles, which formalized, indeed governed, the new relationship between the council and the king.

The Thirty-One Articles expressed in writing and in detail the recommendations which successive parliaments since 1401 had encouraged the king to adopt in order to manage his finances.[10] Little was left to chance. A quorum of councillors was to remain constantly with the king, in effect a buffer between him and those who sought to take advantage of his generosity; all royal grants and appointments were to be subject to conciliar approval; Henry was to restrict his hearing of petitions to two days a week (Wednesday and Friday), at which councillors were always to be present; if anyone tried to sway him, no action was to be taken until the council had been consulted. (It has been estimated that Henry received about four thousand petitions a year.[11]) Councillors were also to undertake a thorough investigation of the royal household 'and all other places and offices in which the revenues of the kingdom are spent', with a mandate to root out excess and restore solvency; in addition the king was not to meddle in common law suits at the instance of the parties involved; above all, Henry was enjoined (in Article 1) to 'govern in all cases with the advice of [his councillors], and to trust in this'. In return, the councillors swore to be impartial in their judgments and not to take advantage of their powers, accept bribes, tolerate corruption by their subordinates or subvert the common law.

If these restrictions on Henry's freedom of action were to be enforced to the letter – which it was soon made clear that they were – the king would become the virtual prisoner of his council. Not surprisingly he sought, if not an escape route, at least a time limit, agreeing to the articles only 'saving his estate and the prerogative of the crown', and only until the next parliament. Yet still the commons remained mistrustful, declaring at the last minute that if it turned out that any taxation they granted had been misspent, they wanted 'certain lords' to be personally responsible for repaying it from their own resources. This the lords absolutely refused to do, while the 'enraged' king finally lost patience and 'vented his anger against them all' (*rex furibundus irascitur contra omnes*). As incoming chancellor and head of the council, Arundel also wanted to cover his back, declaring that only if the commons voted adequate taxes could the councillors honour the trust placed in them. And so, eventually – late into the night, four days before Christmas – the Thirty-One Articles were agreed, and the commons granted a tenth and fifteenth and renewed the wool subsidy for two years.[12]

Arundel may have hoped that by encouraging the commons to be (moderately) generous he could head off demands for taxation from convocation, for Henry was once again putting pressure on the clergy, including those traditionally regarded as exempt. Following the events of June 1405, York was too cowed to do anything but grant a tenth and reduce the exempt minimum to zero, but Canterbury proved more resistant. Initially summoned to St Paul's for 26 April, it was continually postponed and only during about two weeks in June does it appear to have done any real business. On 7 June a delegation from the lords and commons came to the chapter house to explain in the customary apocalyptic terms the king's desperation.[13] The clerics simply 'stood around and listened' (*circumstantibus tunc ibidem et audientibus*). The next day the delegation came again, but nothing was done. Eventually, on 9 June, the clergy bowed to the pressure and granted a tenth plus a subsidy of 6*s*. 8*d*. (one-third of a pound) from each of those friars, chaplains, vicars, chantry priests and other stipendiaries who had formerly been exempt – although only with much grumbling (*murmur*) at the novelty of such a scheme. This additional subsidy does not appear to have yielded more than about £1,700, but Henry needed every penny he could get. No sooner was the second session adjourned (on 19 June) than the exchequer embarked on another round of borrowing, secured on the clerical tenths just granted, which yielded some £16,000 by mid-July – just enough to keep the government afloat over the summer.[14]

Arundel's part in securing the Canterbury convocation's third grant in two years is obscure, but he was clearly instrumental in ensuring the passing in parliament of that curious hybrid of a statute designated by the clerk simply as 'Against the Lollards' (*Contre les Lollardes*). Despite the fact that it was nominally based on a petition from Prince Henry and the lords spiritual and temporal, it was submitted by Tiptoft as a common petition.[15] As with the Thirty-One Articles, it was said to have been agreed only on the last day of the parliament, 22 December, but how long had it been under discussion? And why was it necessary? Apart from the usual trickle of suspects investigated, there had been no significant heretical agitation since 1401. It may have been prompted by a sermon delivered by the Lollard William Taylor at St Paul's Cross on 21 November 1406, in which – hoping, perhaps, to capitalize on parliament's reluctance to grant taxation – he made a forceful case for the disendowment of the Church's temporalities.[16]

Ostensibly, the statute was directed at two seemingly separate problems. The first was those who, 'by public sermons, or by conventicles, or in places called schools', incited others to call for churchmen to be 'evicted' from their temporalities – that is, disendowment. Unless they were silenced, the statute went on, it was likely that before long the Lollards would also start agitating for temporal lords and commons to be deprived of their inheritances. The second target was those who went about 'wickedly' claiming that Richard II was still alive or spreading 'other false prophecies' to stir up dissent. In future, any persons of whatever status who preached or disseminated doctrines contrary to the Catholic faith, or who sought to disendow the Church, or who claimed that Richard II was alive or that he was 'that idiot (*celuy fool*) who lives in Scotland',[17] or published false prophecies should be arrested and imprisoned until they could be brought before the chancellor to receive judgment in the next parliament. Lords, justices, mayors, sheriffs, bailiffs and all other ministers of the king were to have the power to make such arrests and to make enquiries without any further commission, and writs under the great seal were to be issued authorizing these powers. The statute was to be published on 6 January 1407 but was only to remain in force until the next parliament.[18] If Arundel was preparing the ground for his chancellorship, there were some who may not have been entirely comfortable with it.

This is unsurprising. Disendowment in some form was an idea to which almost all Lollards subscribed, but so did many others. Were those 'parliamentary knights' who had argued in favour of it in 1403–4, or those friars and rebels who in 1402–3 had proclaimed that Richard II still lived, or those 'false prophets' who foretold doom for the Lancastrian dynasty or defeat in Wales, now *ipso facto* to be considered heretics too?[19] If the intention was – by sleight of hand, as it were – to elide heresy with treason, that was not spelled out, at least not yet. Nevertheless, the implication that to argue for disendowment was heretical would surely not have been lost on the commons. To wrap the broad spectrum of subversive behaviours into a single bundle and label it 'Lollardy' was, of course, as tempting as it was occasionally effective, not just for chroniclers but also for a king or an archbishop of Canterbury. *Contre les Lollardes* was a catch-all and, although it added next to nothing to the sanctions against heresy already in place – some dating back to 1382, others to 1388 or 1401 – its most significant innovation was that lay authorities, not just prelates and their officials, were now given the power to arrest and imprison suspects – and it would be before Arundel, as chancellor, and then parliament that they would be brought.

Whether the majority of the commons were in favour of the statute or were cajoled into accepting it as part of the compromise hammered out in the days before Christmas is difficult to know. The specious threat to noble inheritances may have encouraged some of the lords temporal to support it, as did Prince Henry, eager to be known as an opponent of Lollardy. The role reversal whereby he sponsored the petition against the Lollards while Arundel sponsored the December act for the inheritance of the crown was a calculated piece of political theatre: the prince would defend the Church, the archbishop would uphold the dynasty.[20] Arundel had also made it clear that he would not hesitate to utilize his chancellorship to further his ecclesiastical agenda.

The Thirty-One Articles and *Contre les Lollardes* provided Arundel with the heavy weaponry he needed to feel confident about returning to the chancery. There are contrasting but not necessarily conflicting views about how the settlement of December 1406 was forged. The traditional view, derived largely from the official record, is that it was a head-on clash between commons and king in which both sides fought each other to a standstill, but the king, weary and in poor health, conceded more than the commons (whose grant was certainly not as generous as he would have hoped).[21] But were the commons as united in their resistance as the official record suggests? In particular, how likely was Tiptoft, a royal chamber knight, to be the fierce critic of the administration that the record portrays? Might he in fact have been the broker of a compromise reform package which allowed him, as a servant of the crown, to head off a hostile house?[22] Alternatively, it has been suggested that the settlement might have been an astute political démarche on Arundel's part.[23] Most likely, perhaps, is that Arundel and Tiptoft worked together, as they would continue to do for a further three years, to find a solution acceptable to both sides. Either way, as Arundel made his way back to Canterbury to commemorate the birth of Christ and the death (on 29 December) of Thomas Becket – who two and a half centuries earlier had given up the chancellorship when he became archbishop of Canterbury, believing the offices to be incompatible – he would have been uncomfortably aware of the trust both sides had placed in him. If this settlement was going to work, it was up to him to make it.

11

Chancellor of England
1407–9

At ten o'clock on the morning of 30 January 1407, 'in a little chapel at the entrance to the chapel of St Mary de la Puwe',[1] Thomas Langley resigned the chancellorship and handed over the great seal, wrapped in a leather bag, to the king, who passed it directly to Arundel, who, after being sworn in, took it back to Lambeth and, at eight o'clock the following morning, in the great hall at Westminster, began sealing writs.[2]

As chancellor, Arundel was not just head of the royal administration and the privy council, 'the second person in the kingdom';[3] he also had *ex officio* duties such as supervision of the king's hospitals, royal free chapels and other churches of the king's patronage; scrutiny of all abbatial appointments; the right to present to benefices valued at less than 20 marks (£13 6*s.* 8*d.*) and grant pardons for felony in royal courts. Mayors or merchants commonly sought his help in recovering debts, while Henry would dash off notes under his signet asking Arundel's advice on the appointment of a sheriff, the correction of an errant nun or a request to deal with a persistent petitioner – for example, 'a woman called D . . .' who wanted letters of protection against her creditors, because he was sick of her importunity, 'and you too will probably get tired of her company and annoying persistence (*nuyeuse pursuite*)'. Much of this kind of work could be delegated, but when, for example, a right of way in London's Bread Street was unlawfully closed off, blocking access to a church under royal patronage, Arundel and the king's justices visited the site in person and gave the offender detailed instructions for its restoration.[4]

Diplomatic affairs – treaties, embassies, mercantile disputes – were also routinely submitted to him for advice, sometimes at the express wish of foreign powers. Thus, in September 1408, the grand master of the Teutonic Knights wrote to Henry suggesting that Arundel be asked to resolve the ongoing dispute between England and the Hanseatic League over compensation claims for piracy. The fact that several memoranda recording English and Hanseatic claims from these years survive in Canterbury cathedral's archives suggests that the archbishop took the job seriously. Five months later, the king wrote to thank him and the council for the good work they had done to satisfy the parties involved.[5] Also time-consuming was the 'great and truly shameful dispute' which broke out in 1404 within the English Franciscan order between the Observants, who advocated a life of strict poverty, and the Conventuals, who preferred a less rigorous lifestyle. After papal, archiepiscopal, royal and civic injunctions failed to settle it, Arundel invited the Franciscan minister-general, Antonio de Pereto, to come to England, although even Pereto, when he came in 1407, failed to find a solution. Not until the cantankerous English provincial minister John de la Zouche was promoted to the bishopric of Llandaff – a deal which may well have been agreed between the king, the minister-general and the archbishop – did the rancour begin to subside.[6]

All this naturally meant that Arundel spent a good deal more time in London than he had during the early years of the reign, although he still managed a few months each year in his diocese, either at Canterbury or in his Kentish palaces. He was lucky in this respect: a chancellor who was also, say, bishop of Durham (Thomas Langley) or of Exeter (Edmund Stafford) found it more difficult to visit his diocese in person. Arundel even managed to undertake occasional provincial visits, for example to the dioceses of Winchester and Salisbury and the abbeys of Bruton (Augustinian) and Glastonbury (Benedictine), and Wells cathedral (all in Somerset) in September 1408. Only in 1409, when the king was more severely incapacitated and conciliar disagreements were escalating, was he more or less tied to London.[7]

In one sense, conciliar debate was a sign of a healthy political climate: frank and independent advice to the king was what the commons had asked for. Yet the disagreements of 1407–9 were – or at least became – about more than policy. Apart from Arundel, the most influential voices on the reshaped council were Prince Henry and the king's half-brothers, John and Henry Beaufort. For much of 1407 and 1408, the prince was still needed in Wales; the Beauforts, however, were regular attenders. It was the collapse of Percy dominance in 1403 which had opened the door to their growing influence. By 1407, the ascendant power in the family was Henry Beaufort: a man of great wealth and ambition, the holder of the rich bishopric of Winchester from 1404 and chancellor from 1403 to 1405, he had remained on the council following his demission of office and he had the king's ear.[8]

Arundel appears to have resented his influence, and perhaps to have mistrusted him. He may have feared a repeat of the Percy debacle – a concentration of family power serving only to whet appetites for more – although, given the Beauforts' dependence on crown patronage rather than inherited land and wealth, that was less likely. More obviously, he found it hard as archbishop to condone the bishop's lack of interest in his episcopal responsibilities and his worldly lifestyle, which included fathering a daughter by Arundel's niece, Alice, in 1402. Henry Beaufort, in turn, is unlikely to have looked kindly on the archbishop's sharp rebuke a few years earlier.[9] Nor did Arundel trust the youngest of the Beaufort brothers, Thomas, who had played such a prominent part in the condemnation of Archbishop Scrope.[10] Thomas was often in the company of Prince Henry, with whom he campaigned in Wales. As yet, he played little part in Westminster politics, focusing on his roles as admiral and captain of Calais, but by mid-1409 he too was a councillor and in January 1410 would replace Arundel as chancellor.[11]

This froideur between Arundel and the Beauforts may explain why, just ten days after he became chancellor, a letter patent (technically an exemplification) was issued amending the 1397 patent by which Richard II had declared them legitimate and capable of inheriting lands and titles as if they had been born in wedlock. The 1397 patent was, ostensibly, unconditional. The exemplification of 10 February 1407, which was said to have been issued at John Beaufort's request, repeated it verbatim but interlined three words: *excepta dignitate regali* – 'the royal dignity excepted'.[12] In other words, the Beauforts and their descendants were explicitly barred from inheriting the crown. In the wider sense, what lay behind this was the concern over Henry IV's health which had induced the 1406 parliament to pass the act vesting the inheritance of the crown in the king's four sons successively. No other potential heirs were named in the 1406 act – not the duke of York, not the Beauforts, certainly not the Mortimers.[13] With four healthy sons approaching adulthood, few could have anticipated that the house of Lancaster would run dry – and even if it did, it was far from clear whether the half-blood Beauforts would merit consideration. Perhaps this was why John Beaufort requested the exemplification, to clarify their position, but if so he and his brothers would surely not have welcomed the outcome, which explicitly denied to them the recognition for which they had presumably been hoping. The king must at the very least have consented to the Beauforts' exclusion from the royal succession, but the timing bears Arundel's fingerprints. Perhaps he thought it was a necessary clarification; perhaps he wanted to keep the Beauforts in their place. Whatever his reasons, an already cool relationship now turned cooler.[14]

Yet, if conciliar rivalries were an unwelcome distraction, Arundel always knew that the real challenge of his fourth chancellorship was to bring some kind of order to the king's chaotic finances, and in this respect he and his council were remarkably successful. The plentiful evidence for the council's fiscal policy and achievements in 1407–9 need only be summarized here.[15] Eschewing the experimental measures which had failed to restore solvency between 1404 and 1406, Arundel and his treasurers – Nicholas Bubwith from April 1407 to July 1408,

John Tiptoft from then until December 1409 – adopted a back-to-basics policy of reducing the level of assignment (revenue anticipation) and increasing the level of cash receipts at the exchequer; drawing up annual budgets allocating predetermined sums according to perceived priorities (Wales, Calais, Guyenne, the royal household, etc.); enforcing reduced expenditure, especially in the household; and exercising central control over the distribution of all crown resources. The last of these meant, for example, that even direct taxation was now used for non-military purposes such as the household, contravening a principle which the commons had long cherished but which they now seemed willing to abandon. To achieve these aims, Arundel was prepared to take strong measures, such as imposing a freeze on disbursements from the exchequer during the first two months of 1407 to allow the council time to work out its priorities and accumulate a cash reserve, and ordering his officials to ignore mandates from the king if they contravened the Thirty-One Articles.[16] As a result, royal grants of landed or monetary resources in 1407 amounted to one-fifth of what they had been in 1406, and almost all of them were sanctioned by the council.[17]

When parliament met at Gloucester in October 1407, the king graciously thanked the council for its work, and the commons, after a private briefing from Arundel on how the council had spent its money, granted one and a half tenths and fifteenths, collection of which was to be staggered between February 1408 and February 1409. Simultaneously, convocation granted one and a half clerical tenths. This assured revenue stream for the next eighteen months allowed the council once again to plan its expenditure; in the event, 1408 turned out to be, financially speaking, the most orderly year of the reign. The reassertion of exchequer supremacy allowed annuities to be paid regularly, arrears to be cleared, debts to be repaid, and failed assignments and borrowing to be greatly reduced. To some extent, Arundel was fortunate to become chancellor when he did: the Welsh rebellion was subsiding; so was piracy in the Channel, meaning that revenue from wool exports surged; King James I and the earl of Douglas were English prisoners, alleviating pressure on the northern border; and in November 1407 the arch-Anglophobe Louis, duke of Orléans, was assassinated in Paris by agents of the duke of Burgundy, much reducing the threat to Guyenne. In 1407, for the first time in nearly a decade, England faced no significant military emergency. Yet if luck played its part, the vital new ingredient was the clear-headedness of conciliar policy.

By the summer of 1409, however, the taxes granted in 1407 were mostly spent, and since they had been secured with a promise to parliament not to ask for any more until March 1410, competition for diminishing resources was accelerating and, with it, conciliar rivalries.[18] The twenty-two-year-old Prince Henry, having more or less accomplished his mission in Wales, was now mainly based at Westminster and presiding over the council. Not surprisingly, he was keen to see his own military priorities, which were different from Arundel's, adequately funded. Around him clustered his supporters, including Henry and Thomas Beaufort, the latter having returned with the prince to Westminster, where he immediately joined the council, and the young earls of Warwick and Arundel (the archbishop's nephew). By late 1409, the council's authority was slipping away: Tiptoft resigned on 11 December, Arundel on the 21st, three years almost to the day since the dismissal of the Long Parliament.[19] Five weeks later, the first parliament since 1407 met and Thomas Beaufort was appointed chancellor, the only lay chancellor of the reign. By the time this assembly was dissolved, a new council under the leadership of Prince Henry had been formed, consisting almost entirely of his supporters, which included neither Tiptoft nor Arundel.

Yet, if the prince appears to have lost confidence in the archbishop, the same was not true of the king – indeed, quite the reverse. Despite formally renouncing the Thirty-One Articles at Gloucester in October 1407, Henry continued to leave the day-to-day management of the country, crown finance included, in Arundel's and Tiptoft's hands. Then, in June 1408, while Henry was staying at the archbishop's manor of Mortlake, he suffered what was probably a coronary thrombosis.[20]

Henry had always trusted Arundel, but he had not thus far been forced into reliance on him. Now, increasingly, he was, and with dependence came a deepening of their friendship. Following his collapse, he remained with Arundel at Mortlake for four weeks, before gradually making his way back to London, but in January 1409, while staying at Greenwich, he suffered a relapse. Believing that he was dying, he drew up his will on 21 January, committing all the arrangements for his funeral to 'the discretion of my cousin the archbishop of Canterbury'. Four days later he issued a general pardon to anyone who had rebelled against him.

Messages between Henry and Arundel now became increasingly affectionate: 'your true friend and child in God', the king signed himself, or 'your true son Henry'; he thanked Arundel for writing to him 'so tenderly and in your own hand', telling him 'with all my true heart, my worshipful and well-beloved cousin, you, next to God, I thank for the good health that I am in'. Arundel wrote back 'in accordance with the affection we bear towards you'.[21] On 10 March 1409, still at Greenwich, Henry granted Arundel the custody of Queenborough castle, the strategic outpost on the Isle of Sheppey, for life, along with all the profits of its lordship – a remarkable commission for an archbishop. The prince evidently did not approve and removed it from Arundel's custody the day after he became king.[22]

By early March the crisis was passing, but in fact Henry IV's health never fully recovered and he remained a semi-invalid for the rest of his life, less involved in the business of government and more inclined to spend his time in friends' houses than in royal palaces.[23] It was with Arundel that he stayed most often, sometimes at Canterbury or Lambeth, sometimes at the archbishop's manors at Croydon or Mortlake.[24] His letters habitually addressed the archbishop as 'Most reverent father in God, dearest and much-loved cousin' (*Tresreverent pere en Dieu, treschier et tresame cousin*), a more intimate form of greeting than to anyone else except his family.[25] This reflected not just their ever closer friendship but also their political alignment. Like the archbishop, the king was sidelined by Prince Henry's assumption of power in January 1410 and largely excluded from influence until the parliament of November 1411.[26] Despite the fact that Prince Henry's administration followed the fiscal policies that Arundel and Tiptoft had put in place (but with different priorities), both king and archbishop disagreed with some of the decisions made by the prince, especially in relation to foreign policy.

It was a fractious time: for the first six or seven years of the reign, threats from domestic rivals and foreign powers had united the Lancastrian royal family. Now, having largely seen off its external rivals, it was dividing internally: one faction led by the king, his second son (Thomas of Lancaster[27]) and the archbishop; the other by Prince Henry, the Beauforts and the earl of Arundel. The archbishop's nephew, now twenty-eight, was less reckless than his father, but similarly belligerent and reputedly an exacting landlord. Before 1407, he was mainly engaged in the suppression of the Welsh rebellion, often alongside Prince Henry, to whom he became close. By the time they returned to Westminster, he was the prince's leading retainer, with an annual fee of £166. But as his stock with the future king rose, his relationship with his uncle became correspondingly strained, even threatening in 1409–10 to turn violent.[28]

Thus it was not just the royal family that fractured in 1409; so did Arundel's. To the archbishop, his nephew's attachment to the prince's party was a threat to the stability of the Lancastrian dynasty, perhaps even a kind of betrayal. To Earl Thomas, the Beauforts and others who supported the prince, it was a sick king increasingly dependent on an overmighty and over-cautious archbishop which represented the real threat: it was with Prince Henry, not his father, that the future lay, and the sooner the better. Fortunately for both dynasty and country, this split was contained – in the sense that it did not lead to civil war, as in France – but it disfigured Henry IV's later years.

12

The Constitutions and the Schism 1407–9

Arundel's three years as chancellor from January 1407 to December 1409 marked the apogee of his contribution to English public life under Henry IV. For the first ten months, until October 1407, his priority was to restore crown solvency. Once this had been achieved and taxation had been secured at the Gloucester parliament, he could turn to other matters – notably, the ongoing defiance of the Lollards and the growing Europe-wide calls to find a solution to the Great Schism.

One of the archbishop's frustrations in combating Lollardy was that the ground upon which he had to fight seemed constantly to be shifting. With hindsight, it is possible to identify three broad types of religious nonconformist in early fifteenth-century England. Firstly, there were the Wycliffite masters and professors at Oxford, the wellspring of 'the English heresy'. Secondly, there were the poor preachers – some clerical, some lay – who taught or advocated Wycliffite or quasi-Wycliffite ideas to any who would listen, sometimes publicly in churches or market places, sometimes privately in 'schools' or 'conventicles', that is, local or familial gatherings often focused on close Bible-reading. Thirdly, there were the knights and lords who, motivated sometimes by Wycliffite logic, sometimes by disgust at institutionalized clerical corruption, had the means to protect or patronize unorthodox chaplains and preachers and the stature to argue in parliament or council for measures such as disendowment; what fuelled their desire for ecclesiastical reform was often experiential as much as ideological.

Arundel probably thought of these groups as the three-headed hound of hell – an image he liked to cite.[1] Bishops and chroniclers sometimes made little distinction between them (not always accidentally), yet in many ways they were quite different. Out-and-out heretics, rich or poor, were often very well read in the Scriptures and irredeemably convinced by Wycliffite logic that, for example, the consecrated host could not possibly have ceased to be bread. Their core beliefs tended to be coherent and consistent. At the other end of the spectrum were those who, not necessarily well versed in the subtleties of theological debate, were fundamentally orthodox but, influenced sometimes by pietistic trends or political considerations, believed that the Church needed urgent moral reform. Consider, for example, the case of John Cheyne, who, according to convocation, was 'under the influence of the Lollards' and 'utterly hostile' to the Church. Yet the evidence for Cheyne's 'Lollardy' is entirely conjectural. What men like him really wanted was to return the Church to its original Christian ideals; but to the monochrome vision of Thomas Walsingham, a monk of wealthy and privileged St Albans, reform was unwelcome – or, at least, that kind of reform.[2]

Cheyne's 'Lollardy' was certainly very different from that of men such as William Sawtre or John Purvey. This is not to deny that some of the Lollard knights – Thomas Latimer, Lewis Clifford, John Montagu – almost certainly held heterodox views on questions such as the Eucharist, papal authority, confession or religious imagery, but they did not make a habit of preaching in public.[3] Moreover, if they patronized radical preachers in their private chapels or gave them benefices to which they held rights of presentation, and if they circulated or commissioned Wycliffite texts, their patrician immunity made it unlikely that they would be arrested, unlike artisans, husbandmen or poor priests. They had also become convinced that the Catholic hierarchy had become so corrupt that only king or parliament was capable of enforcing reform.

Arundel was certainly not opposed to reform – quite the reverse. He constantly urged his clergy to do better. Nor did he object to parliament taking the lead in certain cases. Indeed, one of the striking aspects of parliamentary legislation during Henry IV's reign is how much of it concerned the Church. For example, Arundel welcomed the commons' successful campaign against the appropriations system, with its attendant evils of non-residence and the neglect of pastoral care, despite the fact that appropriations were often sanctioned by bishops (who received a cut of the profits). Appropriation (or impropriation) was the process by which a religious house – typically a monastery – was granted a licence to appropriate the revenues of a parish church to its own use, in return for which it was supposed to provide a vicar, or series of vicars, to perform the priest's functions: saying masses and giving sermons, conducting baptisms and funerals, offering hospitality and almsgiving. It has been estimated that, by this time, at least 40 per cent of the roughly nine thousand English parishes may have been appropriated.[4] The problem was that – at least according to critics of the system – once a licence had been granted, the religious house in question often neglected its obligations, appointing slack, unqualified or non-resident vicars who left the parishioners bereft of pastoral care or even regular services.[5]

Non-residence in particular was a matter which Arundel always took seriously.[6] Yet the rate at which appropriations were sanctioned continued to increase. During the fifty years of Edward III's reign, the papacy had issued about 140 such licences for England, but Boniface IX alone granted 155 during the fifteen years of his papacy (1389–1404), of which the large majority were issued between 1397 and 1402.[7] In 1402, after a decade-long campaign against the system, the commons eventually lost patience and a statute was passed abolishing all appropriations licensed since 1377, which the pope had little option but to endorse. Arundel followed suit, circulating Boniface's bull to his suffragans with orders to make sure it was enforced by Easter 1403. Richard Clifford, for one, took this seriously, initiating a searching review of appropriations in his Worcester diocese to ensure that proper pastoral care was provided.[8]

To out-and-out Lollards, however, this was just tinkering. The whole edifice was institutionally corrupt. Why must the obfuscating superstructure of Catholic liturgy and Latinate mummery deny individuals the right to interpret God's word for themselves or engage in the kind of personal dialogue with God through which they hoped to attain salvation? Why could not individuals work through their own process of understanding the precepts of Holy Scripture (hence the Lollard emphasis on translating the Bible into English)?[9] The implications of this for the priesthood – the medium through which the Catholic Church claimed the exclusive right to interpret the word of God for the laity – were only too obvious. The Latin liturgy was important to the Church, as a signifier of its universality: a symbol, like the papacy, of a unified Christendom, of its superior learning and competence to minister to the laity, the purveyor of international services which any *literatus* in any part of the world (or, at any rate, Christendom) could understand. Not without a fight would the language of Rome by forsworn. Indeed, it was not until the twentieth century that Latin would be replaced by the vernacular as Catholicism's designated liturgical medium.

There was no catch-all way to deal with Lollardy's ever-moving target. The 1401 parliament witnessed considerable religious agitation, but the trial of William Sawtre had no discernible effect on those dangerously influential 'knights who never loved the Church'. In 1402, Arundel recorded a minor success when the veteran Lollard knight Sir Lewis Clifford apparently recanted his beliefs and gave him a list of Lollard preachers and conclusions.[10] Yet the next two years only saw the calls for disendowment grow more insistent.

A further embarrassment was that Wyclif's influence was by now acquiring an international dimension. How much detail Arundel or his suffragans knew about events in Bohemia is difficult to ascertain, but he would certainly have been aware that Wyclif's theological works had begun to circulate in Prague around 1400 and that the Czech reformer John Hus was using them to promote heterodox ideas. Hus had been teaching at Prague university since 1396. In 1401, he became dean of arts, and in 1402 began his ministry (preaching always in Czech) at the Bethlehem chapel. Worse still, in 1403, the new archbishop of Prague, Zajic Zbynek, began supporting Hus, as he continued to do for five years. Zbynek was a noble, more warrior than pastor, one of many Bohemians of his class who favoured the reform movement, or at least a version of it. Around 60 per cent of Bohemian parishes had noble or gentry patrons, who, like England's Lollard knights, used their connections to further their religious convictions. Hussite masters at the university continued to visit Oxford, copy Wyclif's works and carry them back to Prague, corresponding with English Lollards who sent Wycliffite tracts and letters of encouragement. (There are still more manuscript copies of Wyclif's works in Bohemia than in England, where so many were burned.[11]) For an archbishop of Canterbury, the idea that England was becoming the fount of European heresy was a source of acute discomfort, especially as international cooperation to end the Schism gathered pace.

At some point during 1406–7, Arundel became convinced that a Church which always seemed to be on the defensive must move on to the front foot. The poet John Gower appears to have marked the moment. In early 1397, Gower had composed his *Epistle to Arundel*, a fairly conventional encomium for the newly installed primate. Ten or eleven years later, fearing perhaps that he had presented an over-critical view of the prelacy, he made a few minor but significant revisions. Not that Gower had ever had Lollard sympathies – far from it – but in the England of *De Heretico Comburendo* and *Contre les Lollardes* it was important that those in authority should remember this. The archbishop had become 'a different, more dangerous man'.[12]

One reason for this was the revival after nearly a decade of overt Wycliffite sympathies at Oxford. Recent bishops of Lincoln, in whose diocese Oxford lay, may not have been sufficiently vigilant: Henry

Beaufort, bishop from 1398 to 1404, never took much interest in ecclesiastical affairs, while Philip Repingdon, chancellor of the university from 1400 to 1403 and bishop of Lincoln from 1404 to 1419, was an ex-Lollard who, even after his reversion to Catholicism, retained some sympathy for the academic independence of his former associates. Be that as it may, on 5 October 1406, just before parliament's third session got under way, a testimonial under the seal of the chancellor and masters of the university to 'all children of Holy Mother Church' commended the impeccable conduct and unrivalled intellectual acuity 'in heart, in voice and in his writings' of that 'former son of our university and professor of sacred theology', John Wyclif. Wyclif, it pointed out, had never been condemned as a heretic either while he lived or posthumously. (As yet, this was true.) Intended primarily to impress Wyclif's Hussite admirers in Bohemia, the letter was carried back to Prague in 1407 by two Bohemian scholars who had visited Oxford in order to copy the great logician's works, and published there in January 1409. The true author of the letter was almost certainly the Oxford theologian Peter Payne, who, despite making no secret of his admiration for Wyclif, evaded censure and in 1410 even became principal of St Edmund Hall, the epicentre of Oxford Wycliffism at this time.[13]

Seven weeks later, Arundel received another sharp reminder of Oxford's continuing defiance. On 21 November, with parliament still sitting, the known Lollard William Taylor, Payne's predecessor as principal of St Edmund Hall, preached a widely reported sermon at St Paul's Cross in which he stressed that, before the world could become a better place, the clergy must surrender their worldly possessions and allow them to be distributed to the genuinely needy: 'Let your plenty fulfil other men's needs' (2 Corinthians 8:14).[14] The next day, also at St Paul's Cross, another Oxford theologian, Richard Alkrinton of Merton College, preached in refutation of Taylor's arguments, arguing that anyone who advocated disendowment should be excommunicated.[15] Among those listening to him was a former Oxford disciple of Wyclif, the inveterate Lollard William Thorpe, who, by his own admission, walked through the crowd trying to persuade them to disperse, before accosting Alkrinton and upbraiding him as a flatterer and a hypocrite. Also present was Robert Waterton, a long-standing esquire of Henry IV's household and master of the king's horses, who, as the sermon ended, told one of his servants to hand Alkrinton a curry-comb, implying that he had merely been trying to curry favour with prelates. When Arundel heard about this, he went to the king, who apparently found it quite amusing. This infuriated the archbishop: 'This is no joke', he told Henry. 'By St James, the man must make amends to the preacher for the disgrace he inflicted upon him.' What Arundel wanted was for the culprit to apologize publicly and swear to obey the Church, but this was resisted by both Henry and Waterton. In the end it was agreed that the servant (not Waterton himself) should perform penance by walking semi-stripped, carrying a comb and a lighted candle, at the front of an unspecified number of processions.[16]

This scandal may have been one of the reasons why *Contre les Lollardes* was passed. The first suspects to be arrested under the new statute were Alkrinton's abuser, William Thorpe, and John Pollerbache, both described as chaplains. Apprehended by the Shrewsbury civic authorities on 17 April 1407 for preaching heretical opinions in St Chad's church, they were examined by the abbot of Shrewsbury and other 'trustworthy churchmen and scholars'. In mid-June, when news of their arrest reached Westminster, a royal writ was sent ordering the bailiffs to send them to London to be interrogated in chancery. Pollerbache soon recanted and no more was heard of him.[17] It is quite likely that no more would have been heard of Thorpe either had he not compiled a long and detailed account of an interview with Arundel at Saltwood castle, where he was being held in the archiepiscopal gaol, on 7 August 1407. His testimony, which runs to seventy pages in its modern printed edition, is one of the most remarkable documents of the Lollard movement. Almost certainly compiled within days of the interview, it was, so Thorpe claimed, 'as close to the sentence and the words, both that were spoken to me and that I spoke' as he could manage.[18] That his recall was perfect is, of course, impossible, but the circumstantial detail he includes and the picture of Arundel he paints are reassuringly consistent with what can be gleaned from other sources. This was not, as in the case of Sawtre, a formal trial. No lawyers were present. A few of the archbishop's clerks were there, but they barely spoke. Arundel was acting as chancellor as well as archbishop, conducting a wide-ranging interview which at times almost resembled an academic disputation.

What might be learned from 'hearing' Arundel from the other side, the point of view of the accused, is discussed below.[19] But what happened to William Thorpe, and how was his testimony promulgated? His account of the interview, which lasted several hours, ends with him being locked away in solitary confinement in Saltwood castle prison and expressing the hope that 'all who read or hear this writing' might pray to God 'to be united in true faith, steadfast hope and perfect charity. Amen. Amen. Amen', following which he disappears from the records.[20] Perhaps Arundel released him pending a formal trial; perhaps he escaped. In the latter context, it is worth noting that the constable of Saltwood castle, Roger Honyngton, into whose custody Thorpe was delivered after interrogation, left office six weeks later for reasons unexplained.[21] If Thorpe did escape, he probably fled to Bohemia, which might explain why his testimony was circulated in both England and Bohemia, in Latin and English. However, the evidence for this is slight. It is also possible that he died in prison after finding a way to smuggle his testimony out. This is not impossible, for he was apparently able to receive visitors, one of whom turned out to be an agent provocateur.[22] Either way, his wish to be read and heard was granted.

Arundel's interview with Thorpe can only have confirmed his belief that decisive action was needed to restrain the freethinking academics of Oxford. With momentum gathering for a resolution of the Schism, this was now more urgent than ever. Academics from Europe's leading universities had risen to new prominence during the Schism: they wrote widely debated treatises, their opinions were sought by rulers and their pronouncements on the possible paths to reunification were treated, by and large, as coming from somewhere above the political fray (even if this was not always the case). Lawyers and theologians from the university of Paris – Simon de Cramaud, Pierre d'Ailly, Jean Gerson – were especially active in Schism diplomacy, achieving thereby a status comparable to the modern public intellectual. The problem with Oxford was that the only public intellectual of Europe-wide renown that it had produced over the previous thirty years was John Wyclif, who saw the Schism simply as further evidence of the necessity for wholesale reform and who had, in any case, died in 1384.[23] To Arundel, this was deplorable. If a general council were to be held, as seemed increasingly likely, how much respect would be shown to the representatives of a university – a nation – known in Europe for disseminating heresy? On 31 October 1407, therefore, during the Gloucester parliament, Arundel summoned the Canterbury convocation to meet on 28 November at St Frideswide's priory, Oxford (the only Canterbury convocation of the reign to be held outside London). It was here that he drafted his *Constitutions*, the most controversial archiepiscopal enactment of the later Middle Ages.[24]

The *Constitutions* consist of a preamble and thirteen clauses. The preamble, addressed to all clerics and laymen in Canterbury province, resonated with the kind of polemic which flowed so readily from Arundel's pen when addressing heresy, replete with references to the black horse of the Book of Revelation, to Satan's 'perverse doctrines and novelties' and to the need to eradicate such poison from human souls. Orthodoxy and unity were non-negotiable, the authority of the Old and New Testaments unimpeachable. Several of the clauses are similarly wordy but can be summarized as follows:

(1) No person, layman or cleric, may preach in either Latin or English without a licence from his diocesan bishop, for which no payment should be demanded; if he preaches errors or heresies, his licence will be suspended until he purges himself; anyone deliberately disobeying this will automatically be excommunicated; persistent offenders will be treated as heretics, as will their supporters.

(2) Anyone permitting an unlicensed person to preach in their church, cemetery or elsewhere will *ipso facto* have that place put under interdict.

(3) Preachers must preach in a manner appropriate to their audience, such as to the clergy (but only them) about clerical vices, to the laity about the most common types of sin.

(4) Anyone preaching contrary to the Church's teaching on the Eucharist or other sacraments such as marriage or confession, or uttering 'scandalous words' about the Church, shall be excommunicated until they publicly and sincerely recant in their parish church on a Sunday or holy feast day; persistent offenders will be treated as heretics.

(5) It is contrary to the Church's teaching for masters or others who teach pupils (*pueros*) in arts or grammar or other primitive sciences (*scienciis primitivis*) to instruct them about matters concerning the Catholic faith, the Eucharist, other sacraments or any theological question; nor should they allow scholars to dispute matters concerning Holy Scripture, in public or private; offenders will be punished by the diocesan ordinary.

(6) No book or tract by John Wyclif or any other person writing since his time should be read anywhere in the province of Canterbury, including the universities of Oxford and Cambridge, unless it has been examined by twelve members of the university approved by the archbishop and unanimously declared to be orthodox; offenders will be punished as supporters of heresy.

(7) Since translation is a dangerous process, often involving error, no person should, on their own authority, translate any text of Holy Scripture into English by way of any book, libel or tract, nor should any such translation by Wyclif or any other person since his time be read either publicly or privately, in whole or in part, unless that translation has been approved in a provincial council; offenders will be excommunicated.[25]

(8) No person should engage in disputation about the Catholic faith beyond what is necessary for his teaching in the schools or

elsewhere, since such disputation is liable to be misunderstood; offenders will be excommunicated until they purge themselves.

(9) No person should dispute in public or in private the articles determined by the Church, unless it is to arrive at a true understanding of them; especially those concerning worship of the cross, images, the veneration of the saints, pilgrimages, relics or oaths taken on the gospels, all of which should be venerated; offenders will be treated as heretics until they recant.

(10) No chaplain should celebrate mass in Canterbury province without letters testimonial from a diocesan who knows him; anyone who does so or permits another to do so will be punished in a suitable fashion by the diocesan ordinary.

(11) Since various teachings known by 'the damnable name of Lollardy' have spread from Oxford, to the great scandal of the university, an inquisition is to be conducted each month by college officials, including principals, to determine whether any of their scholars are propounding or disseminating opinions critical of the Catholic faith, and warn them to desist; those who will not desist will be excommunicated, suspended or expelled and replaced by a Catholic; negligent officials or principals will similarly be excommunicated; in extreme cases colleges will be deprived by the archbishop or the diocesan ordinary of their scholastic privileges.[26]

(12) Persons who rashly and persistently infringe these Constitutions will be banned from holding benefices in Canterbury province for three years and punished by their superior.

(13) Although heresy and treason are treated as equal in certain laws, heresy is a more serious crime because it offends God as well as human majesty and deserves a graver punishment; those who are denounced or strongly (*vehementer*) suspected of maligning the Catholic faith shall be publicly cited for interrogation by diocesan ordinaries and punished according to the severity of their crimes.

Before the emergence of Lollardy, there had been no need for anything more than ad hoc enquiries into the occasional outbreaks of heretical activity in England. Since 1381–2, measures had been introduced piecemeal, aimed in scattergun fashion sometimes at Oxford university, sometimes at unlicensed preaching, sometimes at suspect books or clandestine gatherings ('schools' or 'conventicles'), sometimes at those knights and lords who argued too vociferously in favour of measures such as disendowment. Arundel's *Constitutions* marked the first systematic attempt to devise a more coordinated strategy for the detection and suppression of heresy, for, as he pointed out in the preamble, the existing statutes and provincial and diocesan decrees were inadequate. He claimed to have the unanimous support of the prelates for his *Constitutions* and to be issuing them at the 'urgent request' (*instantem petitionem*) of proctors for the entire clergy of Canterbury province. Much of what they decreed was familiar, such as the clauses on preaching (nos 1–4), although these went further than before. Even so, they aroused controversy: half a century later, Thomas Gascoigne regarded the stricter controls on preaching as the most pernicious aspect of the *Constitutions*, for by making licences to preach compulsory – and, apparently, hard to obtain – Arundel had 'silenced the word of God' (and not just unorthodox preachers).[27]

More novel, however, and more startling, were the measures proposed to stamp out theological debate at England's premier university. That the *Constitutions* were directed principally at Oxford is beyond doubt. That much had been made clear in the summons Arundel issued on 31 October: 'in the University of Oxford', he wrote, 'where the wisdom of literate men ought to flourish . . . alas! the enemy of man and the old sophist [Satan] has found persons through whom he can deceive the souls of the simple under the cloak of sanctity'.[28] Innovations such as the establishment of a board of censors and monthly inquisitions into students' and masters' orthodoxy introduced controls which he knew would be strongly resisted. So would three further clauses (nos 5, 8, 9) which sought to limit academics' freedom to engage in or teach through the medium of disputations (*determinationes*, or *quaestiones*), the most common and popular way for masters and students to develop their intellectual acuity by testing hypotheses in public debate. During Courtenay's clampdown in 1382, several Oxford academics had been suspected of heresy, but the charge was dismissed after they claimed that they had only put forward Wycliffite propositions as an exercise in disputation – that is, as *quaestiones*. That public disputations continued unchecked during the next twenty-five years is beyond question, as is the continuing support at the university for Wyclif's views.[29] Topics ranged widely: was it right to worship images or undertake pilgrimages; how did 'common religion' compare to 'private religion'; was obedience to the Ten Commandments more admirable than the renunciation of temporal wealth; were pluralities permissible? There were even discussions 'on the Sacrament of the Altar' – the Eucharist. Wycliffite opinions featured prominently and were usually (but not always) rejected. Occasionally, disputations were sponsored by nobles. To Arundel, such freedom to discuss fundamental doctrine was too dangerous (clause 8), but his insistence that the masters and academic authorities abandon their indeterminate attitude to Wycliffite opinions was bitterly resented.

The university, which was represented at the 1407 convocation, would have known about the *Constitutions* almost as they were being drafted. Whether John Gower had heard of them before revising his *Epistle* is unclear, but their fame – or notoriety – soon spread. Lollards excoriated them and so did many scholars apart from Gascoigne (a former chancellor of the university). Twenty-five years later, William Lyndwood, Archbishop Chichele's chancellor and principal auditor of the Court of Arches, included them in his great collection of English ecclesiastical canons, *Provinciale*, although he included precious little else by Arundel.

Their impact has also been the subject of fierce debate between modern scholars, and no clause more than clause 7, which raised the question of theological literature in English.[30] There is little to suggest that the English ('Wycliffite') translation of the Bible, versions of which were produced from the early 1380s and which was in fact a very close translation, had been seen as a problem until shortly before the publication of the *Constitutions*. Richard Rolle's English translation of the psalms and several copies of the Wycliffite Bible were already in circulation, some of them owned by lords, and as recently as 1401 the unquestionably orthodox Oxford theologian Richard Ullerston had engaged in open debate about the necessity for a vernacular Bible without any apparent suggestion that he was a heretic. According to an English tract of *c.* 1401 based on Ullerston's (Latin) determination on the subject, a bill had been presented to one of Richard II's parliaments 'by assent of both archbishops and the clergy' to 'annul' the English-language Bible, but John of Gaunt had responded 'with a great oath' that since other Christian nations had vernacular Bibles, so too should the English. The bill, if such there was, has not survived. The author added that during his sermon at Queen Anne's funeral in 1394, when Arundel was archbishop of York and chancellor, he had commended her for the fact that, although Czech-born, she had an English-language copy of the four gospels with commentaries, which she had sent him for approval, and he had declared them to be 'good and true'. A much later, longer English tract into which this was incorporated added 'but after this he became the cruellest enemy that might be against English books'.[31]

What seems clear is that, by 1407, Arundel and presumably others had come to believe that the circulation of unapproved vernacular translations of the Scriptures was to invite heretical interpretation.[32] An unhealthy dose of intellectual snobbery underpinned this realization. Whether academics and prelates exchanged views in Latin or English mattered little since they communicated in both. Laymen, however – the 'lewd' (unlearned) as they were sometimes referred to – were a different matter: translation into English made all sorts of ideas, all species of texts, *too* comprehensible to them. As the Lollard author of the *Lantern of Light*, written a few years later, put it, restricting translations of theological texts was 'for the more blinding of lewd people'.[33]

What Lollards advocated was opening the eyes of the laity, rich or poor: that the tools for self-determination should be made available to all, thereby undermining the Church's monopoly of scriptural and theological interpretation.

This is what lay behind the Wycliffite Bible project, as well as behind clause 7 of the *Constitutions* (although the modern attention lavished on this clause would surely have puzzled many including Arundel). It also helps to explain why Oxford was the archbishop's main concern, not just because its scholars had been involved in producing the Wycliffite Bible but also because Lollardy was one of the few medieval heresies with its roots in academic controversy rather than popular dissatisfaction with the Church (although it gained a much broader following as a result of the latter). Yet the fact that some 250 manuscripts containing all or part of the Wycliffite Bible survive from fifteenth-century England suggests that the *Constitutions* did not have the 'paralysing effect' on English translation that Arundel might have hoped.[34] This is hardly surprising, not least because the nobility – presumed to be less 'lewd' than their social inferiors – appear to have been considered, or considered themselves, exempt from the ban. Henry IV and his son Thomas both had English Bibles, as did many other lords.

Before Arundel felt ready to publish the *Constitutions* more widely, however, his attention was diverted to a quite different issue – not a new one by any means, but one which was fast approaching its long-awaited resolution: the Schism. This was a task that required unity and cooperation, including that of the university academics against whom the *Constitutions* were principally aimed. For the moment, therefore, the archbishop kept his powder dry.

By 1408, the Great Schism had lasted for thirty years, with support for the rival popes in western Europe more or less equally divided between Rome (England, Italy, the Empire) and Avignon (France, Castile, Scotland and, since 1406, parts of Wales). A scandal to Christianity, an impediment to ecclesiastical reform and international diplomacy, a comfort to heathens and an incitement to heretics, it was decried by clergy and laity alike as 'detestable', 'horrible', 'abominable', but periodic attempts to heal it, usually French-led, foundered on mutual distrust or self-interest, while Henry IV had been too preoccupied to address it seriously. Until now. Gregory XII, the Roman pope elected in November 1406, had promised before his election to do everything he could to heal it, including to resign if his opposite number, 'Pedro de Luna, whom some people call Benedict XIII', did likewise.[35] Negotiations between them began in 1407 but soon broke down, and by the spring of 1408 patience was wearing thin. In May, most of Gregory's cardinals deserted him and announced a general council of the Church to meet at Pisa in March 1409 to depose both popes and elect an agreed successor. The French withdrew obedience from Benedict and the defecting cardinals wrote to Henry IV asking him to withdraw England's obedience from Gregory. Henry was prepared to stop monetary payments to Rome and wrote several warning letters to Gregory exhorting him to honour his promises, but would the king agree to send an English delegation to Pisa? It was to decide this question that, on 29 July 1408, an extraordinary assembly of clergy from both convocations, theologians from Oxford and Cambridge and lords and knights of the realm met at St Paul's to 'celebrate the union of Holy Church' – in other words, to try to end the Schism.[36]

It fell to Arundel as primate to give the opening address, and he did not disappoint. 'We in the kingdom of England', he began, 'especially the prelates and clergy whom it behoves above all to repair and reunify the seamless robe of Christ, the catholic and apostolic church militant,[37] have done little as yet to this end, as a result of which England's reputation has declined.' This was true. Arundel's Church was an insular church, obsessed with its own problems, and for the moment, at any rate, the king was not planning to withdraw obedience from Gregory, a radical and potentially isolating step which filled many in England with the same apprehension, even horror, as it still would do 120 years later.[38] Arundel was probably disappointed by the king's hesitancy. Encouraged by Richard Dereham, who had brought the cardinals' letter back from the Curia, he seems by now to have come to believe that an immediate and total withdrawal of obedience, as the French had done, was the only way forward.[39] Henry, however, who had also spoken with Dereham, was not yet ready to abandon a pope whose weakness he had recently exploited with some success and who now declared – or pretended – that he too intended to call a general council to resolve the Schism.[40]

Yet pressure on the king was growing. The French had already intimated that they would go to Pisa. On 29 October 1408, Cardinal-Archbishop Francesco Uguccione of Bordeaux, representing the cardinals, addressed Henry and a large gathering of nobles and clergy in Westminster great hall. His speech, widely reported and enthusiastically received, enumerated Gregory's broken promises and warned that those who continued to support him would share his guilt as fomenters of schism, which was tantamount to heresy.[41] This was followed within days by letters from the French clergy confirming that they were planning to send a delegation to Pisa and begging the English to come too, for unless they acted together the council stood little chance of success. To facilitate their joint attendance, an Anglo-French truce was quickly agreed. By 12 November, Henry had made up his mind, writing to Gregory XII to inform him that an English delegation would be going to Pisa and urging him to attend as well.

If it was the king who ultimately made this decision, Arundel and many of the English clergy supported it. Among the letters sent by the French clergy was a personal appeal to Arundel, whose 'wise presence' and 'astute qualities of character' they earnestly requested at Pisa to help them. According to Walsingham, Arundel was 'unbelievably delighted' to receive such an invitation and immediately made plans to go, calculating how much money he would need for the journey, how long he would be away and how many servants he would need: so persistently did he beg the king to release him from the chancellorship that eventually Henry agreed. 'But the council of the realm was wiser', Walsingham went on, and, worried about the king's health while Arundel was away, persuaded Henry to revoke his permission and 'compel' the archbishop to remain in England.[42] That Arundel would have loved to lead the English delegation – a once-in-a-lifetime chance to strut the European stage – is easy to believe. And as late as Christmas Eve, when the king drew up a proposed list of English representatives to Pisa, it was headed by the two archbishops, of Canterbury and York, each of whom was to be accompanied by four doctors of law or theology.[43] By mid-January 1409, however, when the Canterbury convocation met to finalize the list, Henry was desperately ill and Arundel's chance had gone. But at least, he might have reflected, he now had the time to deal with more immediate problems: it was almost immediately after this that he published his *Constitutions* more widely, circulating it to the episcopate with strict instructions to enforce it throughout their dioceses.[44]

Walsingham was probably right: Arundel simply could not be spared in a crisis. Nevertheless, the choice of proctors to go to Pisa in his place bears his unmistakable imprimatur: his protégé and confidant Robert Hallum of Salisbury led the Canterbury delegation, accompanied by Henry Chichele of St David's and Thomas Chillenden, prior of Canterbury. The York delegation was led by Thomas Langley of Durham. Also chosen were Nicholas Rishton, representing the king but also one of Arundel's close advisers, and Richard Dereham, representing the university of Cambridge, equally acceptable to the archbishop. It was always clear that Hallum was the leader of the English delegation.[45]

The Council of Pisa did what it had been summoned to do, so that by 26 June 1409 Gregory XII and Benedict XIII had both been deposed and a new pope, Alexander V, unanimously elected. For some there was an expectation, or at least hope, that before it broke up (on 7 August) it would do more, for surely one of the lessons of the past thirty years (to say nothing of earlier times) was how sorely the Church needed reforming, and was not a general council the ideal time and place to start doing so? Hallum certainly expected reform to be discussed at Pisa and had commissioned from the Oxford theologian Richard Ullerston a treatise entitled *Petitiones Quoad Reformationem Ecclesie Militantis*

(Petitions for the Reformation of the Church Militant). What was striking about Ullerston's sixteen petitions – which Henry IV had apparently approved – was the emphasis placed on reform at the diocesan and parish level.[46] Continental reformers tended to be more concerned with reform of the central Curia and its financial arm, the papal *camera*, but the English were evidently just as concerned with local issues such as appropriations, dispensations and exemptions.[47] There was some discussion of reform at Pisa, but little was done about it. After four months, most of the delegates wanted to get home. And after thirty years, they would undoubtedly have counted the council a success.

If a general council of the Church seemed in the circumstances to be the only way to heal the Schism, it is hard to believe that Arundel was a conciliarist at heart: his instinctive authoritarianism would surely have baulked at the idea that the jurisdiction of a general council should, *in normal circumstances*, override that of the pope. Like many in England, he found conciliarism troubling, in part because its repositioning of papal authority came too close to heresy.[48] Yet he was, like Henry IV, and like the majority of Christians, immensely relieved at what appeared to be the ending of the Schism. Wisely, he and the king waited until Hallum's return to England on 15 October before announcing jointly that Alexander V had, 'with the inspiration of the Holy Spirit', been elected unanimously by both the cardinals and the council and that Henry had 'joyfully admitted' him as the true pope.[49] Unfortunately, the joy was brief, for on 3 May 1410, less than a year after his election, Alexander V died, and although a successor was elected (John XXIII), his erstwhile rivals, who had never accepted deposition, seized the moment to reassert their claims. From the summer of 1410, therefore, there were not just two popes, but three. Yet the Council of Pisa had shown the way, and four years later another general council met at Constance which did finally bring the Great Schism to an end.[50]

13

The Disendowment Bill and Wycliffism at Oxford
1410–11

On 2 January 1409, presumably as a consequence of one of the frequent mandates to arrest suspects which Arundel continued to issue from the chancery during 1408, an obscure tailor from Evesham (Worcestershire) called John Badby was interrogated by his diocesan, Bishop Thomas Peverell, for allegedly expressing heretical opinions.[1] Being a layman, he was not said to have preached them, but, according to 'several faithful Christians' – perhaps those local *fidedigni* encouraged by the *Constitutions* to be on the lookout for nonconformity – to have 'taught and publicly maintained' them. What is certain is that they were heretical. The Eucharist, said Badby, was not the body of Christ, whatever words any priest might pronounce; it was simply 'material bread' (*panis materialis*). If the host became Christ's body, why could he not see Christ on the altar? If Jesus was sitting with his disciples at the Last Supper, how could he have handed out bits of his body to them? ('Then the Jews started arguing among themselves: "How can this man give us his flesh to eat?"' (John 6:52)). In other words, Badby did not even believe in consubstantiation, let alone transubstantiation. 'John Rakyer of Bristol', he went on, had as much power to make Christ's body as any priest did.[2] Asked by Peverell whether he wished to renounce his views, Badby replied that he did not, whereupon Peverell declared him a heretic and presumably (although the record is silent on this) committed him to prison. The likelihood is that, like William Thorpe, he was sent to Arundel and held in one of the archiepiscopal gaols. At any rate, the archbishop was able to produce him in public, almost at a moment's notice, when required.

Twelve months later, that moment arrived. The parliament which met at Westminster on 27 January 1410 witnessed the most audacious parliamentary assault on the clerical establishment of the entire Lollard movement – the Disendowment Bill.[3] According to its drafter(s) – 'satellites of Pilate' (*satellites Pilatales*), said Thomas Walsingham – it represented the views of 'all the faithful commons'. That is unlikely, although some of the members were doubtless emboldened by Arundel's dismissal as chancellor five weeks earlier. Yet this was no spur-of-the-moment impulse: the Disendowment Bill was the product of ideas and calculations that had been discussed in Lollard circles for at least twenty years.[4] It claimed that if the king were to confiscate the 'proudly wasted' temporalities of the bishoprics and major monastic houses of England, said to be worth £214,666 a year, these could support 15 new earls, 1,500 knights and 6,200 esquires, all generously endowed with land; 15 universities with 15,000 scholars;[5] and 100 almshouses, each with an annual income of £67. These almshouses were not to replace the provisions for poor relief agreed in the 1388 Statute of Cambridge, which put the onus on towns, but to supplement them. Further confiscations from 'worldly clerks' would add another £100,000 annually, which would support 15,000 (presumably unworldly) priests and clerks. And even if all this were done, it would still leave an annual surplus of £20,000 in the king's treasury 'for defence of his realm' and £143,734 a year of ecclesiastical spiritualities to support the regular and secular clergy. It would be the greatest redistribution of England's landed wealth between the Norman Conquest and the Dissolution of the Monasteries.

If these calculations were optimistic and in places eccentric, they were not entirely divorced from reality (for example, the plausible estimate of around £140,000 for spiritualities). They were designed to appeal to a broad spectrum of society. Not for the first time, clerical disendowment was clothed in the garb of charitable provision and educational opportunity. More tempting in a parliamentary context, it was presented as a way of providing the king with a secure income to enable him to exercise largesse and defend his realm without continually asking for taxation. This was not coincidental, for the 1410 parliament had opened with a request, nominally from the king but perhaps more plausibly from Prince Henry, now head of the council, for a lay and clerical subsidy to be levied each year without the need for parliamentary consent.[6] Although refused, it may well have persuaded the commons, or at least a caucus of MPs, that this was the moment to remind the government that there was another way to secure not just a regular long-term income but much more besides. But the Disendowment Bill was too radical to have any chance of success, and according to Walsingham the 'catholic and orthodox' king had no hesitation in quashing it.[7]

The text of the Bill in the London chronicle ends with the words, 'to this bill at that time no answer was given'.[8] To Arundel, however, it was so outrageous as to call for a terrible example, and who better than the suicidally obdurate John Badby? Convocation had been summoned to meet at St Paul's on 17 February, but only convened twice during the following eleven days, on 21 and 24 February.[9] On 26 February – somewhat ominously – the cathedral was polluted by the spilling of blood, so it was to the cloister of the London Blackfriars' convent that, on Saturday 1 March, Badby was brought to trial. Archbishops Arundel and Bowet were both present, plus eight further bishops and a 'great multitude' of lords temporal, including the duke of York, the chancellor Thomas Beaufort and the former treasurer, William, Lord Roos. Since Badby was a layman, the interrogation was conducted in English throughout.[10] It began with Philip Morgan (Arundel's auditor of causes) reading out the record of Peverell's interrogation and Badby's responses. Arundel asked him whether he wished to recant and promised to pray for his soul at the Last Judgment if he did so. Badby made it abundantly clear that he did not: if every host consecrated on the altar was really the body of Christ, he declared, then there must be 20,000 gods in England;

he preferred, 'if it please the reverend father', to continue believing what he regarded as the truth. Urged by Arundel to think again, he flatly refused. This was quite unlike William Sawtre's trial nine years earlier: no logic-chopping, no scriptural quotations or attempts to lead his interrogator up theological byways. Badby was no theologian; he simply found what he had been told to believe preposterous. Even so, Arundel was prepared to give him more time, and after some discussion it was agreed that Badby would remain at Blackfriars, in a 'secure chamber', the key to which would be kept by the archbishop, until the following Wednesday. Perhaps Arundel hoped to visit him in the meantime to try to persuade him to recant, but there is no evidence that he did so.

By Wednesday 5 March St Paul's had been cleansed and it was here that Badby was brought to be offered a final chance to save himself. Before him stood much the same exalted array of spiritual and temporal lords, headed by Arundel and the duke of York. Once again, the record of his beliefs was read out and he was asked if he wished to recant. Once again, he refused. The duke of York, he asserted defiantly, or any man since the time of Adam, was 'of greater worth and reputation' than the sacrament of the altar. At this point an 'enormous' spider appeared on his face, 'close to his lips', and try as he might Badby was unable to prevent it from disappearing into his mouth. For Arundel, this was unequivocal proof of his degeneracy: 'perceiving that this man . . . completely lacked the grace of the Holy Spirit, and seeing that he had an indomitable and hardened heart, like Pharaoh', he shouted. 'Leave it! Now we shall see who it is that teaches him to speak' – the point being that the devil was often compared to a spider because he set traps for the unwary.[11] No more could be done except formally to declare Badby an unrepentant heretic and hand him over to the secular power, with the customary pious archiepiscopal request that he be spared 'the sting of death' (*mortis aculeo*). That, as Arundel was well aware, was never likely to be, and within an hour or so a royal writ instructed the sheriffs of London to 'commit him to the fire'.[12]

Smithfield thus witnessed its second and last heretical burning of Henry IV's reign. The king was not there, but Prince Henry was, and it was he who provided the main diversion. Strapped to a stake and enclosed within an open-ended barrel, Badby was set atop the pyre. When the faggots were lit, he uttered a cry. Taking this as a last-minute plea for mercy rather than a howl of anguish,[13] the prince ordered the flames to be put out, approached the pyre and offered Badby a pension of threepence a day for life if he would conform. Not having attended the trial, he may not have been aware of Badby's obduracy. Perhaps this was a chance for the prince not only publicly to demonstrate his religious orthodoxy but to perform a fine gesture of mercy, even to show that secular power might save a soul where ecclesiastical power had failed?[14] But when Badby again refused, the prince had no option but to order the flames to be rekindled, and within a few minutes England's second Protestant martyr had been 'completely incinerated' (*totaliter combustus*). According to Walsingham, his ghost, tossed about by violent storms, continued to terrify many who remained at Smithfield that night.[15]

As with Sawtre's burning nine years earlier, Arundel seems not to have gone to Smithfield, presumably not wishing, as a prelate, to witness the spectacle. Also, he had much else to deal with. Like the parliaments of 1401 and October 1404, that of 1410 included a good number of Lollard knights. As well as the Disendowment Bill, the first few days of the session had witnessed the presentation of a commons' petition asking for a relaxation of the penalties for heresy, although precisely how was unclear. On 8 February, two weeks into the session, the commons asked to withdraw this – a most unusual procedure and indicative of conflicting currents of parliamentary opinion on religious policy. The king agreed, but only as long as it did not serve as a precedent. Arundel was probably behind this move, as he had been behind the removal of John Cheyne as speaker of the commons in 1399.[16] Yet at least some of the knights and burgesses persisted, asking that in future arrests made under the terms of *De Heretico Comburendo* should be made by lay rather than clerical authorities so that suspects could be mainperned (released on bail) and purge themselves in lay courts. Further petitions asked that common law matters never be tried in Church courts and – trying perhaps to salvage something from the wreckage of the Disendowment Bill – that holders of benefices with cure of souls be obliged to make a greater financial contribution to the war, since many of them were not fulfilling their duties. The king's responses to these petitions were non-committal, but the message was clear.[17] For three years, ever since his resumption of the chancellorship in January 1407, Arundel had been trying to seize the initiative against those who impugned and derided the clergy. In 1408–9, the preparations for the Council of Pisa appeared to have united the English Church and State in a common enterprise under his guidance, but now, stripped of his secular authority, he must have felt that he was once again reduced to fighting a rearguard action against the Church's critics.

Yet he was not daunted. Before convocation was adjourned, it defiantly reissued *De Heretico Comburendo*, and barely had Badby been executed – with parliament still in session – than Arundel launched an investigation into a chaplain, John (Lay), suspected of preaching heresies at Cooling castle (Kent), the principal seat of his master, Sir John Oldcastle, shortly to become the most notorious English heretic since Wyclif. Simultaneously, the archbishop issued a mandate to the sheriffs of London to arrest several citizens, hold them in prison and search their houses for suspect books. According to one source, parliament also licensed all friars to preach freely throughout England against the Lollards, notwithstanding any earlier restrictions on their activities. Around this time, Arundel circulated to the bishops a new schedule to be followed by recanting heretics: culprits must publicly recite their heresies in detail while holding a copy of the gospels; declare that they now, of their own volition, understood those heretical beliefs to be entirely false; and, having seen the light, swear never again to deviate from the true faith as taught by Holy Mother Church.[18]

Whether or not the January 1410 Disendowment Bill was a calculated riposte to Arundel's *Constitutions* (this being the first parliament since their publication), it was an unmistakable signal that the 'satellites of Pilate', those 'knights who never loved the Church', had no intention of backing off. And, having lost his secular authority as chancellor, Arundel's options for bringing them to account were limited. Instead, while continuing to prowl around the fringes of popular Lollardy, he turned his main attention to the fountainhead of English heterodoxy, the principal target of the *Constitutions*, that 'teeming nest of heretics' as Adam Usk termed it, Oxford university.[19]

Arundel had no wish to be an enemy to his alma mater. No doctor or professor or university chancellor had been responsible for the curtailment of his studies forty years earlier; rather, it had been a family emergency. He continued to donate books to his old college, Oriel, and to the university library, where his name was inscribed on the *grandem et notabilem* honour-board of its major donors.[20] However, he was adamant that the training ground of more than half of England's bishops must not be tainted by even the suspicion of heresy, and the refusal of the masters and students to submit to his authority always irked him.[21]

Oxford's response to the *Constitutions* was predictable. Initially, the university simply omitted to appoint the board of twelve censors required by clause 6. Forcefully reminded by Arundel to do so – and to draw up a comprehensive list of Wyclif's 'heresies and errors' – congregation responded that his writings were so numerous that, to avoid 'strangling the wheat with the tares through unconsidered counsel', progress was bound to be slow.[22] This was transparent obstructionism. In December 1409, Arundel wrote again to the chancellor, regents and scholars, giving them ten days either to silence 'certain persons of the said university' who were continuing to propagate Wycliffite opinions despite their condemnation by the censors, or to hand them over to him in person. The archbishop was also unimpressed by the presence among the censors of Richard Fleming, a 'beardless youth' and a cousin of Robert Waterton, who was accused, possibly spuriously, of dabbling with Wycliffite ideas.[23] Arundel retorted that the board had been established on his orders and was answerable to him alone.

Despite further prompting from both king and archbishop, it was not until the summer of 1410 that the twelve managed to compile even a preliminary – and very incomplete – list of Wyclif's errors, which were duly condemned in a congregation held on 26 June.[24] Even so, in October, the king had to order the university to punish those who were refusing to comply or were even composing 'opprobrious words and rhymes' about the censors and their work.[25] Eventually, in March 1411, they submitted a list of 267 'errors and heresies' extracted from a variety of Wyclif's writings, and some of his books were publicly burned at Carfax in the heart of the city.[26] Meanwhile, several of these 'pestiferous teachings of the son of the old serpent' were sent to Pope John XXIII with a recommendation that Wyclif's bones be exhumed and burned. Arundel also demanded that all members of the university take an oath on the gospels not to teach or defend the condemned propositions. Punning on his name, he declared that he was no reed (*arundo*) to be shaken by the wind.[27]

Thus far Arundel had been able, with royal support, to impose his will on the scholars, but when he announced that he intended to undertake a visitation of the university he was on shakier ground. This was no longer – or no longer primarily – a question of heresy. Despite his victory in 1397 over those who had resisted his right of visitation, there was still a substantial body of opinion among the scholars which viewed it as a threat to academic freedom and the university's ancient privileges. Their response was to write to the king declaring that, if their exemption from visitation was not respected, they were bound by their oath as scholars to disperse, resulting in the closure of the university. Henry IV's reply, in mid-July 1411, was that the alleged privilege had never been confirmed. In fact, as they must have known, it had been explicitly rejected in 1397.[28] Yet, although he continued to support his archbishop in public, the king was becoming concerned at the way events were escalating, and on 24 July he wrote privately to Arundel, warning him of the university's fear that he would extend his enquiries at Oxford beyond matters concerning heresy, and urging him 'with all our heart [to] conduct yourself in such a way that our University can remain in ease and tranquillity, bearing in mind the great divisions, quarrels and troubles which have recently occurred there'. When they next had a chance to speak privately, they could discuss this at length; in the meantime, the king hoped that Arundel would take the advice of his confessor, Roger Coryngham, the bearer of the letter and a man experienced in the university's affairs.[29]

If the tone of Henry's letter was soothing, it came too late to make Arundel change his plans. Despite what some at Oxford probably believed, his decision to visit Lincoln diocese was not simply an excuse to bring the university to heel. It was ten years since he had last conducted a full diocesan visitation, a duty which he always took seriously, and he was as good as his word. Entering the diocese from Norwich at the beginning of June, he visited Spalding (where he conducted institutions and ordinations), Boston, Horncastle, Grimsby and Lincoln (where he presided over the consistory court on 28 June), before moving south to Leicester, Oakham and Northampton. He arrived in Oxford on 26 July – whereupon, as his register records, a 'quarrel and controversy erupted' (*orta fuit lis et controversia*) between the archbishop and the university.[30]

Trouble had been brewing throughout the year. In April, in the aftermath of the bonfire at Carfax, the king had ordered the chancellor of the university to arrest rioters in the city, some of whom were brought before the royal council.[31] Arundel had done his best to prepare the ground, visiting several colleges during the first week of August, commandeering St Mary's church for his use and threatening excommunication against any who resisted him. So too had the university chancellor, Richard Courtenay, who countered by audaciously threatening the archbishop with excommunication should he disturb the university's 'peace and tranquillity'.[32] Thus when the archiepiscopal entourage arrived at St Mary's on the morning of Friday 7 August, they found the door locked, the key 'mislaid' and an angry crowd waiting. The seriousness of the violence which followed is unclear. Arundel ascribed it to 'certain insolent boys'. Beatings and even killings were alleged, but the reports were probably exaggerated.[33] Fortunately, just as his opening sermon was concluding, a letter from the king arrived, summoning both parties to appear before him on 9 September.[34] Bursting (by his own account) into tears of relief at this *deus ex machina*, Arundel suspended his visitation and left Oxford within a day or two, sped on his way by the imprecations of his opponents. These included the dean of his old college, who is alleged to have remarked, 'may the devil break his neck!', and another fellow of Oriel, the university proctor John Birch, who opened the doors of St Mary's and rang the bells despite the fact that Arundel had placed the church under interdict.[35]

The king's letter signalled the beginning of a four-month reconciliation process which largely vindicated Arundel's claims. That this would be the case became apparent much sooner. On 20 August, two weeks after the fracas at St Mary's, the king wrote to Pope John, insisting that the university's alleged bull of exemption from Boniface IX be revoked once and for all.[36] On 9 September, Arundel and Courtenay duly appeared before Henry and the council at Lambeth and, eight days later, without waiting for the papal reply, the king announced his decision: the right of visitation of the university belonged unequivocally to the archbishop of Canterbury and his successors; those who impeded him would be severely punished. Courtenay was dismissed as chancellor, the masters and regents were forbidden to re-elect him, and some of his supporters were consigned to the Tower for a few weeks; in his place, the king appointed Dr Edmund Beckingham, warden of Merton, as acting chancellor. Yet even this failed to heal the divisions among the scholars: while one faction defiantly re-elected Courtenay, another renounced their choice. Not until the king summoned before him those who were still flouting his and Arundel's authority was the resistance broken.

All this took up most of October 1411. On 3 November, parliament met and ratified the king's judgment, and on 20 November the pope confirmed the right of Arundel and his successors to visit the university 'as if [Boniface's bull] had never existed'. In return, neither king nor archbishop raised any objection to Courtenay's – now apparently unanimous – re-election as chancellor on 18 November.[37] This probably cost Arundel little. Despite their very public spat in the summer, the bad blood between them was soon wiped away. Courtenay was one of the rising stars of the English Church, respected in political as well as academic circles and a close friend of Prince Henry, who two years later would secure his provision to Norwich, the first see to become vacant following his accession as king. Nor did Courtenay give any further trouble. On 22 November, he formally signified the university's submission to the king's and parliament's judgment, and two months later told Arundel that congregation had 'cordially and humbly' acknowledged the 'imbecility' of the 'pretended bull'. All this, he added, had been 'done in peace'. It had also been agreed, at Courtenay's suggestion, that the university librarian should include Arundel as well as the king and the prince among those to be remembered at his daily masses. Lollardy at Oxford had not been killed off, but it had been mortally wounded.[38]

Courtenay's role in this whole affair raises a number of questions. As the nephew of William, Arundel's predecessor at Canterbury, he would have known of the close relationship between the two archbishops during the 1390s, but his memories of his uncle's assault on Lollardy at Oxford in 1382 would not have been first hand (he was born in 1381). As chancellor of the university for the first time in 1406–7, he had been slow to discipline Peter Payne and his supporters.[39] By 1410–11, he was firmly established in Prince Henry's circle at Westminster. Also present at St Mary's church on 7 August was Arundel's nephew Earl Thomas, who had recently quarrelled with the archbishop over their respective rights in Sussex. It was in the presence of Earl Thomas, who probably delivered the king's letter, that Arundel and Courtenay swore to submit their quarrel to royal arbitration, and, according to the university's

Chancellor's and Proctors' Book, it was through Prince Henry's mediation that the compromise was agreed.[40] Thus it was Prince Henry, still the effective head of government, who, via Earl Thomas, probably prevented the dispute between Arundel and the university from degenerating into violence, while simultaneously sparing the blushes of a valued supporter.[41]

Yet if it was the prince who brokered the ceasefire, he was not the one who drafted the treaty. One of the reasons why the eventual outcome was so favourable to Arundel was simply that the 'pretended bull' of Boniface IX was just that, and Henry IV had no intention of acknowledging it. But equally germane is the fact that, whereas in August 1411 Prince Henry was still head of the royal council, three months later he was not. On 21 September, the day after the king wrote to the pope requesting the definitive revocation of the bull, parliament was summoned to meet in early November. Henry IV's main concern at this time was not Oxford but foreign policy. France was sliding towards civil war and during the summer of 1411 ambassadors from both sides, Armagnacs and Burgundians, had crossed to England seeking support.[42] The king initially swithered between them, but the prince supported the Burgundians and in late September 1411, contrary to his father's wishes, dispatched 1,000 troops under the earl of Arundel to join Duke John of Burgundy. This was too much for the king, who now determined to reassert his authority. Prince Henry did what he could to hold on to power, even allegedly trying to persuade his father to abdicate. The king retorted that he would continue to rule as long as he drew breath. The upshot was that by the end of the parliament the prince and his supporters had been dismissed from the council and new ministers appointed, among them Arundel, who on 5 January 1412 embarked on his fifth term as chancellor.[43] Prince Henry's presumption had backfired. Whether the outcome of the dispute with Oxford would have been substantially different had the prince held on to power through the winter is questionable, but the university's submission to the archbishop might not have been so abject.

14

Jerusalem: The End of a Reign
1412–13

Arundel's return to the chancery in January 1412 meant that government affairs now once more demanded his attention, as he did his best to steer the stricken king through the final chapter of their lives together. The febrile mood at Westminster and Henry IV's precarious health also meant that he needed to guard against what a new reign might bring. Before parliament adjourned on 19 December 1411, therefore, he sought and was promised a royal pardon for any crime of which he might hitherto have been accused, ranging from treason or insurrection to debt or contempt. This included any suggestion that he had ever been an adherent of Glyn Dwr, Thomas Trumpington (the pseudo-Richard II) or any foreign adversary of the king, in England or abroad. Uppermost in his mind was probably the whispering campaign against him in 1404–5, but anything dating from before 19 December 1411 was covered, excluding (as always) murder and rape.[1]

Yet, although the pardon was authorized 'by the king himself, in parliament', it was not until 15 June 1412 that it was enacted. The date is significant. The great matter vexing the English body politic through the first half of 1412 continued to be the debate over which side to support in the French civil war. Prince Henry still favoured Burgundy, partly to ensure the security of Calais, but the king and his second son, Thomas, prioritized the retention of Guyenne and were persuaded by the chimerical promises of the dukes of Orléans and Berry to ally with the Armagnacs. Arundel supported the king, as did the council, now once again dominated by their friends – John Pelham, Henry Bowet, William Roos and John Prophet. On 18 May the Treaty of Bourges was duly signed with the Armagnacs and the flirtation with Burgundy disaffirmed. According to Thomas Walsingham, the king was so overjoyed at the terms that 'rising from his seat, he clapped his hands and said to [Arundel], "Do you see how Almighty God is providing for us? How welcome is this day for which we have longed!"' Within days if not hours, preparations were in hand for the first major English campaign in France for twenty-five years, to be led not by Prince Henry but by his brother Thomas, soon to be elevated to the dukedom of Clarence.[2] The prince was furious. Apologizing abjectly to Burgundy (as did the earl of Arundel), he retired in early June from Westminster to Coventry. Wild rumours of his intentions circulated: that he was stirring up popular disaffection, raising an army, trying to impede his brother's expedition, even plotting 'with murderous desire' to depose his father. It was this – in reality ephemeral, but in the moment very real – threat of civil war that provided the catalyst for Arundel to secure his royal pardon on 15 June.

Fortunately, the storm blew over. Writing an open letter to his father on 17 June, the prince declared his loyalty to be 'as great as filial humility can express', and by early September they had been reconciled.[3] Meanwhile, on 10 August, Clarence's expedition had landed in Normandy. As many – including Prince Henry – had doubtless predicted, the Armagnacs reneged on their promises and made their peace (for the moment) with the Burgundians. Yet Clarence's campaign was far from fruitless. Settling into Bordeaux for the winter, the English began picking off French-held towns and castles and securing oaths of allegiance. By the time Clarence returned to England in the spring of 1413, the English crown's authority in Guyenne, so long in decline, had been reinvigorated. Ironically, the real gainer from this was Prince Henry, who, once he became king, found himself able to direct his ambitions towards northern France, knowing that the threat to Guyenne was much diminished.[4]

Meanwhile, Henry IV was slowly dying. By the winter of 1411–12, his body was under the constant care of doctors and he could barely walk, let alone ride. The blocked arteries which were probably the root of the problem had left him shrunken and disfigured, his innards ruptured, his limbs bustling with suppurating sores.[5] As death approached, he and Arundel grew closer. During the first decade of the reign, Henry had stayed at Lambeth or Canterbury on fewer than half a dozen occasions. Between February 1410 and January 1413, he stayed at Lambeth on at least seventeen occasions, at Canterbury four times (including six weeks in the spring of 1412 and a week in September 1412) and at the archbishop's palaces or manors at Mortlake, Merton and Croydon on eleven occasions. For three months before Christmas 1412, he was almost exclusively at Croydon or Merton.[6] As the years ebbed away, the ties that bound them – of trust, affection, spiritual kinship – grew ever stronger.[7]

Yet there was only so much that personal friendship could achieve, and when it came to revenue-raising, this was disappointingly little. When parliament met in November 1411, the final tranche of the subsidy granted in the spring of 1410 still had a year to run and the commons would promise no more than a miserly land tax, which apparently raised less than £1,500.[8] It was probably no surprise to the clergy, then, that when convocation met at St Paul's on 1 December 1411, it was visited by the most imposing royal delegation of the reign – the duke of York, the chancellor (still Thomas Beaufort), the treasurer and the king's chamberlain. Beaufort began by announcing, apparently with a straight face, that the king intended personally to lead a campaign to France which would remain overseas for six months or more, for which he would need at least £100,000. The prelates listened 'patiently', conferred for a short time in closed session and recalled the ministers. Arundel must have felt torn. He knew as well as anyone that Beaufort's proposal was fantastical and that the clergy were sick of being taxed; on the other hand, he was about to become chancellor again and had no desire to be hamstrung by insolvency. His 'noble and elegant' reply to the ministers thus steered a middle path, assuring them of the Church's support for the king as a warrior and an 'athlete and defender' of the Catholic faith, but reminding them that the English Church had been reduced to poverty by repeated and excessive demands for money. Convocation needed time to confer.

Once the royal delegation departed, however, they turned instead to discussion of a group of impostors alleged to have issued bulls under a forged papal seal and then drew up a list of thirteen *gravamina*.[9] Not until 21 December, two days after parliament adjourned, did they agree to grant a meagre half tenth. Early in 1412, the York convocation followed suit, though 'with ill-will' (*aegre*). The entire tax yield of the parliament and convocations combined cannot have exceeded £20,000. Arundel's last chancellorship was indeed hamstrung. For Clarence's expedition in the autumn of 1412, loans totalling £16,600 had to be negotiated, to which the archbishop contributed £666. The king's debts at his death were assessed at £16,666; those of the crown were much greater.[10]

During the first nine months of 1412, Arundel remained close to the languishing king while continuing to discharge his archiepiscopal duties. On 30 March and 10 April, they jointly welcomed new members of the Christ Church fraternity.[11] Summer and autumn were filled with Clarence's expedition and Prince Henry's frustration, but once the king and prince were reconciled, time seemed to slacken, waiting for Henry IV to die. From 15 September to 23 December, he stayed continuously with Arundel, firstly at Canterbury, then Merton, Croydon and Merton again. In early December, they made provision for Queen Joan's dower. Arundel acted as her feoffee.[12] By Christmas Day, Henry had returned to his beloved Eltham palace, where he stayed for six weeks, before moving to Greenwich on 5 February 1413 and on to Lambeth and Mortlake. Parliament had been summoned to meet on 3 February, but Henry only arrived at Westminster on 21 February. Convocation, also summoned for February, did not meet until 6 March.[13] Arundel presided at both.

According to John Strecche's chronicle, the king roused himself one last time and 'appeared publicly before all the people', presumably borne on a litter, to ask for a subsidy with which to fulfil his long-cherished desire to revisit Jerusalem – a notion as fanciful as him leading a six-month campaign in France.[14] If subsidies were granted, as Strecche claimed, they were soon cancelled, for Henry's life was spent. He died on 20 March, the feast of St Cuthbert, after collapsing in Westminster abbey, where he had gone to make an offering at the Confessor's shrine. Comatose, he was carried to the Jerusalem Chamber in the abbot's lodging, where he revived for long enough to be told where he was. His time had come, he declared, for it had been prophesied that he would die in Jerusalem. Contemporary accounts focused on his confession to his Dominican confessor and his dying words of advice to his son. Prince Henry's presence at his father's deathbed is well attested. Whether Arundel was there is unknown, but it is highly likely – after all, this was Westminster, and if he was not already in the abbey he could have been summoned within minutes. It would certainly have been fitting for Henry's 'spiritual father', the man with whom he had forged one of the closest friendships between any medieval king and primate, to have been there at the end.

15

The Oldcastle Rising
1413–14

The last eleven months of Arundel's life saw him cast into the political wilderness. On 21 March 1413, the day after Henry V became king, he was replaced as chancellor by Henry Beaufort, dismissed from the council and relieved of Queenborough castle. Other faithful servants of Henry IV negotiated the transition more smoothly. Thomas Langley remained on the council and became chancellor again in 1417; John Prophet retained the privy seal until his death in 1416; Nicholas Bubwith continued as a councillor until sent to Constance as one of the king's principal envoys.[1] But Arundel had been too dominant, too closely identified with the policies that had divided the king and the prince during the previous few years. If asked, he would doubtless have served Henry V loyally, but they probably both knew that he would always be biting his tongue.

Rarely, then, was he now seen at Westminster except on state occasions. On 9 April, a day of fearsome storms and heavy snow, he crowned the new king in the abbey.[2] Summoned as a matter of course to the parliament which met on 15 May 1413, he acted as a trier of petitions, but the only item of business in which he was involved there was an agreement concerning the fulfilment of Henry IV's will. The former king had appointed his eldest son and Arundel as supervisors for its execution, but the executors, chief among whom were Henry Bowet and Thomas Langley, had renounced executry on the grounds that

Henry IV's goods were insufficient to cover his debts, so the task devolved to Arundel. What Henry V now proposed was that all his father's possessions should pass to him and he would pay the executors £16,666 over four years to cover the costs of the funeral and satisfy the creditors. Since the debts of Henry IV's household alone amounted to some £31,000, this was manifestly inadequate, but it suited both sides: Henry V, who in fact paid no more than £4,000 by the time he died nine years later; and Arundel and the executors, who, although charged with assessing and paying the outstanding sums, were 'completely exonerated in perpetuity' from any legal action arising from their commission. It was, predictably, the creditors who suffered. Not until 1429 were the debts cleared, many of them having meanwhile been discounted.[3]

Henry IV's will is a remarkable document.[4] Written in English – unusual but not unprecedented at the time – on 21 January 1409, when he believed he was dying, it reveals both his spiritual affinity with and his implicit trust in Arundel. Eschewing the lavish burial instructions and legacies of so many royal wills – including Richard II's and Henry V's – he declared himself to be a 'sinful wretch' with a 'sinful soul' and begged God's mercy for his 'misspent' life and his subjects' forgiveness, 'if I have mistreated them in any wise'. The language of Arundel's will is more graphic, but the sentiments ('miserable and most unworthy sinner', etc.) are almost identical.[5] Henry's only named legatees apart from the queen were six lowly grooms of his chamber who cared for him during his illness. As for his funeral, he merely said that he wished to be buried in Canterbury cathedral 'after the discretion of my cousin the archbishop of Canterbury' and that a perpetual chantry be established there to pray for his soul 'in such a place and after such ordinance as it seems best to my aforesaid cousin of Canterbury'. In other words, he left it all to Arundel. His choice of Canterbury rather than Westminster may have been influenced by a desire to be interred close to the shrine of Thomas Becket, with whose putative oil he was the first king to be crowned, or even to the tomb of the man whose 'child in God' he had declared himself to be. The interment itself was a hasty and modest affair, effected within a week or two of his death,[6] but once parliament ended a much more lavish memorial service was held at the cathedral on Trinity Sunday (18 June) in the presence of Henry V and his brothers, with Arundel and Prior Wodnesbergh officiating. It was the last service Arundel performed for Henry, and, with parliament and convocation both having concluded, it was also the prelude to his withdrawal from the Westminster bear pit that had consumed so much of his time and energy for the past quarter of a century.[7]

But he was, of course, still archbishop of Canterbury, albeit no longer a primate with the king's ear, as soon became apparent. A week after Bishop Tottington's death on 28 April 1413, Arundel wrote in haste to his *amico carissime* Niccolo Lucca, a Florentine merchant and papal banker who had spent many years in England, begging him to use his influence with Pope John to support the provision to Norwich of his archdeacon, John Wakering, and the promotion of his long-serving secretary, John Bathe. Neither was successful. It was Henry V who prevailed, securing Norwich for Richard Courtenay. In December 1413, Arundel wrote again to Lucca (now *amico confidentissime*) on a matter 'concerning our own person and more special to us than ever before (*specialius quam unquam ante*)', since he trusted him more than anyone else outside England to expedite the matter 'which we so ardently desire'. He and the king had also sent letters to the pope and others begging them to help, copies of which he enclosed, along with a ring which contained a piece of Christ's cross as a gift for the pope. What this urgent personal matter was, he does not reveal, but it is hard to avoid the impression of a man increasingly reliant on others to secure what had once been within his reach, if not always his grasp.[8]

Personal matters aside, Arundel still had a diocese – indeed a province – to run, and during the summer of 1413 that is what he did. As in 1399, the first convocation of a new reign provided him with the opportunity to reiterate various decrees issued by earlier primates and papal legates concerning clerical behaviour in general: rights of visitation; the roles, regimens and apparel of prelates and archdeacons; and the 'honest life' of the clergy regarding such matters as non-residence, charging reasonable fees, preaching, penances, proving wills, observing the Sabbath, presentments to benefices, and much else besides. It was also agreed to elevate the feast days of St George and St Dunstan to double festivals – the latter, apparently, at Arundel's instigation.[9] Following Henry IV's funeral on 18 June, Arundel retired to Saltwood castle, where he remained for around two weeks before moving north-east to Sandwich, back to Saltwood, west to South Malling, on to Chichester for the feast of the Assumption (15 August), then north-east, via Tonbridge Wells, to Maidstone, thereby traversing most of his diocese, conducting ordinations of sub-deacons, deacons and priests and instituting rectors and vicars as he went.[10] By 10 September he had moved a few miles eastwards from Maidstone to Leeds castle. Here he had an assignation of the gravest import.

Ten weeks earlier, on 26 June, following a bonfire of Wyclif's books at St Paul's Cross, the prelates had met to consider the case of one book in particular. Arundel seems not to have been present, for chairmanship of the session was delegated to Richard Clifford, bishop of London.[11] During the recent seizures of Wyclif's books, Clifford told them, an unbound volume containing tracts of a most dangerous nature had been discovered after being left with an illuminator in London's Paternoster Row; it turned out that this book belonged to a man whom Arundel had been keeping an eye on for over three years, Sir John Oldcastle.

Oldcastle came from a gentry family in Herefordshire – a county with a history of Lollard activism – which he represented in parliament in 1404 and of which he had been sheriff in 1406–7. As a Marcher, he had frequently campaigned against the Welsh, serving on occasions under Prince, now King, Henry. It may have been the prince, with whom he was said to be *familiaris*, who arranged his marriage in 1407–8 to Joan, the granddaughter and sole heir of John, Lord Cobham, following which Oldcastle became a substantial landholder and was summoned as a peer to the parliament of 1410. He may well have supported the Lollard Disendowment Bill, for it was around this time that Arundel's suspicions seem first to have been aroused. In April 1410, a chaplain called John (probably John Lay of Nottingham), who was living at Cooling castle (Kent), Oldcastle's principal residence in the south-east, was cited for heresy, and a number of churches where he had been preaching were laid under interdict.[12]

If this was intended as a warning, Oldcastle took no heed. The autumn and winter of 1410–11 saw him writing to Bohemian heretics and even to King Wenzel to tell him about his correspondence with Hus. By early 1413, his heterodox leanings had become so notorious that by June, after his book was found in Paternoster Row, he was summoned to the king's 'inner chamber' at Kennington, where Henry V and Arundel had arranged a reading of various 'toxic and poisonous' extracts from his book. Asked by the king whether he agreed that it deserved to be burned, he replied, 'Yes'. So why was it found in his possession? He had never used it, he said, nor read 'more than a couple of pages' (*ultra duo folia*).[13]

Whether or not the king believed him, Arundel did not, but he knew that with a *familiaris* of the king he must proceed with caution. Initially, Henry asked him to defer the summons, saying that, because of his friendship with Oldcastle and 'out of reverence for the order of knighthood', he would talk to him in private to see if he could persuade him of the error of his ways; if he failed, then the investigations could go ahead. No record of this private conversation between Henry and Oldcastle survives, although they certainly met, for on 1 August Oldcastle brought a party of twenty-six wrestlers to perform before the king at Windsor. Within another two weeks, however, Henry had come to realize that Oldcastle was incorrigible, and he wrote to Arundel telling him to proceed. Oldcastle, 'full of the devil', responded by locking himself away in Cooling castle. Arundel summoned him to Leeds castle on 11 September to face trial as 'the principal receiver, supporter, protector and defender' of Lollards. This was what brought the archbishop to Leeds – but in vain, for Oldcastle did not appear.

Losing patience, Arundel excommunicated him, while the king sent officers to Cooling castle to arrest him. Served with a royal summons, he offered no resistance and was escorted to the Tower of London.[14]

The record of Oldcastle's trial, which began on Saturday 23 September 1413 in the chapter house of St Paul's, was written by Arundel's clerks and stresses throughout the archbishop's desire to give Oldcastle every opportunity to save himself.[15] Flanked by Richard Clifford and Henry Beaufort (now chancellor), Arundel began by telling Oldcastle that he was still prepared to forgive him if he recanted. Oldcastle replied that he had no wish to be absolved. Instead, he produced a written schedule in English of his beliefs, which he proceeded to read out. Calling on God as his witness, he did his best, like Sawtre before him, to bridge the divide between what he believed and what the Church taught, but simply could not do so. He believed in 'all the sacraments that ever God ordained' (not the same as those now approved by the Church); he believed that the Eucharist was 'Christ's body in the form of bread' (not the same as Christ's body transubstantiated *from* bread); he believed that no man might be saved without confessing and performing penance (not the same as confession to a priest). Images, he believed, were useful for the instruction of simple souls, but to worship them was idolatry (*mawmentrie*); as for pilgrimages, he believed that every man was a pilgrim on the road to heaven, but a pilgrimage to Canterbury or Rome was worthless. All these were common, indeed classic, Lollard statements.

Arundel's response was to question him more closely, but he wished to add nothing to his schedule. 'Be careful, Sir John,' warned Arundel, 'for if you do not reply clearly to these objections within the time limit allowed to you, you will be adjudged and declared a heretic.' When Oldcastle remained silent, Arundel produced his own schedule, translated into English 'for easier comprehension', of the Church's approved beliefs on the Eucharist, confession, papal supremacy, pilgrimages and relic worship, appending to each one the question 'How do you respond to this article?' He was given two days to read it, but by the time he appeared again on Monday 25 September at the London Blackfriars' convent before Arundel, who was now accompanied by twelve doctors of law or theology, Oldcastle had had enough. These beliefs, he declared, were contrary to Scripture; the pope and the cardinals were the Antichrist, with no claim on Christians' obedience. Then, raising his voice and opening his arms wide, he cried out, 'These people who judge and wish to damn me are seducing you and themselves and leading you to hell. Beware of them!' Arundel asked him one last time, 'with a tearful face', whether he was prepared to accept the Church's teaching, to which he expressly replied that he was not. 'With bitterness of heart', the archbishop had no option but to proceed to judgment and Oldcastle was handed over to the secular arm, taken back to the Tower and held in chains.

Still the king hesitated. Walsingham said that this was because Arundel begged Henry to respite Oldcastle's sentence for forty days in the hope that he might yet recant, but (as he went on to point out) Henry V took little persuading.[16] To consign his former comrade in arms, a knight of the realm, to the flames was very different from burning an obscure chaplain or country tailor. Arundel and Henry both knew that Oldcastle was far from the first man of knightly rank to believe what he did. And initially it seemed as if their patience would be rewarded, for Oldcastle did apparently promise to accept the Church's teaching and was accordingly released from his chains, though not from his cell.[17] But this, it turned out, was a ruse – or perhaps a moment of weakness soon regretted – for on the night of 19 October, helped by his supporters among the city's Lollard community, Oldcastle escaped and began planning an uprising against both Church and State.

So began the first crisis of Henry V's reign and the last of Arundel's life. Lollard preachers and their 'confederates in holes and corners' distributed handbills and recruited supporters, promising them riches and salvation. Oldcastle remained undetected, sheltering with a parchment-maker in Clerkenwell and coordinating the plot, which involved not just poor priests and artisans but a dozen or so knights and esquires from the home counties, the Midlands and the Marches.[18] On 20 November 1413, when convocation met at St Paul's, much stricter measures against Lollardy were proposed, including the automatic conviction of heretics as traitors, who would thus forfeit all their goods to the king and be drawn and hanged as well as burned.[19] Yet even this proved no deterrent. By mid-December, Arundel and Henry were aware that something was afoot. Rumours circulated that 20,000 or more insurgents would converge on London early in the new year. Juries were empanelled to try them. The Lollards' plan – or so the authorities alleged – was to ambush the king, disguised as mummers, while he was celebrating the Epiphany at Eltham, kill him and his brothers, 'destroy the clergy' and despoil the monasteries, before taking control of the kingdom and setting up Oldcastle as ruler.

The correspondence to the Epiphany Rising of 1400 is unmistakable, but most of the details are confirmed by the timing of subsequent events. From 5 January 1414 onwards, groups of rebels began arriving near the appointed meeting place, St Giles's Fields (or 'Fickett's Field'), between London and Westminster, but there were spies among them and they were quickly seized and interrogated. By the time more arrived, the king was waiting for them. Accompanied by his brothers and Arundel, he left Eltham during the night of 8 January and ordered London's gates to be closed so that rebels in the city could not join the incomers. He arrived at St Giles's Fields, accompanied by a small but well-armed force, on the evening of 9 January. Needless to say, rebel numbers fell far short of what recruiting agents had promised: not 20,000 but probably fewer than 500. Even so, some of his party advised the king not to approach them. He ignored the advice. Intercepted in small groups as they arrived, dismayed at the lack of support from the city, the rebels put up little resistance. A small number were killed; around eighty others were rounded up and marched to the Tower. Some who tried to turn back were pursued and caught but others managed to escape. Oldcastle also avoided capture.

Justice was swift and exemplary. On 10 January, sixty-nine captured rebels were tried for treason in the Tower before juries whose task appears to have been simply to endorse pro forma indictments drawn up by the crown. Not all were convicted. Thirty-eight of them were hanged at St Giles's Fields on 13 January, of whom seven were also burned (after they were already dead).[20] Two days later, Arundel felt confident enough to lead a service of thanksgiving at St Paul's, attended by the king, just as he had done exactly fourteen years earlier for Henry IV after the collapse of the first Epiphany Rising.[21] Yet judicial proceedings continued. A further four rebels were executed on 19 January and another four during the next few weeks. Others died later, while awaiting trial in the Tower, probably including the well-known Lollard John Purvey. In the Home and Midland counties, trials of indicted rebels continued into the summer, although many – often the wealthier sort – purchased pardons, especially after 28 March, when Henry announced a general pardon to all who would sue (and pay) for one. Oldcastle, naturally, was excluded, but he continued to evade capture, sheltering in London for a month after the revolt, before making his way to the Midlands. He remained at large for almost four years before being recaptured and executed by simultaneous hanging and burning on 14 December 1417.[22]

Although only 47 of the 231 rebels known to have been indicted were accused of heresy as well as treason, there is no doubt that this was, in inspiration and in organization, a Lollard rising. It was 'the destruction of the Catholic faith' as well as '[the king's] person' on which they were bent and it was as 'a true Christian prince' that Henry 'made provision against their malice'.[23] As did Arundel. According to Adam Usk, he planned to hold a further convocation at Oxford in 1414, but died before it could meet.[24] Yet the agenda he had laid out was not discarded. Archbishop Chichele continued to adopt a hard line against heresy, not just over the next few years, while Oldcastle remained at liberty and the fear of another Lollard insurrection was ever-present, but throughout his primacy. It has been argued that Arundel took Lollardy too seriously, but that view was not shared by his successor.[25]

In the longer term, Oldcastle's revolt proved decisive. Even if Lollards were not to be *ipso facto* convicted as traitors, heresy was now inextricably associated with treason, and both Church and crown had demonstrated that they would not hesitate to prosecute (and execute) those whose gentility had hitherto afforded them immunity, even those who were *familiaris* with the king. 'Lollard knights' gradually became a distant memory. For the next 120 years, until swept up into the tide of Lutheran reform flowing in from the Continent, Lollardy shed the militancy which had been one of its early hallmarks. During the 1390s, heterodox speculation in its various guises had become public, almost acceptable. Richard II's court was notorious for its Lollard knights and lords; Oxford academics openly debated Wycliffite ideas; a vernacular tract depicting a debate between a friar and a Lollard-leaning secular clerk was dedicated to the duke of Gloucester, the king's uncle.[26]

Arundel knew how and where Lollardy must be disabled: with the poor preachers who propagated its message to any who would listen (William Sawtre, John Seynon); at Oxford, from which it first emanated and which continued to gird it with an aura of legitimacy; and, eventually, at court and in parliament, where those with influence and immunity had become increasingly emboldened in their advocacy of disendowment and Erastianism. It is arguable that his assault on Lollardy wherever it lurked, especially from 1407 onwards, had provoked the desperate gamble of January 1414. If so, he did not live to see, or oversee, the consequences. He was still in London, in *hospicio nostro*, on 21 January, but by the next day he had retired to Maidstone, where his final institution was recorded, an exchange of benefices.[27] This is the last place-datable entry in his register. Within another month, he was dead.

1. This nineteenth-century portrait of Arundel is inscribed (in Latin) 'Thomas Fitzalan, son of the earl of Arundel, archbishop of Canterbury, constable of the castle of Queenborough, 27 April in the tenth year of the reign of Henry the Fourth'. The emphasis on his brief tenure of Queenborough is striking. Arundel was granted custody of Queenborough castle by Henry IV on 10 March 1409 and is known to have visited it on 13 April 1409 (the tenth year of the reign), which suggests that the lost original upon which this portrait is said to be based may commemorate that visit. However, it clearly owes something to later portraitists such as Hans Holbein. The shield of Arundel's arms in the top left corner matches that of his boss in Canterbury cathedral cloister.

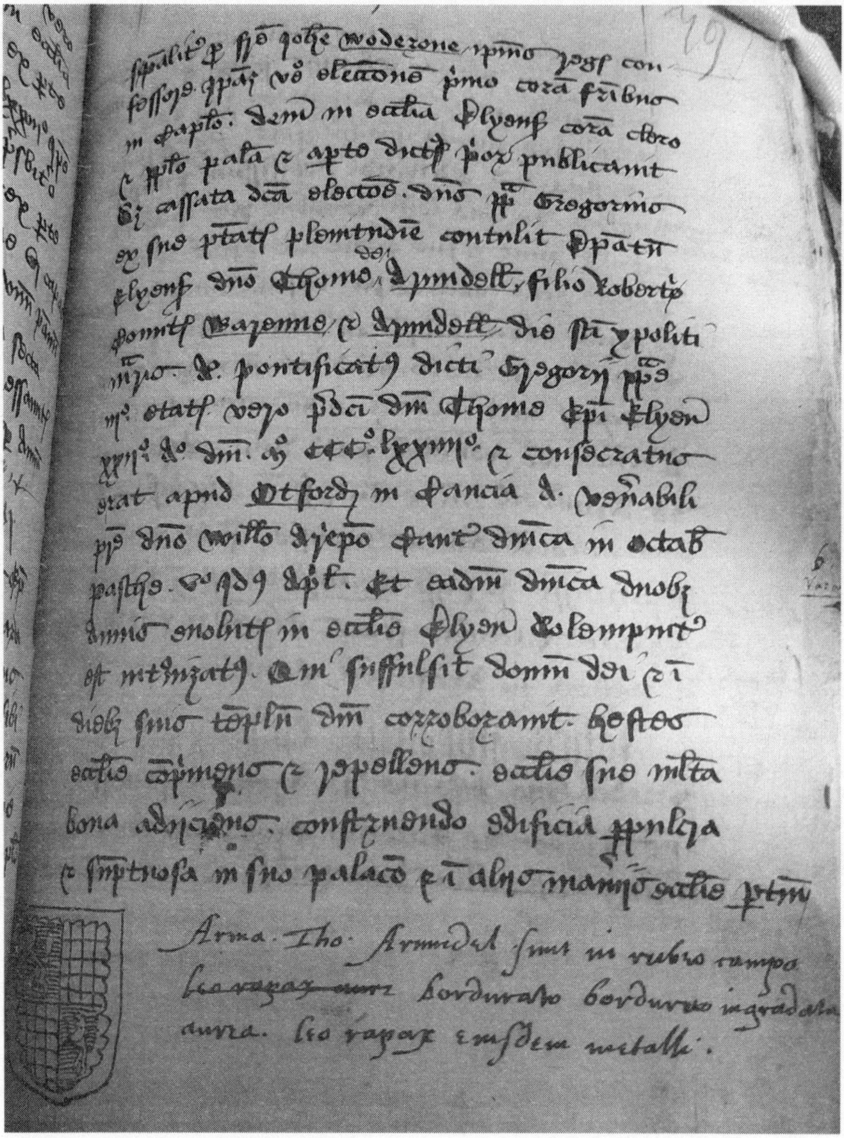

2. The Ely chronicler's account of the episcopal election of 1373 states that after Bishop Barnet's death the chapter first elected Henry de Wakefield, treasurer of Edward III's household, despite the king's advocacy for his confessor, John Woderove. However, Pope Gregory XI quashed the election and provided Thomas, son of Robert (*sic*), earl of Arundel and Warenne. Even so, the chronicler praises Arundel's vigorous rule and generosity to the community. In the bottom margin is a (post-medieval) rough drawing of Arundel's arms with a description: 'The arms of Thomas Arundel are on a red field, bordered with an engrailed border of gold and a lion rampant of the same metal.' Compare the shield of his arms in the cloister bay.

3. Arundel preaching to the Londoners in 1399. This is one of sixteen illustrations in an early fifteenth-century copy of Jean Creton's *Metrical History of the Deposition of King Richard the Second*, which was notably sympathetic to Richard. According to the poem, Arundel is here shown preaching to the Londoners about the evils of Richard's rule, which must have been after the captive king returned to London in early September 1399 (although Creton appears to place this several weeks earlier, which would not have been possible). Arundel was renowned for the emotive force of his preaching. An illustration in the Bodleian Library, Oxford, Ms Laud Misc. 165, also shows him preaching.

4. The tomb of John Trefnant in Hereford cathedral. The scholar, diplomat and lawyer was one of a growing number of legally trained bishops in later fourteenth- and fifteenth-century England. On 29 September 1399 he received Richard II's abdication in the Tower, and on the following day announced it to the meeting of the estates which formally deposed the king. Having also spent several years in papal service in the 1380s, Trefnant was then sent back to Rome by Henry IV to justify the deposition to Pope Boniface IX. An inventory of his goods at death listed around a hundred books, mostly legal texts.

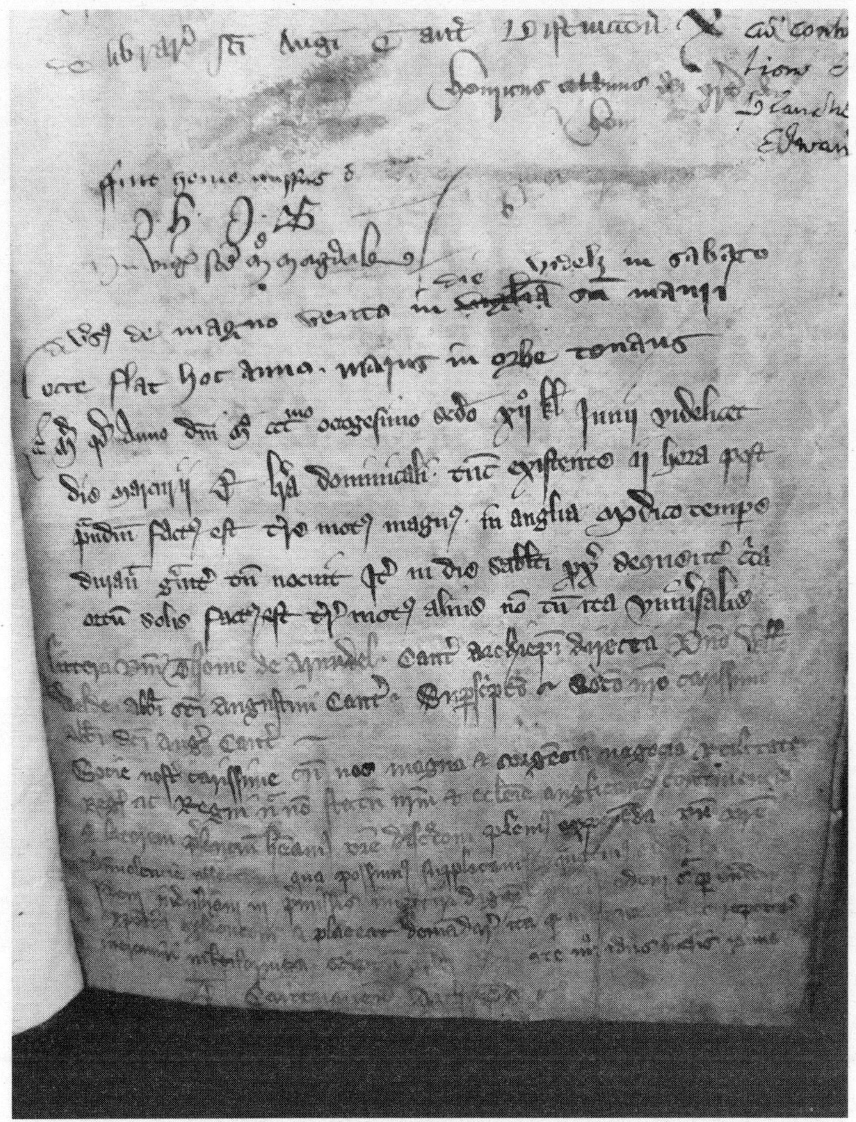

5. The bottom eleven lines of this folio, in effect a flyleaf, reproduce a brief, informal note from Arundel to William Welde, abbot of St Augustine's, Canterbury, dated 9 June, probably 1404, copied into a manuscript of the abbey's chronicles. Arundel maintained friendly relations with the abbots of St Augustine's, addressing Welde here as 'our most dear colleague' (*socio nostro carissimo*), before reminding him of the 'great and urgent business of the king and kingdom' and the English Church, and begging him to help him, presumably financially. It is signed 'T[homas] Cantuarien[sis] Archiepis[copus]'. The five lines above this letter, written in a different hand, record the earthquake of Wednesday 21 May 1382, which significantly delayed the reconstruction of the nave of Canterbury cathedral, begun five years earlier.

6. This view from high up in Canterbury cathedral crossing towards the great west window shows the reconstructed nave in the perpendicular style which was favoured in England at the time. It was largely built between 1391 and *c.* 1403, with considerable financial as well as moral support from Arundel, but due above all to the energy and initiative of his friend Thomas Chillenden, prior from 1391 to 1411. The decision to rebuild the nave had been taken as early as 1377, when the previous Norman nave was demolished by Archbishop Sudbury, but the earthquake of May 1382 set back the work for another decade.

7. The thirty-six bays of Canterbury cathedral cloister were constructed between *c.* 1408 and 1414, with around 850 heraldic bosses decorating the lierne vault. Most of these are of prominent local or national families whose members donated to the cathedral's fabric fund. The 'Arundel Bay', with this boss in the centre, supported by three angels and surrounded by members of Arundel's extended family, is located prominently at the entrance to the cloister from the chapter house.

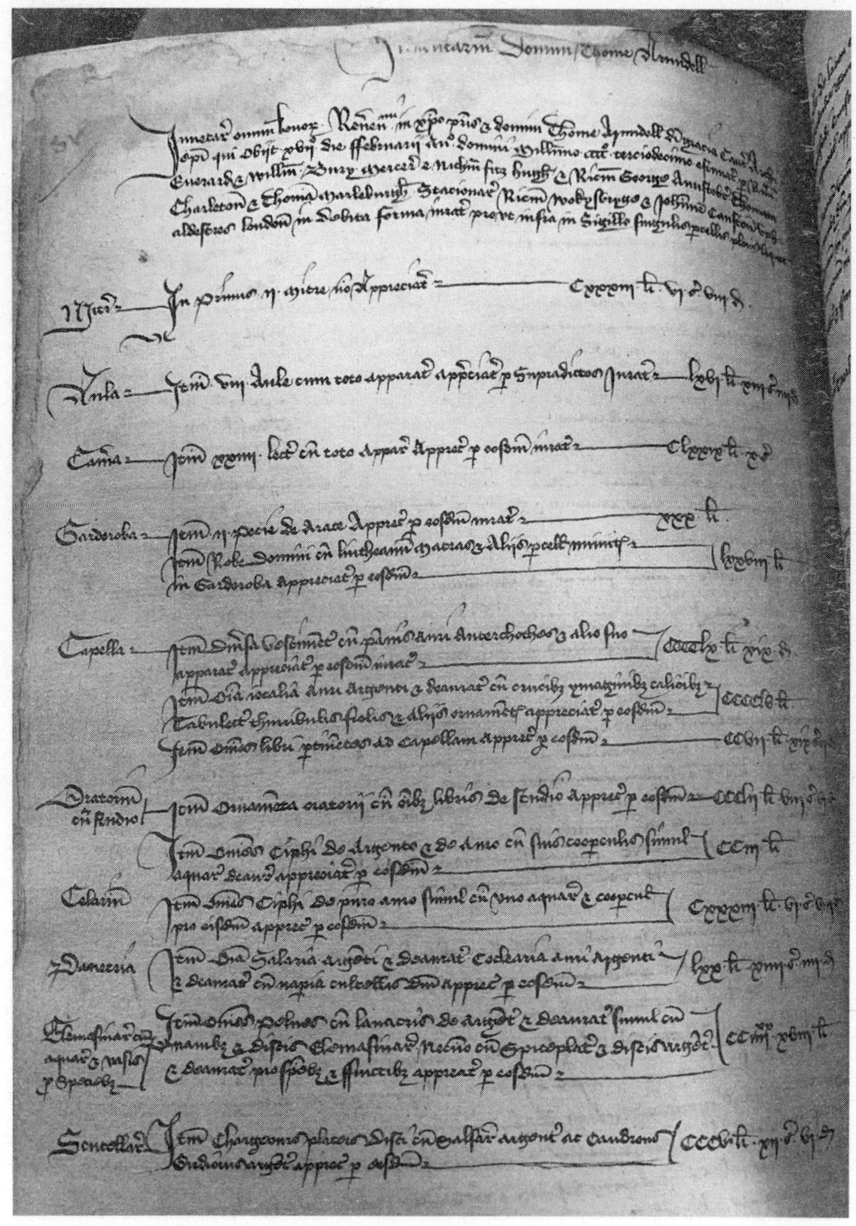

8. Arundel's goods at death were valued at £6,008 in total, around half of which was the live and dead stock and rental value of his archiepiscopal lands, which appear on the next folio. This folio lists his household goods and ceremonial vestments, beginning with his mitres and moving on to list his plate, jewels, ornaments and books. For a full translation of this document, see Appendix I.

Part Two
ARUNDEL THE MAN

16

Canterbury

Arundel's obituary in the register of Canterbury cathedral opens as follows:

> Let it be recalled to memory that there died [in 1414] that most reverend father and lord in Christ, Thomas Arundel, archbishop, primate of all England, legate of the apostolic see, the remarkable (*spectabilis*) son of Lord Richard, earl of Arundel and Warenne; he was firstly bishop of Ely, then archbishop of York, and after that, at the unanimous request of this prior and chapter, translated to this holy church of Canterbury. He was an exceptionally knowledgeable man, manifesting talent in all his undertakings, prudent and circumspect, diligent in the execution of his pontifical office, most dutiful to the kings who reigned in his time and recognized in the kingdom for the maturity of his wise counsel as well as repeatedly being chancellor of the realm.[1]

There follows a list of the jewels, plate, vestments, books and other donations which he gave to the cathedral: for example, his gift of four new bells, 'commonly known as Arundel Ring', to be hung in the central tower; the £666 which he gave towards the rebuilding of the nave; and his annual gift of six shillings and eightpence to each monk of the cathedral in memory of 'the day of the return [to Canterbury] of the precious martyr Thomas' (2 December 1170).[2] More precious still was a piece of 'that seamless robe which the Blessed Virgin Mary is believed to have woven for her son Jesus Christ', which the Byzantine Emperor Manuel had given to Henry IV on his visit to England in 1400. The king divided it into two parts, one of which he gave to Westminster abbey and the other to Arundel, because of his 'great trust and friendship' with the archbishop. Arundel donated it to the high altar of Christ Church, where it was placed in a silver-gilt jewel box also containing a relic from Christ's crown of thorns and a few drops of Becket's blood.[3] Also lauded were Arundel's efforts to curb 'the perfidious sect of Lollards which was then growing stronger in the kingdom'. All this, his obituarist concluded, merited the establishment of a memorial service in his honour.

It is easy to imagine that it was primarily Arundel's generosity that prompted such warm words, and doubtless it was much appreciated, but there is also a mass of evidence pointing to his consistently good relations with the seventy or so monks at Christ Church. This was far from normal in what has been called 'the most touchy and cantankerous chapter in England'.[4] Many archbishops were seen as (and some clearly were) overbearing: externally imposed, often political appointments with little interest in the fortunes of the community, whose privileges and exemptions from primatial authority they ignored or undermined. The saintly Edmund of Abingdon quarrelled so vehemently with his monks that he excommunicated them all.[5] Yet between Arundel and his chapter there is scarcely a hint of disagreement.

At the heart of this cooperative partnership was the archbishop's rapport with Thomas Chillenden, prior from 1391 to 1411. Chillenden was a Kentishman, a monk at Canterbury since 1365 and a doctor of laws from Oxford who had represented the community at the Curia, where he secured from Pope Urban VI the valuable privilege of a processional staff for the priors. Before becoming prior he had been the cathedral's treasurer, and his election by the monks in 1391 was unopposed. Arundel and Chillenden, 'a man well beloved of Archbishop Courtenay, but more dear to his successor Arundel', bonded from the start.[6] In February 1397,

Arundel appointed Chillenden as his commissary-general; eight months later, preparing to go into exile, he made him his vicar-general, a role which Chillenden probably continued to perform under Roger Walden.[7] Two years later, prior and archbishop were among the dozen or so magnates and prelates who personally witnessed Richard II's abdication in the Tower, of which Chillenden probably wrote an independent account.[8] The next twelve years saw him employed by the archbishop on numerous metropolitan visitations, sometimes accompanying him, sometimes with Archdeacon Hallum.[9]

The chapter's privileges, so often a bone of contention with archbishops, never became an issue: they were confirmed by Arundel at the start of his primacy and again on 2 December 1403 and 7 July 1407 – the anniversaries of Becket's return to Canterbury and the translation of his remains in 1220.[10] Arundel also helped the community to compose its quarrels with other churches and on at least two or three occasions each year he and Chillenden jointly welcomed friends, donors, members of the royal family, the nobility and other dignitaries into the cathedral's fraternity. In July 1409, Arundel himself was admitted to the fraternity. In 1404, after John Bottlesham's death, Arundel proposed Chillenden for the see of Rochester but, according to the latter's obituarist, he 'preferred to serve God in this holy church of Canterbury under the noble rule of its pontiffs than to be raised up to the pontifical dignity in a different church'.[11]

Chillenden was the kind of administrator that Arundel favoured: a man who liked to concentrate power in his own hands (he remained treasurer as well as prior after 1391) but did not abuse it.[12] It was as a builder that he was chiefly remembered – 'the greatest Builder of a Prior that ever was in Christes Churche', according to Leland, and it was probably true. His lasting legacy was the rebuilding of the cathedral's magnificent new perpendicular nave, a project begun under Archbishop Sudbury in 1376–7 but all too quickly interrupted by the 1382 earthquake and not taken up again until 1391.[13] When Arundel became archbishop, he helped Chillenden to move it forward, granting licences for the appropriation of two churches to the priory's fabric fund and donating £666 of his own money.[14] Within another two or three years, the nave was substantially complete, but Chillenden did not stop there. The extraordinary energy manifested at Canterbury during the first decade of the fifteenth century also led to the construction of a new choir screen, two new chapels dedicated to the Anglo-Saxon archbishops St Dunstan and St Alphege, a sumptuous new silver reredos (*tabula*) weighing 903 lbs and costing £3,428 (dedicated by Arundel on 7 July 1400), a new roof for the chapter house costing £1,006, a new 'shaving room' (*domum rasture*) in the prior's lodging, and the rebuilding of much of the monastic dormitory and cloister, the latter completed after Chillenden's death.

Granaries, stables, the precinct walls, various priory buildings in and around Canterbury and 'almost all the priory's manors and churches' were renovated; at Oxford, Chillenden built a 'most beautiful' new chapel at Canterbury (later Christ Church) College. He also acquired for the cathedral an array of jewels, vestments and some thirty-five books on canon and civil law.[15] In 1409, he was one of the English delegates to the council of Pisa, but fell ill soon after his return and died on 15 August 1411. He was buried, at his own request, immediately adjacent to the spot Arundel had chosen for his own chantry chapel and tomb-chest, under the third most easterly arch of the new nave arcade. At his feet was buried his successor, Prior John Wodnesbergh, whose unopposed election the archbishop attended and who by 1414 had completed the reconstruction of the cloister and paid off the arrears of some £1,000 from Chillenden's rule. In 1413, Arundel and Wodnesbergh jointly officiated at Henry IV's funeral in the Trinity chapel.[16]

This was an exhilarating time to be at Canterbury, and Arundel gave his wholehearted support to what was in effect the rebirth of England's pre-eminent house of God. Less certain is his contribution to the design of the new work. According to Chillenden's obituarist, the nave was rebuilt with Arundel's 'support and help' (*ope et auxilio*), but this claim did not extend to the cloister, for which Chillenden alone received the credit.[17] Documentary evidence for the cloister's reconstruction is scant, but it is reasonably clear that, although work had begun on the south walk (adjacent to the nave) in the mid-1390s, it was only between 1408 and 1414 that real progress was made. This included the cloister's lierne vault with its 856 heraldic shield bosses distributed across thirty-six bays. Based largely on this heraldic evidence, it has been argued that the arrangement of the bosses was determined by Arundel and that they represented families and individuals 'who were in some way directly associated with the prelate and from whom donations were solicited'. That the bosses commemorated those who contributed to the renovation is highly likely – this was a traditional way to recognize donors – and Arundel's family was indeed prominently represented in some of the bays, but whether the decorative programme 'point(s) unwaveringly to the guiding hand of [Arundel]', and whether he was the prime mover in soliciting donations, is uncertain.[18] Even so, his enthusiasm and generosity must have played a significant part in the great enterprise which, in the space of twenty-five years, created a spectacular western arm to match the soaring eastern arm of the cathedral erected three centuries earlier in the aftermath of Becket's murder.

What his contemporaries remembered about Arundel's architectural contribution was his lavish chantry – the *capella Beate Marie Virginis* mentioned by Chillenden's obituarist. Built between *circa* 1406 and 1408, it was the cathedral's only free-standing chapel and was placed in the north arcade of the nave, as close as possible to the crossing. Endowed by the appropriation of Northfleet rectory, said to be worth £120 a year, it was initially served by two priests. A third priest, based at Maidstone college, was added to the endowment in 1408. By 1411, Arundel's tomb-chest at Canterbury had been constructed and installed. In his petitions to king and pope for foundation licences, Arundel said that he also wanted his chantry to serve as an oratory for lay folk when they were excluded from the choir and Trinity chapel – an interesting example of his desire to facilitate lay participation in services. He ensured that his chantry was well provided for, supplying a reredos of ivory, five suits of vestments, three frontals, a diaper cloth with *corporas* case for the altar and a missal with silver clasps. All this was seized and sold off by Henry VIII's commissioners in 1540, following Archbishop Cranmer's order to demolish the chapel – revenge for his erstwhile predecessor's treatment of Lollards. All that was left was 'a bare gravestone levelled with the floor, with the brass all shamefully torn away'.[19]

Canterbury was always at the heart of English Christianity – in effect, England's Rome. It boasted the primate's palace, the nation's most famous cathedral and most popular pilgrim shrine, and its oldest monastic house, St Augustine's abbey. Founded by King Ethelbert of Kent between 598 and 604, St Augustine's was named after the first missionary sent from Rome to convert the English people to Christianity, but following the building of Christ Church in the wake of the Norman Conquest it was the new cathedral which became the premier religious house in the city. Yet St Augustine's never forgot its precedence, continuing to claim that it was subject to no authority except the pope's, to prove which it produced papal bulls dating back to the seventh century (at least one of which was forged). This led to chronic bickering.[20] According to William Thorne, the late fourteenth-century chronicler and monk of St Augustine's, the fortunes of his house revolved around three persons: 'the king, who endows us with property; the abbot, who preserves what is entrusted to him; the [arch]bishop, who disturbs us who are exempt from him'. It was thus as a kind of *pas de trois* that he presented the abbey's history, focusing especially on the litany of disputes between St Augustine's and a succession of 'vulpine' archbishops. When Archbishop Sudbury tried to visit the abbey, he was warned by the abbot that God would punish him for his temerity – 'and thus it happened', declared Thorne with unchristian relish, when Sudbury was lynched on Tower Hill during the 1381 revolt. His successor, William Courtenay, was no better, attempting to 'enslave (*ancillare*) our church in various ways'. 'Puffed up by pride', he even tried, 'though uninvited', to enter St Augustine's on the day of abbot William Welde's installation in 1389, but was sent back 'with the curse of God to his own place'.[21]

Arundel, however, escaped Thorne's censure. As soon as he became archbishop, he confirmed St Augustine's exemption from episcopal visitation, declared the monks to be subject to the pope *nullo medio* and encouraged them to seek a papal bull confirming this (although, like archbishops Pecham and Stratford before him, he excluded the abbey's appropriated churches). Thus, when he entered St Augustine's on the day of his enthronement, 18 February 1397, he was welcomed by Abbot Welde, at whose 'earnest request' he celebrated high mass in the abbey. This happy state of affairs was confirmed on 16 August 1397, when, perhaps sensing the political storm about to engulf him, Arundel issued a charter confirming the abbey's privileges, exemptions and properties.

With this 'definitive sentence', Thorne brought his chronicle to a close.[22] There is thus no first-hand account from St Augustine's covering the great majority of Arundel's primacy, yet it is clear that he remained on good terms with the abbots. A scribbled note, possibly in his own hand, probably dating from 1403–4, asking for a contribution to the 'great and urgent business of the king and kingdom', was addressed to 'our dearest friend (*socio nostro carissimo*) William Welde, abbot of St Augustine's Canterbury'. It may well also have been the archbishop, about to become chancellor, who on 25 November 1406 secured the abbey's exemption from the payment of tenths during abbatial vacancies.[23] On 31 March 1412, Welde's successor as prior, John Hunden, was received into the cathedral's fraternity.[24]

Equally trouble-free, it seems, were Arundel's relations with the Austin canons of St Gregory's priory, where the archiepiscopal treasury and archives were kept, and the city's house of Franciscan friars, both of which had sometimes been strained.[25] So favourable towards Arundel was the Canterbury Franciscan who compiled the *Continuatio Eulogii* that it has been suggested that parts of it might derive from a lost biography of the archbishop; although this is unlikely, the author's admiration for Arundel is manifest.[26]

Unlike so many of his predecessors, Arundel must have found Canterbury a restful place, a haven of friendship and cooperation where he could escape the pressures of government and the wearying personal and political rivalries of Westminster. To some extent he was lucky: Chillenden was a man for whom his contemporaries (and historians) appear to have had nothing but admiration. Yet it is hard not to think that Arundel's ability to pour balm on troubled waters and his readiness to recognize the legitimate rights of others even if they derogated from his own – the tact and willingness to compromise noted by the Bury St Edmunds chronicler in 1401 – were the main reason why the perennial squabbles of Canterbury's multiple religious houses fell into abeyance during his primacy. Here, indeed, was a model for his successors to emulate.

From Canterbury to Lambeth, at intervals of between fifteen and twenty miles, stretched an almost direct line of archiepiscopal residences, or 'palaces', at which Arundel regularly stayed, conducted ordinations and consecrations, or held his archiepiscopal courts – from east to west, Charing, Maidstone (which had a prison), Otford and Croydon.[27] At each of these he had both a private chamber and an oratory or chapel for his personal devotions or individual interviews. At Lambeth palace, he had both an oratory, where in February 1409 the widow of his friend Lord Lovell placed her hands between his and took a vow of chastity, and, attached to the east side of his chamber, a 'newly constructed' smaller chamber where in September 1407 he consecrated an altar to the Blessed Virgin Mary. In August 1401, he personally received the profession of the hermit John Langfield in his 'small interior oratory' at Canterbury. There are also references to his private chapels in Saltwood castle, built by William Courtenay, and Ford manor, and to his 'oratory or chapel' next to his 'principal chamber' at Queenborough castle. The altars here were invariably dedicated to the Blessed Virgin Mary, sometimes jointly with Edward the Confessor, Becket or St Dunstan. Arundel also occasionally used his private oratories for a 'spiritual ordination' or a bishop's profession of obedience, and they probably served as private studies.[28] There are references too to *hospicio nostro* in London, which may have meant Ely (Holborn) palace, where he still stayed sometimes after his promotion to Canterbury, or perhaps Lambeth, or to another private residence in the city.[29]

When not journeying back and forth to London, his preferred residences were Ford palace, seven miles north of Canterbury in Kent's north-eastern corner, reputedly an archiepiscopal manor since Anglo-Saxon times, and Saltwood castle, twenty miles south of Canterbury on the Channel coast.[30] Rarely did he pass more than a night anywhere else in Kent, despite holding, in addition to his palaces, around forty-five manors in the county. (He also held some fifteen manors in Sussex and eight in Surrey, Middlesex and Hertfordshire.[31]) From roughly 1200 to 1380, many of these manors were directly managed for the archbishops' profit, but by Arundel's time, with the rising cost of labour following the Black Death, the trend throughout England was towards demesne-leasing, and the archiepiscopal estates were gradually farmed out to lessees who paid fixed rents, usually in cash or occasionally in produce (often for the archbishop's household), under the supervision of the steward of the lands.[32] By 1440 almost all the demesne was leased. Although the total income from the archiepiscopal estates varied from year to year, it was probably in the region of £3,000 annually in Arundel's time, about one-third from spiritualities, the remainder from temporalities.[33]

Annual income of this magnitude made Arundel one of the wealthiest men in England. Only three or four of the country's dozen or so dukes and earls could match it, although the greatest of them, usually kings' sons, enjoyed incomes of up to £10,000 a year. Three or four bishoprics – Winchester, Lincoln, Durham, Ely – also yielded annual incomes similar to that of Canterbury, and great London merchants such as John Hende and Richard ('Dick') Whittington probably had liquid assets greater than any of them, as did the occasional soldier of fortune such as Sir Robert Knolles.[34] At his death, Arundel's personal wealth ('all his goods') was valued at £6,008, roughly half of which (£2,934) came from the live and dead stock on his manors, the remainder from his jewels, plate, apparel, furnishings, books and horses.[35]

It was perhaps rumours of his wealth which led in the autumn of 1402 to a robbery on his baggage train as he passed through Rogate (West Sussex), the principal casualty of which was the loss of the register of Archbishop Stratford (1333–48), which was never recovered.[36] There is nothing, however, to suggest that Arundel's wealth was diminished. His lavish gifts to Christ Church – twenty-one copes, a pastoral staff of gilded silver, a gold chalice worth £133, three silver basins to hang before the high altar, a mitre worked with gold and studded with precious gems, the four great bells – speak for themselves; in 1399–1400 he was able simultaneously to give £666 towards the rebuilding of the nave and loan another £666 to the king. He continued to loan substantial sums to the exchequer until the end of the reign: £666 in June 1404 for naval operations and an unspecified sum later in the year; £390 in July 1406 and a further £400 a month later; and £666 for the duke of Clarence's expedition in July 1412.[37] Personal influence probably meant that he would have been repaid promptly, which was far from true for many of those who lent Henry money.

The sources of Arundel's private wealth are unclear, but its foundation was undoubtedly the generosity of his immensely rich father. However, there is no direct evidence that, like his father, he invested money for profit with London merchants.[38] To have done so might have been considered usury, which was forbidden to Christians by the Church – presumably more of a consideration to an archbishop than to an earl. After 1404 he received a fee of £200 a year as a royal councillor, a far from negligible sum but hardly enough to fund his lavish gift-giving. There is no evidence that he exploited his enormous influence to demand monetary bribes, although he doubtless expected favours to be returned. Whatever his enemies called him, no one accused him of peculation.

In a county where no great lay magnate habitually resided, the vast estates and ecclesiastical muscle of the archbishops of Canterbury made them far and away the dominant power in Kent, as they had been for at least six hundred years. This did not mean that they lacked potential challengers. In south and east Kent, the military and judicial power of the constable of Dover castle and warden of the Cinque Ports might easily, in the wrong hands, have presented a threat, as it had done in both the recent and the distant past.[39] Fortunately, it was held between 1399 and 1409 by the lifelong Lancastrian Sir Thomas Erpingham, whose principal estates were in Norfolk, and with whom Arundel appears to have got on well. From 1409 to 1414 it was held firstly by Prince Henry and then by Arundel's nephew, Earl Thomas. Although they certainly had their political differences with the archbishop, they did not exploit the post to impose their authority more widely in the county. In west Kent, the great lordship of Tonbridge, valued at around £450 a year net, presented more opportunity than threat during these years since its Stafford lords suffered a series of untimely deaths and the archbishop was entitled to two-thirds of its wardship during the minority of an heir.[40] It was not in Kent but in neighbouring Sussex where Arundel encountered the only significant challenge to his regional authority – and from an unexpected source.

17

Family

On 21 March 1401, Pope Boniface IX instructed Arundel and Bishop Braybrooke of London to go to the convent of the Minoresses (Poor Clares) at Aldgate, by the Tower of London, and ask the fourteen-year-old Isabella, daughter of Thomas of Woodstock, the duke of Gloucester murdered by Richard II in 1397, whether she wished to remain there. She had been placed in the convent by her father 'in infancy' but had not yet been professed as a nun. The reason cited by Boniface was because 'all her brothers and sisters, with the exception of one sister, have died', and there was a danger 'lest the duke's inheritance devolve to strangers' (*ad extraneos*). This was true: the duke's wife, Duchess Eleanor, their only son and heir, Humphrey, and their daughter Joan all died in 1399–1400. Isabella's remaining sister was Anne, who around 1396 had married Edmund, earl of Stafford. Boniface would not have known this: for the facts, he had to rely on the petition from England on which his mandate was based, which was said to have been presented to him by 'some persons, for a remedy' – that is, to protect the Gloucester inheritance. This was not the only petition on the matter which Boniface had received. Arundel had also sent him one, which claimed simply that 'all her brothers and sisters are dead', without mentioning Anne – which, obviously, was not quite true. Not that it made much difference: the request was the same in each case, but Arundel's petition made a more compelling case for it, and there is just the inkling of a suspicion here that he might not have been quite straightforward with the pope, and that other 'persons', realizing this, felt compelled to set the record straight.[1] Boniface's response was, quite correctly, to tell the archbishop firstly to 'examine' Isabella as to whether she wished to leave the nunnery – which was only to be done once she was 'beyond the jurisdiction of the said friars and nuns' – and subsequently, if necessary, to 'invoke the aid of the secular arm' – for what, exactly, it is not spelled out.

In the end, the question of whether or not Arundel tried to deceive the pope or had simply 'forgotten' about Anne is not that important (except, perhaps, as shining a little sidelight on his character). He was clearly not the only one who thought that one married and as yet childless sister was too slender a thread upon which to hang the fortunes of such a great inheritance. But there was, in this case, a further incentive for him to act, for he was Isabella's great-uncle. This was a family matter. In fact, it may well have been the archbishop's sister, Countess Joan of Hereford, Isabella's grandmother, who was behind it. She had custody of Isabella's lands during her minority, and it was she who, twenty years earlier, had collaborated with John of Gaunt to abduct her own daughter, Mary de Bohun, Duchess Eleanor's sister, from the Minoresses, to whom Mary had been entrusted as a child, and arrange her betrothal at Arundel castle to the then Henry of Bolingbroke, now Henry IV.[2] She may well have reckoned that, what she had done for a daughter, she should also do for a granddaughter. Her motivation was presumably the belief that her daughter and granddaughter should not be consigned to a religious life without being given the option of choosing otherwise. In both cases, it had been Thomas of Woodstock – as Mary's brother-in law, and as Isabella's father – who had placed them with the Minoresses. Whether Arundel shared Joan's belief, or was acceding to the wishes of his sister, is unclear, but like all aristocrats he knew the importance of orchestrating marriage and inheritance at this level, especially where kindred were involved. As it turned out, Isabella opted, after examination, to stay in the nunnery, where twenty years later she became abbess. But at least this was her own decision.[3]

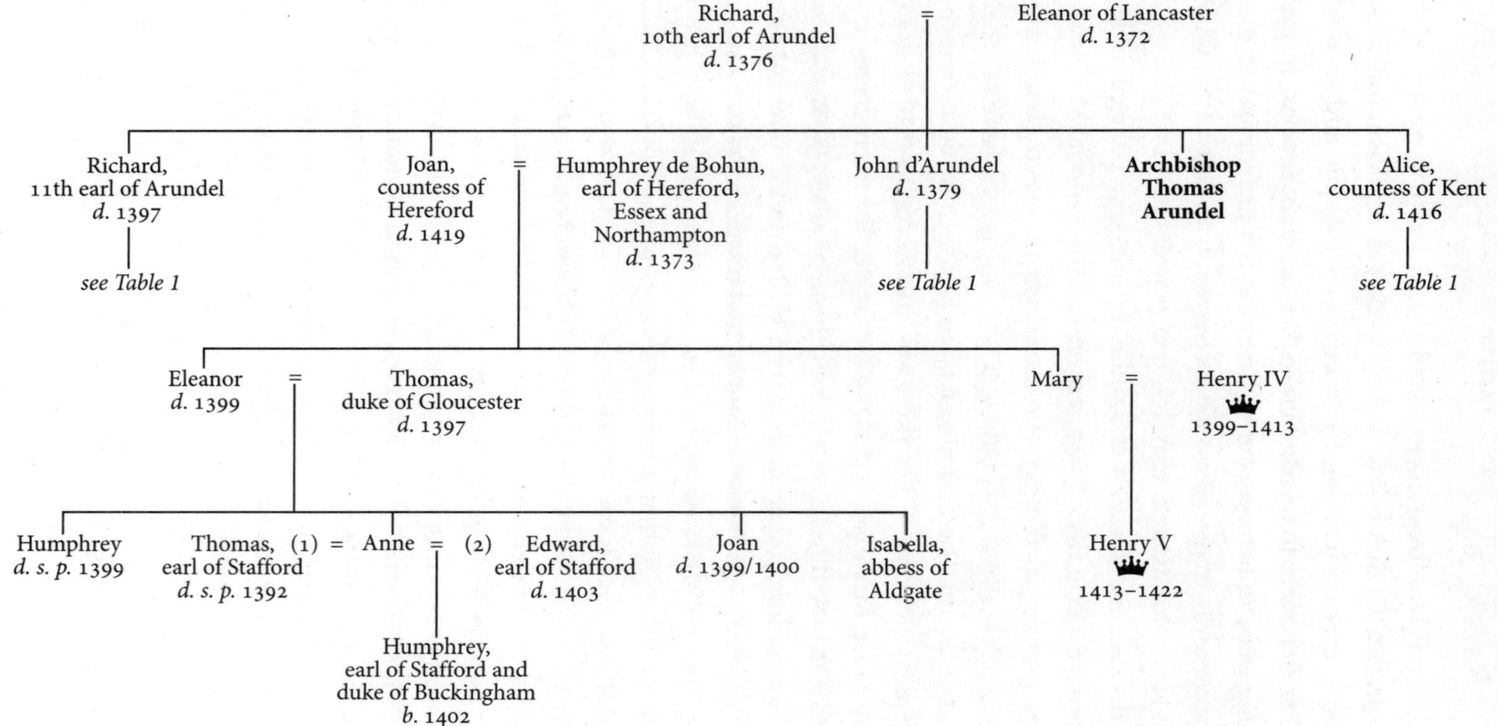

Table 2. The Fitzalans and the Stafford family, *c.* 1400.

Countess Joan, five or six years older than Arundel, was probably his closest friend, and a formidable lady.[4] Married at twelve to Humphrey de Bohun, earl of Hereford, Essex and Northampton, and widowed in 1373 aged twenty-five, she lived until 1419 but never remarried, choosing to carve her own path through a rampantly masculine world from whose innate prejudices and alarming lurches she tried to shield her daughters, Eleanor and Mary. As coheiresses to one of England's greatest patrimonies, they were both paired off before the age of twelve – Eleanor to a king's son; Mary (once abducted from the Minoresses) to a king's grandson.[5] Mother and daughters remained close, regularly exchanging visits and gifts, and it was probably the deepest wound of Joan's life that they both died young, Mary in 1394, aged twenty-five, and Eleanor five years later, aged thirty-three.[6] Her family was the axis around which Joan's life turned. In January 1400, when John Holland, earl of Huntingdon – who in 1397 had helped to condemn her eldest and youngest brothers to death and exile respectively – was captured in Essex following the abortive Epiphany Rising and taken to Pleshey castle, she had him executed on the spot by 'common folk and workmen' (*plebeyos et mecanicos*).[7] Henry IV, of course, had also spoken out against Earl Richard in 1397, but Joan, like Arundel, forgave him – he was, after all, her son-in-law, the father of six of her grandchildren – and from early in his reign she, like Arundel, enjoyed a close friendship with the king and played a prominent part in the affairs of the kingdom.[8]

Joan's dower lands, worth around £1,000 a year, were mainly in Essex, where she held a succession of offices and commissions of the kind rarely entrusted to women and provided a steady hand in a county where anti-Lancastrian sentiment was always latent. In May 1402, when commissions were issued to suppress the 'many lies' being told about the king, Joan was nominated to the Essex bench, the only woman among 300 men appointed throughout England.[9] The previous year, she had been granted the wardship of the underage Richard de Vere, earl of Oxford, which she held until he reached his majority in 1406. De Vere loyalty to the memory of Richard II was always a potent threat: Countess

Maud, the mother of Richard II's favourite Earl Robert and another formidable great lady, was at the centre of an Essex-based conspiracy to dethrone Henry IV in 1403–4 (although the young Earl Richard remained prudently loyal to the Lancastrian dynasty until his death in 1417).[10] Between 1407 and 1410, Countess Joan also held the politically sensitive wardship of John Mowbray, son of Thomas, the rebel earl of Nottingham executed alongside Archbishop Scrope in 1405.[11]

Commissioned in July 1410 to raise government loans in Essex – again, she was the only woman among seventy or so men appointed in England – she generously lent £333 of her own money 'in exoneration of herself and of all other temporal persons in the county of Essex'.[12] She could also be high-handed, as when she apparently demanded money from a London priest, William Hall, before allowing him to enter his church of Newton (Suffolk), of which she was the patron (Arundel asked his registrar, William Milton, to arbitrate the case, which went against her).[13] Forfeited estates, arbitrations and enfeoffments-to-use were continually entrusted to her, and she was even made deputy keeper of Rochester castle in Kent, with permission to come and go whenever she pleased. Perhaps this was to allow her to spend time with her brother in Kent. They spent every Easter together at Canterbury and in April 1405 she was admitted to the Christ Church fraternity.[14] Their closeness is exemplified by the letter she wrote, probably to Hugh Waterton, expressing her fears for herself and Arundel on account of the slander (*male bouche*) being drip-fed to the king about the two of them. She remained high in the confidence of Henry V, to whom she was 'our dearest grandmother'.[15]

When in Essex, Joan usually resided either at her chief residence, Pleshey castle, six miles north-west of Chelmsford, or at her manor of Rochford in the south-east, where she and her daughters maintained a workshop which continued the Bohun tradition of commissioning high-quality illuminated religious manuscripts.[16] As the sister and confidante of an archbishop, her religious practice is of particular interest. Outwardly, she conformed to the well-groomed aristocratic orthodoxies of the time. A generous patron and benefactress of Walden abbey in north Essex, where she and her husband both chose to be buried, she belonged to St Helen's religious guild at Colchester and contributed to the chantry foundations of several Essex lords and gentry.[17] Yet her orthodoxy was of that distinctive kind to which a growing minority of later medieval English lords, ladies and gentry were turning. Influenced by the ever-popular works of Richard Rolle and Walter Hilton, this emphasized, alongside orthodox public worship, private devotional practice focusing on meditative prayer and self-examination. Inwardly, it fed off a desire to come face to face with God rather than trying to discern Him dimly through a miasma of obscurantist vocabulary and a cloud of incense. Its outward signs were the growing popularity of the cults of Corpus Christi, the Blessed Virgin Mary, the Five Wounds of Christ and the Seven Deadly Sins; noble patronage of Carthusian austerity; testamentary self-chastisement and a preference for funerary restraint rather than lavish display; and the late medieval predilection for small, portable and often beautifully illuminated Books of Hours as aids to solitary devotion outside approved places of worship.[18]

This was an age of lay initiative in religion, and Countess Joan and her younger daughter embraced these more individualized forms of expression.[19] At some point, Joan took a vow to fast every Monday, from which Archbishop Chichele released her in 1414 since it might aggravate the 'various infirmities' from which she now suffered. Instead she was to celebrate a weekly 'mass of the angels' at which she would give two pence to a beggar of her choosing.[20] The early fifteenth-century monk of Walden who compiled a history of the abbey singled out for praise her lavish generosity to the abbey, which included re-covering the church roof with lead, erecting a new bell-tower and donating precious vestments, a gold cross and 'various ornaments' for the altar – all this, he added, on account of the intensity of her piety:

> She was the very model of the woman devoted to God, the glory of matrons, meditating, keeping vigil and living chastely like the

widow Anna in the temple of God [Luke 2:37–8] from the time of her husband's death until the end of her days, always, like the olive, keeping back to herself the bitterness of the root while pouring forth to others the sweetness of the fragrance, and with a healthy mind anticipating the face of God in confession and preparing her lamp with true humility in the fashion of virgins.[21]

The danger in these more independent forms of worship was naturally that they might lead to rejection of the Church's institutional practice, ultimately even to Lollardy – and Countess Joan did have slight connections with well-known Lollards. For example, she acquired from the Lollard knight Sir Lewis Clifford (d. 1404) a half-share in a gold brooch studded with precious gems worth £800, which in 1413 she sold for £400 to Henry V. This involved negotiating with Clifford's executors, who included John Cheyne and John Oldcastle.[22]

Joan was certainly not a Lollard but, despite being Arundel's sister, she did not shun Lollards (nor did many others who were never accused or suspected of heresy). Indeed, brother and sister almost certainly held some common views on religious practice, perhaps attributable at least in part to familial influence. Their father, mother and elder brother had all stated in their wills that they wanted 'no armed men, horses, *herce*, or other vanities (*bobaunces*)' placed about them at their funerals.[23] Funerary restraint was a family tradition. One of the first English nobles to request it was Arundel's uncle Henry of Grosmont, the first duke of Lancaster (d. 1361).[24] Such requests, often accompanied by expressions of remorse for a sinful life and contempt for the mortal body, anticipate the penitential self-reflection practised by Joan and Mary de Bohun. Grosmont was also the author of the remarkable *Livre de Seyntz Medicines*, a self-lacerating treatise based on his lived experiences which focused on the sins – pride, lust, avarice – of which he was culpable and the 'cures' (the 'holy medicines' of the title, such as meditation, contrition and full and frank confession) which might help him to curb his desires and find a more personal conduit to salvation.[25] The fact that the future archbishop of Canterbury and his sister grew up with such exemplars may help to explain not only Countess Joan's spirituality but also why, unlike so many of his contemporaries, Arundel did not turn Margery Kempe away when she visited him at Lambeth in 1413, or advise her to suppress the idiosyncratic forms of worship which, she believed, brought her closer to God. There was more than one path by which salvation might be achieved.

Apart from Joan, Arundel's closest living relatives after 1399 were his younger sister Alice, his nephew Thomas, twelfth earl of Arundel (1381–1415), and several nieces. Alice is a curiously absent figure from the archbishop's life.[26] Fratricidal enmity – the curse of a compulsively endogamous ruling class – was probably to blame: married to Richard II's half-brother Thomas Holland, earl of Kent (d. 1397), Alice was closely attached to Richard's court; her son, another Earl Thomas, died in the Epiphany Rising and was posthumously condemned as a traitor. Yet there also seems to have been a lack of personal empathy between Alice and her brother. Even after 1400, when she might have tried to trade on her kinship with the archbishop to mitigate the rigours of her son's forfeiture, there is no evidence of communication, let alone intimacy, between them. Not that she was penurious: her dower rights were generally respected; she had nine children who married into some of England's greatest families; and she held extensive estates in Hampshire, where she usually resided, and elsewhere. Her second son, Edmund, had remained loyal in 1400 and was restored to his father's earldom of Kent. After his death in a naval engagement off Brittany in 1408, she retired to Beaulieu abbey (Hampshire), where the abbot provided her with lodgings until her death in March 1416.[27]

The most notable of Arundel's nieces was Joan Beauchamp (not to be confused with Countess Joan), described by Adam Usk as a 'second Jezebel'. The daughter of Richard, the eleventh earl (d. 1397), she married William Beauchamp, youngest brother of the Appellant earl of Warwick. With such family connections, their relations with Richard II were equivocal at best and they were clearly more comfortable once Henry IV came to the throne. There is some evidence that Joan and William flirted with heterodoxy, although it is equally possible that Joan was influenced by the familial tradition of contemplative piety. There is at any rate no indication that this created a problem for her uncle: it was Arundel who acted as feoffee for her and William's principal seat in the Welsh Marches, the castle and lordship of Abergavenny, and Arundel whom William appointed, along with his wife, as the chief executors of his will. Following William's death in May 1411, Joan proved herself, like her aunt and namesake, to be a powerful presence in the local politics of Lancastrian England, pursuing litigation and defending her rights with vigour for another quarter of a century until her death in 1435. Like his sister, the archbishop's niece was not a woman to be cowed by the gender norms of the age.[28]

Equally strong-willed was Arundel's nephew Thomas, twelfth earl of Arundel. Less reckless than his father, he nevertheless had a reputation for being quarrelsome and harsh to his tenantry, especially those of his Marcher estates. To be sure, Earl Thomas was unlucky that his tenure of the earldom coincided with Owain Glyn Dwr's revolt, which not only shrank drastically the income from his great Marcher lordships but also absorbed the majority of his energy and resources between *circa* 1401 and 1410. Yet he and his officers also found it hard to soften their ways once the revolt was over.[29] More significantly, his prolonged service in Wales led, firstly, to comradeship-in-arms with the young prince of Wales, under whom he served for much of this time, and secondly, the relative neglect of his role in the political society of Sussex. Less testing times would doubtless have seen him residing mainly in central and western Sussex. This – along with the Welsh Marches – was where his power was concentrated, around the honours of Arundel and Lewes. Here, Fitzalan supremacy was rarely contested. Hence his resentment at the pretensions of his close neighbour Thomas Poynings, Lord St John, whose ancestor Sir Edward had been among the most trusted servants of Earl Richard the elder (d. 1376). In 1399, St John married the widowed Countess Philippa of Arundel, Earl Thomas's stepmother, but after her death in 1401 a dispute arose between him and Earl Thomas over the terms of her dower, which Boniface IX had to ask the archbishop to arbitrate.[30]

It was in East Sussex, however, where Earl Thomas's reach overlapped with that of his uncle, that the real challenges to his pre-eminence in the county emerged. When John of Gaunt attempted to consolidate his authority there during the 1380s and 1390s, the thorn in his side was Sir Edward Dallingridge, a retainer of the eleventh earl.[31] Dallingridge died in 1393, and after 1399 local and national circumstances combined to create a new balance of power in Sussex. With Earl Thomas absent for much of the following decade and the Lancastrian affinity in the ascendant, it was one of Henry IV's chief retainers, Sir John Pelham, who rose to prominence, a threat not to Lancastrian influence but to Fitzalan hegemony in the county. Pelham was a lifelong servant of the Lancastrian regime, the son of a coroner from Warbleton (Sussex) who rose through the ranks of Gaunt's and then Henry IV's inner circle to become a knight of the king's chamber, royal councillor, diplomat, treasurer of England in 1412–13, and a local power-broker in Sussex holding duchy and adjacent lands said by 1409 to be worth £870 a year. This probably gave him a landed income in the county greater even than Earl Thomas's. Based at Pevensey castle, of which Gaunt had made him constable in 1394, Pelham received grants from Henry IV over the next decade which included the lordship of the whole rape of Pevensey in tail male, the reversion of the rape of Hastings, the stewardship of all duchy of Lancaster lands south of the Trent, and the keeping of Bramber and Bosham castles (thus also giving him a foothold in the west of the county).[32] He was elected as MP for Sussex in almost every parliament from 1401 to 1407, was sheriff of the county in 1401–2 and was regularly appointed to commissions of the peace. Pelham was no saint, but he was a more than competent administrator, a respected councillor, an utterly dependable Lancastrian, and a friend and colleague of the archbishop.[33]

Earl Thomas disliked upstarts in Sussex: from the spring of 1410, when he joined a royal council now dominated by followers of the prince of Wales,[34] the cascade of royal grants to Pelham abruptly dried up – removed from the peace commissions and other local offices which he had held in the county, he was not reinstated until late 1411, when the king wrested back power and appointed Pelham treasurer. This is not surprising: amid the personal and political squabbles which blighted Henry IV's rule during the last few years of his reign, there was no doubt which side Pelham was on: that of the king. Nor was there any doubt which side Earl Thomas was on: that of the prince.[35] By 1405–6, the relationship between Arundel and his nephew was already becoming strained. A letter from Earl Thomas to his 'most honoured uncle', probably dating from December 1404, was still friendly but indicates that the earl was nervous about what was being said to the king for, 'in this parliament', he wrote, many false 'complaints and suggestions' concerning him had been made to Henry; he asked his uncle not to believe them, and to warn the king not to believe them either, until he had spoken to him in person.[36] Then in June 1405 came the furore surrounding the death of Archbishop Scrope and the leading role which Earl Thomas played in it. His marriage in the same year to Beatrix, the illegitimate daughter of the king of Portugal, against his will but arranged by the king in order to strengthen the Anglo-Portuguese alliance, provided another source of grievance.[37]

Four years later, with political and personal rivalries at Westminster deepening, the relationship between Arundel and his nephew broke down entirely, resulting in a bitter and very public quarrel ostensibly about rights of lordship in Sussex but much exacerbated by events at court. At stake were what may seem relatively minor matters: rights of access or fishing or 'washing of sheep' in certain waterways, views of frankpledge (medieval village community self-policing), levying tolls, organizing town watches, maintaining fences and hunting for venison in specified chases. Most of the locations mentioned were around Lewes and the archbishop's extensive manor of South Malling, but some were in West Sussex, in Arundel forest and Slindon, another archiepiscopal manor.

Such rights were zealously guarded by landholders, and disputes often rumbled on for centuries, periodically breaking out, being patched up and then lying dormant until the next time. This was no exception. Ostensibly settled by compromise in 1258, confirmed in 1274, without good will it was always liable to flare up again.[38] By 18 August 1409, the situation was serious enough for the king to order the earl and archbishop to seal recognizances for £6,666 promising not to 'do or procure any harm or hurt' to each other, their men or servants. On 26 October an arbitration panel was set up, containing four of the king's justices and overseen by the two chief justices, Sir William Gascoigne and Sir William Thirning. Arundel and Earl Thomas each gave sureties of £2,000 that they would abide by the panel's decision.[39] However, after the panel made its award, it was found by one or other party – it is not clear which – to be unacceptable and 'debate arose anew' between them, causing the exasperated king to summon both men personally into his presence at Holborn and read the riot act to them. There were twenty articles of disagreement, fourteen historical and six new.[40] A year later, in November 1410, a more comprehensive settlement was agreed: as far as can be gathered, the justices' verdict favoured the archbishop, but even now some articles were respited until further evidence was forthcoming, so, although it is unlikely that this concluded the matter, it appears to have been accepted by both sides for the moment. What was shocking about this affair was that such a relatively minor local matter, even though it involved two of the greatest men in the land, was allowed to escalate to the point where the king had to call on his chief justices to settle it and even to intervene personally.

Taking the longer viewpoint, Arundel can hardly have considered himself unfortunate to have been born into the great and wealthy Fitzalan dynasty. However, he may well have thought that the Fitzalan lords whose active careers coincided with his own had given him as much trouble as support. Between 1386 and 1389, he was as committed as his brother to draining the swamp of Richard II's court, but during the 1390s, while Arundel was trying to heal past divisions and build a more inclusive polity, it was Earl Richard who proved the main obstacle to reconciliation. The result, for both brothers, was the catastrophe of 1397. Thomas, the twelfth earl, was less pig-headed than his father but no friend to his uncle, at least not after 1405; the intractability of their quarrel in 1409–10 points to an alarming lack of good will between them. Only with his elder sister did Arundel share a real communion. For a more supportive 'family', he had to look elsewhere, to the friends and servants whom he patronized, promoted and relied so heavily upon.

18

Friends and Servants

Medieval epistolary greetings can make it difficult to distinguish a dutiful servant from a cherished friend, or even a lover. A letter written at Pevensey castle (Sussex) on 25 July 1399 to 'my dear lord, dearest and best loved of all earthly lords', signed 'J. Pelham', was for long thought to be a letter from Lady Joan Pelham to her husband, John. In fact, it was from John to his 'earthly lord', Henry of Bolingbroke.[1] Arundel received many letters with similarly effusive salutations from both friends and servants, but few of them were true confidants: his sister Joan, Henry IV and Prior Chillenden of Canterbury, certainly; Coluccio Salutati, probably, despite the brevity of their personal acquaintance. Among secular nobles, his closest friends were John, Lord Lovell, and William, Lord Roos. Lovell, a parliamentary peer from 1375 until his death in 1408, had been a friend since Arundel's Ely days, and although he was close enough to Richard II to be dismissed from court by the Appellants in 1388, this does not appear to have affected their relationship.[2] For much of the time between 1391 and 1406 they were both royal councillors. After Lovell's death on 10 September 1408, Arundel acted as his principal executor, and in February 1409 his widow, Matilda, came before the archbishop in his oratory in Lambeth palace and, placing her hands between his, vowed not to remarry.[3]

With William, Lord Roos, a much younger man who was married to Arundel's niece Margaret, the daughter of his brother John (d. 1379), the archbishop worked even more closely. Perhaps because of this affinity with the Fitzalans, Roos found little favour with Richard II and was committed from the start to the Lancastrian cause. One of the first to join Henry and Arundel in 1399, he served as a royal councillor intermittently until 1410, as treasurer of England 1404–7 and on several occasions as Henry IV's spokesman in parliament.[4] Although sprung from a Yorkshire baronial family, he resided mainly at Belvoir castle (Leicestershire), for which in November 1408 Arundel became his principal feoffee.[5] His close association with both the king and the archbishop meant that, like Arundel, he was excluded from Prince Henry's council in 1410–11, but once the king regained his authority, Roos was reinstated and remained a councillor, under Arundel's chancellorship, until Henry's death. In his will, dated 22 February 1413, he asked, if he should die near London, to be buried 'in Christ Church Canterbury, close to the chantry chapel of the most reverend father in Christ and my lord, Thomas Arundel . . . in the most secret way possible' (*secretiori modo quo poterit*), with only the prior and convent present; if he died in Yorkshire, he was to be buried at Rievaulx abbey; if in Lincolnshire, at Belvoir priory. In the event, he died and was buried in November 1414 at Belvoir.[6]

Those named as testamentary legatees or beneficiaries of chantry foundations are often indicative of close friendship, but in Arundel's case they add little to what can be deduced from other sources. His 1411 chantry endowment nominated members of his own family and the royal family, his predecessor William Courtenay, the successive priors of Christ Church (Chillenden and Wodnesbergh) and three laymen: John Pelham, Simon Felbridge and Gilbert Umfraville.[7] Pelham's collaboration with Arundel has already been noted,[8] but the inclusion of Felbridge and Umfraville is curious. Felbridge was from Norfolk, a knight of Richard II's chamber who found the transition to Lancastrian service unproblematic, but there is nothing to indicate close association with

Arundel.[9] Gilbert Umfraville is a more interesting choice, partly because Arundel also named him in 1414 as the principal executor of his will and partly because, apart from this, much of the surviving evidence would suggest that he and the archbishop were not allies.[10]

Born in 1390 (so barely of age in 1411), Umfraville was the nephew of a Northumbrian knight of the Garter, Robert, who had won renown as the scourge of Scottish insurgents. From the age of eighteen onwards, Gilbert fought with him – the chronicler Hardyng called him Sir Robert's 'whelpe' – gaining similar renown and coming to the attention of Prince Henry, who knighted him and with whom he found great favour.[11] On the day that Arundel drew up the instructions for his chantry, in December 1411, Umfraville was in France, campaigning on the prince's behalf with the earl of Arundel and the Burgundians, contrary to the wishes of the king and archbishop. The only hint of connection between Gilbert and Arundel is that on the day after he became king, Henry V transferred the custody of Queenborough castle from Arundel to Gilbert – surely not a collusive arrangement of some kind, but the repeal of a grant of which the prince had never approved.[12] Perhaps Arundel wanted someone who had Henry V's ear and could ensure the fulfilment of his will. It is noteworthy in this context that, three weeks after the archbishop's death, Gilbert was received into the Canterbury fraternity.[13] Umfraville apart, Arundel's executors were his ministers and servants – those who knew about and managed his affairs.[14]

As chancellor, Arundel did not appoint the royal councillors and ministers with whom he worked, although he could certainly influence appointments. When he handed back the great seal after serving as Henry IV's stop-gap chancellor in August–September 1399, his replacement was his former keeper of the rolls, John Scarle, an unlikely choice at such a critical moment but a man whose loyalty to the archbishop was not to be doubted.[15] Doubtless Arundel also supported the retention as privy seal keeper of Richard Clifford, his first archdeacon of Canterbury. Between March 1404 and January 1410, as councillor and then chancellor, Arundel probably had little say in the king's choice of councillors. Although he would have been happy to work with clerks such as Henry Bowet, Thomas Langley, Nicholas Bubwith and John Prophet, as well as several of the lay lords including Tiptoft, Lovell and Roos, he found the Beauforts and their allies less congenial. Only during the last fifteen months of the reign was Arundel working almost exclusively with the councillors whom he himself would probably have chosen, several of whom he also counted as friends.

As archbishop, however, the appointment of his ministers and servants lay almost entirely with him. Directly or indirectly, a primate employed many thousands of servants: from his archdeacon, chancellor, auditor of causes and official down to the grooms of his household and the bailiffs or reeves of his manors. The latter barely concerned him: those who worked on his estates were appointed and managed by his estates steward.[16] However, his choice of household servants, principal ministers and clerks concerned him (and them) very much, for upon them depended the probity and reputation of his diocesan and provincial governance. As bishop of Ely, Arundel's household establishment numbered around eighty servants. Through the winter of 1383–4, for example, he had ten knights, seven esquires, twenty-two valets, eleven choristers, eighteen grooms and eight pages.[17]

It might be expected that an archbishop's household would be larger than a bishop's, but, with the general tendency for numbers to decline slightly in great households from the mid-fourteenth century, that might not have been the case. Archbishop Stratford's household in 1347 numbered 191 servants, while in 1459 Archbishop Bourgchier had just 68.[18] Unfortunately, no accounts survive for Arundel's household as archbishop of Canterbury, only glimpses: of his long-serving secretary, 'our dear clerk', John Bathe, who was frequently importuned to secure letters from his master and for whom Arundel sought promotion in 1413;[19] of his knight Nicholas Haute, his esquire Peter Hall and his chaplain Richard Hauk, who all witnessed an ordinance at Ford palace in December 1410;[20] of the unnamed marshal of his hall evidently considered to be of insufficient status to marry a Canterbury widow of means;[21] of his groom William Webbe through whose carelessness another of Arundel's servants lost an ear at Charing manor;[22] of the anonymous esquires and valets who accompanied him on his visitations; of William Piers, 'clerk of my household' in 1401, or John Sutton, 'my esquire' and 'Richard, clerk of my kitchen', both named in his will.[23]

These are for the most part just names, enlivened only by the occasional surviving anecdote: for example, Adam Usk's story of the guests at Arundel's dinner table enjoying a snide jest about the unpopular Bishop Burghill having his horde of gold coins stolen by jackdaws; or Margery Kempe's account of walking into his hall at Lambeth one summer afternoon to find 'many of the archbishop's clerks and other reckless men, both squires and yeomen, who swore many great oaths and spoke many reckless words', and a woman in a coarse fur-skin coat (*pylche*) who cursed her for a heretic, before being summoned through to the garden, where Arundel listened to her criticism of his servants 'full benignly and meekly . . . until stars appeared in the firmament'; or the monk of Bury's description of Arundel concluding his visit to the abbey in October 1401 with a farewell dinner in the abbot's palace 'happily mingling with all their servants to the extent that his clerks and esquires said that they had never seen their lord of Canterbury so jolly or cheerful when dining with any other lord during the previous year'.[24]

Through his choice of diocesan or provincial ministers, an archbishop had the power to advance the careers of those whose talents he valued or whose loyalty he wished to reward, leading perhaps to further advancement such as conciliar, diplomatic or ministerial appointment by the king. This was where a great patron exercised his judgement – and Arundel was both 'a good lord and patron' and 'had a remarkable eye for quality'.[25] He inspired loyalty too, not only through patronage but also, it is abundantly clear, through affection. Some bishops (and many popes) viewed their great patronal power as a dispensation for nepotism. Not so Arundel. His favour was earned through intellectual accomplishment and proven competence.

Of those whom he trusted and promoted, he held none in higher regard than Robert Hallum. Hallum was an Oxford doctor of laws who had served as Archbishop Courtenay's registrar from 1389 to 1396, but it was not until Arundel moved to Canterbury that his career really took off. Briefly auditor of causes in 1399–1400, then simultaneously chancellor and archdeacon of Canterbury from 1400 (note again Arundel's preference for combining high offices in one trusted pair of hands, as when he was at York), 'our dear clerk, a zealot for the faith' was regularly assigned challenging and delicate tasks and enjoyed Arundel's total confidence.[26] Mostly he worked within the diocese, but he also acted as the archbishop's eyes, ears and frequently mouthpiece in the province at large. It was he who pointed out to Arundel that Bishop Trevor of St Asaph was exercising his episcopal functions despite not having been enthroned, or that Bishop Medford was negligent, or who spoke on Arundel's behalf at the trial of William Sawtre. Much admired as a scholar, Hallum was also chancellor of Oxford university from 1403 to 1406 and, once provided to Salisbury (in 1407), presided there over the most intellectually distinguished cathedral chapter of its time.[27] As leader of the English delegation to Pisa in 1409 and again at the Council of Constance (1414–17), his powerful speeches against antipopes and recalcitrant cardinals made him a controversial as well as an influential voice, characterized by one attendee as arrogant but by another as 'most industrious and virtuous'. Ironically, he was himself offered a red hat by Pope John XXIII in June 1411, but did not accept it. Nor did Hallum live to see the healing of the Schism. He died near Constance on 4 September 1417, two months before the election of Pope Martin V. His will named Courtenay and Arundel as his principal benefactors (*parentum*).[28]

When Hallum went to Rome in 1406, the pope provided Angelus, bishop of Ostia and cardinal of Florence, as archdeacon in his place – a purely titular appointment held *in absentia* for nearly two years – until John Wakering was appointed in May 1408. Wakering was a different sort of archdeacon from Hallum.[29] He was not a graduate but a long-standing clerk of the duchy of Lancaster who enjoyed both Henry IV's and Henry V's confidence. As keeper of the rolls of the royal chancery from 1405 to 1415, he was also the archbishop's ideal deputy as chancellor but, given his other commitments, probably not the most assiduous archdeacon. Nevertheless, he continued in both offices until 1415 and there is no sign that Arundel was displeased with him. In April 1413, after Bishop Tottington died, the archbishop tried to get Wakering provided to the see of Norwich, but Henry V favoured Richard Courtenay.[30] However, Wakering was made keeper of the privy seal in 1415 and six months later, when Courtenay died, Henry V supported his second bid for Norwich, which he held until his death in 1425. His will showed great concern for paupers and requested a modest funeral.[31]

Apart from his archdeacon, Arundel's chief ministers were his chancellor, official, auditor of causes and registrar. Most of those whom he appointed to these posts were lawyers; some of them were also friends, such as John Bottlesham, his chancellor from September 1399 to April 1400, when Arundel promoted him to the see of Rochester.[32] One of the archiepiscopal chancellor's tasks was to preside at the superior provincial court, the Audiencia. The official presided at the Court of Arches (or Court of Canterbury) at St Mary le Bow in London (although it is often difficult to distinguish between the theoretically original jurisdiction of the Audiencia and the theoretically appellate jurisdiction of the Court of Arches).[33] Arundel's official, John Barnet, held the post from 1376 until his death in late 1407. Although he had been proposed as long ago as 1389 for the see of Rochester, neither he nor William Milton (archiepiscopal registrar from 1399 to 1420) caught the attention of their superiors (or historians) in the way that Hallum or Bottlesham did – a fact perhaps acknowledged in the wording of Barnet's will, where he appointed Arundel as his chief executor, 'if this kind of executry is, as I hope, worthy to be accepted'.[34]

Bottlesham's auditor of causes (and chief executor of his will) was Hallum, who replaced him as chancellor when he went to Rochester and was in turn replaced by Nicholas Rishton, who remained the archbishop's auditor of causes until 1408.[35] Rishton, who had worked extensively at the Curia during the 1390s and studied law at Bologna, was one of the most eminent lawyers of his day, but how he managed to combine his work in the Audiencia with his concurrent employment as a royal diplomat is hard to know. In 1404–5, he spent as much time in Calais and the Low Countries as in England, trying to negotiate a truce with the duchy of Burgundy, sending scores of updates to Henry IV and the council on affairs in France and Flanders, bemoaning the snail-like progress of the talks, seeking further information and complaining about his lack of payment. One caustic letter to Arundel declared it to be a wonder (*mirum est*) that his 'bountiful' council (*vestrum almum concilium*) was too vague, weak and divided (*vagum et infirmum et ab invicem separatum*) even to respond to his pleas. If the tone smacks of arrogance, it does not seem to have affected Rishton's career. Having composed a determination at Oxford on the ending of the Schism, he was sent by Henry IV in 1408–9 firstly to Pope Gregory XII (then at Lucca) and then as the king's legal representative at Pisa.[36]

In 1407–8, following Hallum's provision to Salisbury and Barnet's death, Arundel reshuffled his ministers. Wakering became archdeacon, Henry Ware took over as official and Philip Morgan as auditor of causes. All three were men on the rise, but not until Henry V's reign would they play leading parts on the national stage. Ware became keeper of the king's privy seal (replacing Wakering) from 1416, and bishop of Chichester in 1418; Morgan was appointed as chancellor of Normandy in 1418, bishop of Worcester in 1419 and then of Ely from 1426. Both were prominent in the tortuous Anglo-French-Burgundian diplomacy which consumed so much time and energy between 1414 and 1420. Ware was also appointed as an executor of Henry V's will, while Morgan, 'a man of sensitivity such that the records of his sort of career cannot show', was one of Arundel's executors, to whom he bequeathed a book.[37] Had Arundel lived longer, he and Morgan might have developed a close friendship, for by the latter stages of his archiepiscopacy several of those who were truly friends as well as servants, such as Hallum or Bottlesham, had died or moved on, and those who now served as his leading ministers – Wakering, Ware, Morgan – were also servants of the king or Prince Henry. Their appointment in 1408 hints at the advancement of princely influence among Arundel's ministers.

Given the many other commitments of Arundel's chief ministers, much of the business of the provincial courts must have devolved to Barnet and Milton. Their routine work – hearing suits, arranging compositions, admitting to benefices, proving wills, undertaking visitations, administering vacant sees – was painstaking and time-consuming. Since Arundel was a papal legate too, they also had to deal with appeals to the Curia, especially for absolution from excommunication, of which several were brought forward each year. They both received valuable prebends, such as Milton's archdeaconry of Buckingham.[38] They, too, naturally had their deputies and underlings – apparitors, examiners, advocates, vicars-general, commissaries, deans or simply 'clerks' – some of whom also expressed admiration and affection for Arundel, usually in their wills. Had they cared to indulge themselves at greater length, they might have been more fulsome, like the chronicler Adam Usk. Between 1395 and 1402, Usk worked under Courtenay, Walden and Arundel as an advocate in the Court of Arches, before going to Rome in search of a bishopric and eventually throwing in his lot with Glyn Dwr and the Welsh rebels. This led to his outlawry, excommunication and loss of all his benefices, but in 1411 he was pardoned, restored by Arundel to his post and recovered a few benefices. His gratitude to the man whom he calls 'my lord of Canterbury' was effusive. Arundel's death in February 1414, which Usk claimed to have foreseen in a vision the previous night, had deprived England of 'the strength, lamp and wisdom of the people, the light and delight of church and clergy, and the unshakeable pillar of the Christian faith'.[39] Usk's rehabilitation after 1411 is an example of another facet of Arundel's character which attracted men to his service: his willingness to forgive. The outstanding example of this is his treatment of Roger Walden, but it is far from the only one. The Ricardian bishops Thomas Merks, Henry Despenser and

Guy Mone were treated with similar forbearance, perhaps even, like Walden, to the point of becoming friends – as long as they remained loyal to the Lancastrian regime.

The English Church overflowed with ambitious and competent clerks, managing whose expectations was no easy task. To avoid contention or confusion, it was important for Arundel to clarify what he in turn expected from them. When the industrious and assertive Hallum was appointed as auditor of causes in 1399, the archbishop added, 'we do not intend that the commission to our dear son, John Bottlesham, our chancellor, as already made, should in any way be revoked, but that it should remain in force in the manner stated'.[40] In other words, Hallum was not to step on Bottlesham's toes. Soon after he became primate, Arundel also issued new statutes for the operation of the Court of Arches. For the most part, these confirmed the statutes issued by his predecessors, Robert Winchelsea in the 1290s and John Stratford in the 1340s, with particular emphasis on timely record-keeping and the competence of advocates. The 'scribe of acts' was to keep the court's records no longer than he needed them before handing them to the registrar, who was to keep them together in 'a big book' (*uno magno libro*). The current scribe had 'presumptuously' been retaining them too long. A further statute in 1401 ruled that only formally admitted advocates and their proctors who were 'expert and knowledgeable' (*experti et gnari*) had standing in the Arches, and they were not permitted to practise in inferior courts. Two years later this was revised, since proctors had been 'surreptitiously' (*clanculo*) acting independently of advocates, leading to a loss of respect for the court, which formerly 'shone with great fame' (*multa celebritate fulgebat*).[41]

The insistence on demarcation of responsibilities, the clarification of hierarchy, the avoidance of distractions and punctual record-keeping tallies with the ordinances Arundel had issued for the chancery in the late 1380s.[42] He anticipated and tried to forestall potential problems. Archdeacons, for example, were renowned for quarrelling with their bishops, especially over the proving of wills. To avoid this, a month after his enthronement as primate, Arundel drew up a composition with his first archdeacon of Canterbury, Richard Clifford, setting out precisely how jurisdiction over wills should be shared between them; when Hallum became archdeacon, he confirmed it.[43] Arundel's relations with all his archdeacons appear to have been excellent.

Yet if detailed compositions or statutes promulgated from his central administration create an impression of the prompt and efficacious dispatch of business, Arundel had no illusions about the scale of the task of running a diocese, let alone a province. Many thousands of persons were involved, down to the 'trustworthy men' (*fidedigni*) whose verdicts on shortcomings or disputes in obscure rural parishes hundreds of miles away a bishop and his ministers constantly sought: whether a grange was dilapidated, for example, or a church lacked mass-books, or a vicar kept a concubine or was a persistent absentee, or a parishioner was suspected of heresy.[44] The usual procedure was to ask an official such as the rural dean to assemble a panel, or jury, of local *fidedigni* to investigate the complaint and submit their opinion – to which the almost invariable episcopal response was, of necessity, to accept what they said and issue the appropriate authorization, admonition or reproof. Episcopal registers are full of such cases.

That does not mean that bishops or their ministers necessarily believed what they were told. They were well aware that witnesses acted on hearsay and had their own axes to grind, their local ambitions or vendettas to pursue. But what it did mean was that bishops must be willing to change their minds if new evidence emerged or new witnesses came forward. Popes too were perfectly aware of this, often prefacing their bulls with the words *si ita est* ('if it is as alleged'). For a primate of all England, the arbiter of cases from all parts of a province extending several hundred miles to the north and west, the problem of whom to believe was acute. During the long-running saga of the chapel of Hook (Hampshire), both Arundel and Pope Boniface twice issued definitive judgments backed by threats of major excommunication in favour of each of the warring parties, thus not merely eating their words when new evidence emerged (or different witnesses were consulted), but subsequently having to disgorge them a second time.[45] In an age of slow and often unreliable communication it was well understood that the 'trustworthy men' upon whom the great and grinding administrative machinery of an archbishop, or indeed a king, really had no option but to rely, were not always as trustworthy as might be hoped.

19

Talking, Writing, Reading

There is no one, not even the king, whose publicly spoken words are recorded more often in late fourteenth- and early fifteenth-century English sources – chronicles, memoirs, trial records, parliamentary and conciliar reports – than Arundel's. This was not just because he held great offices. It was also because he was known for the emotional power of his oratory. Between 1377 and 1413, twelve different chancellors, two bishops and one chief justice gave a total of thirty-three opening addresses to parliaments, only four of which elicited any praise from the clerks. Two of these were delivered by Arundel: to the parliaments of 1388, where he spoke 'most wisely and eloquently', and 1391, 'most nobly and wisely'.[1] Arundel's speeches to convocation were similarly praised as 'elegant and serious' (1406), 'noble, elegant and clear' (1411) or simply 'so effective' (*tantum valuit*) (1403).[2] When exhortation or inspiration was the order of the day, it was Arundel who was called upon: to address the warring London factions in 1387 and 1392; to present the reasons for Richard II's deposition to the estates in 1399; to encourage the nobles and prelates to back the cardinals' plan for ending the Schism in 1408; and, initially, to lead the English delegation to Pisa. His sermon at Queen Anne's funeral was praised by some as 'the best sermon that they ever heard'.[3] This rhetorical virtuosity was enhanced by a sense of theatre: rising and bowing before speaking, kneeling before the king to protest his innocence, bursting into tears, threatening 'harsh blows' or offering his head on the block before he would let the Church be deprived of 'the least of its rights'.[4]

It is no coincidence, then, that two of the surviving images of Arundel in manuscripts of the time portray him making speeches.[5] Yet if he was widely acknowledged to be a powerful orator, it was not for his religious preaching or teaching that he was known, as several of his distinguished predecessors were: Lanfranc, for example, whose school at Bec (Normandy) attracted students from all over western Europe; or Stephen 'Thunder-Tongue' Langton, one of Paris university's outstanding early thirteenth-century preachers and theologians; or Edmund of Abingdon, known above all for 'the moral inspiration of his lecturing and preaching'.[6] Arundel's sermons were not remembered as were those of, for example, Thomas Brinton (bishop of Rochester 1373–89) – or indeed many of the Lollard preachers of the time.[7] They did not meander down theological or conceptual pathways. They addressed practical issues, ecclesiastical or political – calls to action rather than to prayer.

Many of Arundel's conversations or debates were reported in a mixture of direct and indirect speech. Direct speech in narrative sources obviously cannot be expected to reproduce the precisely memorized words of the speaker (although striking phrases might do), but tends to be used to sharpen the reader's perception of a character's values, powers of persuasion and larger emotions. Indirect speech, more susceptible to narrative inflection, can achieve a similar effect, but direct speech captures the immediacy of the moment in a more arresting and memorable way. It also makes more demands on the reader: for example, when a character's *ipsissima verba* are open to differing interpretations, or when they appear closer to the words that might be expected of *any* king or archbishop rather than *this* king or archbishop. Direct speech can also be presented ironically, to mock a speaker's folly or to reveal more egregiously a bare-faced lie – for example, when Richard II assured Arundel that 'for as long as we two are both alive nobody except you will be archbishop of Canterbury', then promptly wrote to the pope asking him to provide Roger Walden.[8]

As recorded by the chroniclers – not just in one or two chronicles but across the gamut – Arundel's conversations with Richard II are markedly different in tone from those with Henry IV. Under Richard, he is presented primarily as the defender of England's traditional liberties, a bulwark against autocracy. The fullest articulation of this is Knighton's account of his speech to the king at Eltham in November 1386, when the king was refusing to return to parliament:

> Under an ancient law [he told Richard] which not long since, lamentably, had to be invoked, which provides that if the king, upon some evil counsel, or from wilfulness and contempt, or moved by his violent will, or in any other improper way, estrange himself from his people, and will not be governed by the laws of the land and its enactments and laudable ordinances and the wholesome counsel of the lords and nobles of the kingdom, but wrong-headedly, upon his own unsound conclusions, follows the promptings of his un-tempered will, then it would be lawful, with the common assent and agreement of the people of the realm, to put down the king from his royal seat and raise another of the royal lineage in his place.[9]

This has a performative feel to it, more like a school-room disputation on tyranny than a fervent plea to a foolish young man to avert disaster. Yet they are unmistakably strong words, delivered at a time when Arundel was neither chancellor nor an archbishop but a relatively junior bishop.

In fact, Knighton's speech is untypical of the way in which Arundel's conversations with Richard were usually portrayed by the chroniclers, which was pithy, robust and very much to the point – the words of a man given to oratorical muscularity and unafraid to speak truth to power. According to Thomas Walsingham, when the king asked him why the Appellants had failed to obey his summons to an interview at Westminster in November 1387, Arundel responded tartly, 'they do not consider you trustworthy'. Ten years later, he told Richard that to wish to be anointed a second time smacked of presumption. A few months after this, when about to go into exile, he lambasted the king for the extravagance and arrogance of his court, a theme which he elaborated after Richard's capture: 'You lived a life of debauchery, and by your foul example you besmirched your court and the kingdom.' By now, however, he was speaking truth not to power but to impotence.[10]

Under Henry IV, Arundel is presented as the defender of the Church. In sharp contrast to his conversations with Richard II, the dialogue between him and Henry is, if occasionally robust, generally respectful and supportive. Even during the greatest crisis in their relationship, the trial of Archbishop Scrope, words are exchanged in measured, if emphatic, rather than angry tones: 'My lord, I am your spiritual father and the second person in the kingdom after you, and there is no one whose advice you should take more readily than mine, if it is good.'[11] It was the 'enemies of the Church' for whom he saved his vitriol. Already in 1385, when he clashed with chancellor de la Pole over the question of episcopal temporalities, he had shown himself to be a vigorous champion of clerical privilege, and from the earliest days of Henry's reign this became the leitmotif of his recorded speech.[12] In February 1400, at the synod summoned to protest at the trial of Thomas Merks, he declared that prelates 'were being treated no differently from laymen' and that justices who tried bishops in lay courts should be punished as his predecessor Archbishop Islip (1349–66) had done – that is, excommunicated and denied Christian burial.[13]

'Knights who never loved the Church' – the disendowers, or those who wanted to seize the prelates' horses and valuables and 'send them home on foot' – invariably felt the lash of his tongue. If they did not desist, he berated them, they would suffer 'harsh blows': 'By St James, you will not take anything from me unless you purchase it by violence.'[14] It was at moments such as this that the archbishop looked to the king for support, and when Henry was slow to help, Arundel did not hesitate to pull him up. Witnessing a group of royal knights and esquires turning their back on the Eucharist in 1404, he hurried to tell the king: when Henry apparently 'thought little of it', Arundel 'became more exasperated and rebuked the king for his negligence, saying that the sin of his own servants would assuredly redound upon his own head'. Two years later, when Henry tried to laugh off the disrespect shown to the anti-Lollard preacher Richard Alkrinton, Arundel exclaimed, 'This is no joke. By St James' – evidently his favoured oath – 'the man must make amends to the preacher for the disgrace he inflicted upon him.'[15]

Lollards stretched Arundel's vocabulary to exhaustion: pestiferous, diabolical, damnable, depraved, to name but a few epithets. They were most commonly compared to wolves or foxes; they were sly, hypocritical, sanctimonious and, like the devil, constantly on the lookout for members of the flock to seduce. Like Pharaoh, they had 'hardened hearts'. Like a disease, they were contagious – hence the frequently epidemiological approach to their detection: who had they spoken with, who was feeding or housing them, where did these vagrant preachers come from?[16] Yet his conversations with Lollards reveal another side to Arundel – especially William Thorpe's account of his interrogation at Saltwood castle. The major problem with this text is obviously the one-sided nature of Thorpe's testimony. Arundel, we can be sure, would have written it differently. On the other hand, the circumstantial detail is convincing and, although Thorpe portrayed the archbishop as often impatient and occasionally angry, he does not come across as impulsive. Despite denouncing Thorpe as a *lewed losel* (ignorant wretch) and warning him at the outset that recalcitrance might mean he would 'follow thy fellow [Sawtre] into Smithfield', later on, when several of his clerks urged him to 'make an end with [Thorpe]', to have him 'cursed and burnt' forthwith, Arundel persisted in trying to bring him round to what he saw as the truth.

He seems to have been prepared to spend hours debating with Lollards, even after it became clear that they had no intention of abandoning their views. According to Thorpe, William Taylor had also spent two days being interrogated at Lambeth about his sermon at St Paul's

Cross in November 1406 and successfully 'maintained it before the archbishop and his clerks'. However much Arundel disagreed with what Thorpe said, he continued to debate, largely on ground of Thorpe's choosing, for longer than his clerks thought advisable, even agreeing with him that Wyclif was 'a great clerk' (before adding 'many men also held him to be a perfect liar').[17] Not that their conversation burrowed very deeply down the metaphysical rabbit warrens beloved of scholastic theologians, such as the Aristotelian distinction between substances and accidents.[18] This was 'school matter', said Thorpe, 'subtle sophistry', where scholars 'wade and wander till they know not where they are and understand not themselves'. The archbishop replied that he was not trying to make him understand 'the subtle argument of clerks, since you are unable to', but whether Arundel, no theologian himself, was any better able to is debatable. Usually when he interrogated Lollards he was accompanied by university doctors, who would probably not have allowed Thorpe the same degree of latitude.

Most of the topics they discussed were a good deal more down to earth: the worship of images, the Church's right to take tithes or hear confessions, oath-swearing, the value of pilgrimages, freedom to preach. Arundel insisted throughout that Thorpe must unambiguously acknowledge the Catholic Church's authority in the interpretation of the Scriptures and, consequently, *his* authority as the leader of the English Church. Thorpe agreed that he must accept the authority of the Church but that the Church meant 'Christ and his saints', not the Catholic hierarchy. Quoting copiously in both Latin and English from the Scriptures and the patristic texts – a feat of memory which Arundel seemed unable to match – he insisted on the Bible's paramount authority. Defending the right to preach without a bishop's licence, he cited St Paul: 'How shall they preach, except they be sent?' (Romans 10:15). Sent by God is what Thorpe meant, not licensed by some terrestrial authority. Arundel simply turned to his clerks, exasperated at these *losels* who 'pick out sharp sentences of holy writ and of doctors in order to maintain their sect and their teaching against the determinations of Holy Church'.

Thorpe responded by implying that the archbishop did not understand what St Paul meant: his clerks should know their Scriptures better. Thorpe had deep knowledge of the Scriptures, deeper than Arundel's, for they, not Catholic dogma, were the definitive guide to the Christian life.[19] Nothing in the Bible justified tithes; Christ lived by 'pure alms' – a point which Arundel answered only with generalities. Yet sometimes Thorpe was evasive, or simply remained silent – as he did when Arundel asked him for a list of his fellow Lollards, whom, unlike Sir Lewis Clifford apparently, he refused to betray.[20]

Eventually, one of his clerks said to the archbishop, 'the longer you oppose him the worse he is, for he is of so shrewd a kind'. Arundel asked Thorpe one last time if he was willing to submit to his authority, but he deflected the question and Arundel finally lost patience, 'smiting his fist against a cupboard', declaring, 'By St Thomas, I shall turn your joy to sorrow', and committing him to the constable. A short while later, Thorpe was brought back in and told that even now, if he was prepared to submit, he would 'find it for the best', but he 'stood still and spoke not a word'. Confined once more in Saltwood prison, he gave thanks for his deliverance from the threats and scorn of his enemies and committed himself to God. It is the last that is heard of him.[21]

Thorpe's interrogation was not a formal trial. Reports of Sawtre's, Badby's and Oldcastle's trials, where the equally one-sided narrative was controlled by the archbishop's clerks, show Arundel as patient and persistent, acting with the backing of convocation, yet ultimately insistent, as with Thorpe, that they must acknowledge his and the Church's authority. In each case, the focus was on transubstantiation. Even when the defendants grew 'mocking' (Sawtre), or impudent (Badby), or abusive (Oldcastle), the archbishop gave them time to consider their answers, repeatedly rephrasing questions to offer them another chance. His final, quasi-catechetical, question to Sawtre was

> whether that material bread, round and white, prepared and disposed for the sacrament of the body of Christ upon the altar,

> lacking nothing necessary and required for this, is altered and changed by virtue of the sacramental words, correctly pronounced by the priest, into the true body of Christ, and thereby ceases in future to be actual and material bread; or not?

However hard Sawtre tried to square his view of the Eucharist with Catholic teaching, Arundel would accept nothing less than total compliance. With Badby and Oldcastle this was never going to happen, and Arundel eventually lost patience with them.

Thorpe's picture of Arundel smiting his fist against a cupboard is the only occasion when the archbishop is unambiguously shown as losing his temper, although he came close to doing so at the Worcester councils of 1403 and 1405. For the most part, however, his anger was controlled, tactical. Like kings, prelates tended to express verbal or written anger as part of an admonitory process aimed at securing compliance without resorting to the law or to violence. When a king said he was 'moved to anger', it was a formalized, negotiable way of ramping up the pressure, something that could be assuaged (*remittere*, *dimittere*) by, for example, a fine or a public apology. It did not entail that loss of self-control which was equated with loss of reason, as when Richard II twice punched Arundel's brother.[22]

For prelates, the closest equivalents were sentences of excommunication, which, despite bearing terrifying threats of condign punishment and eternal damnation, usually included a *nisi* ('unless') clause offering absolution (remission) if the culprits were prepared, for example, to restore Church property or offices which had been seized or usurped, perform public penance, or in some other stipulated way make amends for what they had taken or done. Excommunication was thus commonly presented as 'medicinal', to distinguish it from the unconditional anathema or curse, which was punitive and theoretically prohibited by canonists. Not surprisingly, this distinction was easier to maintain in theory than in practice. In reality, sentences of excommunication were sometimes issued in anger and frequently intended to excite anger or even violence; until remitted, they deprived the culprit of his or her legal standing. And the forms of penance demanded in return for absolution were intentionally humiliating and sometimes corporal, such as whipping. The equivalency between royal anger and prelatical excommunication is not exact, but, to the extent that they both represented not so much an explosion of emotion as the initiation of a recognized procedure, it is not without validity.[23]

Arundel's written words – his letters, decrees, pronouncements, prohibitions – were characteristic of the prelacy: preachy, prolix and polemical. Medieval clerical polemic – in common with much political polemic – was not argumentative. It made no pretence of engaging with contrary points of view or seeking compromise.[24] It was a language of violence, the aim of which was to strip opponents of their legitimate right to be heard. It presented its truths as self-evident, and the author's right to enforce compliance as unquestionable, thereby incentivizing or justifying vigorous action. Identifying the author as a member of a righteous (orthodox) community, it also tended to define that community's position in stricter and narrower terms and hence to extend the range of potentially illicit viewpoints. This is to some extent what happened with heresy, as sharper, more proscriptive definitions of what was acceptably orthodox obliged the Catholic Church step by step to squeeze itself into more compact spaces.

In reality, clerical polemic was often addressed at third parties – king, parliament or simply a winnable public audience – rather than at those it attacked, whom it characterized as quite deaf to truth or reason. It was a well-honed art, perfected over many centuries against infidels and laymen who sought to curtail the Church's liberties, usurp its privileges or challenge its doctrinal rigidities, building on stereotypes – the crafty friar, the negligent pastor, the skulking wolf, the weeds ('tares') which strangled the wheat – whose familiarity only made them more believable. Papal invective hurled thunderbolts of indignation across Christendom, and the vehemence of some of Arundel's decrees lacked nothing by comparison. A sentence of excommunication in 1400 against two laymen accused of killing a priest racked up eleven adjectives in one sentence: detestable, inhumane, terrible, unheard of, insidious, wickedest, evil, horrible, odious, cruel and abominable.[25]

Unless accused or suspected of specific crimes, lay folk tended to be depicted as too 'simple' (or *lewd*) to be able to distinguish between truth and falsity. This was what made them vulnerable. Yet much of Arundel's and other prelates' polemic was directed not at the laity but at their own clergy, claiming that laxity, corruption and worldliness were prevalent, setting a pernicious example and making urgent action imperative – all this set out in lurid terms. Archbishop Islip's decree *Effrenata* ('Unbridled'), issued shortly after the Black Death in an attempt to limit the salaries of unbeneficed mass-priests who were trying to keep up with the general rise in wages following population decline, provides an example:

> The unbridled greed of the human race, out of its innate malice, would grow to such a point that charity would be driven off the earth, unless the strength of justice restrained its effects . . . [mass-priests], unashamed that their insatiable avarice is despicably and perniciously taken as an example by other workers among the laity, now take no heed to the cure of souls . . . but rather leave them completely abandoned [and if no remedy is found] the whole province [of Canterbury] will be left completely destitute of the service of priests, [for] their excessive affluence sucks them down into the whirlpool of voluptuousness, with the trimmings of their garments, their fancy hairstyles, their haunting of taverns and gambling dens and their disgusting pursuit of carnal lust.[26]

The fact that such decrees were issued in Latin meant that they might not have percolated very deeply through lay society, but the danger in depicting the clergy in such terms was that it emboldened those who were already inclined towards more radical solutions for what they saw as an institutionally corrupt church. Wyclif would certainly have agreed with many of Arundel's criticisms of his fellow clergy; indeed, it was upon such foundations that much of the Wycliffite view of the clergy was constructed. The problem with polemic was that it not only closed off the possibility of reasoned discussion but also engendered a degree of defensiveness on the part of the Church authorities, who hesitated to sanction reforms that might have been seen as acknowledging heretical criticisms.

Apart from his formally recorded (presumably redacted) speeches, his archiepiscopal mandates (usually drafted by his clerks) and a relatively small number of personal letters, Arundel is not known to have written anything: no tracts on theology or biblical exegesis, no historical, legal, musical, scientific, literary, moral or political works. He was, of course, a busy man, but some of his predecessors had managed to combine the archiepiscopacy with a prolific scholarly output (Anselm and Langton are the outstanding examples) and it is hard to avoid the conclusion that Arundel was simply not a scholar. Even during a year or so of relative leisure in Florence, in the company of intellectual giants, there is nothing to suggest that he was motivated to write anything apart from letters. Of course, he knew his Bible and, given time to prepare, he quoted extensively from it. His speech to the meeting of the estates which agreed to depose Richard II on 30 September 1399 cited 1 Samuel, Isaiah, 1 Maccabees, Joshua and St Paul's first letter to the Corinthians. His preamble to the *Constitutions* included several quotations from the Pentateuch, the Acts of the Apostles (with particular emphasis on Peter, the source of papal authority) and the Book of Revelation.[27] His addresses to parliament and convocation almost always included biblical references. Yet it is telling that, when William Thorpe contradicted him on the meaning of a passage about oath-taking by the patristic author John of Chrysostom, Arundel replied rather feebly that Chrysostom 'might be understood that way' before insisting that all that mattered was obedience to Catholic doctrine. It was left to one of his clerks to challenge Thorpe on theological grounds.[28] One wonders how he would have fared debating with Wyclif.

Arundel's letters were addressed to a wide variety of recipients. Those to Henry IV were generally brief and often affectionate; some are noted as written in his own hand.[29] To his suffragans, even the greatest of them such as Henry Beaufort, he often wrote tetchily. As he made clear in 1399, he expected them to set high standards and did not hide his disappointment when they fell short.[30] More revealing are the letters he wrote at moments of crisis, be they prolonged (his exile) or transient (the ambush at Kingston in 1400, the fracas at Oxford in 1411), which show him at his most emotionally overwrought. Describing his attempt to visit Oxford in 1411, he wrote that

> Arriving that very Friday [7 August] in the church of St Mary in Oxford, with the University in attendance, and having begun a sermon on the theme 'Come into the garden',[31] I was somewhat anxious on account of their unbridled presumption and eagerly hoping for some royal support for our holy church of Canterbury to arrive in that garden, and recalling to my heart the dove which returned with an olive branch to Noah's ark as a sign of God's mercy, when behold!, just as the sermon ended, your serenity sent me the mercy I longed for, a dove with an olive branch . . . that is to say, your royal letters, sweeter to me than the fragrance of all the balsam and frankincense for which my heart has ever pined . . . and my heart leapt for joy and I burst into tears . . .[32]

Equally effusive is the account which he sent to the Canterbury convent of his near-capture by the rebel earls during the Epiphany Rising, which he likened to the tribulations of Odysseus, St Paul's shipwreck off Malta and the tricephalous hound of hell: 'We would say, indeed, that we were with Paul in the perils of journeying alone by sea. We escaped Scylla and fell upon Charybdis. We heard the voices of the Sirens but did not suffer shipwreck. We overcame the Hydra. We crushed the three-headed Cerberus (*Tricerberum*).'[33]

These conceits were hardly obscure, but Arundel liked to showcase his classical as well as his biblical learning, as demonstrated by the letter he sent from Florence to Prior Chillenden in January 1398. This included nine citations from the Bible, one from the Roman Christian poet Aurelius Prudentius Clemens (348–*c.* 405),[34] and an attempt to imitate the elocutionary embellishments of the neoclassical *cursus curie Romane* favoured by the humanists whom he met in Florence. The *cursus* was a stylistic adornment based on assonant syllabic juxtapositions and the rhythmic repetition of words or phrases. Arundel's friend Coluccio Salutati was a noted exponent of the art, his letters praised by the Florentine Signoria as 'marvellously crafted and copied all over the world'. The opening to Arundel's letter includes *vidistis* and *gratissima* twice each, *lacrimabiles* and *lacrimancium*, *pacienciam* and *pacientissimo*, followed by *omne datum optimum et omne donum perfectum.*[35] Yet by relying too heavily on simple word-repetition rather than syllabic rhythm, his 'ambition to impress' was 'markedly unsuccessful', revealing instead his incompetence in the absence of a trained secretary.[36]

Repetition on a larger scale was in part responsible for that preachy prolixity which came so easily to many prelates, Arundel included, especially when addressing questions of ecclesiastical protocol, about which he was punctilious. To cite multiple examples of prolixity would obviously be tedious, so one illustration must serve for many. On 10 February 1402, Arundel sent a mandate to Robert Braybrooke, bishop of London, telling him to inform all his subjects in the city that if they recited the Lord's Prayer and the Hail Mary five times whenever they heard the ringing of the bells at daybreak, they would be granted an indulgence of forty days. However, before getting to the point of the mandate, which is only revealed in the final section, Arundel evidently felt the need for an extended homily on the Blessed Virgin Mary and her special place in England's history:

> To our right reverend brother, Lord Robert, by the grace of God bishop of London, greetings. While we lift our eyes about us and

behold attentively with circumspect consideration how the most high Word that was in the beginning with God chose to him a holy and immaculate virgin of the kingly stock, in whose womb he took true flesh by divine inspiration, that the merciful goodness of the Son of God, who was uncreated, might abolish the sentence of condemnation which all the posterity of mankind, that was created, had by sin incurred: amongst other labours in the vine of the Lord of Hosts ['Lord of Sabaoth'] we sung to God our Saviour with great joy in him, carefully thinking, that though all the people of the Christian religion did extol with voices of praises so worthy a virgin, by whom we received the beginnings of our redemption, by whom the holy day first shone upon us, which gave us hope of salvation; and although all the same people were drawn to reverence her, which, being a happy virgin, conceived the Son of God, the King of Heaven, the Redeemer and Saviour of all nations, ministering light to the people that were miserably drowned in the darkness of death: we truly, as the servants of her own inheritance, and such as are written of to be of her special dowry, as we are by all men's admission acknowledged to be; we, I say, ought to demonstrate more assiduously than any others the endeavours of our devotion in praising her who, being hitherto merciful to us, who are truly cowards, so that our power – being, as it were, spread abroad everywhere through all the coasts of the world with a victorious arm, fears all foreign nations – that our power, being on all sides so defended with the buckler of her protection, might subdue unto her victorious standards, and make subject unto us, nations both near at hand and far off; likewise our happy estate, all the time that we have passed since the beginning of our lives, may properly be attributed only to the help of her medicine; to whom also we may worthily ascribe now of late in these our times, under the mighty government of our most Christian king, our deliverance from the ravening wolves, and the mouths of cruel beasts, which had prepared against our banquets a mess of meat mingled full of gall, and hated us unjustly, secretly lying in wait for us, in recompense for the good will that we showed to them; so that she, therefore, being on high, sitting before the throne of the heavenly Majesty, the defender and patroness of us all, being magnified with all men's praises, may more plentifully exhibit to us, the sons of adoption, the teats of her grace, in all those things that we shall have to do: at the request of the special devotion of our lord the king himself, therefore, we command and enjoin you, brother . . .

And so, at last, he gets to the point.[37] Arundel would probably not have drafted this himself, but he must have given a good indication of what was required, leaving it to his secretary or a well-trained clerk to fashion the flourishes. The object was not just to explain, but also to stimulate devotion, to provide opportunities for the public demonstration of approved forms of worship and, by emphasizing England's special place as the Blessed Virgin Mary's 'dowry', to associate her worship with national pride.[38]

There were times, of course, when prolixity was necessary, because it enhanced precision: the ponderous and repetitive Latin of the *Record and Process of Richard II's Deposition*, of which Arundel was probably the principal author, was not just for clarification but also to make it as legally and constitutionally watertight as was possible in awkward circumstances. The *Constitutions*, likewise, did their best to delineate precisely what was to be permitted, licensed or prohibited, as Arundel had tried to do since he first encountered Lollardy.[39]

Also unavoidably prolix were the numerous arbitrations between disputants which he was called upon to settle, for here too clarity was of the essence. Arundel had an enviable reputation as a conciliator and was in great demand. His excellent relations with the Christ Church community were due in part to the assistance he gave them in settling their quarrels.[40] His preferred method was simple and effective. He demanded pledges beforehand obliging the parties to accept his decision. After hearing the evidence, he drew up as clear and comprehensive a composition as he could, generally tending to favour established authorities (prelates, urban elites), but trying to offer something to both sides, tempering political expedience with humanity in the hope of forestalling defiance. He did his best to avoid vindictiveness.[41] However, if he became convinced of wrongdoing by either side, the sentences he imposed could be harsh, such as forcing priors or archdeacons to resign, expelling or even imprisoning troublemaking monks (as at Ely, or Walsingham, or Glastonbury). In these cases, his authority was indisputable.

When it came to political disagreements at the national or even international level, such tactics were less practicable. Even so, his preference for conciliation did bring rewards, especially when backed by royal authority. If the parliament of 1399 fell short of the reconciliatory panacea he and Henry had hoped for, it would surely have been a bloodier affair without their moderation. In 1406, after months of wrangling, it may well have been Arundel who finally brokered the deal between king and commons.[42] Inevitably, there were times when Arundel's settlements failed, as at Norwich cathedral, which endured two mulish bishops in succession, or when entrenched positions proved insuperable. At Oxford university, it was royal power, not archiepiscopal, which finally brought the dissidents to heel. Arundel had plenty of political spats (how could he not have?) and a few personal ones, but most of his contemporaries seem to have seen in him the conciliatory sagacity expected of the crown's chief counsellor.

At his death in 1414, the books in Arundel's study and the ornaments in his oratory were jointly valued at £352 and the books in his chapel at £207.[43] This was a substantial library, but individual volume titles are not given. Most of the books mentioned in other sources were liturgical or pastoral manuals. His testamentary bequests included two portiforiums (daily service books); a two-volume Bible; a psalter 'corrected according to the Sarum use'; the *Summa Confessorum* of Thomas de Chobham (d. *c.* 1235), one of the most popular confessional manuals circulating in England; the commentaries of the great Italian canon lawyer Johannes Andreae (d. 1348) on the Decretals and the Sext (here called *Johannes in Novella*: Johannes named it after his daughter Novella); and 'my book containing all the books of St Gregory in one volume', presumably the *Cura Pastoralis*, the most widely used medieval pastoral manual.[44] This was probably the copy of Gregory the Great's works bequeathed to him by Roger Walden in 1406. Arundel seems to have treasured it, indicative perhaps of the importance he attached to pastoral care. In his own will, he instructed that it should remain perpetually in Canterbury cathedral, never to be removed from the church, cloister, library or other place of honour within the same church for any reason; if that should happen, it was to be automatically forfeited to the current king of England and his successors, 'to be passed perpetually from king to king'.[45] Despite this, Arundel's principal executor, Gilbert Umfraville, gave it to Henry V '*pour inspection avoir d'ycell*', who loaned it to Sheen Charterhouse. It was still there in February 1424, when the prior of Christ Church successfully petitioned for its return to the cathedral.[46]

Others besides Walden gave Arundel books. The penultimate bequest in his will was for 'all my books which I had from Master John Barnet', his official (d. 1407), to be sold and the proceeds distributed between the friars of London and Canterbury to pray for his soul, but details are again lacking. Bishop Medford of Salisbury left Arundel 'my best pontifical' (a service book for prelates).[47] John Scarborough, rector of Titchmarsh (Northants), who must have met Arundel through John Lovell, gave him his copy of the *Clementines* with two glosses and the *Summa Summarum* of William of Pagula (d. 1332). The latter was a massive compilation of canon law texts with commentary; the former, also a canon law text, consisted of decrees issued in 1314 by Clement V and his two predecessors.[48] No doubt Arundel also appreciated the beauty of lavishly illuminated manuscripts: he borrowed from Christ Church the magnificent Eadwine Psalter, a product of the twelfth-century Canterbury scriptorium, which Chillenden and the chapter loaned him 'for his enjoyment' (*beneplacitum*).[49] He returned the favour by giving the cathedral a copy of the Franciscan William of Nottingham's commentary on Clement of Llanthony's *Unum ex Quattuor*, a popular gospel harmony, in addition to the two missals for his chantry.[50]

Most of these were the conventional vade-mecums of a medieval bishop: Bible and psalter, daily liturgy, guides to canon law and penitence. Although not a lawyer by training, Arundel must have acquired a reasonable knowledge of canon law, but lawyer-bishops such as Henry Bowet or John Trefnant had a great many more legal texts. Others – for example, William Rede of Chichester – collected scientific works. Arundel must have had a good number of books apart from those whose titles are revealed in the surviving sources, but there is no indication, despite his aristocratic upbringing, that he owned or indeed read the kind of works that lay nobles collected, which, as well as religious books, often included histories (of Troy, of Alexander the Great, the *Brut* and the *Polychronicon*) and treatises on hunting, etiquette or heraldry.[51]

The year he spent in Florence extended Arundel's literary interests. It was probably here that he acquired the copy of Augustine's *De Musica Ratione* which Salutati asked to borrow.[52] Arundel approved of religious music,[53] but his interest in the dauntingly technical *De Musica* probably had more to do with Augustine's view that the mathematical certainties of rhythm, harmony and proportion demonstrated that commitment to God required discipline of the soul: just as music followed orderly, divinely inspired, rules, so the world followed patterns laid down at the Creation. Studying music was thus a way to learn how to study the relationship between God, Creation and humanity.[54] Arundel seems to have been reluctant to send *De Musica* back to Florence: Salutati twice asked him to do so. He was, however, keen to read Salutati's *De Nobilitate Legum et Medicinae*, completed in the winter of 1399–1400, which his friend promised in his letter of January 1403 to send to England. This discussed the relationship between will and intellect, arguing that the active life, as long as it was governed by the law, was superior to the purely contemplative life, since virtuous actions were the only sure way to attain understanding of God's essence. Whether Salutati sent the book is unclear.[55]

Doubtless Arundel also read saints' lives, although references to him doing so are fleeting: the collect of St Etheldreda which he recited at Ely in 1401, or the *Life of St Edmund* which fortified him before his confrontation with the Lollard knights in the parliament of October 1404. The passage from the latter which gave him comfort was in fact a meditation on Becket as well as St Edmund, which made it doubly inspirational, for his namesake St Thomas – England's premier saint, Canterbury's patron, the personification of martyrdom in the cause of ecclesiastical liberties – was an object of special devotion to Arundel, as he was to so many of his successors. Becket's several feast days (return to England, martyrdom, translation) were always celebrated at Canterbury with notable acts of public veneration.[56] So too were the many feasts dedicated to the Blessed Virgin Mary, six of which, from her Purification in February to her Conception in December, were included on a list of holy days approved by Arundel in 1400.[57] As a devotee of the Cult of the Virgin, he was in tune with his times: the altars he consecrated in his private oratories and chapels were invariably dedicated to her, usually in conjunction with other (often Canterbury) saints.

It may be that the saint who, after Becket and the Blessed Virgin Mary, especially fired Arundel's imagination was St (King) Louis IX of France (d. 1270), whose 'wise advice' to his son and heir, Philip III, was one of the very few extraneous (non-administrative) entries in his register.[58] Louis's *Enseignements* were among the most popular meditative texts of the late Middle Ages.[59] 'Fix your whole heart upon God and love Him with all your strength', it began, 'for without this no one can be saved or be of any worth'; if God visit tribulations on you, thank Him for them, for you have deserved them; if He grant you prosperity, do not succumb to vainglory. Particular stress was placed by Louis on the importance of frequent confession to confessors who were not afraid to admonish; regular attendance at religious services combined with prolonged meditation; ways to avoid temptation; favouring the Church and consulting men of religion; upholding law and justice; ensuring that royal officers did not oppress the people; giving alms to the poor; and refraining from war against other Christians if at all possible, but if not, trying to spare the Church and the innocent. The emphasis throughout was on duty, on justice, on the exercise of high office in accordance with a code of morality governed by interiorized values derived from God via men of religion. In short, Louis's essay exhorted those in authority never to forget that God was looking over their shoulder and to use that knowledge to synchronize action with thought, body with soul, the public life with the private: an expression of the ideal of a moral world, barely practicable but undeniably inspiriting. For Arundel – not a king, of course, but a kingmaker and the holder for so long of high secular as well as high clerical office – it had undoubted relevance.

Louis's exhortation to 'Fix your whole heart upon God' struck a chord with another book which Arundel certainly read: *The Mirror of the Blessed Life of Jesus Christ* by Nicholas Love, prior of the newly incorporated Carthusian monastery of Mount Grace (Yorkshire) and one of the first authors to comply with clause 7 of the *Constitutions*. Based on an English translation of the pseudo-Bonaventuran *Meditationes Vitae Christi*, the *Mirror* was a retelling of the life of Christ, drawn from the gospels but including apocryphal, characteristically emotive, material arranged so as to provide 'lewd men and women and those who are of simple understanding' with a weekly programme of meditative aids to spiritual devotion. Arundel probably met Love when, as a benefactor of Mount Grace, he was granted confraternity in the house in January 1410. Shortly after this – 'around 1410', according to a memorandum added to several manuscripts of the *Mirror* – Love personally brought 'the original copy of this book' to London so that it could be 'inspected and duly examined' by Arundel 'before it was freely communicated'. Arundel, 'after examining it for several days . . . commended and approved it in detail and further decreed and commanded, in his own voice and by his metropolitan authority, that it should be publicly communicated, for the edification of the faithful and the confutation of heretics or Lollards'.[60] As it came to be circulated, the *Mirror* included several passages explicitly refuting Lollardy, focusing in particular on obedience to ecclesiastical authority, confession and the Eucharist, but whether these passages were inserted following Love's meeting with Arundel or included in his 'original copy' is unclear. Love had an abiding interest in ecclesiastical reform, and he may have included them in order to convince the archbishop to enforce his *Constitutions* more widely.[61]

Yet the real significance of Arundel's endorsement of the *Mirror* is not that it provided him with another stick to beat Lollards, but that it presented him with a way to satisfy the wishes of the many admirably orthodox English Catholics who would have been horrified to be thought of as heretics yet yearned for less ritualized forms of worship, less *distance* between them and God, than the Latinate pomp of the institutional Church allowed them, in order to achieve a more personal, affective dialogue with Jesus. What the circulation of the *Mirror* was intended to inspire was the widely favoured and approved practice of meditation, through which spiritual insight might be nurtured, much as Richard Rolle's *Fire of Love* had also inspired generations of orthodox Catholics. Describing Christ's crucifixion, for example, Love exhorted the reader to

> Take heed now diligently, with all thy heart, all those things that be now to come, and make them present in thy mind, beholding all that shall be done against thy lord Jesus and that be spoken or done against him. And so, with the inner eye of thy soul, behold some [people] setting and fixing the cross fast into the earth, some making ready the nails and the hammers to drive them with, others making ready and setting up ladders and ordaining other instruments that they thought needful, and others fast about to spoil [strip] him and draw off his clothes.[62]

Similar exhortations are repeated throughout the *Mirror*: to focus 'the inner eye of thy soul' on picturing, on *feeling*, the presence of Jesus and the ineffable significance of his ministry on earth. It is possible, though not provable, that Arundel organized some central system for dissemination of the *Mirror*. Its message was indeed for the 'edification of the faithful' as much as for 'the confutation of heretics', especially for the 'simple' faithful. And, like Rolle's work, it became enormously popular. It survives in sixty-four fifteenth-century manuscripts (surpassed only by the Wycliffite Bible, the *Prick of Conscience* and Chaucer's *Canterbury Tales*) and was printed nine times between 1484 and 1530. Emblematic of what has been termed Arundel's 'Counter-Reformation', it was still being recommended by Thomas More in 1532 as one of the books which 'moste may norysshe and increase devocyon'.[63]

Conclusion

Arundel died in the early hours of the morning of Monday 19 February 1414 in his lodge at Hackington, a mile or two north of Canterbury cathedral, and was buried on the following day, Shrove Tuesday, in his chantry chapel in the cathedral.[1] According to Thomas Gascoigne, writing some thirty years later, he was afflicted by a quinsy (distended abscess) in his throat which made it impossible for him either to speak or to swallow. Characteristically, Gascoigne could not resist adding that 'men believed that God had bound his tongue because he had formerly bound the tongues of almost all the preachers on account of a few heretics'.[2] Adam Usk was kinder, claiming to have had a vision that night in which he saw Arundel 'dressed in short clothes and running with great speed as if planning to journey afar; but when I tried, with a great effort, to follow him, he handed me a wax candle, saying "Break this in half between us two", before vanishing'. Realizing what this meant, Usk, 'with sadness in my heart', said a mass for his soul. It was towards 'the bliss of eternal life', he felt sure, that his 'lord of Canterbury' was sprinting.[3]

Arundel must have known for at least a week that he was seriously ill, for on 12 February he drew up his last will and testament. It began as follows:

> In the name of God, Amen. I, Thomas Arundel, a miserable and most unworthy sinner, by the forbearance (*paciencia*) of God, the

> most useless and tepid minister of the holy church of Canterbury, being of good and sound memory and, by divine mercy, in full knowledge of the Catholic faith, but by the same power greatly weakened in body, awaiting nothing apart from God's mercy and the moment of reckoning for this miserable, putrid cadaver, my body (*tempus resolucionis huius miserabilis putredinie et cadaveris corporis mei*) . . . devise, make and ordain my testament, including my last will, as follows. [He commended his soul to God and the Blessed Virgin Mary, to the patronal saints of Canterbury cathedral – Gregory, Augustine, Dunstan, Blaise, Alphege – and to all the saints in heaven, begging them in all humility to intercede with God] to forgive my sins, my faults, my ignorance and negligence, and to permit the soul of this miserable sinner, which he redeemed with his own precious blood, when it departs from this vale of tears and misery and its fleshly prison, to be liberated from the terrifying vision of demons [and] although this fetid and putrid cadaver of mine is too utterly vile to merit burial, especially in the holy church of Canterbury [nevertheless he asks to be buried in his 'new monument', his chantry chapel].[4]

Miserable sinner, putrid cadaver: this was the language of Lollards' wills, but also of many others in the plague-afflicted post-Black Death world who were decidedly not Lollards but upon whom God continued periodically to wreak his fearsome retribution for humanity's sins. A more extreme version of the testamentary self-abasement expressed by several members of his family, it also resonated with the penitential and introspective piety practised by such as his sister Joan. Does it mean that Arundel died believing himself a failure? He had, after all, just a few weeks earlier, received a chilling reminder that one of his driving ambitions, the suppression of Lollardy, remained unfulfilled. But it also suggests that behind the authoritarian and combative archiepiscopal persona lurked a more self-questioning mortal. Here, after all, was a man who, to many, epitomized the worldly, secularized prelacy routinely excoriated not just by Lollards but by so many of the faithful: the son of England's richest aristocrat; promoted to the episcopacy at an uncanonical age, probably simoniacally; an academic lightweight addicted to political office; a lover of jewels and fine vestments, whose goods at his death were valued at £6,008;[5] a man who had perjured himself to depose a legitimate king and who had shown himself willing at times to place the needs of the State above those of the Church – this was not a negligible charge sheet. Arundel's enormously privileged birth and wealth may have given him a layer of padding against what the world might throw at him, but what would God make of it?

Had he been in a position to read the fulsome obituaries of contemporary chroniclers, he would have derived some comfort from them. 'The unshakeable pillar of the Christian faith' who fortified the people and lit up the clergy, wrote Usk. Walsingham called him 'the tallest tower and undefeated champion of the English Church'. The author of the *Gesta Henrici Quinti*, one of Henry V's chaplains, remembered him as 'a man of exalted ancestry and profound wisdom, a noble defender of the Church, whom neither good fortune made proud nor adversity cast down, who more than any man anywhere since ancient times fought Christ's battles against the seditious [Lollards]'. His Canterbury obituarist, as noted above, praised his wisdom, his prudence, his diligence and sense of duty, the maturity of his counsel and his service to the crown, as well as his perseverance in bringing Lollards to book.[6] It was this quality – perseverance – which probably annoyed his enemies the most, and which explains why he was remembered primarily as a defender of the Church.

What contemporaries did not mention was his piety. Lanfranc is said to have wanted to be a hermit; St Edmund of Abingdon was 'by instinct an ascetic and a recluse' who, like Becket, is said to have practised self-maceration, 'a form of heroism which thirteenth-century society admired no less than it did physical prowess'.[7] To Arundel, excessive religious enthusiasm was suspect, liable to slip beyond control; hence his reaction to the Bianchi. Naturally, he believed in miracles, provided they were approved, but he never claimed to have witnessed one apart from the recurring miracle of the mass, the transubstantiation of the host.[8] The Eucharistic rite was the keystone of the Catholic edifice, the umbilical cord tying earth to heaven, the gateway to salvation. Irreverence to the host shocked him deeply, hence his reaction to the knights who turned their backs on it at Coventry, and his mystification at heretics who disparaged it. To imagine that he was not pious (in the best sense of the word) would be absurd, but it was his practical focus on leadership that impressed his fellow clerics. And sanctity, of course, was not always a primate's most helpful attribute. But no one ever accused Arundel of being a saint.

Nor was he a theologian, a logician or an exegete. Too much theological speculation, too much cleverness, was dangerous; that was the problem with Oxford. Arundel's mind was sharper than it was deep. Yet, if he did not have a first-class mind, he had a first-class temperament and a formidable reserve of political guile. Do not allow the archbishop to defend himself in parliament, John Bushy advised Richard II, because 'he is so superior to us in intelligence'. Exiling Henry of Bolingbroke, Richard forbade him from communicating with Arundel because he 'feared his wisdom and counsel'; he had already warned Pope Boniface not to be deceived by his cunning. What Richard was insinuating was low cunning, but in fact Arundel's cunning was of the higher sort. The French clergy longed for his 'astute qualities' and 'wise presence' at Pisa.[9] His reputation as a mediator, based on rhetorical skill, pragmatism, attention to detail and a sense of fairness, was second to none, a voice of reason in a fractious world. His estimation of others could be scathing, but he was also capable of great charm. His clerks and officials expressed uncommon admiration for him. Margery Kempe remarked on how 'benignly and meekly' he listened to her criticism of his servants, and went away 'well comforted and strengthened in her soul'.[10] The monks of Bury St Edmunds, initially alarmed at the idea of an archiepiscopal visit, were amazed at his conviviality and informality, as well as his tact in paying for his own accommodation rather than insisting on accommodation at the abbey.[11] Although keenly aware of the eminence of the offices he held, Arundel did not stand on his dignity. Nor did he exploit high office for personal gain: he did not practice nepotism and was never accused of corruption, sexual immorality or excessive indulgence.

Arundel's four decades as a bishop (1373–1414) coincided almost exactly with a potentially existential crisis for the unity of Christendom (the Great Schism of 1378–1417 and the battle of Nicopolis in 1396[12]) and for the English Church in particular, in the form of Lollardy. It was also a dangerous time for English archbishops, two of whom suffered violent deaths (Simon Sudbury in 1381, Richard Scrope in 1405) and two others exile (Alexander Nevill in 1388, Arundel in 1397), victims of the social and factional rancour which rent the kingdom apart. Following his restoration, Arundel knew that his continuance as primate depended on the continuance of the Lancastrian dynasty. If it fell, so in all probability did he – and he acted accordingly, marshalling his clerics' moral and material support behind Henry IV even at the risk of forfeiting his credibility as their protector. There were some among the clergy who doubtless considered Arundel to be *too* close to the king, yet the cohesion of the English prelacy barely wobbled. One reason for this was because he inherited Archbishop Courtenay's hard line against Lollardy and hardened it further. Yet he never wanted to burn heretics; he wanted them to save themselves. There was always a presumption of innocence for suspects and many continued to preach and disseminate their heterodoxy for years without serious punishment. Those who recanted went free. He certainly did not introduce heretic-burning to England.[13]

It is easy to say with hindsight that he took Lollardy too seriously, that it was never a real threat to either Church or State, that the events unfolding in Bohemia could never happen here. But there is no mistaking the conviction of many contemporaries that it was, that they could. For the Church, Lollard agitation during these decades was an ever-present drumbeat. For the secular authorities, it periodically retreated out of earshot, but they would not have failed to notice that it tended to quicken at times of political crisis, or when the king was absent or vulnerable. Notable upsurges of Lollard agitation (and stricter government measures against it) are detectable in 1381–2 (the Great Revolt), 1388 (the Merciless Parliament), 1395 (Richard II's absence in Ireland), 1399–1401 (the usurpation), 1410 (Henry IV's illness and quarrel with his son) and 1413–14 (Henry V's accession). Apart from Oldcastle's last desperate gamble, these did not aim to overthrow royal authority: they aimed to persuade king and parliament to take a more active role in reforming the Church – the Erastianism advocated by so many of its critics. That is why the Lollards' loudest drum rolls tended to coincide with crisis parliaments, those which appeared to herald change. It also explains why both Henry IV and Henry V lent their support to the Church's campaign to silence them.

Although there is no doubting the close bond between Arundel and Henry IV, this could never be an equal partnership. When the stakes were at their highest, after the arrest of Richard Scrope, the king could afford to dismiss Arundel's pleas for mercy, but the archbishop could not afford to ignore Henry's pleas for money. Although indubitably orthodox, Henry was inquisitive about religious matters and interested in speculative thinking – hence his attempts to restrain Arundel at Oxford in 1411, and his appointment of the ex-Lollard Philip Repingdon as his confessor.[14] There are hints that he found Arundel's fastidious insistence on clerical liberties a little irritating: witness, for example, his reaction to the incident of Richard Alkrinton and the curry-comb. Henry was often suspected of being too lenient on the Church's critics and was not always the first to condemn parliamentary proposals for disendowment, even the revolutionary bill submitted to the parliament of 1410, for which no one appears to have been punished, despite the 1406 statute having ruled that it was an imprisonable offence and strongly associated with heresy.[15] The problem for Arundel was that for everything he held most dear – the suppression of Lollardy, clerical independence from secular encroachment, the resolution of the Schism – he needed royal support, and this came at a price. In the end, the exigencies of the crown outranked those of the Church, and Henry's reign witnessed some erosion of the Church's liberties, especially during the first half of the reign, and with it another lurch towards the integration of the English Church into the apparatus of the State.[16]

From around 1406, however, the English prelacy began to recover its nerve. As chancellor as well as archbishop, Arundel harnessed ecclesiastical and political power in the service of orthodoxy. The most obvious sign of this was the drafting and promulgation of the *Constitutions*, which for decades remained the yardstick by which those suspected of heresy were investigated.[17] Similarly indicative of this renewed confidence was his authorization of Nicholas Love's *Mirror*, arguably the start of what has been characterized as the 'orthodox self-reform' of the English Church under Chichele, or even as 'Thomas Arundel's Reformation'.[18] Veneration of saints – often a marker between orthodoxy and heterodoxy – was actively promoted, along with processions and pilgrimage, as per clause nine of the *Constitutions*.[19]

With Oxford positioning itself as the home of this reinvigoration following the 1411 commotion, a more accessible and digestible style of preaching was developed which included the reclamation of the vernacular 'to make it fit for precise and nuanced theological thought'. The summoning in March 1413 of a new general council of the Church made the task doubly urgent.[20] Anxious to demonstrate their commitment to orthodoxy, the masters and doctors of the university sent Henry V a schedule of forty-six petitions to be forwarded for the council's consideration, based in part on Richard Ullerston's 1408 programme for reform at Pisa, but going considerably further. One of the more notable, indicating their desire to reclaim the vernacular for orthodoxy, was the forty-sixth, which pointed out that 'clumsy and incompetent' translations of books and treatises had misled many 'simple idiots' and recommended their wholesale confiscation until replaced with approved translations by 'scholars who are not suspect'.[21] Arriving at Constance in the spring of 1414, one of the English delegates bullishly informed the council that, thanks to Arundel, every suspect master in England had now abjured Lollardy.[22]

Yet, for all his determination to extinguish what he saw as out-and-out heresy, Arundel was not blind to the fast-shifting patterns of late fourteenth-century belief and worship. He showed greater understanding of Margery Kempe's way of life than most of his contemporaries (as also did Repingdon) and was quite willing to approve a variety of devotional practices as long as ecclesiastical jurisdiction was not compromised.[23] This was the crucial point. Arundel did not set out to make every Christian in England conform to one and only one mode of religious observance; but he did need them to acknowledge the Church's authority and, as he came to realize, the surest way to do this was to gather what was best about the more individualized devotion of late medieval spirituality under the Church's umbrella. This was, after all, the age not just of Lollardy but also, in the Low Countries, of the *Devotio Moderna*, which Arundel probably experienced at first hand during his exile.[24] Like the Lollards, followers of the *Devotio Moderna* hated the wealth and worldliness of the clergy and advocated independent devotional practices, but unlike Lollards – perhaps because they lacked a Wyclif to drive such views to their logical end-point – they stopped short of denying papal supremacy or transubstantiation or rejecting public forms of worship. As a result, rather than being persecuted, they were gradually channelled into the Church's broader current, where their energy and popular appeal strengthened rather than undermined it. To unify the faithful – the most important goal – it was necessary not just to accept a degree of devotional individualism but to foster it and infuse the Church with its enthusiasm.

Although it was not until after Arundel's death, under Henry V and Archbishop Chichele, that this orthodox reformation really began to make a difference, the lines along which it would develop – a more accessible style of preaching to the laity, delivered in the vernacular by graduates under the guidance of bishops such as Philip Repingdon and Richard Fleming, gradually recapturing the ground from the famously down-to-earth Lollard preachers – were already being established. Lincoln College, Oxford, was founded by Fleming – no longer the suspect 'beardless youth' of 1411 – explicitly to be a theological college, a bastion of orthodoxy. It was Oxford masters and doctors and Oxford-trained bishops who led the way here – the enduring consequence of the bruising struggle to purge the university of heresy.[25]

Throughout these wider struggles, Arundel never lost sight of his diocese, to which he returned whenever he could in order to fulfil his pastoral role and, as far as he could, to enforce the kind of reforms – against non-residence, or pluralism – which had troubled him through his years firstly at Ely and then at York. It is perhaps surprising in the light of this – and of his wealth – that Arundel does not appear to have left any provision for clerical education, the prerequisite for effective instruction of the laity, as several of his episcopal contemporaries did: not just the much-vaunted founders of university colleges such as William Wykeham (New College), Richard Fleming (Lincoln College) and Henry Chichele (All Souls), but also the less celebrated such as Richard Clifford, who bequeathed £666 for his scholars at Burnell's Inn in Oxford, Edmund Stafford, a generous benefactor of Exeter College, and Thomas Langley, who founded a song and grammar school for poor children at Durham.[26] It is hard to believe that the education of the clergy at grass-roots level – the parish priest or vicar – was not one of Arundel's priorities, especially given the dearth of priests in the wake of the Black Death. Of course, one of the purposes of his visitations was to ensure that educational opportunities were available in each diocese, but apart from this there is little evidence in his register of concern for it (compared, for example, to non-residence). Most fifteenth-century bishops took a more active interest in clerical education.[27] When Thomas Rotherham, archbishop of York (1480–1500), founded Rotherham School (Yorkshire) in 1483, he explained what motivated him. In his boyhood, he wrote,

> without letters, we would have stood there untaught, illiterate and rough for many years, had it not been that by God's grace a man

> learned in grammar arrived, from whom, as from a primal font, we were, by God's will, instructed and, under God's leadership, came to the state in which we now are, and others arrived at great positions. In order that there always be such a fountain . . . and because that country produces many young men of great sharpness and ability . . . [he established one teacher of grammar, one of music, one for writing and science, and one for theology].[28]

But Arundel, of course, had never been faced with the prospect of 'standing there, untaught, illiterate and rough for many years'.

Had Arundel's term of exile in 1397–9 matched Richard II's intention that it should be for life, he would be remembered primarily not as a prelate but as a politician.[29] More specifically, he would be remembered, as the chroniclers of the time depicted him, as a bulwark against Richard II's incipient tyranny in the mid-1380s, a moderating influence on the king's government during the early 1390s and the undeserving victim of Richard's reckless drive for unfettered power after 1397. Had he suffered the same fate as his closest allies in the Appellant movement, his brother and the duke of Gloucester – and he was, after all, convicted of treason – it is more than likely that he would have become a 'political saint' like Simon de Montfort or Thomas of Lancaster, uncanonized but popularly venerated as sacrificial victims of kings who sought to do away with England's traditional liberties. He might even have been canonized, like Thomas Becket.

Although this high-profile political role during the 1380s and 1390s evolved as a reaction to the folly of an inadequate king and the ineptitude of a venal government, it is highly probable that Arundel's innate political instincts, combined with his aristocratic parentage, would, at almost any time, have propelled him to governmental positions of power and influence.[30] Whether he had what might be termed a 'political programme' is harder to know. The closest approximations to it are the speech he (and Gloucester, which confuses the issue) are alleged to have delivered to Richard II at Eltham in 1386, and the manifesto detailing Richard's crimes, the 'Record and Process', which Arundel is widely assumed to have drafted. The former, as already noted, has a rather contrived feel to it.[31] The latter was first and foremost a justification for Richard's deposition, but it was also implicitly a statement of the moral and legal standards by which Arundel believed the country should be ruled and against which his and Henry's future conduct of government would be measured: not by fear, threats and lies, the imposition of summary financial exactions or disregard for legitimate representational and possessory rights; in short, not by acting, as the 'Record and Process' accused Richard, 'as if the laws were in his mouth, or in his breast'.[32]

To be sure, Arundel's instincts were authoritarian. According to William Thorpe, he declared that 'if a sovereign bids his subject do something that is sinful [*vicious*], this sovereign is to blame for it, but the subject deserves to be rewarded by God, for obedience pleases God more than any sacrifice'.[33] Yet rarely were his actions autocratic. He always tried to carry convocation with him and usually succeeded. With one or two exceptions, his prelates respected and supported his leadership, and several of them had considerable affection for him.

Nevertheless, to argue that Henry IV ruled according to the principles implicit in the 'Record and Process' would be a considerable stretch. For a usurper to hold on to his throne required ruthlessness, military expertise, adequate resources and the avoidance of major errors. Henry made big mistakes and was fiscally imprudent; fortunately for him, he had military expertise in abundance and never shrank from ruthlessness. He survived, though barely at times, never as unpopular as Richard but not infrequently (nor unreasonably) accused of incompetent or arbitrary governance. For all that, there was an unmistakable difference between them: where Richard employed threats and intimidation, Henry recognized the limitations of royal power and sought consensus. There was a qualitatively different *feel* to Henry's kingship.[34] It is tempting to ascribe this in part to Arundel's influence, but it is probably closer to the truth to say that their views on governance were not dissimilar. Their shared experiences under Richard – open opposition in the late 1380s, exile and return a decade later – had created a tight bond between them and must have given them both a sense of how *not* to rule England. Henry knew that his primate was committed to his kingship and Arundel knew that the king was committed to his primacy.

No one was more closely associated with the inception and legitimacy of Henry's rule. His eight years as chancellor under Richard also meant that he had a good understanding of the needs of the crown. Already prominent in the political life of the kingdom before 1399, he now became dominant, 'greater and more powerful than anyone else in the kingdom of England apart from the king', even when not holding high secular office or formally a royal councillor.[35] England between 1399 and 1413 was, in some sense, a diarchy (though not an equal one). In certain respects, such as crown finance, Arundel's influence was crucial. It is no coincidence that the only period of relative exchequer solvency during Henry's reign was in 1407–9, when, as chancellor, the archbishop and the council adopted much the same fiscal principles as he had when, for example, introducing financial reform at Ely in 1401.

The fact that, taking his career as a whole, Arundel is remembered primarily as a churchman rather than a politician is due in part to William Shakespeare. Three of Shakespeare's most frequently performed history plays – *Richard II*, *Henry IV Part 1* and *Henry IV Part 2* – tell the story of the years 1397–1413, but not once does Arundel appear in any of them. There were good dramaturgical reasons for this. In *Richard II*, Henry is shown as a man of action and purpose, bulldozing his way to the crown on his own initiative, thereby providing a starker contrast to the beleaguered, self-doubting, prematurely aged monarch he later becomes. No archiepiscopal midwife or kingmaker is needed; he makes his own history. Of course, he could not do it entirely on his own, but it was the Percies whom Shakespeare credited with the role of his chief comrades-in-arms, thereby amplifying their rejection of his kingship four years later.[36] Brilliant drama this is (much the most important thing), but brilliant history it is not. In reality, Richard's downfall in 1399 was as much Arundel's doing as it was Henry's. It was his most significant contribution to the public life of 'this land where he had been born, and where he wanted to die'; for, as May McKisack concluded sixty-five years ago, if Richard's overthrow was a personal tragedy, his triumph would have been a nation's tragedy.[37]

Appendix I: Arundel's Goods at Death

(Canterbury Cathedral Archives, Register N, fos 221v–222r. Latin original)

[fo. 221v] Inventory of all the goods of the most reverend in Christ father and lord, Thomas Arundel, by the grace of God archbishop of Canterbury, who died on the seventeenth day of February in the year of the Lord 1413 [1414], as reckoned by Richard Everard and William Bury, mercers, and Nicholas Fitz Hugh and Richard George, goldsmiths, Thomas Charlton and Thomas Marlborough, stationers, Richard Wokysbrytte and John Causton, upholsterers, of London, sworn in the accustomed manner, as appears more plainly below under seal in each parcel.

Mitres: Two mitres, not valued, £133 6*s.* 8*d.*

The Hall: Item, eight hangings, with all their apparel, as valued by the aforesaid under oath, £66 13*s.* 4*d.*

The Chamber: Item, twenty-four bed-hangings with all their apparel, as valued under oath by the same, £179 10*s.*

The Wardrobe: Item, two pieces of arras, as valued under oath by the same, £30.

Item, the robes of the lord with linen sheets, mattresses and other small parcels in the wardrobe, as valued under oath by the same, £78.

The Chapel: Item, various vestments with cloths of gold, altar cloths and his other apparel, as valued under oath by the same, £460 19*d.*

Item, all the jewels of gold, silver and gilt, with crosses, images, chalices, panels, thuribles, stoles and other ornaments, valued as above, £455.

Item, all the books pertaining to the chapel, as valued by the same, £207 19*s.* 2*d.*

The Oratory with the Study: Item, the ornaments of the oratory with all the books of the study, as valued by the same, £307 8*s.* 6*d.*

Item, all the cups of silver and of gold with their lids, together with the gilded ewers, as valued by the same, £203.

The Cellar: Item, all the cups of pure gold together with one ewer and the covers for them, as valued by the same, £133 6*s.* 8*d.*

The Pantry: Item, all the salt-cellars of silver and gilt, vases of gold, silver and gilt, with the napery and knives of the lord, as valued by the same, £70 14*s.* 4*d.*

The Almonry, with ewers and vases for spices: Item, all the basins with lavers of silver and gilt, together with the boats and bowls for the almonry, as well as the spice-plates and bowls of silver for spices and fruits, as valued by the same, £298.

The Scullery: Item, chargers, plates, dishes, with salt-cellars of silver and caldrons, gridirons of silver, as valued by the same, £305 12*s.* 6*d.*

[fo. 222r][1] Item, all the pots of copper latten and kettles, together with pans, pipes, side-irons, racks, colanders, flesh-hooks and suchlike, as valued by the same, £19 8*s.* 5*d.*

[*Horses*]: Item, all the palfreys, coursers, sumpters, with the horses for the chariots and carts, with their harnesses and apparatus, as valued by the same, £82.

[*Stock*]: Item, the grains, stock live and dead in the hands of unknown farmers, £1,547 16*s.* 8*d.* and a farthing.

Item, corn in the hands of the lord, by estimation, £566 13*s.* 4*d.*

Item, livestock in the hands of the lord, by estimation, £316 8*d.*

Item, dead stock in the hands of the lord, by estimation, £69 14*s.* 1*d.*

Item, fixed rents and farms and profits from other sources, by estimation, £433 6*s.* 8*d.*

Sum Total Value: £6,008 12*s.* 7*d.* and a farthing.

Appendix II: Arundel's Register

The two volumes of Arundel's register as archbishop of Canterbury, one of the principal sources for this book, are in Lambeth Palace Library, catalogued as Reg. Arundel 1 (561 folios) and 2 (204 folios). The library also holds a microfilm of both volumes (LPL, Ms Film 704), as well as a four-volume handwritten index to their contents compiled by Andrew Ducarel in 1759 (LPL, LR/F/62/12–15). The LPL catalogue entries have brief guides to the layout of each volume;[1] so does David Smith's *Guide to Bishops' Registers of England and Wales* (Royal Historical Society, London, 1981), pp. 10–12.

Episcopal registers, initially adopted by all seventeen English dioceses during the thirteenth century and standardized during the fourteenth century, are the episcopal counterpart to the Patent and Close Rolls compiled by clerks working in the royal chancery. That is to say, they contain copies, sometimes summarized or abbreviated, of the incoming and outgoing correspondence, mandates, decrees, commissions and so forth issued or received by the bishop in the course of administering his diocese: a record of his official acts and a source of reference for future consultation. Archiepiscopal registers included additional material reflecting the primate's provincial responsibilities, such as episcopal consecrations and *sede vacante* administration, mandates to suffragans, metropolitan visitation records and fuller accounts of meetings of convocation.

Registers were compiled by the clerks employed in the bishop's or archbishop's administration under the supervision of his registrar or chancellor. For as long as a bishop held his see, they were written on separate quires of vellum folios according to a fairly well-established division of subject matter. At some point after his death or translation, these quires would be bound together between (usually) leather-covered wooden boards and consecutively foliated. Exactly when Arundel's register was bound in its surviving form is difficult to say. Writing in *circa* 1415–16, the author of the *Gesta Henrici Quinti* noted that the official record of Oldcastle's trial in 1413 'is contained in the archbishop's register', but the fact that the volume which includes it also contains six stray folios recording the proceedings of the convocation of 1444 (*sic*) makes it more likely that the chronicler had access to the copy of the trial record circulated by Arundel to his suffragans than that he had seen any complete or even roughly complete version of the archiepiscopal register.[2]

The inclusion of material from 1444 is symptomatic of the considerable degree of confusion in the final incorporation of Arundel's register. The intention, chronologically, is clear: volume 1 was to cover the years 1397 to 1408/9; volume 2, 1408/9 to 1414. For the most part it was adhered to, but not always. For example, the articles drawn up by convocation in 1399 begin on fo. 52 of volume 1 but are continued on fo. 5 of volume 2.[3] The record of the 1401 convocation begins on fo. 2 of volume 2 but is soon cut off and continues on fos 178–186 of the same volume. A few other examples are noted in the catalogue summaries referenced above. Broadly speaking, Arundel's registers contain quires recording: (1) proceedings of convocations; (2) administrative commissions and appointments of various kinds; (3) institutions and collations to benefices, vicariates, etc.; (4) probate of wills, both diocesan and provincial ('prerogative'); (5) royal writs received (highly selective); (6) compositions and agreements between individuals, churches, or clerics and lay folk; (7) ordinations of sub-deacons, deacons and priests; (8) records of visitations undertaken; (9) reports of suffragan diocesan administration *sede vacante*; and (10) miscellaneous memoranda, sometimes under headings such as *facta diversa* or *littere diverse*, but also including some papal bulls, cardinals' letters, a useful valuation of archiepiscopal benefices (volume 1, fos 258–259) and a record of wills proved between February and May 1414, between Arundel's death and Chichele's provision (volume 2, fos 201–204).

Arundel's register also contains three extraneous (non-administrative) extracts from well-known sources. The first and most interesting is on fo. 208 of volume 1: the 'Note of the wise advice of the king of the French given to his son Philip' (*Nota consilium sanum Regis Francorum datum filio suo Philippo*). The possible significance of this has already been mentioned.[4] It is placed in the middle of a long section on testamentary business and was clearly deliberately inserted into Arundel's register. The second extract appears on the dorse of volume 1, fo. 561, the last folio of a quire of royal writs (fos 550–561). It is a summary of the second article ('*De Clero*') of the well-known early fourteenth-century tract entitled *Modus Tenendi Parliamentum* ('The Way of Holding Parliaments'), which explained the procedure for summoning the clergy to parliament. It probably relates to a writ from the king to Arundel in the same quire (fo. 556r) dated 20 October 1403, a time when Henry was putting great pressure on the clergy to grant additional taxation and had summoned a parliament to meet on 3 December at Coventry (later prorogued to Westminster, January 1404). It ordered Arundel to ensure that not just he and all his bishops attended, but also that the prior and chapter of Canterbury and all the archdeacons and clergy of his diocese were represented there in person by two proctors who had 'full and sufficient power' to make whatever grant of taxation was agreed. In other words, the king was looking to extend the clerical tax base (as much additional evidence indicates), and the archbishop or one of his clerks may have been checking the protocol for clerical representation.[5] The third extract is on the dorses of fos 3–4 of volume 2. It is an abbreviation of the twelfth-century chronicler Henry of Huntingdon's account of the English Church and kings during the second half of the tenth century, emphasizing that this was a great age of monastic foundations, many of which were destroyed when the Danes renewed their attacks.[6] Although this does not appear to be related to the rectos of these folios (a record of the 1401 convocation), it was a theme – the defence of monasticism – which doubtless resonated with Arundel and his clerks at a time when monasticism in particular was under threat of disendowment.

Notes

Abbreviations Used in the Notes

Full titles are given in the Bibliography.

ANLP	*Anglo-Norman Letters and Petitions*
BIHR	*Bulletin of the Institute of Historical Research*
BJRL	*Bulletin of the John Rylands Library*
BL	British Library, London
BRUC	*Biographical Register of the University of Cambridge*
BRUO	*Biographical Register of the University of Oxford*
CA 1 and 2	Churchill, *Canterbury Administration* (2 vols)
CCA	Canterbury Cathedral Archives
CChR	*Calendar of Charter Rolls*
CCR	*Calendar of Close Rolls*
CE	*Continuatio Eulogii*, ed. Given-Wilson
CFR	*Calendar of Fine Rolls*
CIM	*Calendar of Inquisitions Miscellaneous*
CIPM	*Calendar of Inquisitions Post Mortem*
Concilia	*Concilia Magnae Britanniae et Hiberniae*, ed. Wilkins
CP	*Complete Peerage*
CPL	*Calendar of Papal Letters*
CPR	*Calendar of Patent Rolls*
CR	*Chronicles of the Revolution, 1397–1400*, ed. Given-Wilson
EHR	*English Historical Review*
Foedera	*Foedera, Conventiones, Litterae, etc.*, ed. Rymer
Henry IV	Given-Wilson, *Henry IV*
HOC	*House of Commons 1386–1421*
HR	*Historical Research*
ISCA	*Incerti Scriptoris Chronicon Angliae*, ed. Giles
JEH	*Journal of Ecclesiastical History*
Knighton	*Knighton's Chronicle*, ed. Martin
Lit. Cant.	*Literae Cantuariensis*, ed. Sheppard

LPL	Lambeth Palace Library, London
Ms	Manuscript
ODNB	*Oxford Dictionary of National Biography* (online)
POPC	*Proceedings and Ordinances of the Privy Council*
PROME	*Parliament Rolls of Medieval England*
RA 1 and 2	*Register of Archbishop Arundel* (2 vols), Lambeth Palace Library
RHL 1 and 2	*Royal and Historical Letters of Henry IV* (2 vols)
RS	Rolls Series
SAC 1 and 2	*St Albans Chronicle*, ed. Taylor, Childs and Watkiss (2 vols)
Signet Letters	*Signet Letters of Henry IV and Henry V*, ed. Kirby
TA	Aston, *Thomas Arundel*
TNA	The National Archives, Kew
TRHS	*Transactions of the Royal Historical Society*
Usk	*Chronicle of Adam Usk*, ed. Given-Wilson
VCH	*Victoria County History*
Vita	*Historia Vitae et Regni Ricardi Secundi*, ed. Stow
WAM	Westminster Abbey Muniments
WC	*Westminster Chronicle*, ed. Hector and Harvey

Preface

1. Jon di Paolo, 'Mosley, Becket, Jack the Ripper Named on List of 10 Worst Britons', *Guardian*, 27 December 2005, https://www.theguardian.com/uk/2005/dec/27/highereducation.britishidentity.
2. Diarmaid MacCulloch, *Thomas Cranmer: A Life* (New Haven and London, 1996), p. 266; see also this volume, p. 204.
3. E. P. Thompson, *The Making of the English Working Class* (London, 1963), p. 12.
4. Walter was also the king's justiciar, an equally demanding role at that time, from 1193 to 1198. John Stratford was twice chancellor while archbishop (1333–4, and for ten weeks in 1340).
5. The dates in brackets indicate the years during which they acted as archbishop and chancellor simultaneously.
6. *TA*, p. 374.

Introduction

1. *The Book of Margery Kempe*, ed. Barry Windeatt (Cambridge, 2000), pp. 72, 108–11, 274.
2. Two other daughters, Mary and Eleanor, predeceased their father (Chris Given-Wilson, 'Fitzalan, Richard, Earl of Arundel, d. 1376', *ODNB*).
3. Chris Given-Wilson, 'Wealth and Credit, Public and Private: The Fitzalan Earls of Arundel, 1306–1397', *EHR* 106 (1991), pp. 1–26.
4. *Lit. Cant.*, vol. 2, p. 506.
5. *TA*, pp. 15–16; Jonathan Hughes, 'Arundel, Thomas', *ODNB*; *CPL*, vol. 4, pp. 129, 187. (See plate 2.) The earl had tried in the 1340s to secure a bishopric for his younger brother Edmund, treasurer of Chichester cathedral, but Edmund's death in 1349 put an end to this plan (*CPL*, vol. 4, pp. 128, 186, 194).

6. *BRUO*, vol. 1, p. 51: although sometimes described as M.A., he probably did not graduate from Oxford (Thomas Gascoigne, *Loci e Libro Veritatum*, ed. J. Thorold Rogers (Oxford, 1881), p. 181).
7. *TA*, pp. 14–18, 379–80.
8. For Newton's impressive library, see *Testamenta Eboracensia or Wills Registered at York*, ed. James Raine (6 vols, London, 1834), vol. 1, pp. 365–71; E. F. Jacob, *The Fifteenth Century, 1399–1485* (Oxford, 1961), p. 286.
9. The remains of the bishop's 'palace' at Downham are still a grade II listed site.
10. In June 1383 he visited King's Hall (the royal college) at Cambridge to settle a dispute between the warden and scholars; he removed the warden and appointed a new one (*CPR 1381–5*, pp. 352, 560).
11. *TA*, pp. 25–33 (for example, *Petitions to the Crown from English Religious Houses, c. 1272–1485*, ed. Gwilym Dodd and Alison McHardy (Woodbridge, 2010), no. 63).
12. *TA*, pp. 217 (quote), 422; C. M. Woolgar, *The Great Household in Late Medieval England* (New Haven and London, 1999), p. 16, reckoned the average cost per person per day in his household to be significantly higher than those of other lords or ladies.
13. Four of Arundel's household accounts from the early 1380s survive (*TA*, pp. 167–216); details here are from TNA, E 101/400/28, the account for November–December 1383. For Lovell, see *TA*, p. 182.
14. LPL, Ms 448, fos 78–79; the reliquary was probably given to the Black Prince by King Pedro of Castile (d. 1369) after the battle of Nájera (1367) in part-payment for the prince's military support.
15. For 'Arundel's group of clerks' in the Ely diocesan administration in the 1370s and 1380s and their influence upon his thinking, see Jonathan Hughes, *Pastors and Visionaries* (Woodbridge, 1988), pp. 174–250. Cf. Joy Russell-Smith, 'Walter Hilton and a Tract in Defence of the Veneration of Images', *Dominican Studies* 7 (1954), pp. 180–214.
16. Jonathan Hughes, 'Rolle, Richard', *ODNB* (revised 2008). Rolle's best-known work was *Incendium Amoris* ('The Fire of Love').
17. Hughes, *Pastors and Visionaries*, pp. 127–73, 184–8, 213.
18. Anthony Kenny, *Wyclif* (Oxford, 1985), is the best short introduction to Wyclif's life and theology.
19. For measures against Wycliffites in 1382, see J. Dahmus, *William Courtenay, Archbishop of Canterbury, 1381–1396* (University Park, PA, 1966), pp. 78–106; for 1388, see *WC*, pp. 318–20, 330; H. G. Richardson, 'Heresy and the Lay Power under Richard II', *EHR* 51 (1936), pp. 1–28; Ian Forrest, *The Detection of Heresy in Late Medieval England* (Oxford, 2005), pp. 40–7.
20. G. A. Holmes, *The Good Parliament* (Oxford, 1975).
21. *PROME*, vol. 6, pp. 8, 72, 112, 147, 189, 213, 218 (1381 commission), 270, 281, 310.
22. Chris Given-Wilson, *The Royal Household and the King's Affinity: Service, Politics and Finance in England, 1360–1413* (New Haven and London, 1986), pp. 117–18.
23. J. R. Highfield, 'The English Hierarchy in the Reign of Edward III', *TRHS* 6 (1956), pp. 115–38, at pp. 120–1.
24. *TA*, pp. 4–5, 15–16; *CP*, vol. 1, pp. 242–4. Edmund's heirs only reached a final settlement with the eleventh earl in 1396 (*CCR 1396–9*, pp. 72, 84). Two

other daughters, Alice and Philippa, probably the children of Eleanor and her first husband, John, Lord Beaumont (d. 1342), had no claim on the Fitzalan inheritance.
25. *CCR 1374–77*, pp. 413–14, 511.
26. *Henry IV*, pp. 26–8, 32.
27. *SAC* 1, pp. 325–39.
28. *WC*, 68–9.
29. Chris Given-Wilson, 'The Earl of Arundel, the War at Sea, and the Anger of King Richard II', in *The Medieval Python*, ed. R. F. Yeager and Toshiyuki Takamiya (New York, 2012), pp. 27–38.
30. Despenser, the 'warlike bishop', had been advised before departing that he should be accompanied by an experienced secular commander such as Arundel's brother Earl Richard, but refused to have him: *PROME*, vol. 6, pp. 311–12; *CPR 1385–89*, p. 34; *TA*, pp. 147–60.
31. *TA*, p. 159; *SAC* 1, pp. 778–80.
32. *SAC* 1, pp. 782–3.
33. Given-Wilson, *Royal Household*, pp. 103–5; *SAC* 1, pp. 792–6.
34. A tenth and fifteenth, the standard lay subsidy on movable wealth, normally raised about £37,000.
35. *Knighton*, pp. 352–62; *PROME*, vol. 7, pp. 31–4.
36. Knighton's phraseology (*Knighton*, p. 360) makes it clear that he believed that the 'statute' referred to Edward II's deposition, although it has also been suggested that Arundel and Gloucester were referring to the establishment of the lords ordainers in the 1310 parliament (*CE*, p. 52).
37. *CPR 1385–89*, p. 271.
38. For his assertion of his episcopal rights in Ely diocese, see, for example, *CCR 1377–81*, pp. 302–3; *CCR 1381–5*, pp. 42, 146, 182, 255, 464. Comparing him to de la Pole, Walsingham called Arundel a man 'who preferred justice to gold and equity to fine gold' (*SAC* 1, pp. 806–7).
39. Nigel Saul, *Richard II* (New Haven and London, 1997), pp. 148–204; Anthony Tuck, *Richard II and the English Nobility* (London, 1973), pp. 87–138; *Henry IV*, pp. 41–60.
40. Technically, Pope Urban VI translated Nevill to St Andrews, but since Scotland recognized the Avignon papacy this was ineffective. Rushook was moved to the 'modest' (impoverished) see of Kilmore (Ireland); he died in 1392. Nevill, too, died in 1392, having spent three years as a mass-priest in Louvain.
41. The monks of Westminster had some misgivings about Arundel, who had refused to support them in a dispute with St Stephen's Chapel. Another case involving sanctuary led a clerk, William Chesterton, to write a defamatory letter to the pope about Arundel; this seems to have been a case of disappointed expectation of a benefice (*WC*, pp. 303, 324, 336, 378–80; *CPR 1388–92*, p. 92; *TA*, pp. 346–8).
42. *TA*, p. 340; *WC*, pp. 10, 226, 232, 286; *Knighton*, pp. 408–12; *SAC* 1, pp. 832–4; *PROME*, vol. 7, p. 63; see also this volume, p. 235.
43. To mark his new status, Arundel purchased for £333 the mitre forfeited by Rushook following his conviction (T. F. Tout, *Chapters in the Administrative History of Medieval England* (6 vols, Manchester, 1920–33), vol. 4, p. 321, n. 1).
44. *CCR 1385–9*, p. 459 (confirmation by the king on 20 November 1387, when the Commission mandate ended).

45. Given-Wilson, *Royal Household*, pp. 104–5.
46. Tout, *Chapters*, vol. 3, pp. 417, 441–51; Saul, *Richard II*, p. 126; Gwilym Dodd, 'Clerical Chancellors of Late Medieval England', in *The Prelate in Late Medieval England and Europe*, ed. Martin Heale (Woodbridge, 2016), pp. 17–49.
47. B. Wilkinson, *The Chancery under Edward III* (Manchester, 1929), pp. 214–23.
48. Wilkinson, *Chancery*, pp. 215–16. It was granted on 16 October and cancelled on 12 November. It would have brought considerable financial benefit to Burley (*PROME*, vol. 7, pp. 37, 40–2, 46, 52; *CPR 1385–9*, p. 225).
49. Tuck, *Richard II and the English Nobility*, pp. 70, 131.
50. Dodd, 'Clerical Chancellors', p. 41.
51. *TA*, p. 351.
52. *Knighton*, pp. 528–30; *SAC* 1, pp. 864–6; *CPR 1385–9*, p. 676; Arundel's brother Earl Richard was likewise dismissed from his post as admiral.
53. Gilbert was restored to the treasury in August 1389, where he was succeeded by Waltham in May 1391.
54. *TA*, pp. 286–7; Hughes, *Pastors and Visionaries*, p. 190.
55. *TA*, pp. 244–5, 304–19; *CPR 1385–9*, p. 503.
56. *TA*, pp. 278–82, 290–3; *CPR 1385–9*, p. 483; *PROME*, vol. 7, p. 79; R. B. Dobson, 'Neville, Alexander', *ODNB*.
57. See Chapter 4 for visitations.
58. R. N. Swanson, 'Archbishop Arundel and the Chapter of York', *BIHR* 54 (1981), pp. 254–7; *TA*, pp. 277–8, 285–93; *Chronica Monasterii de Melsa*, ed. E. A. Bond (3 vols, RS, London, 1866–8), pp. xxix–xxx, 219–22.
59. William Courtenay also apparently rejected the offer of a cardinalate (by Urban VI, not Boniface), as other English bishops did around this time (*CE*, pp. xvi (and n. 1), 66; *CCR 1392–6*, pp. 399, 401–2; *CPR 1396–9*, p. 61).
60. *PROME*, vol. 7, pp. 190–1, 208–9; the same restrictions were placed on guilds, fraternities and civic corporations.
61. *Vita*, p. 132; *Knighton*, pp. 538–41; *Chronica Monasterii de Melsa*, vol. 3, pp. 217–19 and 218, n. 9; *WC*, pp. 482–3; Given-Wilson, *Royal Household*, pp. 106, 127–8, 140.
62. *TA*, p. 294; R. G. Davies, 'Thomas Arundel as Archbishop of Canterbury', *JEH* 14 (1973), pp. 9–21, at p. 12.
63. *WC*, pp. 498–500; *SAC* 1, pp. 924–38; Sarah Rees-Jones and Paul Dryburgh, eds, *The Church and Northern English Society in the Fourteenth Century* (Woodbridge, 2024), pp. 33–6; Nigel Saul, 'Richard II and the City of York', in *The Government of Medieval York*, ed. Sarah Rees-Jones (York, 1997), pp. 1–13; Caroline Barron, 'The Quarrel of Richard II with London', in *The Reign of Richard II*, ed. C. Barron and R. du Boulay (London, 1971), pp. 173–201; Christopher Fletcher, *Richard II: Manhood, Youth and Politics, 1377–1399* (Oxford, 2008), p. 211.
64. Dodd, 'Clerical Chancellors', p. 37, calls Arundel's 1391–6 term 'one of the most successful chancellorships' of the late Middle Ages.
65. Arundel was also technically 'Primate of England'; after centuries of dispute, it was agreed in 1352 that the archbishop of York was styled 'Primate of England' and the archbishop of Canterbury 'Primate of All England'. Michael Wilks, 'Thomas Arundel of York: The Appellant Archbishop', in *Life and Thought in the Northern Church: Essays in Honour of Claire Cross, Studies in Church History*, ed. Diana Wood, subsidia 12 (1999), pp. 67–86, argued that the episcopacy in the 1380s and

1390s was essentially divided between papalists and royalists, with Arundel one of the papalists, but it would be hard consistently to maintain such a viewpoint.

66. Peter Heath, *Church and Realm, 1272–1461* (London, 1988), pp. 213–18; *TA*, pp. 353ff; Dahmus, *Courtenay*, pp. 177–82; *PROME*, vol. 7, p. 147. The first 'anti-papal' statutes of Provisors and Praemunire were passed in 1351 and 1353, since when the issue had surfaced periodically, especially in the 1360s. The 1390 statute proposed harsher penalties for those who sought benefices from the pope.
67. *PROME*, vol. 7, pp. 227, 233–4.
68. Dodd, 'Clerical Chancellors', pp. 33–4.
69. Although he did deliver a sharp rebuke to the bishops in October 1389 when they agreed to allow the pope to tax the English clergy, 'at which the king marvels', saying tax should not to go to Rome (*CPR 1389–92*, p. 27).
70. *PROME*, vol. 7, pp. 258–9.
71. *SAC* 1, pp. 960–2; *CCR 1392–6*, p. 368.
72. *WC*, p. 520.
73. *ANLP*, no. 30 (probably 1393) and no. 266. Carpenter was presented to the vicarage in November 1395 (*CPR 1391–96*, p. 368).
74. On 25 November 1394 Arundel deposited these in Westminster abbey for safe-keeping. The cache also included an 'obligation' of the earl of Arundel, perhaps the surety for £40,000 of a few months earlier. The king's first will has not survived: *WAM* 9584; *CCR 1392–6*, p. 370; *CPR 1391–6*, pp. 587, 578, 596, 612, 615, 689, 706; *CPR 1396–9*, p. 13; *SAC* 2, pp. 8–28; Alison McHardy, 'Richard II: A Personal Portrait', in *The Reign of Richard II*, ed. Gwilym Dodd (Stroud, 2000), pp. 11–32, at p. 11 (and Appendix, p. 155).
75. A codicil to Courtenay's will shortly before his death declared that he thought himself unworthy to be buried in his cathedral or indeed any church, and asked that he be interred in the graveyard of Maidstone church. Arundel expressed similar sentiments in his will: Dahmus, *Courtenay*, p. 229; K. B. McFarlane, *John Wyclif and the Beginnings of English Nonconformity* (London, 1952), pp. 71–3.
76. *CE*, p. 72; *SAC* 2, p. 50.
77. It was apparently Arundel who recommended that he be replaced as chancellor by Edmund Stafford, dean of York 1385–95 (*TA*, pp. 362–3).

1 Exile (1397–9)

1. T. F. Tout, *Chapters in the Administrative History of Medieval England* (6 vols, Manchester, 1920–33), vol. 4, p. 9; *CPR 1396–9*, p. 50. The cross of Canterbury was transferred to him by Prior Thomas Chillenden at Westminster on 5 January, in the king's presence (*RA* 1, fos 3–5); *Vita*, p. 137. His transfer of 8,000 crowns (*c.* £1,333) to the Florentine Albertini bankers for the 'furtherance of certain business' on 1 February 1397 was presumably to pay his annates to the papal *camera* (*CCR 1396–9*, pp. 30, 43; W. E. Lunt, *Financial Relations of the Papacy with England II* (Cambridge, MA, 1962), pp. 728–9).
2. *PROME*, vol. 7, pp. 306, 312–13.
3. Richard may still have hoped that his half-brother, the earl of Huntingdon, would take an English force to Italy (*CPL*, vol. 4, p. 294).
4. *PROME*, vol. 7, pp. 306–7, 313–18, 329.

5. Alison McHardy: 'Haxey's Case, 1397: The Petition and Its Presenter Reconsidered', in *The Age of Richard II*, ed. James Gillespie (Stroud, 1997), pp. 93–114; Gwilym Dodd, 'Richard II and the Transformation of Parliament', in *The Reign of Richard II*, ed. Gwilym Dodd (Stroud, 2000), pp. 78–80, points out that, since Haxey sat with the lords in this parliament as proctor for the abbot of Selby, it is possible that his bill first emerged in discussions among the lords rather than the commons; it was not a common petition.
6. *PROME*, vol. 7, pp. 317–18, 321–2; *RA* 1, fos 8v–9. Tonbridge castle and lordship were the inheritance of the earl of Stafford, a minor in the archbishop of Canterbury's wardship. This grant (8 March) asserted the archbishop's rights against the executors but was reversed six months later (*CPR 1396–9*, pp. 92, 262).
7. J. Dahmus, *William Courtenay, Archbishop of Canterbury, 1381–1396* (University Park, PA, 1966), pp. 78–106.
8. *TA*, pp. 320–35. One of the first cases he had to deal with after moving to York was that of a Nottinghamshire chaplain and suspected Lollard sent to him as chancellor as well as archbishop (*CCR 1385–9*, p. 550).
9. Originally summoned for 19 February, it was delayed until the 26th to leave time for Arundel's enthronement.
10. *RA* 1, fos 44r–47v; *Snappe's Formulary*, ed. H. E. Salter (Oxford, 1924), pp. 144–56; *TA*, pp. 329–34; Jeremy Catto and Richard Evans, eds, *The History of the University of Oxford II: Late Medieval Oxford* (Oxford, 1992), pp. 232–4, 282–4.
11. *RA* 1, fos 44r–47v.
12. *CPR 1396–9*, p. 143.
13. *RA* 1, fo. 8v, 12 April at Canterbury. For the suggestion that Arundel and the archbishop of York also drew up a petition in early 1397 asking for the death penalty for heresy, see this volume, p. 90.
14. He held ordinations at Canterbury on 17 March and 7 April (*RA* 1, fos 324ff).
15. He also tried to resolve a dispute between Bishop Despenser and his Norwich chapter: R. G. Davies, 'Thomas Arundel as Archbishop of Canterbury', *JEH* 14 (1973), pp. 9–21, at p. 13; *TA*, p. 389; *CPL*, vol. 5, pp. 10, 11; *CPR 1396–9*, p. 107.
16. *SAC* 2, pp. 236–40; *CE*, pp. 86–8.
17. *PROME*, vol. 7, pp. 318–21; *CR*, p. 72.
18. *Vita*, p. 137.
19. *SAC* 2, pp. 64–72; *CE*, p. 72–4; *The Major Latin Works of John Gower*, ed. E. W. Stockton (Seattle, 1962), p. 302.
20. Michael Wilks's comment that Arundel 'was apparently willing to sacrifice his brother to save himself' ('Thomas Arundel of York: The Appellant Archbishop', in *Life and Thought in the Northern Church: Essays in Honour of Claire Cross, Studies in Church History*, ed. Diana Wood, subsidia 12 (1999), pp. 67–86, at p. 84) flies in the face of the evidence.
21. *SAC* 2, pp. 2–4.
22. *CE*, p. 76. Two thousand is probably a more realistic figure.
23. *TA*, p. 389. He was at Dunmow (Essex) on 24 July and at Croydon on 18 August. On 14 August he was told to summon convocation to grant the king a subsidy (*CCR 1396–9*, p. 213; Davies, 'Thomas Arundel', p. 13; *PROME*, vol. 7, pp. 331–430, *Usk*, pp. 20–37; *CR*, pp. 54–62; *SAC* 2, pp. 74–104).

24. *Major Latin Works of John Gower*, p. 308.
25. *CR*, p. 56; *PROME*, vol. 7, p. 347; *CE*, p. 80; *Usk*, p. 22; *SAC* 2, p. 80.
26. *SAC* 2, p. 94. Indicative of Earl Richard's enormous wealth is the list of his forfeited goods delivered into the treasury by the sheriff of Shropshire in April 1398: *Antient Kalendars and Inventories of the Treasury of His Majesty's Exchequer*, ed. F. Palgrave (3 vols, London, 1836), vol. 3, pp. 303–7.
27. It is uncertain whether he was convicted on the charge of being a party to the trials of some victims of the Merciless Parliament (*PROME*, vol. 7, pp. 349–50; *Usk*, p. 26; *CE*, p. 80).
28. *CE*, pp. 80–2. A fuller version of this conversation – or conversations – was later appended to the 'Record and Process', where it was stated that the archbishop warned the king that 'the consequences of these actions would ultimately fall upon his own head', and that Richard also tricked Arundel into handing over to him 'all the jewels and other goods of his chapel', which he swore upon the cross of Thomas Becket to keep safe for him until he was recalled, which would be before Easter 1398 at the latest. Later, however, Richard opened the chests containing Arundel's valuables and 'disposed of the goods as he wished' (*CR*, pp. 183–4).
29. *CPR 1396–9*, pp. 205–6, 244, 267, 307–8; *CCR 1396–9*, pp. 149, 184; *CIM 1392–9*, nos 215–366 (commissions to seize Arundel's lands, stock and movable possessions, 3 October onwards).
30. *CE*, p. 82; *CPR 1396–9*, pp. 217, 246 (24 October, protection to the scholars of Merton Hall, Oxford, since their visitor, Thomas, archbishop of Canterbury, was 'in remote parts'); the register of Prior Chillenden, appointed as his vicar-general, began on 24 October (*TA*, p. 373).
31. *Diplomatic Correspondence of Richard II*, ed. E. Perroy (Camden Society, London, 1933), no. 238.
32. Letters between London and Rome took from two to four weeks. Walden was provided to Canterbury on 8 November. By 21 January 1398 Arundel was 'late archbishop' and Walden had received his temporalities (*CPR 1396–9*, pp. 280, 286, 352).
33. *CE*, p. 86.
34. A. L. Brown, 'The Latin Letters in All Souls Ms 182', *EHR* 87 (1972), pp. 565–73; see *The Deposition of Richard II*, ed. D. Carlson (Toronto, 2007), p. 75, for another letter from Richard to Boniface, preserved only in a sixteenth-century copy, expressing equal amazement that Boniface had given Arundel any hope that he might be restored to his see, since the king knew his character 'to the marrow' (*ad medullas*).
35. *Lit. Cant.*, vol. 3, pp. 70–2; *Deposition of Richard II*, Appendix 4; see also this volume, p. 247.
36. In late January 1399 William was absolved by Pope Boniface from the excommunication imposed on him (by Roger Walden?) for joining Arundel at the Curia without his prior's permission, and was granted leave to remain with Arundel, 'whose chaplain and member of his household he was and is' for as long as he wished and to return when he pleased (*CPL*, vol. 5, p. 202).
37. One of Salutati's later letters to Arundel reminded him that he had conducted a visitation of the house of Sancta Maria degli Angeli at Florence and approved the way of life there. For the letters, see *Epistolario di Coluccio Salutati*, ed. F. Novati

(Fonti de la Storia d'Italia, 6 vols, Rome, 1896), vol. 3, pp. 360–3, 497–501, 618–21; D. Vittorini, 'Salutati's Letters to the Archbishop of Canterbury: A Note on Humanism in the Fourteenth Century', *Modern Languages Journal* 36 (1952), pp. 373–7.

38. Jonathan Hughes, *Dante's Divine Comedy in Early Renaissance England* (London, 2021), Chapter 2 *passim*.
39. G. Holmes, *The Florentine Enlightenment, 1400–1450* (Oxford, 1969), pp. 6–18, 94, 265; *Coluccio Salutati: Political Writings*, ed. S. Baldassari, trans. R. Bagemihl (London, 2014), esp. pp. 79, 95–101 (English translation of *De Tyranno* at pp. 65–143); *Epistolario*, vol. 3, pp. xiv–xvi.
40. Mannini was a Florentine merchant with commercial interests in England who had evidently hoped to profit from the turbulent politics of Richard II's later years (*Epistolario*, vol. 3, pp. 499–500).
41. Robert Brentano, *Two Churches: England and Italy in the Thirteenth Century* (Princeton, 1968), p. 225.
42. D. Bornstein, *The Bianchi of 1399: Popular Devotion in Late Medieval Italy* (Ithaca, NY, 1993), pp. 7, 50, 87–91, 162–87 (quote at p. 163); Alexandra Lee, 'Holy Macharoni? Miracles Encouraging Participation in the Bianchi Devotions of 1399', *Medieval Journal* 10, no. 2 (2020), pp. 43–68.
43. *PROME*, vol. 8, p. 37.
44. *SAC* 2, pp. 281–2.
45. *SAC* 2, pp. 426–7.
46. As suggested by the pope's absolution of William London in late January 1399.

2 Kingmaker (1399)

1. *SAC* 2, p. 60.
2. Nigel Saul, *Richard II* (New Haven and London, 1997), pp. 394–404.
3. *CR*, pp. 71, 76; Saul, *Richard II*, pp. 383–94.
4. Chris Given-Wilson, *Royal Household and the King's Affinity: Service, Politics and Finance in England, 1360–1413* (New Haven and London, 1986), pp. 270–1; *CE*, pp. xix–xli.
5. *CR*, p. 154; *Henry IV*, p. 123.
6. *Henry IV*, pp. 114–15; *CR*, pp. 89–91; *CE*, pp. 86–7.
7. *CR*, pp. 92–3; *CPR 1396–9*, pp. 425, 487.
8. *CR*, pp. 75, 92–3; *Henry IV*, pp. 115–16. Coincidentally, Duchess Margaret of Norfolk died on 24 March.
9. *Henry IV*, p. 124. With him was his seventeen-year-old nephew Thomas, eldest son of Earl Richard, who after his father's execution was placed in the custody of the king's half-brother, John Holland, but escaped and fled abroad: Thomas apparently joined Arundel at Cologne (*Historical Collections of a Citizen of London*, ed. J. Gairdner (Camden Society, London, 1876), p. 101).
10. The story of Arundel's vision is found in only one manuscript of Walsingham's chronicle (Oxford, Bodleian Library, Bodley Ms 462), and must have been written within a year of the revolution. Walsingham believed it had occurred at Utrecht on the night Gaunt died (3 February), but he also apparently believed that Arundel spent his entire exile in Utrecht. The details were in any case less important than the message the story conveyed (*SAC* 2, pp. xxxi, lii, lvi, 122,

138); neither Adam Usk nor the *CE* author, both personally closer to Arundel than Walsingham, mentions it.

11. R. L. Storey, 'Episcopal King-Makers in the Fifteenth Century', in *The Church, Politics and Patronage in the Fifteenth Century*, ed. R. B. Dobson (Gloucester, 1984), pp. 82–98; Saul, *Richard II*, pp. 405–24; *Henry IV*, pp. 123–47; *CR*, *passim*.
12. Whether or not Arundel accompanied Northumberland to Conway has been much debated. Jean Creton, who was with Richard at Conway and provides the fullest record of this meeting, does not mention him, but almost every other chronicler and the official record (the 'Record and Process') said he was with Northumberland, and the balance of probability is that he was (*CR*, pp. 123, 129, 136, 143–4, 155–6, 159; *Henry IV*, p. 135; J. W. Sherborne, 'Perjury and the Lancastrian Revolution of 1399', *Welsh History Review* 14 (1988), pp. 217–41; cf. Saul, *Richard II*, p. 416 (who thought Arundel was probably not at Conway)).
13. *CR*, pp. 162–72, 184–9; *PROME*, vol. 8, pp. 9, 25–6. Christopher Fletcher, *Richard II: Manhood, Youth and Politics 1377–1399* (Oxford, 2008), pp. 1–3, argued that Arundel's sermon was influential in establishing the trope of Richard's childishness (although he also demonstrates *passim* that this accusation was commonly levelled against Richard while he still reigned).
14. *CR*, pp. 38–40, 159, 169–70.
15. *CE*, p. 90. (See plate 3.)
16. *CCR 1396–9*, p. 520.
17. *Usk*, pp. xv, 80; R. G. Davies, 'Walden, Roger, Bishop of London', *ODNB*; *SAC* 2, pp. 86, 280, 298; *CE*, p. 82, called him 'a literate layman'.
18. *Usk*, pp. 60, 78–82; *CE*, p. 90; *Chronique de la traison et mort de Richart deux roy dengleterre*, ed. B. Williams (London, 1846), p. 227.
19. *Usk*, pp. 78–82; *CE*, p. 96; *CPR 1399–1401*, pp. 97, 215. He was also closely watched and arrested at the time of the Epiphany Rising in January 1400, but released after six weeks (*CPR 1399–1401*, p. 224).
20. *CPR 1399–1401*, p. 328 (granted two tuns of wine by the king, July 1400); Davies, 'Walden, Roger', *ODNB*.
21. The bull simply annulled his translation to St Andrews, since he had been translated unwillingly (*Concilia*, vol. 3, p. 246). *Usk*, p. 82, said Arundel's restoration had been foretold in an 'ancient prophecy'.
22. *RA* 1, fo. 51r: *Registrum de quarto anno reverendi in Christo patris et domini Thome dei gratia Cantuariensis archiepiscopi tocius Anglie primatis et apostolice sedis legati post exilium suum ad Angliam reversi* (see also *CA*, vol. 1, pp. 569–70, where it is suggested that Prior Chillenden of Canterbury acted throughout Arundel's exile as his vicar-general, even with Walden's acquiescence).
23. Arundel gave the opening sermon on 6 October, headed the list of triers of petitions and acted as their spokesman, presented the assembly with the 'Record and Process' of Richard's deposition and sought formal consent from the commons for the creation of the king's heir as prince of Wales and duke of Aquitaine (Guyenne). At times, he shared this role with the earl of Northumberland. Only when he petitioned for annulment of the sentence passed on him in 1397 and restitution of his arrears did he speak on his own behalf; both were granted without difficulty by 21 October (*CPR 1399–1401*, pp. 28, 37, 215, 269; *CE*, p. 97; *Usk*, p. 79; *ANLP*, no. xix).

24. *PROME*, vol. 8, pp. 9–11, 33–35; *SAC* 2, 242, 260, 262–5; *Usk*, p. 69; *CE*, p. 93, claimed incorrectly that 'Thomas Arundel, with the assent of all, condemned [Richard II] to perpetual prison'. The trial in parliament of a former king (in whose name it had been summoned) would have raised serious constitutional issues.
25. *SAC* 2, pp. 246–76.
26. *PROME*, vol. 8, pp. 85–6; *The Major Latin Works of John Gower*, ed. E. W. Stockton (Seattle, 1962), p. 323. A letter found in the king's chamber threatened rebellion if they were not put to death, but no one would admit to placing it there (*SAC* 2, pp. 276–8). The lords in question were demoted to their former titles (Rutland, Huntingdon, Kent, Somerset and Lord Despenser).
27. Henry's cousin the earl of Rutland, former duke of Aumale and future duke of York, was also suspected of plotting with them, which he may initially have done before betraying the conspiracy, although accounts varied as to how the plot was uncovered; either way, the king gave him the benefit of the doubt.
28. On a 'fine hill' outside the town, according to John Strecche (BL Add. Ms 35,295, fo. 262r).
29. *CR*, pp. 224–39; *Henry IV*, pp. 160–3; *CE*, pp. 96–9; *Usk*, pp. 86–9; *Traison et mort*, p. 247.
30. Richard died around 14 February, perhaps starved to death, but accounts varied.

3 The Episcopate (1399–1401)

1. Joel Rosenthal, 'Richard II's Bishops: Fair Weather Friends?', in *Creativity, Contradictions and Commemoration in the Reign of Richard II: Essays in Honour of Nigel Saul*, ed. J. A. Lutkin and J. S. Hamilton (Woodbridge, 2022), pp. 179–202.
2. For Rede, see Michael Bennett, *Richard II and the Revolution of 1399* (Stroud, 1999), p. 89.
3. John Fordham was first promoted to the see of Durham in 1381, when acting as the young king's keeper of the privy seal; he was translated to Ely – arguably a demotion, but a move to which he probably did not object – at the behest of the Appellants in 1388 (R. G. Davies, 'The Episcopate and the Political Crisis in England of 1386–1388', *Speculum* 51 (1976), pp. 659–93, at p. 683). A rough ranking order of the twenty-one English and Welsh bishoprics, reckoning prestige as well as financial value, suggests four tiers: (i) Canterbury, York, Durham, Winchester, Lincoln, London, Ely; (ii) Bath and Wells, Salisbury, Norwich, Exeter; (iii) Worcester, Coventry and Lichfield, Hereford; (iv) Chichester, Rochester, Carlisle, St David's, Llandaff, St Asaph, Bangor.
4. Peverell, a Carmelite friar, had been the child-queen Isabella's chancellor in 1399; after 1402 the Welsh rebellion made it too dangerous for him to live in his diocese, and in 1407 he was translated to Worcester (R. G. Davies, 'Peverell, Thomas, Bishop of Worcester', *ODNB*).
5. R. M. Haines, 'Erghum, Ralph, Bishop of Bath and Wells', *ODNB*; R. G. Davies, 'Bottlesham, William, Bishop of Rochester', *ODNB*.
6. H. Summerson, 'Strickland, William, Bishop of Carlisle', *ODNB*; he lived until 1419, but left little impression on national affairs.
7. This was at the behest of Gaunt, who wanted to see Beaufort provided for before he died. Buckingham was offered the less prestigious see of Coventry and Lichfield,

but refused translation; he retired to Canterbury for the last few months of his life, where he lived in Meister Omers, a house attached to Christ Church's monastic infirmary (A. McHardy, 'Buckingham, John, Bishop of Lincoln', *ODNB*).

8. G. L. Harriss, *Cardinal Beaufort* (Oxford, 1988), *passim*.
9. M. G. Snape, 'Skirlaw, Walter, Bishop of Durham', *ODNB*.
10. Since Scrope was promoted while in Rome, he may not have been Richard II's choice for York, although the reason why he was at the Curia was because he had been entrusted with a project close to the king's heart, the canonization of Edward II (P. McNiven, 'Scrope, Richard, Archbishop of York', *ODNB*).
11. A. Tuck, 'Stafford, Edmund, Bishop of Exeter', *ODNB*; *SAC* 2, p. 142.
12. R. R. Davies, 'Trevor, John, Bishop of St Asaph', *ODNB*.
13. R. G. Davies, 'Young, Richard, Bishop of Rochester', *ODNB*; *Henry IV*, pp. 459–60.
14. R. G. Davies, 'Trefnant, John, Bishop of Hereford', *ODNB*. (See plate 4.)
15. R. G. Davies, 'Mone/Mohun, Guy, Bishop of St Davids', *ODNB*; possibly one of the Mohuns of Dunster.
16. *RA* 1, fo. 13.
17. *RA* 1, fo. 246v. Before his promotion to the episcopacy, he held the living of All Saints, Maidstone, worth some £133 a year (*Lit. Cant.*, vol. 3, p. 48, n. 1).
18. See pp. 125–6.
19. *RA* 1, fos 23, 31v, 227r–228r (*qui me de sub pedibus hominum iacentem et pulvere ad London' ecclesie apicem sublimavit*); *Testamentary Records of the English and Welsh Episcopate, 1200–1413*, ed. C. M. Woolgar (Canterbury and York Society 102, Woodbridge, 2011), pp. 66–71. Walden also left Arundel a volume with the *Pastoralia* of Gregory the Great '*cum aliis*' and a red cape embroidered with gold thread, floral motifs, and images of archbishops of Canterbury and the martyrdom of Becket: R. G. Davies, 'Walden, Roger, Bishop of London', *ODNB*, and this volume, p. 327 n.46.
20. Arundel had the bull of Pope Gregory IX (1227–41) confirming this copied into his register: *RA* 1, fo. 14r–v.
21. *CA* 1, pp. 241–78; M. D. Knowles, 'The English Bishops, 1070–1532', in *Medieval Studies Presented to Aubrey Gwynn*, ed. J. A. Watt, J. B. Morrall and F. X. Martin (Dublin, 1961), pp. 283–96; Katherine Harvey, 'The First Entry of the Bishop: Episcopal *Adventus* in Fourteenth-Century England', in *Fourteenth-Century England VII*, ed. J. S. Hamilton (Woodbridge, 2014), pp. 43–58.
22. The removal of John Buckingham from Lincoln in 1398 was remarkable in this context.
23. *RA* 1, fo. 166; *Testamentary Records*, pp. 90–1 (William Bottlesham's will, dated 16 February).
24. *CA* 1, pp. 279–87.
25. *CPL*, vol. 5, pp. 8, 177, 288, 340. Papal provision had already been secured: *BRUC*, p. 76; *TA*, pp. 295, 316–18, 395; *Usk*, p. 95; *RA* 1, fo. 11 (consecration in Canterbury cathedral, 4 July 1400).
26. *RA* 1, fos 93 (appointment as Arundel's chancellor in 1399) and 206r–v (John Bottlesham's will: *ut idem dominus meus in cuius ditatione fiduciam gero specialem sit michi et executoribus meis infrascriptis in execucione testamenti huiusmodi sublevator, pater et protector*; he called Arundel *domino meo spiritualissimo*).

27. For Erghum's will, see *RA* 1, fo. 168v. For the contest for Bath and Wells, see R. G. Davies, 'Clifford, Richard, Bishop of London', *ODNB*; J. J. N. Palmer, 'Bowet, Henry, Archbishop of York', *ODNB*; R. G. Davies, 'Richard II and the Church in the Years of Tyranny', *Journal of Medieval History* 1 (1975), pp. 329–62.
28. *The Register of Richard Clifford, Bishop of Worcester: A Calendar*, ed. Waldo Smith (Toronto, 1976), no. 142 (entertainment at his enthronement).
29. Davies, 'Richard II and the Church in the Years of Tyranny', p. 333.
30. *BRUC*, pp. 83–4.
31. *RA* 1, fo. 11v.
32. *ANLP*, no. 290. He added that the patent for Niccolo Lucca, another member of the Albertini, had been sealed the same day, for which he thanked Arundel.
33. First fruits, the income of the first year from any benefice, routinely claimed by the late medieval papacy, would presumably have been passed to the papal *camera* (*ANLP*, no. 289).
34. *PROME*, vol. 8, pp. 111–12.
35. *CPR 1399–1401*, p. 470 (in theory, the temporalities were to remain in royal hands for the moment).
36. *CPR 1399–1401*, pp. 448, 508, 547–8 (confirmation of temporalities of both sees, August–September).
37. Two months later, after consecration on 20 November, Bowet repeated his profession in person (22 November): *RA* 1, fos 11v–13v; *CA* 1, pp. 265–6.
38. *Register of Richard Clifford*, pp. 28–9. However, Henry supported Clifford's release from paying the first fruits of Bath and Wells, which he had never held (*ANLP*, no. 289, presumably late 1401).
39. Thomas Gascoigne, *Loci e Libro Veritatum*, ed. J. Thorold Rogers (Oxford, 1881), pp. lxiii–lxiv, 21–2. For corroboration of Bowet's simony, see Margaret Harvey, *Solutions to the Schism: A Study of Some English Attitudes, 1378–1409* (St Ottilien, 1983), p. 162. Such stories were a medieval trope: Philip Augustus of France (1180–1223) was said to have asked the great scholar Peter the Chanter 'why we had so many bishops who were saints in the old days, and have none now?' Peter's answer was rather different (F. M. Powicke, *Stephen Langton* (Oxford, 1928), p. 57).

4 Visitations (1400–1)

1. *CA* 1, pp. 289–92; cf. *The Visitation of Hereford Diocese in 1397*, ed. Ian Forrest and Christopher Whittick (Canterbury and York Society 111, Woodbridge, 2021), pp. xv–xxi. *RA* 1, fos 14v–15r, records early objections to the practice of visitation dating from 1233 (Evesham) and 1244 (Norwich). Arundel was careful to cite thirteenth-century papal legates to England for his authority to undertake visitations (*RA* 1, fos 271r–274v, 279v).
2. To judge from their modern biographers in the *ODNB*, a majority of medieval English bishops were 'conscientious diocesans'. The survival of so many episcopal registers from the thirteenth century onwards allows such judgements to be made.
3. J. Dahmus, *William Courtenay, Archbishop of Canterbury, 1381–1396* (University Park, PA, 1966), pp. 107–60; *CA* 1, pp. 315–29. See also Bishop Trefnant's resistance to Courtenay (*Visitation of Hereford Diocese*, p. xx); *The Metropolitan Visitations of William Courtenay Archbishop of Canterbury, 1381–1396*, ed. J. H. Dahmus, Illinois Studies in the Social Sciences 31, no. 2 (1950). For a particularly unpleasant

story of a mid-thirteenth-century visitation by Archbishop Boniface of Savoy to St Bartholomew's in London, see Robert Brentano, *Two Churches: England and Italy in the Thirteenth Century* (Princeton, 1968), pp. 202–4.

4. *RA* 1, fo. 496r–v.
5. *CA* 1, pp. 145, 331; R. G. Davies, 'Thomas Arundel as Archbishop of Canterbury', *JEH* 14 (1973), pp. 9–21.
6. *RA* 1, fos 326r, 470r–473v (ordinations at Chichester, 12 June).
7. He sometimes went to London for council meetings (TNA, C 49/48/1, 16 June 1400; J. L. Kirby, 'Councils and Councillors of Henry IV, 1399–1413', *TRHS* 14 (1964), pp. 35–65, at p. 46), or the council sent messengers asking his advice (TNA, E 28/7, no. 70).
8. While at Shrewsbury, Arundel settled a dispute about financial safeguards to ensure honest dealing by the bailiffs and chamberlains of the town (*CPR 1401–5*, pp. 48–9; *VCH, Shropshire*, vol. 6, part 1: *Shrewsbury*, ed. E. Williamson (London, 2014), pp. 97–9).
9. There may have been a difference of opinion over the appropriation of the church of Denford (Northamptonshire) to Burghill's episcopal *mensa*, settled in his favour by the pope in December 1402, but he did not obstruct Arundel (*CPL*, vol. 5, pp. 369, 371, 473–4; Davies, 'Thomas Arundel', p. 18). Visitations often had an afterlife, with 'corrections' still needing to be made years later (*CPL*, vol. 5, pp. 509–10; *RA* 1, fo. 139r).
10. His response to a letter from the king in June 1403 concludes, 'May your royal highness flourish in prosperity and happiness for a very long time!' (*RHL* 1, p. 137).
11. *Usk*, pp. 248–50, retailed a story told at Arundel's dinner table about Burghill (*vir avarissimus*) hiding some gold which was found by nesting jackdaws and scattered far and wide, thus 'providing a lot of people with a windfall'; R. N. Swanson, 'Burghill, John, Bishop of Coventry and Lichfield', *ODNB*; A. McHardy, 'The Clergy in Parliament', in *The Reign of Henry IV: Rebellion and Survival, 1403–1413*, ed. G. Dodd and D. Biggs (York, 2008), pp. 136–61, at pp. 153–5.
12. Ten days later, Henry wrote to Arundel from Windsor asking his advice about his responses to the ambassadors of the Byzantine emperor and the king of France, and sending the lawyer and papal auditor Nicholas Rishton – soon to become Arundel's auditor (*ANLP*, no. 410, correctly 25 October).
13. *RA* 1, fos 476–489v (cf. *CA* 2, pp. 151–2; Davies, 'Thomas Arundel', p. 13). Arundel personally visited the cathedral churches at Lichfield and Coventry; major monastic houses including Shrewsbury, Haughmond, Chester and Nuneaton; and several colleges.
14. *CA* 1, pp. 332–5; *RA* 1, fo. 480.
15. Davies, 'Thomas Arundel', pp. 15–16.
16. While at Cambridge he issued statutes for the governance of Trinity College (*RA* 1, fo. 361v).
17. *RA* 1, fo. 101r. Fordham seems to have lost his grip; although he lived until 1425, when he must have been close to ninety, all that the Ely chronicler found to say about him was that he was 'old and full of days' and his gifts to the cathedral were less valuable than those of Arundel (LPL, Ms 448, fo. 79).
18. 'Metropolitical Visitation of Archbishop Thomas Arundel, 1401', in *Ely Chapter Ordinances and Visitation Records*, ed. S. J. Evans (Camden Miscellany 17,

London, 1940), pp. 44–51: *recognescens suam insufficienciam et inhabilitatem ad tantam regendam ecclesiam . . . renunciavit ad statim . . . non vi, non metu aut dolo ductus, sed puro, sponte, simpliciter et absolute*. See also *RA* 1, fos 20v, 491–497; *CA* 2, p. 152; P. Meadows and N. Ramsay, eds, *A History of Ely Cathedral* (Woodbridge, 2003), pp. 397–8. Ely had forty to fifty monks at this time (Meadows and Ramsay, *History of Ely*, p. 63).

19. Meadows and Ramsay, *History of Ely*, p. 398. Powcher was abbot of Walden (Essex), under the patronage of Arundel's sister Joan, who may have recommended him.
20. *RA* 1, fo. 101r.
21. *TA*, pp. 83–132.
22. *RA* 1, fos 353r, 356v; *Foedera*, vol. 8, pp. 238–40, summarized in *CPR 1401–5*, p. 51; *TA*, 130 ('in one breath the archbishop had swept away all the archdeaconry's pretensions to jurisdictional equality'). Archdeacons had a dubious reputation: cf. Geoffrey Chaucer, *The Canterbury Tales, General Prologue*, ll. 655–60.
23. *RA* 1, fos 20v–21r, 496v (*Ely Chapter Ordinances*, pp. 52–6, xiii–xv); dated 24 April 1403 at Otford.
24. Sarah Rees-Jones and Paul Dryburgh, eds, *The Church and Northern English Society in the Fourteenth Century* (Woodbridge, 2024), pp. 33–6 ('a significant concentration of authority' in the hands of his three main officials); this volume, p. 201.
25. A. Goodman, *Margery Kempe and Her World* (London, 2002), 23–30; *HOC*, vol. 1, p. 525; L. Attreed, *The King's Towns* (New York, 2001), pp. 40–2, 113; I. Atherton, E. Fernie, C. Harper-Bill and H. Smith, eds, *Norwich Cathedral: Church, City and Diocese* (London, 1996), pp. 207, 297–8.
26. R. G. Davies, 'Despenser, Henry, Bishop of Norwich', *ODNB*; Margaret Aston, 'The Impeachment of Bishop Despenser', *BIHR* 26 (1953), pp. 127–48.
27. *CR*, pp. 118–20, 127.
28. *ANLP*, no. 64.
29. *ANLP*, no. 64. Possibly written to Hugh le Despenser (d. 1401). The bishop asked him not to reveal the contents of this letter unless it became necessary, *car nous ne vouldrons esveiller le chien que dort* ('for let sleeping dogs lie').
30. Davies, 'Despenser, Henry', *ODNB* ('there was something bovine about him').
31. *ANLP*, nos 31, 62, 287. De la Warre sought permission to send a servant to 'ease and comfort' Despenser (probably in 1400, when the bishop was at Canterbury); see this volume, pp. 12–13, for Arundel's support for Despenser in 1385.
32. Atherton, Fernie, Harper-Bill and Smith, *Norwich Cathedral*, p. 297 (which dates the pope's prohibition eighteen months too late).
33. *PROME*, vol. 8, pp. 103–4, including a public act of reconciliation with Erpingham, engineered by Arundel, although this proved hollow.
34. *CPL*, vol. 5, pp. 318–19, 586–7. Boniface only amended the award in one respect, reserving any future consideration of the case to himself rather than to the primate (*CA* 1, pp. 337–8).
35. *RA* 1, fos 359, 497, 521–49; *CA* 1, pp. 337–8.
36. *Memorials of Bury St Edmunds*, ed. T. Arnold (3 vols, RS, London, 1896), vol. 3, pp. 183–8.
37. *multum animose et gratanter . . . hilarem et bonum vultum coram omnibus exhibendo* (*Memorials of Bury*, vol. 3, p. 184).

38. Antonia Gransden, *A History of the Abbey of Bury St Edmunds I, 1182–1256* (Studies in the History of Medieval Religion 31, Woodbridge, 2007), p. xiii. Bury was one of just five monasteries in England under direct papal authority and thus exempt from episcopal or archiepiscopal interference.
39. Michael de la Pole, earl of Suffolk, son of the chancellor whom Arundel had ousted in 1386.
40. Cf. *SAC* 1, pp. 888–91.
41. *RA* 2, fos 70r–71r; several Somerset knights, including Hugh Luttrell and Thomas Broke, came to the abbey to assent to Arundel's measures, which they did 'with one voice'.
42. *RA* 1, fos 499–518 (Winchester, including ordination list), 521–549 (Norwich); *RA* 2, fos 73v–77 (Salisbury), 77v–78v and 187–198 (Norwich).
43. *RA* 1, fo. 410r: in February 1401 the king asked Arundel to 'govern' Amesbury convent in Wiltshire, where the nuns were at odds with the high-handed aristocratic prioress Sybil Montague, sister of the former earl of Salisbury (*CCR 1399–1402*, p. 461; *VCH, Wiltshire*, vol. 3, ed. R. B. Pugh and Elizabeth Crittall (London, 1956), pp. 252–3); he delegated the task to Hallum and Chillenden: *RA* 2, fo. 116v (Pylton). Local commissaries were also used: in January 1405, Arundel asked the abbot of Abingdon to visit Winchester College, Oxford (*RA* 1, fo. 116v).

5 William Sawtre: A Candle Lit (1401)

1. *Two Wycliffite Texts*, ed. Anne Hudson (Early English Text Society, Oxford, 1998), p. 91. The reference to Acle (east Norfolk) is obscure, possibly no more than an indication of its out-of-the-way location. Foxe translated this as 'I shall pursue you so narrowly' (*TA*, p. 335).
2. 'There is complete unanimity amongst the Lollards about the primary function of all the clergy: this is the preaching of the gospel to all and, in so far as it contributes to that but no further, the study of the Bible and of aids to its understanding' (Anne Hudson, *The Premature Reformation* (Oxford, 1988), pp. 145, 196–7, 268–73, 353–6).
3. Ian Forrest, *The Detection of Heresy in Late Medieval England* (Oxford, 2005), pp. 60–8 (quote at p. 65, 'much more practical and far-sighted' than other contemporary episcopal mandates, including Archbishop Courtenay's).
4. *CCR 1399–1402*, p. 185.
5. Hudson, *Premature Reformation*, pp. 145n, 275, 361, 385, doubted that he was a friar, but Forrest, *Detection of Heresy*, p. 133, pointed out that his abjuration was sent to the four orders of friars.
6. *RA* 1, fos 407v–408r.
7. TNA, C 66/362, m. 5 (writ of protection, inadequately calendared in *CPR 1399–1401*, p. 404). This John Beket was described as 'literate, a citizen of London'. On 23 November 1401, Arundel made him apparitor-general of his prerogative court, responsible for summonses in testamentary cases (*CA* 1, p. 417; *CA* 2, p. 182).
8. He may have come from Chatteris, on the Norfolk–Cambridgeshire border.
9. C. Kightly, 'Sawtre, William', *ODNB*; Lollard beliefs varied, but Anne Hudson, 'The Examination of Lollards', in *Lollards and Their Books* (London, 1985), pp. 125–40, gives several lists for the interrogation of suspects.

10. *Concilia*, vol. 3, pp. 257–8.
11. *CPR 1399–1401*, p. 190. The only other known reference to Sawtre before February 1401 was his appearance in chancery as a mainpernor (pledge, or bail bondsman) on 20 March 1400 (Alison McHardy, 'De Heretico Comburendo, 1401', in *Lollardy and the Gentry in the Later Middle Ages*, ed. Margaret Aston and Colin Richmond (Stroud, 1997), pp. 112–26, at p. 120).
12. *Henry IV*, pp. 174–89; *PROME*, vol. 8, pp. 93–153.
13. *Usk*, p. 8.
14. *PROME*, vol. 8, pp. 98, 110, 121.
15. *RA* 2, fos 2–3, 178–186; *Concilia*, vol. 3, pp. 254–63.
16. *SAC* 2, p. 308 (*durante adhuc parliamento captus est*).
17. For chronicle accounts of his trial, see *Usk*, p. 122; *CE*, p. 100; *SAC* 2, pp. 308–11; *Vita*, p. 169.
18. Peter McNiven, *Heresy and Politics in the Reign of Henry IV* (Woodbridge, 1987), pp. 82–3.
19. *Usk*, p. 122.
20. This protest cannot have been made at the outset of his trial in convocation since the answers he gave there were included: *Fasciculi Zizaniorum Magistri Johannis Wyclif cum Tritico*, ed. W. W. Shirley (London, RS, 1858), pp. 408–11.
21. *PROME*, vol. 8, pp. 122–5, 139.
22. Although the initial petition came from the clergy, the statute (which basically repeated the petition and the king's response verbatim) was passed at the request of the commons as well as the clergy (*Statutes of the Realm* (11 vols, Record Commission, 1810–28), vol. 2, pp. 125–8). Walsingham (*SAC* 2, p. 308) even thought that the statute was passed at the commons' request.
23. *Concilia*, vol. 3, p. 259, wrongly gives 24 February.
24. *SAC* 2, p. 310; *Concilia*, vol. 3, p. 260.
25. *Foedera*, vol. 8, p. 178 (*CCR 1399–1402*, p. 265); sent 'by the king himself and the council in parliament'.
26. Anne Hudson, 'Purvey, John', *ODNB*.
27. *Usk*, pp. 122–3; there were 'many onlookers' (*SAC* 2, p. 310).
28. Diarmaid MacCulloch, *Thomas Cranmer: A Life* (New Haven and London, 1996), p. 582; S. Wabuda, 'Latimer, Hugh, Bishop of Worcester', *ODNB*.
29. *Concilia*, vol. 3, pp. 260–2.
30. *RA* 1, fo. 290v (new incumbent admitted to West Hythe in October 1403, after Purvey's 'free resignation').
31. *CE*, p. 100.
32. *Concilia*, vol. 3, pp. 262–3; *RA* 2, fo. 186r. One case of clerical immorality was also dealt with on 8 March: Robert Bowlond, rector of St Anthony's, London, who had impregnated a nun (*Usk*, p. 120). It is possible that Bowlond was also suspected of Lollardy.
33. A. E. Larson, 'Are all Lollards Lollards?', in *Lollards and Their Influence in Late Medieval England*, ed. F. Somerset, J. Havens and D. Pitard (Woodbridge, 2003), pp. 59–72; *Henry IV*, 184–6; McHardy, 'De Heretico Comburendo', p. 114; *SAC* 1, pp. 882–3. Burnings for heresy were cited as common law precedents in thirteenth-century English legal treatises: see Paul Cavill, 'Heresy, Law and the State: Forfeiture in Late Medieval and Early Modern England', *EHR* 129 (2014), pp. 270–95, at p. 274.

34. It has been suggested that Arundel was behind an undated petition in French requesting the death penalty for heretics, which is preserved in a parliamentary formulary but was not submitted to parliament, and that this petition must date from the parliament of January 1397 – his first as primate. The petition came from the two (unnamed) archbishops and the bishops and addressed the problem of 'a new sect recently arisen in the realm', rapidly increasing in number and spreading heresies in order to destroy the unity of the Catholic faith. Several members of the sect had been found guilty of heresy and error, but they could not be silenced without the help of the secular power. In other realms, the petition argued, heretics condemned by the Church were handed over to the secular power and put to death (*mys a mort*); the king was asked to help by providing a 'statutory remedy' in this parliament, so that the sect would be destroyed and heretics dissuaded from 'insurrection'. There is no good reason to date the petition to 1397; it is preceded and followed by letters dating from the 1350s and 1360s and could date from any parliament between 1382 and 1401. More significantly, the petition did not ask for the *introduction* of the death penalty for heresy, let alone burning, but for statutory force to be added to the existing sanctions. As William Swinderby knew in 1382, and as Henry IV stated in his writ to the sheriffs, it was already the 'customary' punishment (BL Add. Ms 24,062, fo. 189r–v, printed in H. G. Richardson and G. O. Sayles, 'Parliamentary Documents from Formularies' *BIHR* (1934), pp. 147–62, at pp. 152–4). Finally, it should be noted that neither the clergy's nor the commons' petitions against heretics in the 1401 parliament asked for the death penalty; it was the king's response which specified burning 'in a high place'.
35. Northumberland did tell the 1399 convocation (but not parliament) that Henry would help the clergy to deal with heretics (*Concilia*, vol. 3, p. 239); and before parliament met, on 1 October 1399, at the request of the friars, the king issued a proclamation forbidding the propagation of 'wicked and nefarious opinions contrary to sacred doctrine', which attacked the friars and discouraged people from giving them alms. This was repeated in May 1400, again with specific reference to the friars (*CCR 1399–1402*, pp. 1, 30).
36. Eighteen months later, he was before convocation again, answering for two opinions, neither of which was common among Lollards: that the Sabbath should be observed as it was in the Old Testament, 'according to the rite of the Jews'; and that the meat of pigs should not be eaten because pigs were unclean. His earlier denial of transubstantiation was not mentioned. He was committed to the bishop of London's prison and disappears from the records (*Concilia*, vol. 3, pp. 248–9 (19 April 1401), 271 (21 October 1402); *RA* 1, fos 54–55).
37. *RA* 1, fos 105r (Calais), 125r (Bristol), 390r (Norwich) 432r (Lincolnshire); *Concilia*, vol. 3, pp. 271 (London), 282 (Norwich); *CCR 1402–5*, p. 221.

6 Liberties and Franchises (1399–1402)

1. *PROME*, vol. 8, pp. 9–10.
2. R. H. Helmholz, *The Oxford History of the Laws of England: The Canon Law and Ecclesiastical Jurisdiction from 597 to the 1640s* (Oxford, 2004), Chapter 9.
3. Benjamin Thompson, 'Locality and Ecclesiastical Polity: The Late Medieval Church between Duality and Integration', in *Political Society in Late Medieval*

England: A Festschrift for Christine Carpenter, ed. Benjamin Thompson and John Watts (Woodbridge, 2015), pp. 113–45.

4. Nigel Saul, 'Cheyne, Sir John', *ODNB*; *HOC*, vol. 2, pp. 549–52; K. B. McFarlane, *Lancastrian Kings and Lollard Knights* (Oxford, 1972), pp. 168–76, 191, 211–15.
5. *SAC* 2, pp. 222–5, 244–5; *PROME*, vol. 8, p. 29; Cheyne declared that 'his voice could not be heard because of his weakness' – no small consideration for a speaker.
6. *SAC* 2, pp. 216–17 (issued on Friday 3 October).
7. *SAC* 2, pp. 220–3. However, he acknowledged that students and professors needed to hold more than one benefice to support their studies. For Bishop Bottlesham's sermon on the theme 'My heart rejoices in the governors of Israel' (Judges 5:9), a cautionary tale on Richard's downfall, see R. L. Storey, 'Episcopal King-Makers in the Fifteenth Century', in *The Church, Politics and Patronage in the Fifteenth Century*, ed. R. B. Dobson (Gloucester, 1984), pp. 82–98, at p. 86; *Records of Convocation*, ed. Gerald Bray (20 vols, Woodbridge, 2006), vol. 4, p. 192.
8. *SAC* 2, pp. 224–5; *Concilia*, vol. 3, pp. 238–9.
9. *Concilia*, vol. 3, pp. 238–45. *RA* 1, fos 51–53, has the first twenty-nine articles; articles 30–65 were bound into *RA* 2 at fos 5–6, following the proceedings of the January 1401 convocation. *RA* 1, fo. 53v, breaks off in the middle of article 29 (after the words *destructiones merito dici*) and the sentence continues on *RA* 2, fo. 5r, with the word *possunt*, completing the sentence. This is noted on both folios with a cross reference in an early modern hand, presumably following the publication of Wilkins's *Concilia* in 1737, since he does not mention the separation (although *Records of Convocation*, vol. 4, p. 201, does so).
10. The papal tax-collector, Lewis of Volterra, was present and advised the clergy to write to Pope Boniface about the never-ending problem of provisions and the authorization of a festival of St George; he also promised to write to Boniface himself on these matters.
11. Taken from Boniface VIII's famous bull *Clericis Laicos*, quoting the Sext 3.23.3.
12. *Records of Convocation*, vol. 4, pp. 196–7.
13. For the Court of Arches, or 'Court of Canterbury', which met in London and heard appeals from the whole province, see p. 232.
14. However, one petition to parliament begged the king to stay his hand in disputed cases until his right of presentation had been tried in a court of law; Henry's response was equivocal (*PROME*, vol. 8, p. 61) and the complaint appears to have been ineffective. Immediately after the parliament, the king began sending a succession of writs of prohibition to Arundel, citing parliamentary statutes, precedents and the prerogative rights of the crown, ordering him not to meddle with royal rights of presentation to specified benefices, including royal free chapels, or to support litigants hoping to use ecclesiastical courts to overturn decisions in royal courts. In many cases, the reason given was because the benefice already had an incumbent. These inhibitory writs continued throughout the reign (*RA* 1, fos 149v–150r, 550r–561r).
15. Maudelyn had already been questioned about his involvement in the murder of the duke of Gloucester, whose corpse he had escorted from Calais back to London. He was also interrogated by convocation on 16 October about a scroll found in his possession containing 'magic arts'. He admitted that Richard II had given it to him but had no idea what it signified and was released: *SAC* 2, p. 242; Chris Given-Wilson, 'Maudeleyn, Richard', *ODNB*.

16. *CR*, pp. 50, 233.
17. *Decretum* 17.4.29, the standard writ against those who flouted the *privilegium canonis*.
18. *RA* 1, fo. 404v. Undated, but among a group of documents dated January, probably 1400 and certainly before 1404 (when Braybrooke died). Perhaps Rede, a known supporter of the former king, was suspected of complicity in the rising: four Londoners confessed to his arrest and submitted to Arundel.
19. *SAC* 2, pp. 264–9; R. G. Davies, 'Merk, Thomas, Bishop of Carlisle', *ODNB*.
20. *Usk*, pp. 92–4 (*Ecce, Libertas Ecclesie*).
21. BL, Ms Cotton Cleopatra E II, fo. 255, item 51.
22. *Foedera*, vol. 8, pp. 150, 165.
23. *Henry IV*, pp. 349–50; Merks was dead by January 1410.
24. *Henry IV*, pp. 174–244.
25. *Usk*, pp. 136–43; Chris Given-Wilson, 'The King's Confessors and the Royal Conscience in Late Medieval England', in *Fourteenth-Century England XII*, ed. J. Bothwell and J. S. Hamilton (Woodbridge, 2022), pp. 1–28.
26. When elected as chancellor of Oxford university in 1400, Repingdon was described as *clericus specialissimus illustrissimi principis domini nostri regis Henrici, vir potens et Deum timens, amans veritatem, et detestans avariciam* (the most special clerk of the illustrious prince, our lord king Henry, a powerful man who feared God, loved truth and hated greed) (*Statuta Antiqua Universitatis Oxoniensis*, ed. Strickland Gibson (Oxford, 1931), pp. 190–1).
27. *Henry IV*, pp. 204–11.
28. *CPR 1401–5*, p. 126.
29. *CE*, pp. 102–12, said the jurors later approached the warden of the Franciscans in tears to apologize.
30. The rumours that Richard II was alive only abated after Henry IV's death (P. McNiven, 'Rebellion, Sedition and the Legend of Richard II's Survival in the Reigns of Henry IV and Henry V', *BJRL* 76 (1994), pp. 93–117).
31. R. L. Storey, 'Clergy and Common Law in the Reign of Henry IV', in *Medieval Legal Records in Memory of C. A. F. Meekings*, ed. R. Hunnisett and J. Post (London, 1978), pp. 342–408, at pp. 353–7.
32. Arundel may not have been with the king during the first two weeks of June: on 15 June, Henry wrote to him from Windsor (*ANLP*, no. 282). However, the Franciscan author of *CE* says (p. 104) that Arundel managed to placate (*pacificavit*) the king to spare the 'aged' Dominican friar John Lakenheath from Cambridge, accused of uttering critical remarks about the king. Arundel was a friend of Lakenheath.
33. *PROME*, vol. 8, pp. 154–220.
34. *Concilia*, vol. 3, pp. 270–2; *RA* 1, fos 54r–56v.
35. These were John Seynon (see p. 91), Richard Herbert and Emmota Wylly (who both recanted). A 'pretended chaplain' accused of living with a woman for twenty-five years was committed to Arundel's gaol.
36. *PROME*, vol. 8, pp. 177–9.
37. Storey, 'Clergy and Common Law', *passim*; *PROME*, vol. 8, pp. 32–3.
38. *PROME*, vol. 5, pp. 35–6, 44–5, 57–8. The king's 'majesty' extended the definition of high treason to the killing of royal ministers 'when they are in their places performing their offices'. 'Lesser' treason encompassed such crimes as a servant killing his master, a wife killing her husband or a cleric killing a prelate. Doubtful

cases were to be determined by the king in parliament. In cases of high treason, forfeitures fell to the king; in cases of felony, they fell to the chief lord of the fee.

39. J. G. Bellamy, *Criminal Law and Society in Late Medieval and Tudor England* (Gloucester, 1984), pp. 115–72.
40. *Concilia*, vol. 3, p. 274.
41. During the winter of 1403–4, three abbots in Essex and Suffolk who had been accused of conspiring with Ricardian partisans to kill the king and bring a French army into England were simply fined and pardoned, as was the leader of the conspiracy, Maud, countess of Oxford (*Henry IV*, pp. 262–4).

7 Clerical Wealth: The Shepherd and the Wolf (1403–4)

1. *Original Letters Illustrative of English History*, ed. H. Ellis (4 vols, London, 1824–7), vol. 1, pp. 24–5; *Henry IV*, pp. 221–32. Arundel was not at Shrewsbury; he spent Easter at Canterbury and the next two months between Canterbury, Lambeth and Westminster, before retiring to Saltwood for what he probably hoped would be a quiet summer (*POPC*, vol. 1, p. 191; *Concilia*, vol. 3, pp. 274).
2. Details of the taxes collected from both laity and clergy at this time can be found in The National Archives, E 179 Database (https://www.nationalarchives.gov.uk/E179/default.asp).
3. *SAC* 2, p. 380, claims he was *destitutus*. On 5 September, Arundel, the duke of York and other magnates dined with the king at Worcester (TNA, E 101/404/21, *dieta*, 5 September 1403).
4. *SAC* 2, pp. 381–5. For similar comments about Richard II's courtier knights in the 1380s, see *SAC* 1, p. 814.
5. *Concilia*, vol. 3, p. 274, records no other business at the convocation. It is not mentioned in Arundel's Register; Wykeham's register notes that it was summoned by royal writ. Two weeks later, the king again begged Arundel to provide some relief (*RA* 1, fo. 556r; see also this volume, Appendix II).
6. This was not a normal tenth and fifteenth but a 'new and extraordinary' tax (*SAC* 2, pp. 392–3; *Henry IV*, pp. 282–3); it was not repeated.
7. *RA* 1, fos 57–59.
8. York only agreed to a grant after assurances that the king would cease his recent distraints and inquisitions in the province and declare the Church immune from the subsidy granted in parliament (*Calendar of Richard Scrope, Archbishop of York 1398–1405*, ed. R. N. Swanson (2 vols, Borthwick Texts and Calendars, York, 1981), vol. 2, pp. ii–iii, 8, 19–22); *Concilia*, vol. 3, pp. 279–80; *SAC* 2, p. 410; *Foedera*, vol. 8, p. 353 (orders dated 16 March and 6 May 1404 to summon York convocation in order to grant a subsidy, stressing the urgency of the king's needs).
9. *Henry IV*, pp. 284–91. Henry put great pressure on the clergy to make further grants, writing twice in three days to Arundel in August 1404 to persuade them to do so (*RA* 1, fo. 557v, 25 and 27 August).
10. Dante Alighieri, *Inferno*, canto 19, ll. 115–17; *Polychronicon Ranulphi Higden*, ed. C. Babington (9 vols, RS, London, 1865–86), vol. 6, pp. 465–6, one of Trevisa's many additions to Higden's Latin text.
11. Wendy Scase, *Piers Plowman and the New Anticlericalism* (Cambridge, 1989), pp. 84–5, 110; R. Rex, *The Lollards* (Basingstoke, 2002), pp. 37–8; Margaret Aston, 'Caim's Castles: Poverty, Politics and Disendowment', in *The Church,*

Politics and Patronage in the Fifteenth Century, ed. R. B. Dobson (Gloucester, 1984), pp. 45–81, at p. 52; Anthony Kenny, *Wyclif* (Oxford, 1985), pp. 76–8.

12. Miri Rubin, *Charity and Community in Medieval Cambridge* (Cambridge, 1986), pp. 95–9; Aston, 'Caim's Castles'; Anne Hudson, *The Premature Reformation* (Oxford, 1988), pp. 334–46.
13. Simon Forde, 'Repyndon, Philip, Bishop of Lincoln', *ODNB*; K. B. McFarlane, *John Wycliffe and the Beginnings of English Nonconformity* (London, 1952), pp. 108–14.
14. Chris Given-Wilson, 'Service, Serfdom and English Labour Legislation, 1350–1500', in *Concepts and Patterns of Service in the Later Middle Ages*, ed. A. Curry and E. Matthew (Woodbridge, 2000), pp. 21–37; Scase, *Piers Plowman*, p. 71.
15. *The Peasants' Revolt of 1381*, ed. R. B. Dobson (London, 1983), pp. 164–5.
16. Rubin, *Charity and Community*, pp. 70, 99 (quote), 297–8.
17. Richard FitzRalph, bishop of Armagh 1344–60, had argued in a similar vein: Scase, *Piers Plowman*, p. 63; Rubin, *Charity and Community*, pp. 72–3.
18. Aston, 'Caim's Castles', pp. 59–60; Scase, *Piers Plowman*, pp. 109–10.
19. V. H. Galbraith, 'Articles Laid Before the Parliament of 1371', *EHR* 34 (1919), pp. 579–82; Aston, 'Caim's Castles, pp. 51 and 73, nn. 26–9.
20. The 'alien priories' were daughter houses founded in England by French monasteries in the aftermath of the Norman Conquest. The expulsions of 1378 led to some of them being farmed to laymen, a practice against which the 1399 convocation protested, whereupon Henry IV restored a number of French priors to their English possessions. In 1402–4, many of these restorations were reversed, largely in response to the anti-alien stance of the commons at a time when war with France loomed and the priories were accused of harbouring spies and sending their profits abroad. In general, Arundel was not wrong to say later in the year that the profits of alien priories went to lay lords and courtiers rather than the crown, but it was a complex picture (*PROME*, vol. 8, pp. 92, 105, 128, 239–40, 243; Benjamin Thompson, 'The Prelates and the Alien Priories', in *The Prelate in England and Europe, 1300–1560*, ed. Martin Heale (Woodbridge, 2014), pp. 50–75); Alison McHardy, 'The Alien Priories and the Expulsion of Aliens from England in 1378', *Studies in Church History* 12 (1975), pp. 133–41.
21. This provoked Arundel into his first significant parliamentary intervention (*SAC* 1, pp. 778–80).
22. The 1371 articles were copied at Bury abbey; the 1385 dispute is mentioned only by Walsingham.
23. Walsingham provided two accounts (*SAC* 2, pp. 418–24 and 794–802; *Concilia*, vol. 3, pp. 281–2).
24. Cheyne was not elected to the commons on this occasion, so presumably attended as a councillor.
25. This was Matthew Paris's life of Edmund (archbishop of Canterbury 1233–40). The passage in question comes from the time when Edmund faced 'enemies everywhere', including the king. He turned for inspiration to his seal, in the centre of which was an image of Thomas Becket, which encouraged Edmund to welcome a corresponding martyrdom (C. H. Lawrence, *St Edmund of Abingdon* (Oxford, 1960), p. 260; *SAC* 2, p. 420).
26. *SAC* 2, p. 798, said that this was in return for clerical support for the lords when the knights proposed that lands held by lay lords by royal grants should also be

resumed. During this parliament, the treasurer, Lord Roos, ordered various bulls of Pope Gregory IX (1227–41) to be sent to Coventry; these concerned the revocation of 'alienations contrary to the dignity or prejudice of the crown', or statutes and ordinances made by English magnates 'in diminution of the royal power' (*Antient Kalendars and Inventories of the Treasury of His Majesty's Exchequer*, ed. F. Palgrave (3 vols, London, 1836), vol. 2, p. 70).

27. *CPR 1401–5*, p. 183.
28. *SAC* 2, p. 422. According to Walsingham, this (unnamed) bishop of Rochester 'was said to be Canterbury's Mercury, because whatever the archbishop thought, he would loudly voice'. This is probably an error: Richard Young had been provided by Pope Boniface to Rochester on 28 July 1404 (see p. 126), but Arundel refused to recognize him and he was often abroad on embassies. There is no other evidence that he attended the Coventry parliament.
29. The improbability of Walsingham's account of penitential knights is underlined by an incident he recounted concerning disrespect to the Eucharist during the Coventry parliament (see p. 260).
30. *Concilia*, vol. 3, pp. 201–2.
31. Indirect taxes on trade in 1404–5 similarly reached their highest level for over sixty years: Mark Ormrod, 'The Rebellion of Archbishop Scrope and the Tradition of Opposition to Royal Taxation', in *The Reign of Henry IV: Rebellion and Survival, 1403–1413*, ed. G. Dodd and D. Biggs (York, 2008), pp. 162–79 (table of taxation, p. 168); Mark Ormrod, 'An Archbishop in Revolt: Richard Scrope and the Yorkshire Rising of 1405', in *Richard Scrope: Archbishop, Rebel, Martyr*, ed. P. J. P. Goldberg (Donington, 2007), pp. 28–44.
32. BL, Ms Cotton Cleopatra E II, fo. 152 (*RHL*, vol. 1, pp. 413–14). On 2 May 1405, Henry sent a letter to all the bishops instructing them to do this (*Signet Letters*, no. 328).

8 Archbishop Scrope: Thy Son's Coat, or No? (1404–5)

1. He received an annual fee of £200 (TNA, E 403/591, 2 May 1404).
2. *PROME*, vol. 8, p. 244; A. L. Brown, 'The Commons and the Council in the Reign of Henry IV', *EHR* 79 (1964), pp. 1–30, at p. 30. He attended ten of thirty-four recorded meetings in 1403, but was not regularly at Westminster even during the second half of 1403, spending several weeks at Maidstone in November and December (*Concilia*, vol. 3, p. 277; *RA* 1, fos 21v, 371, 386v; R. G. Davies, 'Thomas Arundel as Archbishop of Canterbury', *JEH* 14 (1973), pp. 9–21, at p. 16). Curiously, from April 1404 to March 1405, Arundel is named as attending only nine out of sixty-one meetings, although he was a privy councillor throughout the year (J. L. Kirby, 'Councils and Councillors of Henry IV, 1399–1413', *TRHS* 14 (1964), pp. 35–65, at pp. 50–1, 62).
3. In this parliament, he announced the king's wishes with regard to the financing of his much-pilloried household, arranged for the expulsion of aliens and supervised the receipt of the *novam et exquisitam* tax granted by the commons (*PROME*, vol. 8, pp. 239–41; *SAC* 2, pp. 394–7).
4. For this and the following paragraph, see *PROME*, vol. 8, pp. 231–5, 279 (newsletter on the early weeks of the parliament, and official roll).

5. He also had to clear his name concerning an exchequer demand for £200 during his time as archbishop of York (*PROME*, vol. 8, p. 243).
6. *CPR 1401–5*, pp. 183, 236–7.
7. *SAC* 2, pp. 430–3.
8. BL, Add. Ms 35,295, fo. 263v.
9. R. Horrox, 'Edward of Langley, Duke of York', *ODNB*; *SAC* 2, pp. 431–7; *Henry IV*, pp. 264–5; *CE*, p. 126; *ANLP*, no. 62, for Constance's desolation at her husband's death in the Epiphany Rising.
10. *PROME*, vol. 8, p. 291; vol. 9, p. 40.
11. *SAC* 2, pp. 432–5.
12. *CE*, p. 134; see also this volume, pp. 184–6.
13. Sophie Ambler, *Bishops in the Political Community of England, 1213–1272* (Oxford, 2017), pp. 4–10, 105.
14. *Henry IV*, pp. 266–77; Simon Walker, 'The Yorkshire Risings of 1405: Texts and Contexts' in *Henry IV: The Establishment of the Regime, 1399–1406*, ed. Gwilym Dodd and Douglas Biggs (York, 2003), pp. 161–84; Mark Ormrod, 'An Archbishop in Revolt: Richard Scrope and the Yorkshire Rising of 1405', in *Richard Scrope: Archbishop, Rebel, Martyr*, ed. P. J. P. Goldberg (Donington, 2007), pp. 28–44.
15. *ISCA*, pp. 43–4 (Scrope's sermons).
16. Scrope's manifesto is in *SAC* 2, pp. 442–4, translated 'word for word' into Latin from the English in which it was circulated. Another version alleging that Scrope called for Henry IV to be deposed is probably a *post factum* justification for his condemnation: see Walker, 'The Yorkshire Risings'; Ormrod, 'An Archbishop in Revolt'; *Henry IV*, pp. 275–6.
17. Arundel was with Henry at Worcester on 10 May (*Signet Letters*, nos 335, 346A), but not at Pontefract.
18. *Historians of the Church of York and Its Archbishops*, ed. J. Raine (3 vols, London, 1879–94), vol. 3, pp. 289–90.
19. Sir William Plumpton, Scrope's nephew and follower, was also executed.
20. Walsingham adds that the king treated Arundel kindly and avoided distressing him further. Before leaving York, he was consulted by Henry about his daughter Philippa's marriage to Eric, heir to the kingdom of Denmark, Norway and Sweden (*SAC* 2, pp. 456–8).
21. *Henry IV*, pp. 275–6.
22. *ISCA*, pp. 46–7.
23. Danna Piroyansky, '"Martyrio pulchro finitus": Archbishop Scrope's Martyrdom and the Creation of a Cult', and Christopher Norton, 'Richard Scrope and York Minster', in Goldberg, *Richard Scrope: Archbishop, Martyr, Rebel*, pp. 100–12 and 138–213. This was principally a local (York and Yorkshire) cult; letters to suppress it are in *Historians of the Church of York*, vol. 3, pp. 291–3 (December 1405, April and September 1406).
24. *PROME*, vol. 8, pp. 411–13; Walker, 'The Yorkshire Risings', pp. 164–6.
25. He was at Canterbury and west Kent through July (*RA* 1, fo. 21r–v; Davies, 'Thomas Arundel', p. 16).
26. In 1405, the exchequer sent memoranda, rolls and tallies *predicti thesauri intime tangenti* (relating directly to the aforesaid treasure) to inform the gathering of the state of royal finances (TNA, E 403/582, 18 July 1405).

27. *SAC* 2, p. 462; *ANLP*, nos 343–5; *Signet Letters*, no. 939. After the council, Arundel made his way back to London with his friend and former archdeacon Richard Clifford (Davies, 'Thomas Arundel', p. 18).
28. *ANLP*, no. 334 (28 October, probably 1405).
29. *Usk*, pp. xxviii–xxix, 204–6.
30. The bull was presumably brought by the papal nuncios mentioned by Walsingham. 'Because of the frequent taxes in the realm', Arundel raised a loan 'like a beggar' to cover their expenses (*SAC* 2, pp. 468–70).
31. *Historians of the Church of York*, vol. 3, pp. 291–2.
32. F. M. Powicke, *Stephen Langton* (Oxford, 1928), p. 128.
33. *CE*, p. 136 (quote); *ISCA*, p. 48; *English Chronicle, 1377–1461*, ed. W. Marx (Woodbridge, 2003), p. 37; *SAC* 2, p. 470.

9 Bishops Old and New (1404–7)

1. Including translations when relevant: M. D. Knowles, 'The English Bishops, 1070–1532', in *Medieval Studies Presented to Aubrey Gwynn*, ed. J. A. Watt, J. B. Morrall and F. X. Martin (Dublin, 1961), pp. 283–96, counted 461 consecrated bishops in England in 462 years (1070–1532); the longest tenure was Henry Beaufort's, from 1398 to 1447.
2. BL, Ms Arundel 68, fo. 58.
3. For Hallum, see p. 228.
4. *RHL* 1, pp. 415–16; Henry IV was apparently told that, when Hallum realized he was not going to get the see, he and Arundel secretly supported Walden in order to block Langley, but the details are hazy: R. G. Davies, 'Walden, Roger, Bishop of London', *ODNB*; R. N. Swanson, 'Hallum, Robert, Bishop of Salisbury', *ODNB*; C. M. Fraser, 'Langley, Thomas, Bishop of Durham', *ODNB*.
5. *RA* 1, fo. 32; *CA* 1, p. 266 (*Set semper presto sum antiquam consuetudinem ecclesie Cantuar' usque ad minimum iota in omnibus observare*). This 'custom' included Canterbury's primacy over York: in 1401, Arundel took the precaution of copying several ancient charters confirming its superiority into his register (*RA* 1, fos 13v–14r).
6. R. G. Davies, 'Young, Richard, Bishop of Rochester', *ODNB*; Arundel also reproached Young with negligence at Bangor: in February 1404 he appointed a vicar-general to act in the diocese because the bishop, currently 'in remote parts', had not appointed anyone to act for him during his absence and people in the diocese had complained of the *culpa et negligencia ipsius venerabilis fratris nostri* (culpability and negligence of this venerable brother of ours) (*CA* 2, p. 158).
7. *Register of Henry Chichele, Archbishop of Canterbury, 1414–1443*, ed. E. F. Jacob (4 vols, London, 1943), vol. 1, pp. 96–7, and vol. 4, p. 28. Arundel and Henry may have wanted to keep Young at Bangor to prevent it being occupied by Lewis Byford, whom Boniface provided to the see in July 1404 but who was a supporter of Glyn Dwr (Christopher Allmand, 'A Bishop of Bangor During the Glyn Dwr Revolt: Richard Young', *Journal of the Historical Society of the Church in Wales* 18 (1968), pp. 47–56).
8. J. Dahmus, *William Courtenay, Archbishop of Canterbury, 1381–1396* (University Park, PA, 1966), pp. 165–77.

9. *RA* 1, fo. 428 (*CA* 1, p. 278). Yet Arundel had also shown kindness to Trevor: after St Asaph cathedral was gutted in 1403–4, he offered him a home at Canterbury (*SAC* 2, pp. 426–8).
10. R. R. Davies, 'Trevor, John, Bishop of St Asaph', *ODNB.* Arundel's undated monition must be after April 1400, when Hallum became archdeacon of Canterbury (*RA* 1, fo. 267).
11. *RA* 1, fo. 388v: *vestra insuper negligencia remanentibus, ut dicitur, incorrectis certis personis insufficientibus* (moreover, by your negligence, so it is said, certain insufficient persons remain uncorrected).
12. All Souls College, Oxford, Ms 182, fo. 54r–v. Wykeham died on 27 September 1404; Beaufort was provided on 19 November and received the temporalities on 14 March 1405. Arundel's letter is unprinted and worth citing: 'Venerable brother, etc. . . . Justice rightly desires and authority declares to men that the real burdens and cares of things are borne by those persons who receive benefits. Be aware, then, that we have heard, although we do not know whether to believe it, that during the time that your fraternal person has been in charge of the honourable church of Lincoln, numerous serious defects in the manors, houses, granges, closes and other things belonging to the bishopric of Lincoln have been left uncorrected; indeed now, more recently, perhaps with the hope of a future promotion, your negligence has permitted the fruits, rents and profits to be squandered, so that unless God, showing greater diligence, rapidly extends a helping hand to the bishopric, it will be exposed to manifest ruin (*et presertim iam noviter, spe forsan promocionis future, vestra incuria fructus, redditus et proventus dilapidare permisit ut, nisi Deus cum meliore industria celeriter manum supponat, ipse episcopatus patebit manifeste ruine*). We do not say that all of this is true but, struck with bitterness of heart, we report it, hoping thereby to appeal to your good character, so that justice might thrive unsullied, the rights of the church of Lincoln remain unharmed, the prick of conscience be quietened and your and my good name be upheld in all things. Appealing through advice to your fraternal love, we ask, urge and require you (*rogamus hortandoque requirimus*), by any ways and means which are appropriate and convenient for this, since we have already heard encouraging rumours (*bonis rumoribus*) of your translation to the church of Winchester, to undertake with care these repairs, restorations and defects of the bishopric of the church of Lincoln so that your future successor should not have cause to complain, the scandalous reverberating language of the people should cease, and your friendship and ours remain in peace (*ut imposterum surrogatus cum causa non clamet et popularis lingua palpitans scandalosa subticeat, vestraque et nostra amicicia remaneat subquiete*). Be aware, venerable brother, if the aforesaid things are true and remain uncorrected, that, because of the offense to the divine majesty, we cannot perform the duty of our office by averting our eyes and leave this reform to your successor in Christ, as aforesaid, together with other men zealous for justice. Let us not therefore restrict the augmentation of the church of Lincoln, so that like a stepfather we can continue to pursue with good will Saint Swithun and the bishopric of Winchester (*Non tum sit ecclesie Linc' affectamus augmentum ut Sanctum Swithunum et episcopatum Wynton' novercali prosequamus affectu*)'. Thanks to Bob Yeager for images of these folios.
13. A. McHardy, 'The Clergy in Parliament', in *The Reign of Henry IV: Rebellion and Survival, 1403–1413*, ed. G. Dodd and D. Biggs (York, 2008), pp. 136–61, at

p. 155 (Wykeham); *RA* 1, fo. 61v; *Concilia*, vol. 3, p. 279; Virginia Davis, *William Wykeham* (London, 2007), p. 163.

14. *Usk*, p. 248.
15. *RA* 1, fo. 23; R. G. Davies, 'After the Execution of Archbishop Scrope: Henry IV, the Papacy and the English Episcopate, 1405–8', *BJRL* 59 (1977), pp. 40–74; *Henry IV*, pp. 354–60.
16. Tottington, elected on 14 September, was a local man with no interest in national affairs. His legacies were almost entirely for the repair of local churches and convents (will dated 20 April 1413, when he claimed to be 'in complete health of mind and body', but he died eight days later: *RA* 1, fo. 165r).
17. Christopher Harper-Bill, 'Tottington, Alexander, Bishop of Norwich', *ODNB*; *ANLP*, nos 316, 344; *Signet Letters*, no. 943. Arundel was still referring to Norwich as *sede vacante* in early October 1407 (*RA* 1, fos 315r–316v).
18. For the complications over temporalities caused by these rapid translations, see *PROME*, vol. 8, pp. 375–6.
19. C. M. Fraser, 'Langley, Thomas, Bishop of Durham', *ODNB*; R. G. Davies, 'Bubwith, Nicholas, Bishop of Bath and Wells', *ODNB*. Henry's letter to the pope supporting Bubwith described him as a fervent supporter of the Church and a man of outstanding merit, 'virtuous life, wise counsel, immense discretion and circumspect maturity' (All Souls College, Oxford, Ms 182, fo. 75r).
20. In October 1407, at the Gloucester parliament, the new or translated bishops made their formal professions of obedience to Arundel (*RA* 1, fos 37v–42v).
21. *CPL*, vol. 6, p. 98 (12 April 1408). Gregory XII's craven order, technically the papal absolution of all those involved in Scrope's death, was sent to Langley and Repingdon and repeated the royalist line that Scrope had been taken in arms and given a fair trial, and that his execution was justified for the safety of the realm.
22. Chichele and Cheyne were sent to Rome in August 1406 to negotiate episcopal appointments and plans to heal the Schism. By the time they arrived, Innocent VII had died, so it was Gregory XII they dealt with for the next year (*Henry IV*, pp. 357–61, 459–61).
23. The story of appointments to the four Welsh sees was even more complex than those to the English sees, largely because of the revolt. Llandaff and Bangor cathedrals both suffered major arson attacks. After John Trevor of St Asaph defected to Glyn Dwr he was not replaced, his diocese being inaccessible to an English-appointed candidate. Boniface IX's choice for Bangor, Lewis Byford, was never recognized by the king; he too defected and was forced to resign after rebelling in 1408. In September 1405, Arundel appointed deputies to St Asaph and Bangor, claiming that they were vacant and needed to be reconciled following pollution by blood, but whether this had any effect is doubtful (*RA* 1, fos 137v–138r). Following the Pennal declaration of March 1406, by which Glyn Dwr switched allegiance to the Avignon papacy, the two popes appointed rival candidates (including the chronicler Adam Usk to Llandaff). After 1408, when Glyn Dwr's fortunes waned and Guy Mone died, the king appointed new candidates to St David's (Chichele), Bangor (Benedict Nicholls), St Asaph (Robert Lancaster) and Llandaff (John de la Zouche). Only Chichele had any real impact on English affairs (*Henry IV*, pp. 355, 359–60; for Zouche, see *CE*, pp. xxiii–xxv).
24. J. R. Highfield, 'The English Hierarchy in the Reign of Edward III', *TRHS* 6 (1956), pp. 115–38, at p. 135, cites as examples of this William Zouche of York

(in office 1340–52), Alexander Nevill of York (1373–88) and Thomas Hatfield of Durham (1345–81).

25. Bowet took part in Bishop Despenser's expedition to Flanders in 1383 and was constable of Bordeaux and chief justice of Guyenne from 1396 to 1399: *BRUC*, pp. 83–4; Henry Summerson, 'Strickland, William, Bishop of Carlisle', *ODNB*.
26. Margaret Aston and Colin Richmond, eds, *Lollardy and the Gentry in the Later Middle Ages* (Stroud, 1997), pp. 14, 25; Dereham was *in persona viri discreti*, a professor *sacre pagine* (expert in the Scriptures), chancellor of Cambridge 1404–9; he had been on embassies to Denmark and the Roman Curia, and would represent the university at the Council of Pisa and act as apostolic protonotary for the English at Constance. The letter described him as 'virtuous, peace-loving and modest, zealous for harmony and concord, free from illicit dealings and an upholder of the liberty and immunity of the Church' (*RA* 1, fo. 528r; *RHL* 2, p. 45; *BRUC*, pp. 184–5; Davies, 'After the Execution', p. 65).
27. *CPL*, vol. 6, p. 299.
28. Knowles, 'The English Bishops', p. 290; *The Register of Richard Clifford, Bishop of Worcester: A Calendar*, ed. Waldo Smith (Toronto, 1976), p. 22. Examples of scholarly bishops at this time are John Trefnant of Hereford (whose personal library contained around a hundred legal, liturgical and religious books), John Bottlesham of Rochester, Thomas Merks of Carlisle and William Rede (bishop of Chichester 1368–85, not to be confused with his probable relative Robert Rede, bishop of Chichester 1396–1415; for William, a theologian and astronomer of renown, see J. D. North, 'Rede, William, Bishop of Chichester', *ODNB*; cf. *SAC* 2, p. 429). This is not to question the theological expertise of men such as Hallum or Repingdon or Bowet (whose library at his death contained over thirty volumes of philosophical, theological, legal and pastoral works: *BRUC*, p. 84), but each had other strings to his bow. Highfield, 'English Hierarchy', p. 26; R. Rex, *The Lollards* (Basingstoke, 2002), p. 4; Robert Brentano, *Two Churches: England and Italy in the Thirteenth Century* (Princeton, 1968), p. 211, on scholar-bishops in thirteenth-century England.
29. F. M. Powicke, *Stephen Langton* (Oxford, 1928), p. 12. Fifteen of the eighty-five bishops provided during Edward III's reign were monks and eight friars, but they were not as influential as they had been in the twelfth and thirteenth centuries (Highfield, 'English Hierarchy', pp. 25, 132; Knowles, 'The English Bishops', pp. 291–2).
30. See his comment to the Lollard William Thorpe in August 1407, that 'no bishop of this land now pursues more sharply those that hold such [Lollard] beliefs than he [Repingdon] does' (*Two Wycliffite Texts*, ed. Anne Hudson (Early English Text Society, Oxford, 1998), pp. 39–42). In fact, Repingdon, an ex-Lollard, was not an assiduous persecutor of his former fellows, however much they despised him for his betrayal of the cause (Simon Forde, 'Repyndon, Philip, Bishop of Lincoln', *ODNB*).
31. Davies, 'After the Execution', pp. 54, 58.
32. Brentano, *Two Churches*, p. 206.
33. Hugh of Lincoln, Thomas Cantilupe (Hereford), Richard Wyche (Chichester) and Edmund of Abingdon (Canterbury).
34. See p. 265; however, several late medieval bishops were great educational benefactors.

35. R. G. Davies, 'The Episcopate', in *Profession, Vocation and Culture in Later Medieval England*, ed. C. Clough (Liverpool, 1982), pp. 51–89, at p. 63; Highfield 'English Hierarchy', p. 115. Others had held equivalent offices in the households of great nobles such as the Black Prince or John of Gaunt: see Helen Jewell, 'English Bishops as Educational Benefactors in the Later Fifteenth Century', in *The Church, Politics and Patronage in the Fifteenth Century*, ed. R. B. Dobson (Gloucester, 1984), pp. 146–67.
36. The other was John Scarle, appointed as a stopgap on 5 September 1399 and kept on until March 1401; he was a former chancellor of the duchy of Lancaster: Alison McHardy, 'John Scarle: Ambition and Politics in the Late Medieval Church', in *Image, Text and Church, 1380–1600: Essays for Margaret Aston*, ed. Linda Clark, Maureen Jurkowski and Colin Richmond (Toronto, 2009), pp. 68–93.
37. The line between the roles of Church and State in heresy trials wavered briefly in 1414, but by 1428 the investigation of heresy was once again 'firmly in the church's hands' (Ian Forrest, *The Detection of Heresy in Late Medieval England* (Oxford, 2005), pp. 39–47).
38. Langley had acted as chancellor of the palatinate of Lancaster (C. M. Fraser, 'Langley, Thomas, Bishop of Durham', *ODNB*); Bubwith may have studied briefly at Oxford but did not graduate (*BRUO*, vol. 2, pp. 294–6).
39. *Usk*, pp. xxv–xxxvi, 176–8, 188–90, claimed that initially Boniface provided him to Hereford, but that, when the king and his 'enemies in England' objected, Mascall was provided instead.

10 Arundel, the King and the Commons (1406)

1. Three independent chroniclers (*CE*, *SAC* and *ISCA*) all mentioned it, but government records did not.
2. *PROME*, vol. 8, pp. 318–25.
3. *PROME*, vol. 8, p. 331.
4. *Henry IV*, pp. 293–4.
5. *PROME*, vol. 8, pp. 326–7, 335, 337, 338, 339–40, 350, 354, 366.
6. One of them, Arundel's long-time friend John, Lord Lovell, immediately stood down, saying he was involved in too many lawsuits to make his position as a councillor appropriate (*PROME*, vol. 8, pp. 339–40).
7. J. L. Kirby, 'Councils and Councillors of Henry IV, 1399–1413', *TRHS* 14 (1964), pp. 35–65; and A. L. Brown 'The Commons and the Council in the Reign of Henry IV', *EHR* 79 (1964), pp. 1–30. Both stress the radical nature of the changes in the composition and powers of the council in 1406. Those appointed in December were Arundel; the duke of York; the earl of Somerset (John Beaufort); bishops Henry Beaufort, Thomas Langley and Nicholas Bubwith; Hugh, Lord Burnell; William, Lord Roos; Thomas Furnivall (treasurer); Grey; Stanley; Tiptoft; and John Prophet, the privy seal keeper. For a petition from Arundel supporting Prophet's promotion, see TNA, E 28/23, no. 14.
8. Henry's first recorded attendance was on 8 December and he first witnessed a royal charter on 25 November. But he was too exalted to take the oath sworn by other members (Kirby, 'Councils and Councillors', pp. 54–5).
9. *SAC* 2, pp. 494–6.

10. Text in *PROME*, vol. 8, pp. 366–75.
11. A. L. Brown, 'The Authorization of Letters under the Great Seal', *BIHR* 37 (1964), pp. 125–56, at p. 154.
12. *SAC* 2, pp. 480–2.
13. The duke of York had already been sent to convocation in May, without success (*RA* 1, fo. 66v).
14. The full account in *RA* 1, fos 65r–69r, is greatly abbreviated in *Concilia*, vol. 3, p. 284 (E. F. Jacob, 'Canterbury Convocation of 1406', in *Essays in Medieval History Presented to Bertie Wilkinson*, ed. T. A. Sandquist and M. R. Powicke (Toronto, 1969), pp. 345–53); *SAC* 2, pp. 470–2 (Walsingham jibed that no previous king had managed to get so many priests to pray for him); TNA, E 401/638, 12 and 28 July 1406, for £1,694 from the subsidy on unbeneficed clergy and loans raised.
15. *PROME*, vol. 8, pp. 361–3.
16. Maureen Jurkowski, 'The Arrest of William Thorpe in Shrewsbury and the Anti-Lollard Statute of 1406', *HR* 75 (2002), pp. 273–95, at p. 283; see also this volume, p. 156.
17. Arundel used this phrase (*illud fatuum se dicentem Regem Ricardum*) in a letter of 23 March 1407 (*RHL* 2, pp. 159–61).
18. *CPR 1405–8*, p. 352.
19. In 1403, the king had the prophet William Norham beheaded for criticizing him (*SAC* 2, p. 380).
20. *PROME*, vol. 8, pp. 354, 361.
21. Brown, 'The Commons and the Council', *passim*; G. L. Harriss, *Shaping the Nation: England, 1360–1461* (Oxford, 2005), p. 73, considered the 'collapse of the king's health' to be crucial.
22. A. J. Pollard, 'The Lancastrian Constitutional Experiment Revisited: Henry IV, Sir John Tiptoft and the Parliament of 1406', *Parliamentary History* 14 (1995), pp. 99–119, at p. 108. Pollard questioned the unity of the shire knights, many of whom were royal retainers or servants, and suggested that it might have been an alliance between a minority of disgruntled knights and the burgesses who were the most vocal critics, while Tiptoft did not necessarily share their views but was bound as speaker of the commons to report them; Linda Clark, 'Tiptoft, John, First Baron Tiptoft', *ODNB*, endorses this view.
23. Kirby, 'Councils and Councillors', p. 60, thought it might be 'the work of an astute political manager, who without consciously planning the changes could take advantage of events. Such a man was perhaps Archbishop Thomas Arundel'.

11 Chancellor of England (1407–9)

1. The chapel in Westminster abbey, not the king's private oratory by St Stephen's chapel.
2. *Foedera*, vol. 8, p. 464; *CCR 1405–9*, p. 250.
3. For the chancellor as the second person in the kingdom, see Anne Duggan, *Thomas Becket* (London, 2004), p. 16; Gwilym Dodd, 'Clerical Chancellors of Late Medieval England', in *The Prelate in Late Medieval England and Europe*, ed. Martin Heale (Woodbridge, 2016), pp. 17–49, at p. 17.

4. *CPR 1405–8*, pp. 354, 474; *CCR 1405–9*, pp. 441–2; *RHL* 2, pp. 200, 213–14; *Signet Letters*, nos 758, 933, 948; *ANLP*, no. 374. His new-found authority also gave him the opportunity to right old wrongs such as the claim of the monastery of Meaux (Yorkshire) for exemption from subsidies because their lands had been flooded, as Arundel personally testified in 1407 since he had witnessed the floods with his own eyes when he landed at Ravenspur in 1399 (*Chronica Monasterii de Melsa*, ed. E. A. Bond (3 vols, RS, London, 1866–8), vol. 3, pp. 304–6). This exemption was issued within a few days of him becoming chancellor, on 24 January 1407; later on, he was often 'too much occupied by arduous business' to deal with cases personally.
5. *Henry IV*, pp. 337–8; *Signet Letters*, nos 692–741; *Lit. Cant.*, vol. 3, pp. 78–107.
6. *CE*, pp. xxiii–xxv; *RHL* 2, p. 179.
7. J. L. Kirby, 'Councils and Councillors of Henry IV, 1399–1413', *TRHS* 14 (1964), pp. 35–65, at p. 56; R. G. Davies, 'Thomas Arundel as Archbishop of Canterbury', *JEH* 14 (1973), pp. 9–21, at pp. 15–19.
8. G. L. Harriss, *Cardinal Beaufort* (Oxford, 1988), pp. 23–67; John Beaufort, earl of Somerset, was Henry IV's half-brother and probably the king's closest personal friend among the nobility, but he was ailing and died in March 1410. For his will, appointing his brother Henry as his executor, see *RA* 2, fos 48–49.
9. Alice was the daughter of Arundel's brother Earl Richard, and the widow of John, Lord Charlton (d. 1401): Harriss, *Cardinal Beaufort*, p. 16; Peter McNiven, *Heresy and Politics in the Reign of Henry IV* (Woodbridge, 1987), pp. 129–34; and see this volume, pp. 127–8.
10. *SAC* 2, pp. 448–50, for Thomas Beaufort wrenching Scrope's crozier from his hands.
11. Harriss, *Cardinal Beaufort*, p. 48.
12. *PROME*, vol. 7, pp. 322–3 (parliamentary and papal legitimation in 1397); the amended version of 10 February 1407 (but not the interlineation) is in *CPR 1405–8*, p. 284.
13. Two acts for the inheritance of the crown were passed in 1406: in June, restricting the succession to the king's sons and their male heirs only; and in December, declaring this a mistake and extending it to the four sons and their heirs general, female as well as male: *Henry IV*, p. 298.
14. Harriss, *Cardinal Beaufort*, p. 40; McNiven, *Heresy and Politics*, p. 134.
15. Edmund Wright, 'Henry IV, the Commons and the Recovery of Royal Finance in 1407', in *Rulers and Ruled in Late Medieval England: Essays Presented to Gerald Harriss*, ed. Rowena Archer and Simon Walker (London, 1995), pp. 65–81; Harriss, *Cardinal Beaufort*, pp. 37–50; *Henry IV*, pp. 308–16.
16. TNA, E 175/11/32: writ telling the exchequer to ignore any mandate from the king which was contrary to the Articles, signed by Henry personally. (There is little evidence that he tried to evade his promises.)
17. A. L. Brown, 'The Commons and the Council in the Reign of Henry IV', *EHR* 79 (1964), pp. 1–30, at p. 23 and n. 2, gives the following figures: grants of land or custody of land, 36 in 1406, 9 in 1407; grants of goods, 16 in 1406, 1 in 1407; grants of money, 46 in 1406, 8 in 1407. Grants which did not diminish crown revenue remained at the same level – clearly a financial, not a political, policy; the expenses of the royal household fell by some 20 per cent.
18. Harriss, *Cardinal Beaufort*, pp. 48–50; *Henry IV*, pp. 315–16.

19. *CCR 1409–13*, pp. 115–16 (Arundel's resignation).
20. *SAC* 2, pp. 534–7; *Henry IV*, pp. 304–5, 533.
21. *Signet Letters*, nos 717, 726, 735, 736, 952; *RHL* 2, p. 179; TNA, E 28/23. For Arundel as Henry's 'spiritual father', see *CE*, p. 134.
22. 'A quite extraordinary grant' (McNiven, *Heresy and Politics*, pp. 149–50). Built in the 1360s to defend the Thames, Queenborough was held in the 1370s and 1380s by John of Gaunt and Robert de Vere. Arundel visited it on 13 April 1409 and in October received £67 for repairs (*RA* 2, fo. 12v; TNA, E 404/25, no. 2). An indication of the sensitivity of this grant is that Arundel handed the great seal to the king and left the room while it was sealed. Prince Henry was not present (although Thomas Beaufort witnessed it). On 21 March 1413, Henry V committed it to his retainer Gilbert Umfraville (*CPR 1408–13*, p. 59; *CCR 1405–9*, p. 498; *CCR 1413–16*, p. 10).
23. Peter McNiven, 'The Problem of Henry IV's Health, 1405–1413', *EHR* 100 (1985), pp. 747–72; *Henry IV*, pp. 293–5, 302–6, 517, 533.
24. *Henry IV*, pp. 513, 545. From early 1410, the king often preferred Lambeth to Westminster when in London.
25. *Signet Letters*, no. 7.
26. *Henry IV*, pp. 495–6; Harriss, *Cardinal Beaufort*, pp. 55–9.
27. Thomas of Lancaster had been largely occupied with military emergencies during the first half of the reign (especially in Ireland), but returned to Westminster in spring 1409 and was soon at odds with his elder brother: McNiven, *Heresy and Politics*, pp. 151–2; *Henry IV*, pp. 465–6.
28. G. Harriss, 'Fitzalan, Thomas, Earl of Arundel', *ODNB*; McNiven, *Heresy and Politics*, pp. 152–3. See also this volume, pp. 220–1.

12 The Constitutions and the Schism (1407–9)

1. See p. 240.
2. *SAC* 2, pp. 222, 418, 794–9 ('an enemy of the Church'); apart from his call for disendowment in 1404, the evidence for Cheyne's 'Lollardy' is: (1) that he was acquainted with other 'Lollard knights' (though neither Walsingham nor Knighton named him as a 'Lollard knight'); (2) that his will was remorseful and penitential (but so were those of Henry IV and Arundel); (3) that he had a psalter once owned by Richard Rolle; (4) that he had allegedly started out on a clerical career but abandoned it; and (5) that he held lands confiscated during the Anglo-French war from an alien priory (Beckford, Gloucestershire), sometimes seen as an indication of heterodoxy (Nigel Saul, 'Cheyne, Sir John', *ODNB*; *HOC*, vol. 2, pp. 549–52; K. B. McFarlane, *Lancastrian Kings and Lollard Knights* (Oxford, 1972), pp. 168–76, 191, 211–15; J. A. F. Thomson, 'Knightly Piety', in *Lollardy and the Gentry in the Later Middle Ages*, ed. Margaret Aston and Colin Richmond (Stroud, 1997), pp. 95–111).
3. McFarlane, *Lancastrian Kings*, pp. 192–7.
4. W. K. Jordan, *Philanthropy in England, 1480–1660* (London, 1959), pp. 80–3; R. A. Hartridge, *A History of Vicarages in the Middle Ages* (Cambridge, 1930), especially pp. 117–25, 155–62.
5. *Henry IV*, pp. 368–9; Margaret Aston, 'Caim's Castles: Poverty, Politics and Disendowment', in *The Church, Politics and Patronage in the Fifteenth Century*,

ed. R. B. Dobson (Gloucester, 1984), pp. 45–81, at p. 64; *PROME*, vol. 7, 213, and vol. 8, pp. 126, 191, 203, 272; *SAC* 2, pp. 341–56.

6. In November 1403, he ordered twenty-two habitually non-resident vicars in Canterbury diocese to be apprehended and their livings sequestrated; the accrued profits were to be used to repair manses, churches, granges and enclosures which were dilapidated: *ANLP*, no. 282 (correctly dated 1403, as in *Signet Letters*, no. 929); *PROME*, vol. 8, p. 194; *RA* 1, fos 386v–387r (further references to non-residence on fos 100v, 129r, and *RA* 2, fo. 121r); *Concilia*, vol. 3, pp. 275–7. For the 'astonishing growth of appropriations between 1378 and 1402', see *Register of Henry Chichele, Archbishop of Canterbury, 1414–1443*, ed. E. F. Jacob (4 vols, London, 1943), vol. 1, p. cxlviii; *Henry IV*, pp. 368–9.
7. The total number may have been half as much again, for some appropriations were licensed by the king without reference to the pope (E. F. Jacob, 'A Note on the English Concordat of 1418', in *Medieval Studies Presented to Aubrey Gwynn*, ed. J. A. Watt, J. B. Morrall and F. X. Martin (Dublin, 1961), pp. 349–58; Peter Heath, *Church and Realm, 1272–1461* (London, 1988), pp. 263–5).
8. *The Register of Richard Clifford, Bishop of Worcester: A Calendar*, ed. Waldo Smith (Toronto, 1976), pp. 128–37, 161–2.
9. Thomson, 'Knightly Piety', p. 97, calls it a 'do-it-yourself religion'.
10. *SAC* 2, pp. 334–7; McFarlane, *Lancastrian Kings*, p. 212, thought Walsingham's account of Clifford's recantation to be 'fishy'.
11. Matthew Spinka, *John Hus: A Biography* (Princeton, 1968), pp. 34–85; John Klassen, *The Nobility and the Making of the Hussite Revolution* (New York, 1978), pp. 2–3, 27–46, 98; Anthony Kenny, *Wyclif* (Oxford, 1985), p. 102.
12. R. F. Yeager, 'Gower's "Epistle to Archbishop Arundel": The Evidence of Oxford, All Souls College, MS 98', in *Manuscript and Print in Late Medieval and Early Modern Britain: Essays in Honour of Professor Julia Boffey*, ed. Tamara Atkin and Jaclyn Rajsic (Cambridge, 2019), pp. 13–34 (quote on p. 28). Gower also dedicated the final version of his *Vox Clamantis and Cronica Tripertita* to Arundel, addressing him as 'Thomas, successor to Thomas (Becket)': *The Major Latin Works of John Gower*, ed. E. W. Stockton (Seattle, 1962), pp. 13, 47.
13. Payne probably had this letter approved by a snatch vote in a congregation attended by his supporters, rather than a full congregation of masters, as it claimed. It is possible, though unlikely, that he forged it: *Concilia*, vol. 3, p. 302, taken from BL, Ms Cotton Faustina C. vii, fo. 125r–v. In 1412 or 1413, fearing that he would be apprehended, Payne fled to Prague, where, as 'Peter Engliss', he played a leading part in Hussite war and diplomacy until his death in 1455 (F. Smahel, 'Payne, Peter', *ODNB*; Anne Hudson, *The Premature Reformation* (Oxford, 1988), pp. 99–103; A. B. Emden, *An Oxford Hall in Medieval Times* (Oxford, 1927), pp. 138–43).
14. Taylor's sermon circulated in both Latin and English: *Two Wycliffite Texts*, ed. Anne Hudson (Early English Text Society, Oxford, 1998), pp. xi–xxv, 3–23; *SAC* 2, pp. 478–81; Emden, *An Oxford Hall*, p. 127. Thorpe was not an Oxford master, but probably studied under Wyclif; cited by Bishop Braybrooke for heresy in the mid-1390s, he spent time in prison before being released (*John Lydford's Book*, ed. Dorothy Owen (London, 1974), pp. xlvii–l and nos 206, 209).
15. *BRUO*, vol. 1, p. 25.

16. *SAC* 2, pp. 478–81; although excommunicated by Arundel for his fox-like (*vulpeculis*) heresies in March 1410, Taylor avoided condemnation until March 1423, when he was convicted and burned (*Two Wycliffite Texts*, pp. xvii–xxv; *RA* 1, fo. 118v).
17. Maureen Jurkowski, 'The Arrest of William Thorpe in Shrewsbury and the Anti-Lollard Statute of 1406', *HR* 75 (2002), pp. 273–95.
18. *Two Wycliffite Texts*, pp. xxvi–l, 24–93, 105–32.
19. See pp. 239–41.
20. *Two Wycliffite Texts*, pp. 92–3.
21. On 19 September 1407, when he also surrendered his offices of keeper of Saltwood park and bailiff of Hythe; he was replaced by John Sutton on 24 September (*RA* 2, fo. 111r; *CCR 1405–9*, p. 291).
22. *Two Wycliffite Texts*, pp. liii, 80.
23. R. N. Swanson, *Universities, Academics and the Great Schism* (Cambridge, 1979), pp. 2, 202–12; Margaret Harvey, *Solutions to the Schism: A Study of Some English Attitudes, 1378–1409* (St Ottilien, 1983), p. 196; Hudson, *Premature Reformation*, pp. 333–4.
24. *Concilia*, vol. 3, p. 306: parliament ended on 2 December 1407; convocation met from 28 November to 10 December. In 1382, when Archbishop Courtenay first tackled Wycliffism at Oxford, he too summoned the convocation to St Frideswide's. For the *Constitutions*, see *RA* 2, fos 10r–12v; *Concilia*, vol. 3, pp. 314–19; *Records of Convocation*, ed. Gerald Bray (20 vols, Woodbridge, 2006), vol. 4, pp. 311–18.
25. For the implications of this most controversial clause, see Anne Hudson, 'Lollardy: The English Heresy?', *Studies in Church History* 9 (1982), pp. 261–83, at pp. 267–9. It is sometimes incorrectly paraphrased as 'That no text of Holy Scripture shall be translated into English'.
26. According to Hudson, 'this was the final defeat in Oxford's longstanding dispute over the right of the metropolitan to interfere in the university's affairs' ('Lollardy: The English Heresy?', p. 267).
27. Thomas Gascoigne, *Loci e Libro Veritatum*, ed. J. Thorold Rogers (Oxford, 1881), pp. 34, 180–1.
28. *Register of Robert Mascall, Bishop of Hereford, 1404–1416*, ed. J. H. Parry (Hereford, 1916), p. 105; *Register of Bishop Philip Repingdon, 1405–1419*, ed. Margaret Archer (Lincoln Record Society, 2 vols, 1963), vol. 1, p. 101.
29. Hudson, *Premature Reformation*, pp. 82–103; Jeremy Catto and Richard Evans, eds, *The History of the University of Oxford II: Late Medieval Oxford* (Oxford, 1992), pp. 244–5.
30. Much has been written by historians and literary scholars on the broader question of the *Constitutions*' impact on fifteenth-century literature, especially theological literature in English. This vast subject is marginal to the question of the reception of the *Constitutions* before 1414 but of central importance to Arundel's perceived legacy. See especially Nicholas Watson, 'Censorship and Cultural Change in Late Medieval England: Vernacular Theology, the Oxford Translation Debate, and Arundel's Constitutions of 1409', *Speculum* 70 (1995), pp. 822–64; Hudson, 'Lollardy: The English Heresy?'; Catto and Evans, *Late Medieval Oxford*, pp. 224–5; Hudson, *Premature Reformation*, pp. 82–5, 431.
31. W. R. Cooper, 'A Newly Identified Fragment in the Handwriting of William Tyndale', *Reformation* 3 (1998), pp. 323–47 (quotes at pp. 338, 343); Anne

Hudson, *Lollards and Their Books* (London, 1985), pp. 67–84. Arundel is also alleged to have blamed 'the negligence of prelates and other men, insomuch that some said he would on the morrow leave his office as chancellor and forsake the world'; the latter point, if correctly reported, was surely a rhetorical flourish.

32. Hudson, 'Lollardy: The English Heresy?'; Annie Sutherland, 'Psalms as Polemic: The English Bible Debate', in *Polemic: Language as Violence in Medieval and Early Modern Discourse*, ed. Almut Suerbaum, George Southcombe and Benjamin Thompson (Farnham, 2015), pp. 149–63; Catto and Evans, *Late Medieval Oxford*, pp. 224–5.
33. *Chichele's Register*, ed. Jacob, vol. 1, p. cxxxix, n. 8.
34. Watson, 'Censorship and Cultural Change', p. 862; Lotte Hellinga and J. B. Trapp, eds, *Cambridge History of the Book in Britain 3: 1400–1557* (Cambridge, 1999), pp. 25–6; Catto and Evans, *Late Medieval Oxford*, p. 251.
35. *RA* 1, fos 23r–v, 36r, 71r–91r.
36. TNA, E 403/595, 11 July 1408 (*pro unione ecclesie sancte celebrandum*); *Concilia*, vol. 3, p. 309; Bray, *Records of Convocation*, vol. 4, pp. 323–5; *SAC* 2, pp. 536–7.
37. *militantis ecclesiae*, or the Church on earth.
38. . . . *non incipiendo a subtractione obedientiae ab ipso domino nostro papa Gregorio XII . . . sed volumus, ut decet, et debemus, ipso domino papae in licitis et canonicis obedire ac reverentiam debitam obedire* (*Concilia*, vol. 3, p. 309). The French had long advocated withdrawal of obedience from both popes, but the English had never favoured it (Harvey, *Solutions to the Schism*, p. 192).
39. Harvey, *Solutions to the Schism*, pp. 131–46.
40. For example, the lifting of Innocent's sentence of excommunication and the episcopal appointments of 1407. Yet Henry probably had genuine doubts about the legitimacy of a general council not supported by the pope, for which there was no precedent.
41. *SAC* 2, pp. 538–55.
42. *SAC* 2, pp. 556–65.
43. *Foedera*, vol. 8, pp. 567–9; Harvey, *Solutions to the Schism*, p. 150, n. 18. Another five bishops, representatives of religious orders, universities and cathedral chapters, and several dozen doctors were envisaged.
44. For the promulgation of the *Constitutions* between January and April 1409, see *RA* 2, fo. 12v; *Concilia*, vol. 3, p. 320; *Register of Robert Hallum, Bishop of Salisbury*, ed. Joyce Horn (Canterbury and York Society 72, 1982), p. 141.
45. *Concilia*, vol. 3, pp. 311–14. There were about thirty-five English delegates plus their household servants (Harvey, *Solutions to the Schism*, p. 158). Convocation imposed levies to cover their considerable expenses: Langley took 100 servants; Richard Holme, canon of York, took 24 (*Signet Letters*, nos 728–9; *Hallum's Register*, pp. 99–102).
46. Harvey, *Solutions to the Schism*, pp. 162–6; E. F. Jacob, *Essays in the Conciliar Epoch* (Manchester, 1963), pp. 74–84; Catto and Evans, *Late Medieval Oxford*, pp. 238–45.
47. E. F. Jacob, *Archbishop Henry Chichele* (London, 1967), pp. 10–13.
48. Alexander Russell, 'Conciliarism and Heresy in England', in *After Arundel: Religious Writing in Fifteenth-Century England*, ed. Vincent Gillespie and Kantik Ghosh (Turnhout, 2011), pp. 155–65.

49. *CCR 1409–13*, pp. 2–3 (royal mandate to the archbishops, 17 October 1409); *Concilia*, vol. 3, pp. 321–2 (Arundel's mandate to his diocesans, 22 October 1409, same wording).
50. The Council of Constance (Germany) elected Pope Martin V in 1417.

13 The Disendowment Bill and Wycliffism at Oxford (1410–11)

1. *CPR 1405–8*, p. 476 (mandates to sheriffs of Norfolk, Suffolk, Warwick and Leicester and the dioceses of London and Bath and Wells, April–August 1408).
2. 'John Rakyer', perhaps just 'everyman', has not been identified. For Badby's initial interrogation and trial, see *RA* 2, fos 16–18; *Concilia*, vol. 3, pp. 324–9; *Records of Convocation*, ed. Gerald Bray (20 vols, Woodbridge, 2006), vol. 4, pp. 360–7.
3. As with all the disendowment agitation of the previous forty years, the Bill was not mentioned in the official records, but the text was preserved, with slight variations, by two chroniclers. *Selections from English Wycliffite Writings*, ed. Anne Hudson (Cambridge, 1978), pp. 135–7, 203–7, provides the London chronicler's English text, with notes; Walsingham's Latin text is in *SAC* 2, pp. 582–9 (modern English translation in *PROME*, vol. 8, p. 509). The London chronicler assigned the Bill to the 1407 parliament, but Walsingham's 1410 is generally agreed to be much more likely.
4. Anne Hudson, *The Premature Reformation* (Oxford, 1988), pp. 114–15, 174, 339–42.
5. *SAC* 2 has five universities, but fifteen is probably correct.
6. *SAC* 2, pp. 590–2.
7. Peter McNiven, *Heresy and Politics in the Reign of Henry IV* (Woodbridge, 1987), pp. 195–7; *SAC* 2, p. 592, says that it was Henry's former treasurer and close friend John Norbury who led the lay opposition to the Bill, having warned Arundel what was coming. A very similar request based on this petition was submitted to the parliament of 1431 (*PROME*, vol. 10, p. 480).
8. Hudson, *English Wycliffite Writings*, p. 137.
9. They were asked for a subsidy on 21 February. On the 24th, John Whitehead, an Irish professor of Scripture at Oxford, defended himself from charges laid against him by the Dominican friars – for example, that he had criticized their right to hear confessions (*BRUO*, vol. 3, p. 2037).
10. A point reiterated five times: *in vulgari* (three times), *in lingua materna* and *in Anglicis* (*Concilia*, vol. 3, p. 327).
11. The spider appears in the official record and two chronicles (*SAC* 2, p. 580; *CE*, p. 150). Twenty years later, on trial for heresy, Joan of Arc was accused of familiarity with the devil in the guise of insects.
12. *Foedera*, vol. 8, p. 627 (*igni committi*); *CCR 1409–13*, p. 30.
13. *CE*, p. 152, says that he cried out, 'Have pity on me!' but whether to God or to the crowd is unclear.
14. McNiven, *Heresy and Politics*, pp. 199–219.
15. *SAC* 2, p. 582 (*umbra*, usually 'shadow', but in this case signifying his ghost).
16. *PROME*, vol. 8, pp. 456–7.
17. *PROME*, vol. 8, pp. 464–5, 506–7; *SAC* 2, p. 590, where the details differ from the text of the petitions.

18. *Concilia*, vol. 3, pp. 328–30 (3 April); *CPR 1408–13*, p. 224 (5 April); *CE*, p. 152. Schedule in *Register of Thomas Langley of Durham 1406–1437*, ed. R. L. Storey (2 vols, Durham, 1956–7), p. 51 (John XXIII is identified as pope, so after May 1410).
19. *Usk*, pp. 248–9.
20. *Munimenta Academica Oxoniensis*, ed. H. Tasker (2 vols, London, RS, 1868), vol. 1, pp. 266–7; *CPR 1408–13*, p. 191 (*ex gratia* payment to Oriel of 50 marks); Lotte Hellinga and J. B. Trapp, eds, *Cambridge History of the Book in Britain 3: 1400–1557* (Cambridge, 1999), p. 317.
21. Forty-five of the eighty-five bishops during Edward III's reign were from Oxford, seven from Cambridge (J. R. Highfield, 'The English Hierarchy in the Reign of Edward III', *TRHS* 6 (1956), pp. 115–38, at p. 128). Arundel visited Cambridge in 1401, found no evidence of heresy and in October 1404 discharged it (*RA* 1, fo. 388v); Jeremy Catto and Richard Evans, eds, *The History of the University of Oxford II: Late Medieval Oxford* (Oxford, 1992), p. 244.
22. A. B. Emden, *An Oxford Hall in Medieval Times* (Oxford, 1927), pp. 143–7; Catto and Evans, *Late Medieval Oxford*, pp. 244–53; *Snappe's Formulary*, ed. H. E. Salter (Oxford, 1924), pp. 95–115, 115–180 (quote at p. 120); *RA* 1, fo. 127r–v.
23. *Concilia*, vol. 3, p. 322; *Snappe's Formulary*, pp. 95–100. Fleming, reputedly a brilliant scholar, was actually about twenty-six; he later became an outspoken opponent of Lollardy and bishop of Lincoln, and he founded Lincoln College (Catto and Evans, *Late Medieval Oxford*, pp. 243–6; Emden, *An Oxford Hall*, p. 145).
24. *SAC* 2, pp. 568–79.
25. *Snappe's Formulary*, pp. 136–8; *Signet Letters*, no. 745. A letter to the chancellor of the university, Richard Courtenay, in December 1410, insisted on the elimination of heresy there (*RA* 2, fo. 127).
26. *Concilia*, vol. 3, pp. 339–49; *Henry IV*, pp. 488–90; J. Wylie, *History of England under Henry the Fourth* (4 vols, London, 1884–98), vol. 3, pp. 442–9; Catto and Evans, *Late Medieval Oxford*, p. 247. Wyclif's books were also burned at St Paul's Cross (*RA* 2, fos 26v–27v).
27. *Snappe's Formulary*, pp. 133–5, 156–8; Wylie, *Reign of Henry IV*, vol. 3, p. 435.
28. *Snappe's Formulary*, pp. 158–60; *Signet Letters*, no. 749.
29. *Snappe's Formulary*, pp. 160–1; Coryngham had been Henry's confessor since 1405 and was as deeply trusted as most royal confessors were (Chris Given-Wilson, 'The King's Confessors and the Royal Conscience in Late Medieval England', in *Fourteenth-Century England XII*, ed. J. Bothwell and J. S. Hamilton (Woodbridge, 2022), pp. 1–28).
30. *RA* 2, fos 83v–92v; *Snappe's Formulary*, p. 102. He visited several religious houses in Oxford before 7 August and several more in Oxfordshire, Bedfordshire and Buckinghamshire after leaving, before arriving back in London on 24 August; *ISCA*, pp. 58–9, says he visited the university *cum manu forti*.
31. *CPR 1408–13*, pp. 316–18 (April–May 1411).
32. *Snappe's Formulary*, pp. 161–2, addressed to 'you, reverend father in Christ etc, and graduate of the said university . . . who is known to be within the territory of the said university'.
33. *Snappe's Formulary*, p. 110; *Usk*, pp. 244–5, says that there were 'several deaths' and that local dignitaries (*patrie proceres*) took Arundel's side; Catto and Evans, *Late Medieval Oxford*, p. 249.

34. *Snappe's Formulary*, pp. 110, 163–6; his sermon was on the theme 'Come into the garden'.
35. *Snappe's Formulary*, p. 111.
36. *Snappe's Formulary*, pp. 166–80.
37. *PROME*, vol. 8, pp. 523–6; *CPL*, vol. 6, pp. 302–4; *Signet Letters*, no. 758.
38. Peter Payne left for Prague in 1412 or 1413 and in January 1413 a general papal monition ordered more of Wyclif's works to be burned, including his *Dialogus* and *Trialogus* (*CPL*, vol. 6, p. 174; Catto and Evans, *Late Medieval Oxford*, p. 249; *Snappe's Formulary*, pp. 174–80; *Concilia*, vol. 3, p. 336).
39. Catto and Evans, *Late Medieval Oxford*, p. 248; *Henry IV*, pp. 489–90.
40. *PROME*, vol. 8, p. 524. For their quarrel, see this volume, pp. 220–1; *Munimenta Academica Oxoniensis*, vol. 1, pp. 251–2.
41. Courtenay did not live to fulfil his promise, dying at Harfleur in 1415, aged thirty-four. Henry V attended his deathbed, personally closed his eyes and arranged for his burial next to the shrine of Edward the Confessor in Westminster abbey, next to the spot where he himself chose to be buried (R. G. Davies, 'Courtenay, Richard, Bishop of Norwich', *ODNB*.)
42. *Henry IV*, pp. 493–500.
43. As in 1409–10, there was a hiatus between Thomas Beaufort's resignation and Arundel's reinstatement as chancellor, during which the great seal was entrusted to John Wakering; TNA, E 28/23, nos 35 and 36 (28 December 1411 and 18 January 1412) are orders from the king originally addressed to Wakering, 'keeper of the great seal', whose name was crossed out and replaced (*reformatur*) with Arundel's. The first meeting of the new council was on 6 January (TNA, E 403/610, 6 February and 17 March 1412).

14 Jerusalem: The End of a Reign (1412–13)

1. LPL, CM XI/26 (*Foedera*, vol. 8, p. 753), granted at the 'special request' of the lords and commons in parliament.
2. *SAC* 2, pp. 603–11; *Henry IV*, pp. 493–512.
3. *SAC* 2, pp. 611–15.
4. *Henry IV*, pp. 508–12.
5. *Henry IV*, pp. 513–16.
6. TNA, E 403/611, 3 November 1412; *Henry IV*, pp. 542–5. A meeting of the great council of the realm was held at Lambeth on 19 March 1411 (*POPC*, vol. 2, pp. 6–10).
7. See p. 149 for spiritual kinship; for their wills, see pp. 187–8, 257–8.
8. *Henry IV*, pp. 495–6. TNA, E 28/23, no. 53, dated 19 December, is an order from the king to the treasurer to produce, by 8 January, a full account, with supporting documentation, of all income and expenditure 'during the time that you have been treasurer of England'. The year is probably December 1411, but could possibly be 1406 or 1409.
9. These gravamina dealt with traditional clerical grievances (separation of lay and ecclesiastical courts, harassment of clerics by royal officials) and pleaded for exemption of poor vicars and rectors from taxation. The last and longest railed against Oxford university's failure to suppress heterodoxy and urged Arundel to

finish the job. A friar claiming to be a bishop was also imprisoned (*RA* 2, fos 22–24; *Concilia*, vol. 3, pp. 334–7).

10. *SAC* 2, pp. 603–11; *Henry IV*, pp. 493–512, 522–3. Clarence's captains also took out loans to pay their retinues; Arundel helped the duke of York to do so (*CPR 1408–13*, pp. 401, 406, 410, 421, 451).
11. BL, MS Arundel 68, fo. 57r–v. The visitation of Norwich dated in Arundel's register as March–April 1412 took place the previous year (*RA* 2, fos 77–78; *CA* 1, p. 338, n. 1).
12. *CPR 1408–13*, p. 453.
13. *CCR 1409–13*, p. 415; TNA, E 403/611, 25 January 1413; *Concilia*, vol. 3, p. 338; *Henry IV*, p. 515, n. 11.
14. BL, Add. Ms. 35,295, fo. 264v.

15 The Oldcastle Rising (1413–14)

1. Gwilym Dodd, ed., *Henry V: New Interpretations* (York, 2013), pp. 41–2.
2. *SAC* 2, pp. 620–2, and *Usk*, p. 242, for varying interpretations of the significance of the unseasonal weather.
3. *PROME*, vol. 9, pp. 9–10; *Henry IV*, pp. 522–3; TNA, E 404/29, no. 3. The agreement was dated 15 May 1413 and ratified by parliament on 3 June.
4. *A Collection of all the Wills of the Kings and Queens of England*, ed. J. Nichols (Society of Antiquaries, London, 1780), pp. 203–7. He later wrote a second will, or perhaps a codicil, but it has not survived (Chris Given-Wilson, 'Royal Wills, 1376–1475', in *The Fifteenth Century XVII*, ed. Linda Clark (Woodbridge, 2020), pp. 1–16, at pp. 8–9.
5. See pp. 187–8.
6. Perhaps on 31 March, when Arundel was at Canterbury to help with the admission to the cathedral fraternity of Thomas Langley (here designated 'principal executor of King Henry IV') and others: BL, Ms Arundel 68, fo. 57v.
7. Parliament ended on 9 June and convocation probably on 6 June. This was a continuation of the convocation summoned under Henry IV, which last met on 6 March; apparently no new summons was thought necessary following his death. Canterbury agreed to grant one tenth, as did the York convocation when it met on 27 July, though only *post magnam altercationem et varias excusationes* (after great disagreement and various excuses) (*Concilia*, vol. 3, p. 358).
8. LPL, Ms 1999 (i) and (ii), 6 May and 30 December 1413. Twelve years earlier, when Lucca was the chief factor of the great Florentine merchant company of the Alberti (or Albertini), Arundel had secured export licences at denizen rates for him. LPL, Ms 1999 (iii) is a letter from Robert Hallum to the cardinal of Santa Croce, dated Thursday 16 July, possibly 1401, asking him to counteract rumours at the Curia that Lucca had been acting contrary to the pope's interests, which was untrue. Lucca in turn facilitated the canonization of St John of Bridlington (also in 1401) and arranged payments to Englishmen abroad (George Holmes, 'Florentine Merchants in England, 1346–1436', *Economic History Review* 13 (1960), pp. 193–208; *ANLP*, nos 290, 355; *CCR 1399–1402*, pp. 373, 452, 546; *CCR 1409–13*, pp. 439–40; *CPL*, vol. 4, pp. 103, 107, 112, 149–51).
9. *SAC* 2, p. 620 and n. 896; whether St Dunstan's feast was in fact elevated is unclear.

10. *RA* 2, fos 68r–69r, 141v, 95r–101v; R. G. Davies, 'Thomas Arundel as Archbishop of Canterbury', *JEH* 14 (1973), pp. 9–21, at pp. 16–19.
11. *Concilia*, vol. 3, pp. 338, 351–2.
12. *RA* 2, fos 13–14; John Thomson, 'Oldcastle, John, Baron Cobham', *ODNB*.
13. *Concilia*, vol. 3, pp. 352–3.
14. J. H. Wylie and W. Waugh, *The Reign of Henry V* (3 vols, Cambridge, 1914–29), vol. 1, pp. 244–57, at p. 246, n. 2.
15. *RA* 2, fos 26v–27v, 142v–145r; *Concilia*, vol. 3, pp. 353–7.
16. Walsingham's account (*SAC* 2, pp. 622–35) is heavily based on the trial record circulated by the archbishop and stresses that Arundel acted with propriety, speaking to Oldcastle 'graciously', 'patiently' and 'modestly', offering many chances to save himself and only eventually, 'with heaviness in his heart', condemning him.
17. *Gesta Henrici Quinti*, ed. Frank Taylor and John Roskell (Oxford, 1975), p. 6.
18. For the Lollard Rising, see *SAC* 2, pp. 636–42; *Gesta Henrici Quinti*, pp. 6–11; *Usk*, pp. 244–7; Wylie and Waugh, *Henry V*, vol. 1, pp. 258–92; Maureen Jurkowski, 'Henry V's Suppression of the Oldcastle Revolt', in Dodd, *Henry V*, pp. 103–29; Edward Powell, *Kingship, Law and Society: Criminal Justice in the Reign of Henry V* (Oxford, 1989), pp. 141–67.
19. *Usk*, pp. 248–9, is the main source for this convocation, which is not noted in *Concilia*, but for the summons see *Register of Bishop Philip Repingdon, 1405–1419*, ed. Margaret Archer (Lincoln Record Society, 2 vols, 1963), vol. 2, p. 367. Usk implied that the Statute of Lollards passed in the parliament of April 1414 was based on these ordinances, but the automatic conviction of heretics as traitors and complementary hanging and burning were not included, although forfeiture was, for the first time (*PROME*, vol. 9, pp. 55–7). The November 1413 convocation was evidently the spur to Philip Repingdon to begin moving towards a more proactive policy of heretical investigation in his diocese, a significant shift of emphasis which foreshadowed the provincial and parliamentary legislation of 1416 (Ian Forrest, *The Detection of Heresy in Late Medieval England* (Oxford, 2005), pp. 86–90).
20. *SAC* 2, p. 640 (*et post infelicia fata cremati*); *CCR 1413–19*, pp. 56–7. Presumably they were relapsed heretics, but there is nothing to suggest that Arundel or other prelates were involved.
21. On 27 January, Arundel was pardoned his contribution to the clerical tenth granted by the last convocation because of his 'great expense on the king's service' (*CPR 1413–16*, p. 157).
22. *SAC* 2, pp. 726–31.
23. *CCR 1413–19*, pp. 114–15; Powell, *Kingship, Law and Society*, pp. 154–5.
24. *Usk*, pp. 248–9.
25. *Register of Henry Chichele, Archbishop of Canterbury, 1414–1443*, ed. E. F. Jacob (4 vols, London, 1943), vol. 1, pp. cxxxii–cxxxix; *Concilia*, vol. 3, p. 378; cf. Davies, 'Thomas Arundel', p. 20.
26. Jill Havens, 'A Curious Erasure in Walsingham's Short Chronicle and the Politics of Heresy', in *Fourteenth Century England II*, ed. Chris Given-Wilson (Woodbridge, 2002), pp. 95–106; Anne Hudson, *The Premature Reformation* (Oxford, 1988), p. 12.
27. *RA* 2, fos 69v, 176r.

16 Canterbury

1. BL, Ms Arundel 68, fo. 59r: *Erat autem vir eximie sciencie, clari ingenii in singulis agibilibus, providus et circumspectus atque in pontificalis officii executione sedulus et multum devotus regibus ipsius temporis regnantibus, ac regno pro sui maturitate sani consilii multipliciter acceptatus, necnon eiusdem regni vicibus iteratus sepius cancellarius.*
2. *RA* 1, fo. 410v; C. E. Woodruff and W. Danks, *Memorials of Canterbury Cathedral* (London, 1912), p. 460. The bells, blessed by Arundel on 8 April 1409 and later moved to the north-western tower, were named St John the Evangelist, St Blaise, St Gabriel and St Mary; Prior Chillenden added a fifth, St Thomas. Arundel also bequeathed £100 to distribute between the monks at the prior's discretion.
3. LPL, Ms 78; my thanks to Rob Bartlett for this reference.
4. C. H. Lawrence, *St Edmund of Abingdon* (Oxford, 1960), pp. 155, 166–9.
5. Anne Duggan, *Thomas Becket* (London, 2004), p. 216; *VCH Kent*, vol. 2, pp. 115–17.
6. Woodruff and Danks, *Memorials of Canterbury Cathedral*, pp. 194–5.
7. *TA*, p. 373; *CA* 1, pp. 569–70.
8. *CR*, pp. 162–7.
9. *RA* 1, fos 128r–129r; *RA* 2, fo. 71r.
10. *RA* 1, fos 10r, 371r, 446r.
11. BL, Ms Arundel 68, fos 53–58 (fo. 58 for Chillenden's obituary); *CPR 1408–13*, pp. 32–3; CCA-DCc-ChAnt/B/351–89, 1098, G/171, H/157.
12. For his 'outstanding financial acumen' and other qualities, see R. A. Smith, *Canterbury Cathedral Priory: A Study in Monastic Administration* (Cambridge, 1943), pp. 190–4; Mavis Mate, 'Chillenden, Thomas', *ODNB*.
13. Tim Tatton-Brown, 'The Rebuilding of the Nave and Western Transepts, 1377–1503', in *Canterbury Cathedral Nave: Archaeology, History and Architecture*, ed. Kevin Blockley, Margaret Sparks and Tim Tatton-Brown (Canterbury, 1997), pp. 128–46. (See plate 6.)
14. Woodruff and Danks, *Memorials of Canterbury Cathedral*, pp. 167–8; CCA-DCc/ChAnt/W/30.
15. Woodruff and Danks, *Memorials of Canterbury Cathedral*, pp. 172–81; BL, Ms Arundel 68, fo. 58.
16. *RA* 2, fo. 132r. For Wodnesbergh, see Smith, *Canterbury Cathedral Priory*, pp. 194–7; Woodruff and Danks, *Memorials of Canterbury Cathedral*, pp. 187–9.
17. Chillenden's obituarist says that, with the *ope et auxilio* [of Arundel], *navem istius ecclesie cum capella Beate Marie Virginis . . . totaliter renovavit* (he completely renovated the nave of this church, together with the chapel of the Blessed Virgin Mary), but then goes on, referring to Chillenden alone, *Claustrum quoque, domum capitularem, magnum dormitorium cum nova via versus ecclesiam et subtus domum rasture, de novo fieri fecit* (he also had the cloister, chapter house and great dormitory, along with a new passage towards the church and, below it, a shaving room, made again from new) (BL, MS Arundel 68, fo. 58r); Woodruff and Danks, *Memorials of Canterbury Cathedral*, pp. 187–8.
18. Paul A. Fox, *Great Cloister: A Lost Canterbury Tale* (Oxford, 2020), pp. 1–34 (quotes at pp. 2 and 12). Bay 1, by the door leading to the Martyrdom, and bay 33, by the door leading to the chapter house, both celebrate the archbishop's close family. Bay 33 has the shields of Arundel's parents, sisters, nephews, nieces, great-nieces,

great-nephews, sisters-in-law, brother-in-law and cousin (Fox, *Great Cloister*, p. 14). (See plate 7.) Yet the connections between many of the other 121 individuals or shields said to be 'linked directly' to Arundel are quite tenuous. It is worth noting that the original paintwork on the shields has almost entirely disappeared.

19. *RA* 2, fo. 58v; *Lit. Cant.*, vol. 3, pp. 123–31; *CPL*, vol. 6, pp. 133–4 (royal and papal licences); Patrick Collinson, Nigel Ramsay and Margaret Sparks, eds, *A History of Canterbury Cathedral* (Oxford, 1995), pp. 475–6 (Arundel may have planned the effigy for his tomb-chest while archbishop of York); Woodruff and Danks, *Memorials of Canterbury Cathedral*, p. 194; *Inventories of Christ Church Canterbury*, ed. J. Wickham Legg and W. H. St John Hope (London, 1902), pp. 177–9. Each priest received £10 a year and they lived in a house south of the church. Maidstone church was re-founded as a college for a master and twenty-four chaplains and clerks by Archbishop Courtenay shortly before his death (*Lit. Cant.*, vol. 3, pp. 45–8).
20. *VCH Kent*, vol. 2, pp. 128–30.
21. *William Thorne's Chronicle of St Augustine's Abbey Canterbury*, ed. A. H. Davis (Oxford, 1934), pp. 2, 26–9, 39–40, 55, 58, 95, 103, 132, 293, 304–13, 347, 387. Thorne's work continued from 1272 the history of St Augustine's written by Thomas Sprott, although Thorne rearranged it and added much new material. Thomas Elmham, a monk at St Augustine's from 1379 to 1414, also provides some details of these disputes under the Anglo-Saxon and Norman kings (Antonia Gransden, *Historical Writing in England II* (London, 1982), pp. 344–55).
22. *William Thorne's Chronicle*, pp. 613–15 (Sudbury), 670 (Courtenay), 676–81 (Arundel); *CA* 1, pp. 148–9.
23. LPL, Ms 419; *CPR 1405–8*, p. 276 (Welde had died in 1405). (See plate 5.)
24. BL, Ms Arundel 68, fos 53v, 57v. In July 1412, Hunden was licensed to appoint attorneys in the king's courts because his 'great infirmities' did not allow him to appear in person; a month later he was licensed to go on pilgrimage to Jerusalem, but probably did not go. He remained abbot until 1420 (*CPR 1408–13*, pp. 409, 418).
25. *RA* 2, fo. 122r (confirmation of William Canterbury's election as prior of St Gregory's). The archbishops often visited the treasury and archives at St Gregory's (*CA* 1, pp. 34, 123, 139–44, 546; *CA* 2, pp. 38–9; I. Churchill, 'Table of Canterbury Archbishopric Charters', *Camden Miscellany* 15 (London, 1929), pp. vii–ix).
26. Gransden, *Historical Writing II*, p. 141, n. 166; *CE*, pp. xvi–xvii.
27. About half of Arundel's ordination ceremonies were conducted at Canterbury; others were held at Lambeth, Maidstone, Ford, Dover, Otford, Mortlake, Croydon and in London at St Paul's, St Mary Arches and All Saints church in Bread Street (*RA* 1, fos 324–343; *RA* 2, fos 95ff).
28. *RA* 1, fos 324 (Canterbury), 395r (Otford), 409v (Saltwood), 13r (profession of Guy Mone, 9 October 1401), 147v (new altar); *RA* 2, fos 98v (Ford), 125v (Queenborough), 95r (ordination, December 1413), 111r (Matilda Lovell); see also Appendix 1 (oratories as studies).
29. *TA*, p. 276; *RA* 2, fos 69v, 176r.
30. H. Gough, 'The Archbishop's Manor at Ford, Hoath', *Archaeologia Cantiana* 121 (2001), pp. 251–68. He spent several weeks at Ford in October–December 1410, visiting Queenborough castle on 26 October to dedicate a new chapel 'next to the

entrance to the hall of the castle' to the Blessed Virgin Mary and St Dunstan, and Hoath on 9 December to dedicate a chapel of ease for Reculver church to the Virgin 'and her Cross'; he also conducted ordinations at Ford (*RA* 2, fos 127r–128r). At Saltwood, on 6 August 1401, he dedicated a new chapel built by Archbishop Courtenay to the Blessed Virgin Mary and St Thomas (*RA* 1, fo. 409v).

31. F. R. H. Du Boulay, *The Lordship of Canterbury* (London, 1966), pp. 195–6.
32. Du Boulay, *Lordship of Canterbury*, pp. 269–70.
33. Du Boulay, *Lordship of Canterbury*, pp. 218–46; E. F. Jacob, *Archbishop Henry Chichele* (London, 1967), p. 30. This was net income, allowing for deductions at source for wages, stock and running costs; in his petition to appropriate Northfleet church in 1405, Arundel stated that his *mensa* (episcopal income) was worth 'not more than 6,000 marks (£4,000)' (*CPL*, vol. 6, pp. 133–4). This would have included the profits of the liberty, around £250 a year. The liberty of Canterbury was a mark of superior lordship, including rights such as return of writs, shipwreck and chattels of felons and fugitives. The archbishops also had a mint at Canterbury, located in the High Street, and the right to issue their own coinage, the income from which varied greatly but was £200–£300 a year at most and often much less (Du Boulay, *Lordship of Canterbury*, pp. 284, 314–26, Appendix B; for the 'warden of the exchange of Canterbury', see *CCR 1402–5*, p. 197). In 1384 the temporalities and spiritualities of the archbishopric were said to be worth £2,105 a year, but this was an under-valuation for taxation (*William Thorne's Chronicle*, pp. 623–4; *Monasticon Anglicanum*, ed. William Dugdale (6 vols, London, 1846–9), vol. 1, pp. 89–91; Walsingham noted that, in 1404, severe flooding in Kent cost the archbishop and chapter around £1,000: *SAC* 2, p. 424). 'Benefices belonging to the collation or presentation of the archbishop of Canterbury' in Arundel's register listed 113 churches, rectories and vicarages grouped under sixteen deaneries (*RA* 1, fos 258r–259r). These were his spiritualities.
34. Michael Jones, 'Knolles, Sir Robert', *ODNB*; Knolles's two wills are in *RA* 1, fos 245–247. The average episcopal income in the early fourteenth century was £1,590 (B. M. S. Campbell, 'The Agrarian Problem in the Early Fourteenth Century', *Past & Present* 188 (2005), pp. 3–70, at p. 12).
35. CCA-DCc/Register N, fos 221v–222r; see also Appendix I in the present volume. I am grateful to Cressida Williams, Archives and Library Manager at Christ Church, for supplying me with an image of this inventory. (See plate 8.)
36. Alison McHardy, 'The Loss of Archbishop Stratford's Register', *HR* 70 (1997), pp. 317–21. The culprits seem never to have been apprehended.
37. TNA, E 403/564, 10 December 1399; E 401/638, 28 July 1406; *CPR 1401–5*, p. 400; *CPR 1405–8*, p. 215; *CPR 1408–13*, p. 421; *Henry IV*, pp. 285–6.
38. See pp. 2–3. He had connections with John Philpot, one of his father's executors, and Richard Whittington, but their nature is unclear (*TA*, pp. 195, 243; TNA, E 403/574, 27 October 1401).
39. Nigel Saul, *Richard II* (New Haven and London, 1997), pp. 163–4; *WC*, pp. 272–6; David Carpenter, *Henry III, 1258–1272* (New Haven and London, 2023), pp. 384–5.
40. Richard II deprived Arundel of this right in 1397, but Henry IV restored it (see p. 31); Carole Rawcliffe, *The Staffords, Earls of Stafford and Dukes of Buckingham* (Cambridge, 1978), pp. 105–8). After Edmund, earl of Stafford's death in 1403,

two-thirds of the lordship was put in the archbishop's wardship and one-third given to Countess Anne in dower (*CCR 1402–5*, pp. 260–1).

17 Family

1. *CPL*, vol. 5, pp. 385 (Arundel's petition), 387 (other 'persons" petition). Isabella was a minor in the king's wardship (*CFR 1399–1405*, pp. 79, 99). It was obviously the deaths in quick succession of Humphrey, Eleanor and Joan that prompted this concern for the inheritance (*CFR 1399–1405*, pp. 70, 79, 99). Anne's son, another Humphrey, the eventual Stafford heir, was not born until December 1402. Her husband, Earl Edmund, was killed at Shrewsbury in July 1403. She married again and remained countess of Stafford until her death in 1438 (Anthony Tuck, 'Thomas of Woodstock, Duke of Gloucester', *ODNB*; Carole Rawcliffe, *The Staffords, Earls of Stafford and Dukes of Buckingham* (Cambridge, 1978), pp. 7–27).
2. *Women of the English Nobility and Gentry, 1066–1500*, ed. Jennifer Ward (Manchester, 1995), pp. 21–2; this volume, p. 11; *Henry IV*, pp. 25–7; *CCR 1399–1402*, pp. 161–4.
3. By June 1402, Isabella had made her profession as a nun (*CFR 1399–1405*, p. 105; Jennifer Ward, *English Noblewomen in the Later Middle Ages* (London, 1992), pp. 143–4; *CPR 1416–22*, p. 364).
4. *TA*, pp. 171–3, 181–207.
5. Mary married Henry (later Henry IV) in February 1381, but continued to live with her mother until 1384.
6. *Henry IV*, p. 77; Ward, *Women of the English Nobility*, p. 115.
7. *Usk*, pp. 88–9; *SAC* 2, pp. 290–4; and *Chronique de la traison et mort de Richart deux roy dengleterre*, ed. B. Williams (London, 1846), 96–9, give different accounts of this, the latter two focused on Joan's role in his execution (*Signet Letters*, no. 919; *CCR 1399–1402*, pp. 34, 43).
8. *Henry IV*, p. 420.
9. *CPR 1401–5*, pp. 126–9. Jennifer Ward, 'Joan de Bohun, Countess of Hereford, Essex and Northampton, c. 1370–1419: Family, Land and Social Networks', *Essex Archaeology and History* 32 (2001), pp. 146–53; *ANLP*, no. 352; *CCR 1399–1401*, p. 349. She was active from early in her widowhood in defence of her rights (*PROME*, vol. 5, p. 428; vol. 6, p. 66).
10. James Ross, 'Seditious Activities: The Conspiracy of Maud de Vere, Countess of Oxford, 1403–4', in *The Fifteenth Century III*, ed. Linda Clark (Woodbridge, 2003), pp. 25–41, at p. 36; James Ross, 'De Vere Richard, Eleventh Earl of Oxford', *ODNB*. In 1411, Joan and Arundel were jointly appointed as arbitrators of a dispute arising from the will of Earl Richard's father, Aubrey (*CCR 1409–13*, p. 305). My thanks to James Ross for additional information on the de Veres.
11. TNA, E 403/602, 2 December 1409; E 403/611, 19 November 1412; she had £200 a year for his upkeep. In March 1410 he moved into the royal household as a ward of the queen (*CPR 1405–8*, p. 375; *CPR 1408–13*, p. 220).
12. *CPR 1408–13*, pp. 204–5, 216; *POPC*, vol. 2, p. 348. This would have spared those with less influence than Joan from having to wait for repayment. Her commission covered Essex, Hertford, Cambridge and Huntingdon.

13. *CPL*, vol. 6, p. 139 (April 1408). Joan was supporting another candidate, Robert Hunt, whom Hall accused of bribing her.
14. *ANLP*, no. 38, a letter from Joan to Arundel apologizing for being unable to join him for Easter as usual (dated Wednesday 11 April, either 1403 or 1408, the only two years in the reign which match that day of the week).
15. *CCR 1409–13*, p. 395; Jennifer Ward, *Women in England in the Middle Ages* (London, 2006), p. 109; K. B. McFarlane, *Lancastrian Kings and Lollard Knights* (Oxford, 1972), p. 115; *ANLP*, no. 334; Ward, *Women of the English Nobility*, pp. 153, 185–6. Her councillors included Essex gentry who were also notable servants of the king, such as the king's knight John Howard and the royal councillor and speaker of the commons John Doreward (Ffiona Swabey, *The Medieval Gentlewoman: Life in a Gentry Household in the Later Middle Ages* (Stroud, 1999), pp. 105–6); BL, Ms Arundel 68, fo. 53v. For other royal grants to Joan, and her transactions with leading Essex gentry such as William Marny and Gerard Braybrook, see *CPR 1399–1401*, pp. 34, 60, 468; *CPR 1405–8*, pp. 102, 122, 319–20; *CCR 1399–1402*, pp. 215, 306, 396; *CCR 1409–13*, p. 171.
16. Lucy Freeman Sandler, *The Lichtenthal Psalter and the Manuscript Patronage of the Bohun Family* (Studies in Medieval and Renaissance Art History 38, London, 2004); *Henry IV*, pp. 78–80, and works by Sandler cited there. Especially notable are the three psalters she commissioned for Mary's marriage to Henry of Bolingbroke, one of which had the Bohun and Lancaster arms with their tendrils embracing, symbolizing the union of the families.
17. *TA*, p. 191; Ward, *Women in England*, pp. 108–9; *CPR 1405–8*, pp. 386, 389; *VCH Essex*, vol. 2, p. 112; *CPR 1408–13*, p. 411 (chantry for Lord FitzWalter). Around 1406 she wrote to Arundel's registrar, William Milton, informing him that Great Bricett priory (Suffolk), 'which is under our patronage', was 'very badly governed' and needed investigation (*ANLP*, no. 323).
18. *Women's Books of Hours in Medieval England*, ed. Charity Scott-Stokes (Cambridge, 2006), pp. 1–7.
19. Ward, 'Joan de Bohun', p. 151. Joan's elder daughter, Eleanor, was also a great patron of illuminators, although her religious practice appears to have been conventional; for her will, see *A Collection of All the Wills of the Kings and Queens of England*, ed. J. Nichols (Society of Antiquaries, London, 1780), pp. 177–86. For Joan's and Mary's piety, see Jeremy Catto, 'The Prayers of the Bohuns', in *Soldiers, Nobles and Gentlemen: Essays in Honour of Maurice Keen*, ed. Peter Coss and Christopher Tyerman (Woodbridge, 2009), pp. 112–25; Jeremy Catto, 'Religion and the English Nobility in the Later Fourteenth Century', in *History and Imagination: Essays in Honour of H. R. Trevor-Roper*, ed. Hugh Lloyd-Jones, Valerie Pearl and Blair Worden (London, 1981), pp. 43–55. For Mary, see also *Henry IV*, pp. 79–80.
20. *Register of Henry Chichele, Archbishop of Canterbury, 1414–1443*, ed. E. F. Jacob (4 vols, London, 1943), vol. 1, pp. 96–7.
21. *Erat enim forma mulierum Deo devotarum, decus matronarum, meditans ac vigilans in templo Dei, vivens caste cum Anna vidua a morte viri omnibus diebus vitae suae. Sibi semper olivae more retinens radicis amaritudinem, ac aliis infundem odoris suavitatem, mente enim sana praevenit facie Dei in confessione, atque per satisfactionem condignam, cum virgines aptavit lampadem suam* (*Monasticon Anglicanum*, ed. William Dugdale (6 vols, London, 1846–9), vol. 4, pp. 134, 140).

22. TNA, E 403/612, 24 July 1413 (*firmaculo auri lapidibus preciosis ornati*). Clifford's executors also included Richard Colfox, one of the leaders of the 1414 Lollard Rising (Edward Powell, *Kingship, Law and Society: Criminal Justice in the Reign of Henry V* (Oxford, 1989), pp. 145, 236); the supervisor of Clifford's will was John Cheyne.
23. The tenth earl's lengthy will of 1375, which stated that his wife had made the same request, is calendared in *The Register of Simon Sudbury, Archbishop of Canterbury, 1375–1381*, ed. F. Donald Logan (Canterbury and York Society 110, Woodbridge, 2020), pp. 150–60; original in LPL, Reg. Sudbury, fo. 92v; cf. *TA*, 16. The eleventh earl said that he *ne vuile en nulle manere qe nulls genz armez, chivalx, herce, n'autre qe je n'ay devise pardevant, ne nul autre bobaunce, soient faitz entour de moi* (*Collection of Wills*, p. 121). A *herce* was an iron candle-frame large enough to enclose the bier, displaying hundreds of candles, also known in France as a *chapelle ardente*. Militaristic vanities such as the display of coats of arms and weaponry and the appearance in churches of mounted horses in trappings of war had been popular at noble and knightly funerals since the middle of the thirteenth century.
24. Grosmont wanted nothing *de bobaunce, come des homes armeez, ne des chivals couvertz, ny autres choses veines* (*Collection of Wills*, pp. 83–5).
25. J. A. F. Thomson, 'Knightly Piety', in *Lollardy and the Gentry in the Later Middle Ages*, ed. M. Aston and C. Richmond (Stroud, 1997), p. 98: 'the most famous pious layman of the mid-fourteenth century'.
26. She is barely mentioned in *TA* (but see pp. 5, 18n).
27. M. M. Stansfield, 'Holland, Thomas, Earl of Kent', *ODNB*; *CPR 1408–13*, p. 98. She did not remarry (Paul A. Fox, *Great Cloister: A Lost Canterbury Tale* (Oxford, 2020), p. 188, confuses her with the daughter of the eleventh earl).
28. *CIPM 1407–13*, no. 854; Margaret Aston and Colin Richmond, eds, *Lollardy and the Gentry in the Later Middle Ages* (Stroud, 1997), pp. 13–14; J. A. F. Thomson, 'Knightly Piety', in Aston and Richmond, *Lollardy and the Gentry*, pp. 95–111, at pp. 105–6; Christine Carpenter, 'Beauchamp, William, First Baron Bergavenny', *ODNB*; Christine Carpenter and Ed Walker, 'Beauchamp, Joan, Lady Bergavenny', *ODNB* ('perhaps the most formidable woman in England over the next twenty-four years', namely, 1411–35); *Usk*, p. 132; *CCR 1409–13*, p. 144; *RA* 2, fo. 155 (William's will); *ANLP*, no. 358 (letter from Joan to Arundel asking her 'lord and uncle' to help an esquire of Hereford who was being hounded by ill-wishers).
29. R. R. Davies, *The Revolt of Owain Glyn Dwr* (Oxford, 1995), pp. 109, 240–4, 307–8; G. L. Harriss, 'Fitzalan, Thomas, Earl of Arundel', *ODNB*; Powell, *Kingship, Law and* Society, pp. 216–24; *CCR 1409–13*, pp. 481–3.
30. Earl Thomas's mother died in 1385; in 1390, Earl Richard married Philippa, daughter of the earl of March and widow of the earl of Pembroke. After Philippa's death, St John, her executor, petitioned the pope alleging that the earl was wrongfully withholding 'movables and immovables' which should pertain to her dower. Boniface told Arundel to adjudicate between them, but his decision is not recorded: *CPL*, vol. 4, p. 352 (October 1402). See *Usk*, p. 114, for a fulsome obituary of Philippa; Earl Richard bequeathed many valuable jewels, plate and furnishings to her (*Collection of Wills*, pp. 128–30). For Poynings, see *CP*, vol. 11, p. 328.

31. Dallingridge was also the builder of Bodiam castle; Gaunt was eager to demonstrate the limits of the eleventh earl's patronage in Sussex (Simon Walker, *The Lancastrian Affinity, 1361–1399* (Oxford, 1990), pp. 127–41).
32. For Pelham, see *HOC*, vol. 4, pp. 39–44; Nigel Saul, *Scenes from Provincial Life: Knightly Families in Sussex, 1280–1400* (Oxford, 1986), pp. 70–2; Alastair Dunn, *The Politics of Magnate Power* (Oxford, 2003), p. 173; G. L. Harriss, *Shaping the Nation: England, 1360–1461* (Oxford, 2005), pp. 27, 173. Sussex was divided from west to east into six 'rapes': Chichester, Arundel, Bramber, Lewes, Pevensey and Hastings.
33. Julian Lock, 'Pelham, Sir John', *ODNB*.
34. TNA, E 404/27, no. 169; this volume, p. 148.
35. See pp. 149–50; also *Henry IV*, pp. 448–9.
36. Letter dated 9 December (probably 1404, possibly 1406) at the earl's manor of Dawley (Shropshire). The Coventry parliament of 6 October 1404 ended on 25 November. The earl was present when it opened but was probably called away to deal with affairs in the March: *POPC*, vol. 2, p. 117; *PROME*, vol. 8, p. 287.
37. *Henry IV*, pp. 448–9; although married for ten years, they had no children.
38. F. R. H. Du Boulay, *The Lordship of Canterbury* (London, 1966), p. 292; *CChR*, vol. 2, pp. 188–9.
39. *CCR 1405–9*, p. 525; *CCR 1409–13*, p. 59.
40. *CCR 1409–13*, pp. 183–5.

18 Friends and Servants

1. Simon Walker, 'Letters to the Dukes of Lancaster in 1381 and 1399', *EHR* 106 (1991), pp. 68–79.
2. Simon Walker, 'Lovell, John, Fifth Baron Lovell', *ODNB*.
3. *RA* 1, fo. 255v; *RA* 2, fos 103, 111; *CP*, vol. 8, pp. 219–21. Arundel facilitated the Lovells' landed transactions, enfeoffing them (collusively) with five manors in Wiltshire, Oxfordshire and Northamptonshire (*CCR 1405–9*, pp. 414–25). Lovell's wife Matilda, daughter and heiress of Sir Robert Holland, brought Lovell substantial landholdings, and he styled himself 'Lord of Titchmarsh and Holland'.
4. *CR*, pp. 35, 127, 170. Roos was born in the early 1370s: *CP*, vol. 11, pp. 102–3; TNA, E 404, no. 546.
5. *CPR 1408–13*, p. 25.
6. *Register of Henry Chichele, Archbishop of Canterbury, 1414–1443*, ed. E. F. Jacob (4 vols, London, 1943), vol. 2, pp. 22–7. Roos left £66 to Christ Church's fabric fund, to be used at Arundel's discretion, and to the archbishop personally a gold cup with a white rose enamelled on the cover. He wanted his sons to be educated *in grammatica et sciencia et disciplina* (*Register of Bishop Philip Repingdon, 1405–1419*, ed. Margaret Archer (Lincoln Record Society, 2 vols, 1963), vol. 1, p. l). His excellent tomb effigy was removed after the Dissolution to St Mary's church in Bottesford (Leicestershire). His request to be buried close to Arundel is not mentioned in his original will of 22 February 1413, since the archbishop was still alive then (*Testamenta Eboracensia or Wills Registered at York*, ed. James Raine (6 vols, London, 1834), vol. 1, pp. 357–60).
7. CCA-DCc/ChAnt/C/148; *Lit. Cant*, vol. 3, pp. 123ff.
8. See p. 219.

9. Chris Given-Wilson, *Royal Household and the King's Affinity: Service, Politics and Finance in England, 1360–1413* (New Haven and London, 1986), pp. 201–2.
10. *Sede Vacante Wills, Canterbury*, ed. C. E. Woodruff (Kent Archaeological Society Records Branch, Canterbury, 1914), pp. 81–5.
11. *Henry IV*, pp. 483–4; Henry Summerson, 'Umfraville, Sir Robert', *ODNB*; Gwilym Dodd, ed., *Henry V: New Interpretations* (York, 2013), pp. 45–6, 56–7; Malcolm Vale, *Henry V: The Conscience of a King* (New Haven and London, 2016), pp. 128–9.
12. *CPR 1413–16*, p. 10.
13. BL, Ms Arundel 68, fo. 57v.
14. For his will, see pp. 257–8.
15. In Scarle's will, dated 22 April 1403, he called Arundel 'his dearest lord' (*carissimo domino meo*) and bequeathed him a golden cup or a pair of bowls (*RA* 1, fo. 200v); see Alison McHardy, 'John Scarle: Ambition and Politics in the Late Medieval Church', in *Image, Text and Church, 1380–1600: Essays for Margaret Aston*, ed. Linda Clark, Maureen Jurkowski and Colin Richmond (Toronto, 2009), pp. 68–93, at p. 68, for the rarity of such affectionate language in wills. Gwilym Dodd, 'Clerical Chancellors of Late Medieval England', in *The Prelate in Late Medieval England and Europe*, ed. Martin Heale (Woodbridge, 2016), pp. 17–49, at p. 39, called Scarle 'very much the creature of Thomas Arundel'.
16. William Makenade, a local Kentish man, was appointed steward of the archiepiscopal lands in 1397, to 'survey, inquire and ordain concerning the state of all manors belonging to the archbishopric, to receive recognitions and entry-fines from tenants, to hold courts everywhere in the see's properties and do all that is necessary, appoint and remove bailiffs, sub-bailiffs, parkers, warreners, woodwards, reeves, reapers and other ministers however called, and do whatever he thinks is useful to the archbishop and the church of Canterbury'. He was succeeded by the esquire Gregory Ballard from 1400 to 1412, then by Bartholomew Brokesby until Arundel's death (*RA* 1, fo. 4r).
17. TNA, E 101/400/28, m. 2d; *TA*, pp. 168ff; C. M. Woolgar, *The Great Household in Late Medieval England* (New Haven and London, 1999), p. 12.
18. Woolgar, *Great Household*, pp. 12–15. The royal household bucked this trend, rising from 400–700 in the late fourteenth century to around 800 by the mid-fifteenth – although numbers fluctuated rapidly, for example, from 522 in 1402–3 to 644 in 1405–6.
19. LPL, Ms 1999 (i); BL, Add. Ms 19,398, fo. 23 (quote); *CPL*, vol. 6, p. 324. Bathe held canonries at Salisbury and Wells and was admitted to the Christ Church fraternity in 1402 (BL, Ms Arundel 68, fo. 53v); *ANLP*, nos 33, 35, 37, 41; *CA* 2, pp. 147–8.
20. CCA-DCc/ChAnt/R/21. For Haute and Hall, see also Paul A. Fox, *Great Cloister: A Lost Canterbury Tale* (Oxford, 2020), pp. 367–8, 385–7. Arundel's will mentioned his esquire John Sutton.
21. *ANLP*, no. 68 (letter from the London draper Roger Kegworth to Robert Hallum asking him to intervene, since Kegworth himself 'firmly desired' to marry her).
22. *CPR 1408–13*, p. 437.
23. *RA* 2, fo. 178v (Piers).
24. *Usk*, pp. 248–50; *The Book of Margery Kempe*, ed. Barry Windeatt (Cambridge, 2000), pp. 109–11; *Memorials of Bury St Edmunds*, ed. T. Arnold (3 vols, RS, London, 1896), vol. 3, p. 8.

25. *TA*, pp. 318–19; McHardy, 'John Scarle: Ambition and Politics', p. 68; R. G. Davies, 'Ryssheton, Nicholas', *ODNB*.
26. BL, Ms Add. 19,398, fos 23r–24v (quote from Arundel's petition to the king for Hallum's ratification as archdeacon, April 1400); *RA* 1, fos 11, 13, 93, 100, 267; *CA* 2, p. 245; R. N. Swanson, 'Hallum, Robert, Bishop of Salisbury', *ODNB*; Sarah Rees-Jones and Paul Dryburgh, eds, *The Church and Northern English Society in the Fourteenth Century* (Woodbridge, 2024), pp. 35–6.
27. *Register of Robert Hallum, Bishop of Salisbury*, ed. Joyce Horn (Canterbury and York Society 72, 1982), pp. ix–xiv, no. 1125. At Constance, he and Nicholas Bubwith commissioned a Latin translation of Dante's *Divina Commedia* from the humanist Giovanni di Serravalle, bishop of Fermo.
28. For the effect of his absence on his episcopal estates, see *Chichele's Register*, vol. 2, pp. 127–30; vol. 4, p. 62. His executors were only to act with the assent of Bishop Clifford of London.
29. *CPR 1405–8*, p. 60; *RA* 1, fo. 320v, for Wakering's appointment on 13 July 1408. He was admitted to the fraternity of Christ Church in the same year (BL, Ms Arundel 68, fo. 56v).
30. See p. 189.
31. LPL, Ms 1999 (i); R. G. Davies, 'Wakeryng, John, Bishop of Norwich', *ODNB*. After his provision to Norwich, the king sent him to join Hallum at Constance, where he remained until February 1418, when he finally entered his diocese.
32. See p. 62.
33. The third main archiepiscopal court was the consistory court, which dealt with diocesan suits.
34. *RA* 1, fo. 247r (*si omne executione huiusmodi dignetur, ut desidero, acceptare*); R. G. Davies, 'Bottlesham, John, Bishop of Rochester', *ODNB*; *The Medieval Court of Arches*, ed. F. Donald Logan (Canterbury and York Society 95, Woodbridge, 2005), p. 48.
35. *RA* 1, fo. 206r.
36. *RA* 1, fo. 100r; Davies, 'Ryssheton, Nicholas'. He came from Lancashire. The two volumes of *Royal and Historical Letters* include dozens of letters from Rishton; *RHL* 1, p. 367, 6 October 1404 (quote).
37. R. G. Davies, 'Ware, Henry, Bishop of Chichester', *ODNB*; R. G. Davies, 'Morgan, Philip, Bishop of Worcester and Ely', *ODNB*. Gascoigne considered Morgan to be a 'rare example of an honest bishop' (Thomas Gasgoine, *Loci e Libro Veritatum*, ed. J. Thorold Rogers (Oxford, 1881), p. lxviii).
38. Barnet, for example, was deputed by Arundel to settle the bilious dispute between the bishop and prior of Ely in 1401 (*RA* 1, fo. 101v); Milton administered the troublesome see of Norwich during the vacancies of 1406–7 and 1413 (*RA* 1, fos 521–549; *RA* 2, fo. 187).
39. *Usk*, pp. xv–xvii, 246–9.
40. *RA* 1, fo. 93.
41. *Medieval Court of Arches*, pp. 48–52. The statutes were dated 14 August 1397, 28 June 1401 and 5 March 1403. For Stratford's statutes, see Roy Haines, *Archbishop John Stratford* (Toronto, 1986), pp. 385–94. Latin was the language of the court: on 4 October 1399, Arundel appointed Thomas Baryn 'master of grammar for the *regimen* of the scholars at the Arches in London' (*RA* 1, fo. 93).
42. See p. 19.

43. *CPL*, vol. 5, pp. 483–5.
44. Ian Forrest, *Trustworthy Men: How Inequality and Faith Made the Medieval Church* (Princeton, 2018).
45. Chris Given-Wilson, 'The Bishop of Winchester, the Abbey of Titchfield and the "Pretended Chapel" of Hook, 1375–1405', in *People, Power and Identity in the Late Middle Ages: Essays in Memory of W. Mark Ormrod*, ed. Gwilym Dodd, Helen Lacey and Anthony Musson (New York, 2021), pp. 137–56.

19 Talking, Writing, Reading

1. *moult sagement et eloquentement*; *moult noblement et sagement*. In 1410, Henry Beaufort spoke 'most discreetly and wisely' (*molt discretement et sagement*); William Courtenay in 1381 had to make do with 'a good collation in English' (*bone collacioun en Engleys*): *PROME*, vol. 7, pp. 63, 193, 454; vol. 6, pp. 212–13.
2. *eleganter et seriose*; *nobiliter, eleganter ac distincte*: *Concilia*, vol. 3, pp. 308, 334; *SAC* 2, p. 382. For Arundel's eloquence (*facundia*), see *SAC* 2, p. 422.
3. W. R. Cooper, 'A Newly Identified Fragment in the Handwriting of William Tyndale', *Reformation* 3 (1998), pp. 323–47, at p. 338.
4. *SAC* 2, pp. 382, 432, 796–800; *Snappe's Formulary*, ed. H. E. Salter (Oxford, 1924), pp. 110–11.
5. Bodleian Library, Ms Laud Misc. 165, fo. 5r; BL, Harleian Ms 1319, fo. 12r.
6. Margaret Gibson, *Lanfranc of Bec* (Oxford, 1978), pp. 34–5; F. M. Powicke, *Stephen Langton* (Oxford, 1928), pp. 34, 41, 74; C. H. Lawrence, *St Edmund of Abingdon* (Oxford, 1960), p. 129.
7. *The Sermons of Thomas Brinton, Bishop of Rochester*, ed. Mary Aquinas Devlin (2 vols, Camden Society, London, 1954); Gloria Cigman, *Lollard Sermons* (Early English Text Society, Oxford, 1989).
8. *CE*, pp. 80–4.
9. *Knighton*, pp. 354–60; Knighton attributes this speech jointly to Arundel and the duke of Gloucester, but Arundel is the more likely speaker; he adds that he is reporting 'words such as these' (*tali sensu verborum*).
10. *SAC* 1, pp. 832–5; *CE*, pp. 82, 90; *SAC* 2, p. 240. This tone was not reserved for a wayward king: see the Westminster chronicler's accounts of his admonitions to the citizens of London in 1387–8 and 1392 (*WC*, pp. 232–4, 498–500; see also this volume, pp. 16, 23).
11. *CE*, p. 134; *SAC* 2, p. 450.
12. *SAC* 1, p. 778.
13. *Usk*, pp. 92–4.
14. *SAC* 2, pp. 382–4, 462.
15. *SAC* 2, pp. 424–6, 480, 800.
16. *CE*, p. 150; *Concilia*, vol. 3, p. 327; *RA* 1, fo. 480; Ian Forrest, *The Detection of Heresy in Late Medieval England* (Oxford, 2005), pp. 143–59.
17. *Two Wycliffite Texts*, ed. Anne Hudson (Early English Text Society, Oxford, 1998), pp. 24–93 (quotes in the remainder of this discussion are at pp. 36, 39, 42, 51–2, 55, 66–8, 71, 74, 77, 79, 85–93).
18. Wyclif the logician considered it to be 'quintessentially absurd' that an 'accident' could remain without a 'substance', an idea which was central to the theory of transubstantiation – namely, that the body of Christ (the 'accident') inhered in

the bread (the 'substance') while the substance itself entirely disappeared. Nor could he find any compelling evidence for transubstantiation in the Scriptures (Anthony Kenny, *Wyclif* (Oxford, 1985), pp. 80–90).

19. His defence when cited for heresy by Bishop Braybrooke included quotes from several psalms, Amos, Numbers, Mark, Luke, Jerome, the Acts of the Apostles and Paul's Epistle to the Romans, as well as Gratian's *Decretum* (*John Lydford's Book*, ed. Dorothy Owen (London, 1974), no. 209).
20. *SAC* 2, pp. 334–7. But Clifford was no exception: those accused of heresy often seem to have sought leniency by naming others (Forrest, *Detection of Heresy*, p. 178).
21. For his possible fate, see p. 158.
22. See p. 242. J. E. A. Jolliffe, *Angevin Kingship* (London, 1963), pp. 87–109; Chris Given-Wilson, 'The Earl of Arundel, the War at Sea, and the Anger of King Richard II', in *The Medieval Python*, ed. R. F. Yeager and Toshiyuki Takamiya (New York, 2012), pp. 27–38.
23. Felicity Hill, *Excommunication in Thirteenth-Century England* (Oxford, 2022), pp. 14, 30–3, 55–8, 111–14, 195–6.
24. Almut Suerbaum, George Southcombe and Benjamin Thompson, 'Introduction', and Benjamin Thompson, 'The Polemic of Reform in the Later Medieval English Church', in *Polemic: Language as Violence in Medieval and Early Modern Discourse*, ed. Almut Suerbaum, George Southcombe and Benjamin Thompson (Farnham, 2015), pp. 1–14 and 183–222; Forrest, *Detection of Heresy*, pp. 113–68.
25. *RA* 1, fo. 406r.
26. Translation from *The Black Death*, ed. Rosemary Horrox (Manchester, 1994), pp. 307–9.
27. *PROME*, vol. 8, pp. 9–10; Christopher Fletcher, *Richard II: Manhood, Youth and Politics, 1377–1399* (Oxford, 2008), pp. 1–3; *Concilia*, vol. 3, p. 314.
28. *Two Wycliffite Texts*, pp. 76–8.
29. *RHL* 2, p. 179 (1407, Henry thanks Arundel for writing 'so tenderly about this and in your own hand').
30. See pp. 95–6.
31. Perhaps from Song of Solomon 4:16; gardens were a popular medieval symbol of love and reconciliation.
32. *Snappe's Formulary*, pp. 163–4.
33. *Lit. Cant.*, vol. 3, pp. 73–5.
34. *Lit. Cant.*, vol. 3, pp. 70–2 (1 Corinthians 16:13–14; Ephesians 6:10–11; Job 2:10, 5:17–18; Romans 2:4, 11:15; Revelation 2:23; Matthew 24:11–13; Philippians 4:7; Aurelius Prudentius Clemens, *Hymnum ante Somnem*); see also this volume, p. 41.
35. Quoting Theophylact, the fourth century biblical commentator: *omne datum optimum desuper est descendens de te* ('every good thing descends from you above').
36. *The Deposition of Richard II*, ed. D. Carlson (Toronto, 2007), pp. 13–15, 79–86 (quotes), who adds that Bishop Repingdon in his letter to the king in 1401 used 'the same effects, but with greater success'.
37. John Foxe chose this passage 150 years later as an example of 'The Insufferable Pride and Vainglory of the Prelates' (www.exclassics.com/foxe/foxe96.htm); cf. *RA* 1, fos 362r (an agreement on the ringing of bells at Spalding (Lincs)), 441r

(an order to Worcester cathedral chapter, *absque contradictione*, to ring their bells when Bishop Clifford visited).

38. England under the special protection of Mary as her 'dowry' was stressed by Richard II during the Great Revolt of 1381 and again in the Wilton Diptych (*c.* 1395). For a rededication service at the outbreak of the pandemic in March 2020, see https://parish.rcdow.org.uk/hitchin/wp-content/uploads/sites/60/2020/02/Dowry-of-Mary-article.pdf.
39. *Deposition of Richard II*, pp. 7–10; Forrest, *Detection of Heresy*, p. 65.
40. For example, *CPR 1408–13*, p. 32.
41. See his visitations to Ely and Norwich in 1400 and 1401 (pp. 70–5); at Shrewsbury, King's Lynn and elsewhere he was called upon to settle urban disputes (p. 289 n.8; also Kate Parker, 'Politics and Patronage in Lynn, 1399–1416', in *The Reign of Henry IV: Rebellion and Survival, 1403–1413*, ed. G. Dodd and D. Biggs (York, 2008), pp. 210–27; Anthony Goodman, *Margery Kempe and Her World* (London, 2002), pp. 21–48).
42. See pp. 54–5, 141–2 (1399, 1406, 1408–9). For Hansa, see *Henry IV*, pp. 336–9.
43. CCA-DCc/Register N, fos 221v–222r; see also this volume, Appendix I.
44. The portiforiums went to his registrar, William Milton, and Edward, duke of York; the Bible to his estates steward, Bartholomew Brokesby; the psalter to his esquire John Sutton; the *Summa Confessorum* to his secretary John Bathe; *Johannes in Novella* to his auditor, Philip Morgan. The Sarum Use was the Latin liturgy developed at Salisbury cathedral some 300 years earlier and finally adopted at all houses in the early fifteenth century.
45. This portion of the text is damaged and some words are missing, but the meaning is clear.
46. *Foedera*, vol. 10, pp. 317–18. See Walden's will: *Item lego dicto domino meo Cantuariensis unum librum in quo continentur Pastoralia Beati Gregorii cum aliis* (Also, I bequeath to my aforesaid lord of Canterbury a book containing St Gregory's *Pastoralia*, with other things) (*RA* 1, fo. 227r).
47. B. Golding, 'Medford, Richard, Bishop of Salisbury', *ODNB*.
48. *Testamenta Eboracensia or Wills Registered at York*, ed. James Raine (6 vols, London, 1834), vol. 3, pp. 1–8 (October 1395, when Arundel was archbishop of York). Scarborough also left £20 to Arundel for his (anticipated) 'diligence and care' in fulfilling his last will, and asked that, 'if his reverence should accept it, out of charity', he should act as supervisor of the will; he further asked that a debt of £36 to Arundel be paid. Scarborough was a notary public and had an impressive collection of religious, legal and historical texts, many of which he directed to be sold.
49. The enjoyment was presumably from the superb illustrations, but he may have been interested in the text: three Latin versions of each psalm with translations into Old English and Anglo-Norman (Dominique Verfaillie-Markey, 'Deux inscriptions grattées dans le psautier d'Eadwine', *Scriptorium* 39 (1985–6), pp. 97–102).
50. It is now in the Bodleian Library, Oxford (Ms Laud Misc. 165); it has an image of Arundel preaching: N. R. Ker, *Medieval Libraries of Great Britain* (London, 1964), pp. 238, 383.
51. E. F. Jacob, *The Fifteenth Century, 1399–1485* (Oxford, 1961), pp. 663–7.
52. *Deposition of Richard II*, p. 86.

53. When Thorpe said that churches and pilgrimages should be silent apart from preaching, Arundel robustly defended church organs and singing: *Two Wycliffite Texts*, pp. lv, 64–6.
54. *Augustine on Music* (*De Musica*), ed. and trans. Robert Catesby Taliaferro (Rhode Island, no date, available at https://archive.org/details/augustine-on-music-de-musica/mode/2up); see, for example, pp. 377–8.
55. See p. 43.
56. See pp. 142, 201.
57. *Concilia*, vol. 3, p. 252; this volume, p. 329.
58. *RA* 1, fo. 208r (marginal: *Nota consilium sanum Regis Francorum datum filio suo Philippo*); sections referring specifically to Philip's imminent kingship were omitted. Cf. Jacques Le Goff, *Saint Louis*, trans. G. E. Gollrad (Notre Dame, IN, 2009), pp. 330–40; this volume, Appendix II.
59. Jeremy Catto, 'The Prayers of the Bohuns', in *Soldiers, Nobles and Gentlemen: Essays in Honour of Maurice Keen*, ed. Peter Coss and Christopher Tyerman (Woodbridge, 2009), pp. 112–25, at pp. 120–2.
60. *The Mirror of the Blessed Life of Jesus Christ by Nicholas Love: A Full Critical Edition*, ed. Michael Sargent (Exeter, 2005), p. 7 and introduction p. 29 (grant of confraternity, from *RA* 2, fo. 121), text p. 10.
61. Michael Sargent, 'Nicholas Love as an Ecclesiastical Reformer', *Church History and Religious Culture* 96 (2016), pp. 40–64, at pp. 58–62; several of these passages were highlighted in the *Mirror* with marginals such as *Nota Contra Lollardos* (*The Mirror*, pp. 25, 90, 132, 138, 142, 151).
62. *The Mirror*, p. 174 (English modernized); Michael Sargent, 'Bishops, Patrons, Mystics and Manuscripts: Walter Hilton, Nicholas Love and the Arundel and Holland Connections', in *Middle English Texts in Translation*, ed. Simon Horobin and Linne Mooney (Woodbridge, 2014), pp. 159–76.
63. *The Mirror*, pp. xvii–xviii, 89, 95–6.

Conclusion

1. The customary fee for 'dilapidations' was set at £466; Henry Chichele was postulated by the chapter on 12 March and papally provided on 27 April (*Register of Henry Chichele, Archbishop of Canterbury, 1414–1443*, ed. E. F. Jacob (4 vols, London, 1943), vol. 1, pp. xxxiii, 3, 7–13).
2. *Fuit obtrusus in suo gutture quod non potuit nec bene loqui nec deglutire et sic moriebatur.* Gascoigne repeats this several times (Thomas Gascoigne, *Loci e Libro Veritatum*, ed. J. Thorold Rogers (Oxford, 1881), pp. 34, 61, 180–1). The inventory of Arundel's goods (Appendix I) gave 17 February as his date of death, but the 19th is more widely recognized. Ironically, Wyclif's death thirty years earlier was preceded by a stroke which likewise rendered him speechless.
3. *Usk*, pp. 248–9.
4. *Sede Vacante Wills, Canterbury*, ed. C. E. Woodruff (Kent Archaeological Society Records Branch, Canterbury, 1914), pp. 81–5.
5. Arundel's love of jewels is attested in various sources: *Memorials of Bury St Edmunds*, ed. T. Arnold (3 vols, RS, London, 1896), vol. 3, p. 184; *CCR 1402–5*, p. 431; *RA* 1, fo. 215 (gifts of jewels and beads inscribed *Jhesus est amor meus* from Bishop Wykeham); for his goods at death, see Appendix I.

6. *Usk*, pp. 246–9; *SAC* 2, p. 642; *Gesta Henrici Quinti*, ed. Frank Taylor and John Roskell (Oxford, 1975), pp. 4–5; BL, Ms Arundel 68, fo. 59r.
7. Margaret Gibson, *Lanfranc of Bec* (Oxford, 1978), p. 25; C. H. Lawrence, *St Edmund of Abingdon* (Oxford, 1960), p. 129 (quote).
8. *Two Wycliffite Texts*, ed. Anne Hudson (Early English Text Society, Oxford, 1998), pp. 60–1.
9. *SAC* 2, pp. 80, 560; *CE*, p. 86. Anthony Goodman, *The Loyal Conspiracy* (London, 1971), p. 9, described him as 'the earl's brilliant clerical brother'.
10. *The Book of Margery Kempe*, ed. Barry Windeatt (Cambridge, 2000), pp. 108–11.
11. *Memorials of Bury*, vol. 3, pp. 186–7.
12. In fact, the Turkish threat to Christendom did not materialize until the 1430s, but it was never far from the minds of popes or of Christian kings and prelates (*Henry IV*, pp. 398–9).
13. See pp. 90, 293 n.34. Many more heretics were burned in England between 1414 and 1536 (approximately seventy-five) than during his primacy (R. Rex, *The Lollards* (Basingstoke, 2002), p. 113).
14. *Henry IV*, pp. 376–82.
15. Badby was burned for heresy during the parliament, but he had nothing to do with the bill.
16. Benjamin Thompson, 'Locality and Ecclesiastical Polity: The Late Medieval Church between Duality and Integration', in *Political Society in Late Medieval England: A Festschrift for Christine Carpenter*, ed. Benjamin Thompson and John Watts (Woodbridge, 2015), pp. 113–45, at pp. 144–5 and *passim*; *Henry IV*, p. 382.
17. Ian Forrest, *The Detection of Heresy in Late Medieval England* (Oxford, 2005), pp. 225, 239–40.
18. Vincent Gillespie and Kantik Ghosh, eds, *After Arundel: Religious Writing in Fifteenth-Century England* (Turnhout, 2011), especially Vincent Gillespie, 'Chichele's Church', pp. 3–42; David Lepine, 'Let Them Praise Him in Church: Orthodox Reform at Salisbury Cathedral in the First Half of the Fifteenth Century', pp. 167–85; and Sheila Lindebaum, 'London after Arundel', pp. 187–208. See also several further articles by Jeremy Catto: 'Thomas Arundel's Reformation', in *Image, Text and Church, 1380–1600: Essays for Margaret Aston*, ed. Linda Clark, Maureen Jurkowski and Colin Richmond (Toronto, 2009), pp. 94–108; 'The King's Government and the Fall of Pecock', in *Rulers and Ruled in Late Medieval England: Essays Presented to Gerald Harriss*, ed. Rowena Archer and Simon Walker (London, 1995), pp. 201–22; 'Religious Change under Henry V', in G. L. Harriss, *Henry V: The Practice of Kingship* (Oxford, 1987), pp. 97–115; 'Wyclif and Wycliffism at Oxford', in *The History of the University of Oxford II: Late Medieval Oxford*, ed. Jeremy Catto and Richard Evans (Oxford, 1992), pp. 257–61.
19. The promotion of new, 'English', saints' cults has been presented as integral to Henry V's and Chichele's programme of reformed orthodoxy, but the saints usually mentioned in this context (Chad, Winifred, George, John of Beverley) had in fact all been promoted by Arundel within a few months of his restoration, when he issued a directive naming forty-nine days in the year as *festa ab omnibus operibus*; these included a dozen feasts associated with Christ's Life (principally Easter and Christmas), six associated with the Blessed Virgin Mary, and a number

of notable martyrs, the apostles, the evangelists, All Souls, All Saints, etc. Some of these had also been promoted by Richard II. For Arundel's promotion of St George, see pp. 96, 190; for St John of Beverley (not to be confused with St John of Bridlington, canonized in 1401), see *Foedera*, vol. 8, p. 369, 23 August 1404 (*Concilia*, vol. 3, p. 252; Catto, 'Religious Change', pp. 107–9; Gillespie, 'Chichele's Church', p. 15; Nigel Saul, *Richard II* (New Haven and London, 1997), p. 324).

20. *CPL*, vol. 6, p. 174. This was the first intimation of what became the Council of Constance, which met after Arundel's death.
21. *Concilia*, vol. 3, pp. 360–5; Gillespie, 'Chichele's Church', pp. 19, 36 (quote), concludes that Wyclif 'had more impact on the language and attitudes of the English Church in the fifteenth century than his arch enemy Thomas Arundel', which arguably underplays the sustained criticism by Arundel and several of his suffragans – notably Robert Hallum and Philip Repingdon – of clerical abuses.
22. J. H. Wylie and W. Waugh, *The Reign of Henry V* (3 vols, Cambridge, 1914–29), vol. 1, p. 293.
23. In 1401, in his private chapel at Otford, he accepted the profession of John Langfield of Northfleet as a hermit, and Langfield agreed to accept his jurisdiction (*RA* 1, fo. 395r).
24. Albert Hyma, *The Christian Renaissance: A History of the Devotio Moderna* (Hamden, CT, 1965).
25. See Gascoigne's comments on the way in which the style of orthodox preaching had changed between *c.* 1415 and 1440 (Gascoigne, *Loci e Libro Veritatum*, pp. 34–5); R. N. Swanson, 'Flemming/Fleming, Richard, Bishop of Lincoln', *ODNB*.
26. *The Register of Richard Clifford, Bishop of Worcester: A Calendar*, ed. Waldo Smith (Toronto, 1976), p. 35; Anthony Tuck, 'Stafford, Edmund, Bishop of Exeter', *ODNB*; C. M. Fraser, 'Langley, Thomas, Bishop of Durham', *ODNB*.
27. Helen Jewell, 'English Bishops as Educational Benefactors in the Later Fifteenth Century', in *The Church, Politics and Patronage in the Fifteenth Century*, ed. R. B. Dobson (Gloucester, 1984), pp. 146–67; E. F. Jacob, *Archbishop Henry Chichele* (London, 1967), p. 73. William Bateman, bishop of Norwich, had founded Trinity Hall, Cambridge, specifically to train more clergy after the Black Death.
28. E. F. Jacob, 'Founders and Foundations in the Later Middle Ages', in *Essays in Later Medieval History* (Manchester, 1968), pp. 154–74, at p. 173.
29. Despite Margaret Aston's meticulous work on his role as a bishop and archbishop from 1373 to 1396 (*TA*), general histories of Richard II's reign focus almost exclusively on Arundel's political role.
30. Arundel's role as a 'political revolutionary' has been compared to earlier and later archbishops such as John Stratford (archbishop 1333–48) and Thomas Bourgchier (archbishop 1454–86). Bourgchier was also of aristocratic birth but Stratford was the son of a prosperous burgher in Stratford-upon-Avon; his involvement in Edward II's deposition in 1326–7 was, however, considerably less prominent than Arundel's part in Richard's overthrow (Roy Haines, *Archbishop John Stratford* (Toronto, 1986), pp. 164–91; R. L. Storey, 'Episcopal King-Makers in the Fifteenth Century', in *The Church, Politics and Patronage in the Fifteenth Century*, ed. R. B. Dobson (Gloucester, 1984), pp. 82–98).
31. See p. 237.

32. *CR*, pp. 168–89.
33. *Two Wycliffite Texts*, p. 49.
34. *Henry IV*, pp. 526–33.
35. See p. 76 (quotation).
36. Richard: 'Northumberland, thou ladder wherewithal / The mounting Bullingbrooke ascends my throne' (*Richard II*, Act 5, Scene 1, ll. 55–6).
37. May McKisack, *The Fourteenth Century* (Oxford, 1959), p. 496; this volume, p. 39.

Appendix I

1. The headings on the recto folio have been obscured by the binding.

Appendix II

1. https://archives.lambethpalacelibrary.org.uk/CalmView/Record.aspx?src=CalmView.Catalog&id=V%2fA%2f9Arundel1.
2. *Gesta Henrici Quinti*, ed. Frank Taylor and John Roskell (Oxford, 1975), pp. 8–9; *RA* 2, fos 28–33 (1444 convocation), 142–5 (Oldcastle trial record).
3. As noted on p. 294 n.9, this might suggest that the register was re-bound in the eighteenth or nineteenth century.
4. See p. 253.
5. See pp. 105–7. The king's writ was in fact worded very much in line with what the *Modus* prescribed, although the *Modus* added that the proctors should come 'with their warrants in duplicate sealed with the seals of their superiors that they have been elected and sent to act as proctor' (*Parliamentary Texts of the Later Middle Ages*, ed. Nicholas Pronay and John Taylor (Oxford, 1980), pp. 41–3, 67–8, 80–1).
6. *Henry Archdeacon of Huntingdon: Historia Anglorum*, ed. Diana Greenway (Oxford, 1996), pp. 319ff.

Bibliography

Manuscripts

London, British Library (BL)

Additional Mss 19,398; 24,062; 35,295
Harleian Ms 1319
Ms Arundel 68
Ms Cotton Cleopatra E II
Ms Cotton Faustina C. vii

Kew, The National Archives (TNA)

Classes of Mss consulted:

- C 49 Chancery, Council and Parliament Files
- C 66 Patent Rolls
- E 28 Exchequer, Council and Privy Seal Records
- E 101 Exchequer, King's Remembrancer, Accounts Various
- E 175 Exchequer, Parliamentary and Council Proceedings
- E 401 Exchequer, Receipt Rolls
- E 403 Exchequer, Issue Rolls
- E 404 Exchequer, Warrants for Issue

London, Lambeth Palace Library (LPL)

Register of Archbishop Thomas Arundel (2 volumes)
Reg. Sudbury
CM XI/26
LR/F/62/12–15
Ms 78
Ms 419
Ms 448
Ms 1999
Ms Film 704

Canterbury Cathedral Archives (CCA)

Classes of Mss consulted:
CCA-CC
CCA-DCc/ChAnt
CCA-DCc/Register N
CCA-U39

Oxford, All Souls College

Ms 182

Oxford, Bodleian Library

Bodley Ms 462
Ms Laud Misc. 165

London, Westminster Abbey Muniments

Muniment 9584

Printed Sources

Anglo-Norman Letters and Petitions, ed. Dominica Legge (Oxford, 1941)
Antient Kalendars and Inventories of the Treasury of His Majesty's Exchequer, ed. F. Palgrave (3 vols, London, 1836)
Augustine on Music (*De Musica*), ed. and trans. Robert Catesby Taliaferro (Rhode Island, no date, available at https://archive.org/details/augustine-on-music-de-musica/mode/2up)
Biographical Register of the University of Cambridge to 1500, ed. A. B. Emden (Cambridge, 1963)
Biographical Register of the University of Oxford to 1500, ed. A. B. Emden (3 vols, Oxford, 1957)
The Black Death, ed. Rosemary Horrox (Manchester, 1994)
The Book of Margery Kempe, ed. Barry Windeatt (Cambridge, 2000)
Calendar of Charter Rolls in the Public Record Office, 1257–1300 (London, 1906)
Calendar of Close Rolls in the Public Record Office, 1377–1422 (13 vols, London, 1914–38)
Calendar of Fine Rolls in the Public Record Office, 1399–1405 (London, 1931)
Calendar of Inquisitions Miscellaneous in the Public Record Office, 1392–99 (London, 1963)
Calendar of Inquisitions Post Mortem in the Public Record Office, 1405–13 (London, 1992)
Calendar of Papal Letters Relating to Great Britain and Ireland (vols 4–6, London, 1902–4)
Calendar of Patent Rolls in the Public Record Office, 1377–1422 (12 vols, London, 1895–1911)
Calendar of Richard Scrope, Archbishop of York, 1398–1405, ed. R. N. Swanson (2 vols, Borthwick Texts and Calendars, York, 1981)

Chronica Monasterii de Melsa, ed. E. A. Bond (3 vols, RS, London, 1866–8)
Chronicle of Adam Usk, 1377–1421, ed. C. Given-Wilson (Oxford, 1997)
Chronicles of the Revolution, 1397–1400, ed. C. Given-Wilson (Manchester, 1993)
Chronique de la traison et mort de Richart deux roy dengleterre, ed. B. Williams (London, 1846)
A Collection of All the Wills of the Kings and Queens of England, ed. J. Nichols (Society of Antiquaries, London, 1780)
Coluccio Salutati: Political Writings, ed. S. Baldassari, trans. R. Bagemihl (London, 2014)
Complete Peerage, ed. G. E. Cockayne and V. Gibbs (12 vols, London, 1910–59)
Concilia Magnae Britanniae et Hiberniae, ed. D. Wilkins (3 vols, London, 1737)
Continuatio Eulogii: The Continuation of the Eulogium Historiarum, ed. C. Given-Wilson (Oxford, 2019)
The Deposition of Richard II, ed. D. Carlson (Toronto, 2007)
Diplomatic Correspondence of Richard II, ed. E. Perroy (Camden Society, London, 1933)
English Chronicle, 1377–1461, ed. W. Marx (Woodbridge, 2003)
Epistolario di Coluccio Salutati, ed. F. Novati (Fonti de la Storia d'Italia, 6 vols, Rome, 1896)
Fasciculi Zizaniorum Magistri Johannis Wyclif cum Tritico, ed. W. W. Shirley (RS, London, 1858)
Foedera, Conventiones, Literae, etc., ed. Thomas Rymer (20 vols, London, 1727–35)
Gascoigne, Thomas, *Loci e Libro Veritatum*, ed. J. Thorold Rogers (Oxford, 1881)
Gesta Henrici Quinti, ed. Frank Taylor and John Roskell (Oxford, 1975)
Henry Archdeacon of Huntingdon: Historia Anglorum, ed. Diana Greenway (Oxford, 1996)
Historia Vitae et Regni Ricardi Secundi, ed. George Stow (Philadelphia, 1977)
Historians of the Church of York and Its Archbishops, ed. J. Raine (3 vols, London, 1879–94)
Historical Collections of a Citizen of London, ed. J. Gairdner (Camden Society, London, 1876)
House of Commons, 1386–1421, ed. J. Roskell, L. Clark and C. Rawcliffe (4 vols, London, 2006)
Incerti Scriptoris Chronicon Angliae de Regnis Trium Regum Lancastriensum, ed. J. Giles (London, 1848)
Inventories of Christ Church Canterbury, ed. J. Wickham Legg and W. H. St John Hope (London, 1902)
John Lydford's Book, ed. Dorothy Owen (London, 1974)
Knighton's Chronicle, 1337–1395, ed. G. Martin (Oxford, 1995)
Literae Cantuariensis, ed. J. B. Sheppard (3 vols, RS, London, 1887–9)
Lollard Sermons, ed. Gloria Cigman (Early English Text Society, Oxford, 1989)
The Major Latin Works of John Gower, ed. E. W. Stockton (Seattle, 1962)
The Medieval Court of Arches, ed. F. D. Logan (Canterbury and York Society 95, Woodbridge, 2005)
Memorials of Bury St Edmunds, ed. T. Arnold (3 vols, RS, London, 1896)
The Metropolitan Visitations of William Courtenay Archbishop of Canterbury, 1381–1396, ed. J. H. Dahmus, *Illinois Studies in the Social Sciences* 31, no. 2 (1950)

'Metropolitical Visitation of Archbishop Thomas Arundel, 1401', in *Ely Chapter Ordinances and Visitation Records*, ed. S. J. Evans (Camden Miscellany 17, London, 1940)
The Mirror of the Blessed Life of Jesus Christ by Nicholas Love: A Full Critical Edition, ed. Michael Sargent (Exeter, 2005)
Monasticon Anglicanum, ed. William Dugdale (6 vols, London, 1846–9)
Munimenta Academica Oxoniensis, ed. H. Tasker (2 vols, RS, London, 1868)
Original Letters Illustrative of English History, ed. H. Ellis (4 vols, London, 1824–7)
Parliament Rolls of Medieval England, 1275–1504, ed. P. Brand, A. Curry, C. Given-Wilson, R. Horrox, G. Martin, W. M. Ormrod and J. R. S. Phillips (16 vols, Woodbridge, 2005; and online)
Parliamentary Texts of the Later Middle Ages, ed. Nicholas Pronay and John Taylor (Oxford, 1980)
The Peasants' Revolt of 1381, ed. R. B. Dobson (London, 1983)
Petitions to the Crown from English Religious Houses, c. 1272–1485, ed. Gwilym Dodd and Alison McHardy (Woodbridge, 2010)
Polychronicon Ranulphi Higden, ed. C. Babington (9 vols, RS, London, 1865–86)
Proceedings and Ordinances of the Privy Council of England, ed. N. Nicolas (6 vols, Record Commission, London, 1834)
Records of Convocation, ed. Gerald Bray (20 vols, Woodbridge, 2006)
Register of Bishop Philip Repingdon, 1405–1419, ed. Margaret Archer (2 vols, Lincoln Record Society, 1963)
Register of Henry Chichele, Archbishop of Canterbury, 1414–1443, ed. E. F. Jacob (4 vols, London, 1943)
The Register of Richard Clifford, Bishop of Worcester: A Calendar, ed. Waldo Smith (Toronto, 1976)
Register of Robert Hallum, Bishop of Salisbury, ed. Joyce Horn (Canterbury and York Society 72, 1982)
Register of Robert Mascall, Bishop of Hereford, 1404–1416, ed. J. H. Parry (Hereford, 1916)
The Register of Simon Sudbury, Archbishop of Canterbury, 1375–1381, ed. F. Donald Logan (Canterbury and York Society 110, Woodbridge, 2020)
Register of Thomas Langley of Durham, 1406–1437, ed. R. L. Storey (2 vols, Durham, 1956–7)
Royal and Historical Letters During the Reign of Henry IV, ed. F. Hingeston (2 vols, RS, London, 1860–5)
St Albans Chronicle, 1376–1422: The Chronica Maiora of Thomas Walsingham, ed. J. Taylor, W. Childs and L. Watkiss (2 vols, Oxford, 2003–11)
Sede Vacante Wills, Canterbury, ed. C. E. Woodruff (Kent Archaeological Society Records Branch, Canterbury, 1914)
Selections from English Wycliffite Writings, ed. Anne Hudson (Cambridge, 1978)
The Sermons of Thomas Brinton, Bishop of Rochester, ed. Mary Aquinas Devlin (2 vols, Camden Society, London, 1954)
Signet Letters of Henry IV and Henry V, ed. J. L. Kirby (London, 1978)
Snappe's Formulary, ed. H. E. Salter (Oxford, 1924)
Statuta Antiqua Universitatis Oxoniensis, ed. Strickland Gibson (Oxford, 1931)
Statutes of the Realm (11 vols, Record Commission, London, 1810–28)
Testamenta Eboracensia or Wills Registered at York, ed. James Raine (6 vols, London, 1834)

Testamentary Records of the English and Welsh Episcopate, 1200–1413, ed. C. M. Woolgar (Canterbury and York Society 102, Woodbridge, 2011)
Two Wycliffite Texts, ed. Anne Hudson (Early English Text Society, Oxford, 1998)
The Visitation of Hereford Diocese in 1397, ed. Ian Forrest and Christopher Whittick (Canterbury and York Society 111, Woodbridge, 2021)
Westminster Chronicle, 1381–1394, ed. L. Hector and B. Harvey (Oxford, 1982)
William Thorne's Chronicle of St Augustine's Abbey Canterbury, ed. A. H. Davis (Oxford, 1934)
Women of the English Nobility and Gentry, 1066–1500, ed. Jennifer Ward (Manchester, 1995)
Women's Books of Hours in Medieval England, ed. Charity Scott-Stokes (Cambridge, 2006)

Secondary Works

Allmand, Christopher, 'A Bishop of Bangor During the Glyn Dwr Revolt: Richard Young', *Journal of the Historical Society of the Church in Wales* 18 (1968), pp. 47–56
Ambler, Sophie, *Bishops in the Political Community of England, 1213–1272* (Oxford, 2017)
Aston, Margaret, 'Caim's Castles: Poverty, Politics and Disendowment', in *The Church, Politics and Patronage in the Fifteenth Century*, ed. R. B. Dobson (Gloucester, 1984), pp. 45–81
— 'The Impeachment of Bishop Despenser', *BIHR* 26 (1953), pp. 127–48
— *Thomas Arundel: A Study of Church Life in the Reign of Richard II* (Oxford, 1967)
Aston, Margaret and Colin Richmond, eds, *Lollardy and the Gentry in the Later Middle Ages* (Stroud, 1997)
Atherton, I., E. Fernie, C. Harper-Bill and H. Smith, eds, *Norwich Cathedral: Church, City and Diocese* (London, 1996)
Attreed, L., *The King's Towns* (New York, 2001)
Barron, Caroline, 'The Quarrel of Richard II with London', in *The Reign of Richard II*, ed. C. Barron and R. du Boulay (London, 1971), pp. 173–201
Bellamy, J. G., *Criminal Law and Society in Late Medieval and Tudor England* (Gloucester, 1984)
Bennett, Michael, *Richard II and the Revolution of 1399* (Stroud, 1999)
Bornstein, Daniel, *The Bianchi of 1399: Popular Devotion in Late Medieval Italy* (Ithaca, NY, 1993)
Brentano, Robert, *Two Churches: England and Italy in the Thirteenth Century* (Princeton, 1968)
Brown, A. L., 'The Authorization of Letters under the Great Seal', *BIHR* 37 (1964), pp. 125–56
— 'The Commons and the Council in the Reign of Henry IV', *EHR* 79 (1964), pp. 1–30
— 'The Latin Letters in All Souls Ms 182', *EHR* 87 (1972), pp. 565–73
Campbell, B. M. S., 'The Agrarian Problem in the Early Fourteenth Century', *Past & Present* 188 (2005), pp. 3–70
Carpenter, David, *Henry III, 1258–1272* (New Haven and London, 2023)
Catto, Jeremy, 'The King's Government and the Fall of Pecock', in *Rulers and Ruled in Late Medieval England: Essays Presented to Gerald Harriss*, ed. Rowena Archer and Simon Walker (London, 1995), pp. 201–22

— 'The Prayers of the Bohuns', in *Soldiers, Nobles and Gentlemen: Essays in Honour of Maurice Keen*, ed. Peter Coss and Christopher Tyerman (Woodbridge, 2009), pp. 112–25
— 'Religion and the English Nobility in the Later Fourteenth Century', in *History and Imagination: Essays in Honour of H. R. Trevor-Roper*, ed. Hugh Lloyd-Jones, Valerie Pearl and Blair Worden (London, 1981), pp. 43–55
— 'Religious Change under Henry V', in G. L. Harriss, *Henry V: The Practice of Kingship* (Oxford, 1987), pp. 97–115
— 'Thomas Arundel's Reformation', in *Image, Text and Church, 1380–1600: Essays for Margaret Aston*, ed. Linda Clark, Maureen Jurkowski and Colin Richmond (Toronto, 2009), pp. 94–108
— 'Wyclif and Wycliffism at Oxford', in *The History of the University of Oxford II: Late Medieval Oxford*, ed. Jeremy Catto and Richard Evans (Oxford, 1992), pp. 257–61
Catto, Jeremy and Richard Evans, eds, *The History of the University of Oxford II: Late Medieval Oxford* (Oxford, 1992)
Cavill, Paul, 'Heresy, Law and the State: Forfeiture in Late Medieval and Early Modern England', *EHR* 129 (2014), pp. 270–95
Churchill, Irene Josephine, *Canterbury Administration* (2 vols, London, 1933)
— 'Table of Canterbury Archbishopric Charters', *Camden Miscellany* 15 (1929), pp. 1–19
Collinson, P., N. Ramsay and M. Sparks, eds, *A History of Canterbury Cathedral* (Oxford, 1995)
Cooper, W. R., 'A Newly Identified Fragment in the Handwriting of William Tyndale', *Reformation* 3 (1998), pp. 323–47
Dahmus, J., *William Courtenay, Archbishop of Canterbury, 1381–1396* (University Park, PA, 1966)
Davies, R. G., 'After the Execution of Archbishop Scrope: Henry IV, the Papacy and the English Episcopate, 1405–8', *BJRL* 59 (1977), pp. 40–74
— 'The Episcopate', in *Profession, Vocation and Culture in Later Medieval England*, ed. C. Clough (Liverpool, 1982), pp. 51–89
— 'The Episcopate and the Political Crisis in England of 1386–1388', *Speculum* 51 (1976), pp. 659–93
— 'Richard II and the Church in the Years of Tyranny', *Journal of Medieval History* 1 (1975), pp. 329–62
— 'Thomas Arundel as Archbishop of Canterbury', *JEH* 14 (1973), pp. 9–21
Davies, R. R., *The Revolt of Owain Glyn Dwr* (Oxford, 1995)
Davis, Virginia, *William Wykeham* (London, 2007)
Di Paolo, Jon, 'Mosley, Becket, Jack the Ripper Named on List of 10 Worst Britons', *Guardian*, 27 December 2005, https://www.theguardian.com/uk/2005/dec/27/highereducation.britishidentity
Dobson, R. B., *The Peasants' Revolt of 1381* (London, 1983)
Dodd, Gwilym, 'Clerical Chancellors of Late Medieval England', in *The Prelate in Late Medieval England and Europe*, ed. Martin Heale (Woodbridge, 2016), pp. 17–49
— ed., *Henry V: New Interpretations* (York, 2013)
— 'Richard II and the Transformation of Parliament', in *The Reign of Richard II*, ed. Gwilym Dodd (Stroud, 2000), pp. 71–84
Du Boulay, F. R. H., *The Lordship of Canterbury* (London, 1966)

Duggan, Anne, *Thomas Becket* (London, 2004)
Dunn, Alastair, *The Politics of Magnate Power* (Oxford, 2003)
Emden, A. B., *An Oxford Hall in Medieval Times* (Oxford, 1927)
Fletcher, Christopher, *Richard II: Manhood, Youth and Politics, 1377–1399* (Oxford, 2008)
Forrest, Ian, *The Detection of Heresy in Late Medieval England* (Oxford, 2005)
— *Trustworthy Men: How Inequality and Faith Made the Medieval Church* (Princeton, 2018)
Fox, Paul A., *Great Cloister: A Lost Canterbury Tale* (Oxford, 2020)
Galbraith, V. H., 'Articles Laid Before the Parliament of 1371', *EHR* 34 (1919), pp. 579–82
Gibson, Margaret, *Lanfranc of Bec* (Oxford, 1978)
Gillespie, Vincent, 'Chichele's Church', in *After Arundel: Religious Writing in Fifteenth-Century England*, ed. Vincent Gillespie and Kantik Ghosh (Turnhout, 2011), pp. 3–42
Gillespie, Vincent and Kantik Ghosh, eds, *After Arundel: Religious Writing in Fifteenth-Century England* (Turnhout, 2011)
Given-Wilson, Chris, 'The Bishop of Winchester, the Abbey of Titchfield and the "Pretended Chapel" of Hook, 1375–1405', in *People, Power and Identity in the Late Middle Ages: Essays in Memory of W. Mark Ormrod*, ed. Gwilym Dodd, Helen Lacey and Anthony Musson (New York, 2021), pp. 137–56
— 'The Earl of Arundel, the War at Sea, and the Anger of King Richard II', in *The Medieval Python*, ed. R. F. Yeager and Toshiyuki Takamiya (New York, 2012), pp. 27–38
— *Henry IV* (New Haven and London, 2016)
— 'The King's Confessors and the Royal Conscience in Late Medieval England', in *Fourteenth-Century England XII*, ed. J. Bothwell and J. S. Hamilton (Woodbridge, 2022), pp. 1–28
— *The Royal Household and the King's Affinity: Service, Politics and Finance in England, 1360–1413* (New Haven and London, 1986)
— 'Royal Wills, 1376–1475', in *The Fifteenth Century XVII*, ed. Linda Clark (Woodbridge, 2020), pp. 1–16
— 'Service, Serfdom and English Labour Legislation, 1350–1500', in *Concepts and Patterns of Service in the Later Middle Ages*, ed. A. Curry and E. Matthew (Woodbridge, 2000), pp. 21–37
— 'Wealth and Credit, Public and Private: The Fitzalan Earls of Arundel, 1306–1397', *EHR* 106 (1991), pp. 1–26
Goodman, Anthony, *The Loyal Conspiracy* (London, 1971)
— *Margery Kempe and Her World* (London, 2002)
Gough, H., 'The Archbishop's Manor at Ford, Hoath', *Archaeologia Cantiana* 121 (2001), pp. 251–68
Gransden, Antonia, *Historical Writing in England II* (London, 1982)
— *A History of the Abbey of Bury St Edmunds I, 1182–1256* (Studies in the History of Medieval Religion 31, Woodbridge, 2007)
Haines, Roy, *Archbishop John Stratford* (Toronto, 1986)
Harriss, G. L., *Cardinal Beaufort* (Oxford, 1988)
— *Shaping the Nation: England, 1360–1461* (Oxford, 2005)
Hartridge, R. A., *A History of Vicarages in the Middle Ages* (Cambridge, 1930)

Harvey, Katherine, 'The First Entry of the Bishop: Episcopal *Adventus* in Fourteenth-Century England', in *Fourteenth-Century England VII*, ed. J. S. Hamilton (Woodbridge, 2014), pp. 43–58
Harvey, Margaret, *Solutions to the Schism: A Study of Some English Attitudes, 1378–1409* (St Ottilien, 1983)
Havens, Jill, 'A Curious Erasure in Walsingham's Short Chronicle and the Politics of Heresy', in *Fourteenth-Century England II*, ed. C. Given-Wilson (Woodbridge, 2002), pp. 95–106
Heath, Peter, *Church and Realm, 1272–1461* (London, 1988)
Hellinga, Lotte and J. B. Trapp, *Cambridge History of the Book in Britain 3: 1400–1557* (Cambridge, 1999)
Helmholz, R. H., *The Oxford History of the Laws of England: The Canon Law and Ecclesiastical Jurisdiction from 597 to the 1640s* (Oxford, 2004)
Highfield, J. R., 'The English Hierarchy in the Reign of Edward III', *TRHS* 6 (1956), pp. 115–38
Hill, Felicity, *Excommunication in Thirteenth-Century England* (Oxford, 2022)
Holmes, George, *The Florentine Enlightenment, 1400–1450* (Oxford, 1969)
— 'Florentine Merchants in England, 1346–1436', *Economic History Review* 13 (1960), pp. 193–208
— *The Good Parliament* (Oxford, 1975)
Hudson, Anne, 'The Examination of Lollards', in *Lollards and Their Books* (London, 1985), pp. 125–40
— *Lollards and Their Books* (London, 1985)
— 'Lollardy: The English Heresy?', *Studies in Church History* 9 (1982), pp. 261–83
— *The Premature Reformation* (Oxford, 1988)
Hughes, Jonathan, *Dante's Divine Comedy in Early Renaissance England* (London, 2021)
— *Pastors and Visionaries* (Woodbridge, 1988)
Hyma, Albert, *The Christian Renaissance: A History of the Devotio Moderna* (Hamden, CT, 1965)
Jacob, E. F., *Archbishop Henry Chichele* (London, 1967)
— 'Canterbury Convocation of 1406', in *Essays in Medieval History Presented to Bertie Wilkinson*, ed. T. A. Sandquist and M. R. Powicke (Toronto, 1969), pp. 345–53
— *Essays in the Conciliar Epoch* (Manchester, 1963)
— *The Fifteenth Century, 1399–1485* (Oxford, 1961)
— 'Founders and Foundations in the Later Middle Ages', in *Essays in Later Medieval History* (Manchester, 1968), pp. 154–74
— 'A Note on the English Concordat of 1418', in *Medieval Studies Presented to Aubrey Gwynn*, ed. J. A. Watt, J. B. Morrall and F. X. Martin (Dublin, 1961), pp. 349–58
Jewell, Helen, 'English Bishops as Educational Benefactors in the Later Fifteenth Century', in *The Church, Politics and Patronage in the Fifteenth Century*, ed. R. B. Dobson (Gloucester, 1984), pp. 146–67
Jolliffe, J. E. A., *Angevin Kingship* (London, 1963)
Jordan, W. K., *Philanthropy in England, 1480–1660* (London, 1959)
Jurkowski, Maureen, 'The Arrest of William Thorpe in Shrewsbury and the Anti-Lollard Statute of 1406', *Historical Research* 75 (2002), pp. 273–95
— 'Henry V's Suppression of the Oldcastle Revolt', in *Henry V: New Interpretations*, ed. Gwilym Dodd (York, 2013), pp. 103–29

Kenny, Anthony, *Wyclif* (Oxford, 1985)

Ker, N. R., *Medieval Libraries of Great Britain* (London, 1964)

Kirby, J. L., 'Councils and Councillors of Henry IV, 1399–1413', *TRHS* 14 (1964), pp. 35–65

Klassen, John, *The Nobility and the Making of the Hussite Revolution* (New York, 1978)

Knowles, M. D., 'The English Bishops, 1070–1532', in *Medieval Studies Presented to Aubrey Gwynn*, ed. J. A. Watt, J. B. Morrall and F. X. Martin (Dublin, 1961), pp. 283–96

Larson, A. E., 'Are All Lollards Lollards?', *Lollards and Their Influence in Late Medieval England*, ed. F. Somerset, J. Havens and D. Pitard (Woodbridge, 2003), pp. 59–72

Lawrence, C. E., *St Edmund of Abingdon* (Oxford, 1960)

Le Goff, Jacques, *Saint Louis*, trans. G. E. Gollrad (Notre Dame, IN, 2009)

Lee, Alexandra, 'Holy Macharoni? Miracles Encouraging Participation in the Bianchi Devotions of 1399', *Medieval Journal* 10, no. 2 (2020), pp. 43–68

Lepine, David, 'Let Them Praise Him in Church: Orthodox Reform at Salisbury Cathedral in the First Half of the Fifteenth Century', in *After Arundel: Religious Writing in Fifteenth-Century England*, ed. Vincent Gillespie and Kantik Ghosh (Turnhout, 2011), pp. 167–85

Lindebaum, Sheila, 'London after Arundel', in *After Arundel: Religious Writing in Fifteenth-Century England*, ed. Vincent Gillespie and Kantik Ghosh (Turnhout, 2011), pp. 187–208

Lunt, W. E., *Financial Relations of the Papacy with England II* (Cambridge, MA, 1962)

MacCulloch, Diarmaid, *Thomas Cranmer: A Life* (New Haven and London, 1996)

McFarlane, K. B., *John Wyclif and the Beginnings of English Nonconformity* (London, 1952)

— *Lancastrian Kings and Lollard Knights* (Oxford, 1972)

McHardy, Alison, 'The Alien Priories and the Expulsion of Aliens from England in 1378', *Studies in Church History* 12 (1975), pp. 133–41

— 'The Clergy in Parliament', in *The Reign of Henry IV: Rebellion and Survival, 1403–1413*, ed. G. Dodd and D. Biggs (York, 2008), pp. 136–61

— 'De Heretico Comburendo, 1401', in *Lollardy and the Gentry in the Later Middle Ages*, ed. M. Aston and C. Richmond (Stroud, 1997), pp. 112–26

— 'Haxey's Case, 1397: The Petition and Its Presenter Reconsidered', in *The Age of Richard II*, ed. James Gillespie (Stroud, 1997), pp. 93–114

— 'John Scarle: Ambition and Politics in the Late Medieval Church', in *Image, Text and Church, 1380–1600: Essays for Margaret Aston*, ed. Linda Clark, Maureen Jurkowski and Colin Richmond (Toronto, 2009), pp. 68–93

— 'The Loss of Archbishop Stratford's Register', *HR* 70 (1997), pp. 317–21

— 'Richard II: A Personal Portrait', in *The Reign of Richard II*, ed. Gwilym Dodd (Stroud, 2000), pp. 11–32

McKisack, May, *The Fourteenth Century* (Oxford, 1959)

McNiven, Peter, *Heresy and Politics in the Reign of Henry IV* (Woodbridge, 1987)

— 'The Problem of Henry IV's Health, 1405–1413', *EHR* 100 (1985), pp. 747–72

— 'Rebellion, Sedition and the Legend of Richard II's Survival in the Reigns of Henry IV and Henry V', *BJRL* 76 (1994), pp. 93–117

Meadows, P. and N. Ramsay, eds, *A History of Ely Cathedral* (Woodbridge, 2003)

Norton, Christopher, 'Richard Scrope and York Minster', in *Richard Scrope: Archbishop, Martyr, Rebel*, ed. P. J. P. Goldberg (Donington, 2007), pp. 138–213

Ormrod, W. Mark, 'An Archbishop in Revolt: Richard Scrope and the Yorkshire Rising of 1405', in *Richard Scrope: Archbishop, Rebel, Martyr*, ed. P. J. P. Goldberg (Donington, 2007), pp. 28–44

— 'The Rebellion of Archbishop Scrope and the Tradition of Opposition to Royal Taxation', in *The Reign of Henry IV: Rebellion and Survival, 1403–1413*, ed. G. Dodd and D. Biggs (York, 2008), pp. 162–79

Oxford Dictionary of National Biography, ed. C. Matthew and B. Harrison (Oxford, 2004; and online)

Parker, Kate, 'Politics and Patronage in Lynn, 1399–1416', in *The Reign of Henry IV: Rebellion and Survival, 1403–1413*, ed. G. Dodd and D. Biggs (York, 2008), pp. 210–27

Piroyansky, Danna, '"Martyrio pulchro finitus": Archbishop Scrope's Martyrdom and the Creation of a Cult', in *Richard Scrope: Archbishop, Rebel, Martyr*, ed. P. J. P. Goldberg (Donington, 2007), pp. 100–12

Pollard, A. J., 'The Lancastrian Constitutional Experiment Revisited: Henry IV, Sir John Tiptoft and the Parliament of 1406', *Parliamentary History* 14 (1995), pp. 99–119

Powell, Edward, *Kingship, Law and Society: Criminal Justice in the Reign of Henry V* (Oxford, 1989)

Powicke, F. M., *Stephen Langton* (Oxford, 1928)

Rawcliffe, Carole, *The Staffords, Earls of Stafford and Dukes of Buckingham* (Cambridge, 1978)

Rees-Jones, Sarah and Paul Dryburgh, eds, *The Church and Northern English Society in the Fourteenth Century* (Woodbridge, 2024)

Rex, R., *The Lollards* (Basingstoke, 2002)

Richardson, H. G., 'Heresy and the Lay Power under Richard II', *EHR* 51 (1936), pp. 1–28

Richardson, H. G. and G. O. Sayles, 'Parliamentary Documents from Formularies', *BIHR* (1934), pp. 147–62

Rosenthal, Joel, 'Richard II's Bishops: Fair Weather Friends?', in *Creativity, Contradictions and Commemoration in the Reign of Richard II: Essays in Honour of Nigel Saul*, ed. J. A. Lutkin and J. S. Hamilton (Woodbridge, 2022), pp. 179–202

Ross, James, 'Seditious Activities: The Conspiracy of Maud de Vere, Countess of Oxford, 1403–4', in *The Fifteenth Century III*, ed. Linda Clark (Woodbridge, 2003), pp. 25–41

Rubin, Miri, *Charity and Community in Medieval Cambridge* (Cambridge, 1986)

Russell, Alexander, 'Conciliarism and Heresy in England', in *After Arundel: Religious Writing in Fifteenth-Century England*, ed. Vincent Gillespie and Kantik Ghosh (Turnhout, 2011), pp. 155–65

Russell-Smith, Joy, 'Walter Hilton and a Tract in Defence of the Veneration of Images', *Dominican Studies* 7 (1954), pp. 180–214

Sandler, Lucy Freeman, *The Lichtenthal Psalter and the Manuscript Patronage of the Bohun Family* (Studies in Medieval and Renaissance Art History 38, London, 2004)

Sargent, Michael, 'Bishops, Patrons, Mystics and Manuscripts: Walter Hilton, Nicholas Love and the Arundel and Holland Connections', in *Middle English Texts in Translation*, ed. Simon Horobin and Linne Mooney (Woodbridge, 2014), pp. 159–76

— 'Nicholas Love as an Ecclesiastical Reformer', *Church History and Religious Culture* 96 (2016), pp. 40–64

Saul, Nigel, *Richard II* (New Haven and London, 1997)

— 'Richard II and the City of York', in *The Government of Medieval York*, ed. Sarah Rees-Jones (York, 1997), pp. 1–13

— *Scenes from Provincial Life: Knightly Families in Sussex, 1280–1400* (Oxford, 1986)

Scase, Wendy, *Piers Plowman and the New Anticlericalism* (Cambridge, 1989)

Sherborne, J. W., 'Perjury and the Lancastrian Revolution of 1399', *Welsh History Review* 14 (1988), pp. 217–41

Smith, David, *Guide to Bishops' Registers of England and Wales* (Royal Historical Society, London, 1981)

Smith, R. A., *Canterbury Cathedral Priory: A Study in Monastic Administration* (Cambridge, 1943)

Spinka, Matthew, *John Hus: A Biography* (Princeton, 1968)

Storey, R. L., 'Clergy and Common Law in the Reign of Henry IV', in *Medieval Legal Records in Memory of C. A. F. Meekings*, ed. R. Hunnisett and J. Post (London, 1978), pp. 342–408

— 'Episcopal King-Makers in the Fifteenth Century', in *The Church, Politics and Patronage in the Fifteenth Century*, ed. R. B. Dobson (Gloucester, 1984), pp. 82–98

Suerbaum, Almut, George Southcombe and Benjamin Thompson, 'Introduction', in *Polemic: Language as Violence in Medieval and Early Modern Discourse*, ed. Almut Suerbaum, George Southcombe and Benjamin Thompson (Farnham, 2015), pp. 1–14

Sutherland, Annie, 'Psalms as Polemic: The English Bible Debate', in *Polemic: Language as Violence in Medieval and Early Modern Discourse*, ed. Almut Suerbaum, George Southcombe and Benjamin Thompson (Farnham, 2015), pp. 149–63

Swabey, Ffiona, *The Medieval Gentlewoman: Life in a Gentry Household in the Later Middle Ages* (Stroud, 1999)

Swanson, R. N., 'Archbishop Arundel and the Chapter of York', *BIHR* 54 (1981), pp. 254–7

— *Universities, Academics and the Great Schism* (Cambridge, 1979)

Tatton-Brown, Tim, 'The Rebuilding of the Nave and Western Transepts, 1377–1503', in *Canterbury Cathedral Nave: Archaeology, History and Architecture*, ed. Kevin Blockley, Margaret Sparks and Tim Tatton-Brown (Canterbury, 1997), pp. 128–46

Thompson, Benjamin, 'Locality and Ecclesiastical Polity: The Late Medieval Church between Duality and Integration', in *Political Society in Late Medieval England: A Festschrift for Christine Carpenter*, ed. Benjamin Thompson and John Watts (Woodbridge, 2015), pp. 113–45

— 'The Polemic of Reform in the Later Medieval English Church', in *Polemic: Language as Violence in Medieval and Early Modern Discourse*, ed. Almut Suerbaum, George Southcombe and Benjamin Thompson (Farnham, 2015), pp. 183–222

— 'The Prelates and the Alien Priories', in *The Prelate in England and Europe, 1300–1560*, ed. Martin Heale (Woodbridge, 2014), pp. 50–75

Thompson, E. P., *The Making of the English Working Class* (London, 1963)

Thomson, J. A. F., 'Knightly Piety', in *Lollardy and the Gentry in the Later Middle Ages*, ed. M. Aston and C. Richmond (Stroud, 1997), pp. 95–111

Tout, T. F., *Chapters in the Administrative History of Medieval England* (6 vols, Manchester, 1920–33)

Tuck, Anthony, *Richard II and the English Nobility* (London, 1973)
Vale, Malcolm, *Henry V: The Conscience of a King* (New Haven and London, 2016)
Verfaillie-Markey, Dominique, 'Deux inscriptions grattées dans le psautier d'Eadwine', *Scriptorium* 39 (1985–6), pp. 97–102
Victoria History of the Counties of England, volumes consulted:
Essex, vol. 2, ed. William Page and J. Horace Round (London, 1907)
Kent, vol. 2, ed. William Page (London, 1926)
Shropshire, vol. 6, part 1: *Shrewsbury*, ed. E. Williamson (London, 2014)
Wiltshire, vol. 3, ed. R. B. Pugh and Elizabeth Crittall (London, 1956)
Vittorini, D., 'Salutati's Letters to the Archbishop of Canterbury: A Note on Humanism in the Fourteenth Century', *Modern Languages Journal* 36 (1952), pp. 373–7
Walker, Simon, *The Lancastrian Affinity, 1361–1399* (Oxford, 1990)
— 'Letters to the Dukes of Lancaster in 1381 and 1399', *EHR* 106 (1991), pp. 68–79
— 'The Yorkshire Risings of 1405: Texts and Contexts', in *Henry IV: The Establishment of the Regime, 1399–1406*, ed. Gwilym Dodd and Douglas Biggs (York, 2003), pp. 161–84
Ward, Jennifer, *English Noblewomen in the Later Middle Ages* (London, 1992)
— 'Joan de Bohun, Countess of Hereford, Essex and Northampton, c. 1370–1419: Family, Land and Social Networks', *Essex Archaeology and History* 32 (2001), pp. 146–53
— *Women in England in the Middle Ages* (London, 2006)
Watson, Nicholas, 'Censorship and Cultural Change in Late Medieval England: Vernacular Theology, the Oxford Translation Debate, and Arundel's Constitutions of 1409', *Speculum* 70 (1995), pp. 822–64
Wilkinson, B., *The Chancery under Edward III* (Manchester, 1929)
Wilks, Michael, 'Thomas Arundel of York: The Appellant Archbishop', in *Life and Thought in the Northern Church: Essays in Honour of Claire Cross, Studies in Church History*, subsidia 12 (1999), pp. 67–86
Woodruff, C. E. and W. Danks, *Memorials of Canterbury Cathedral* (London, 1912)
Woolgar, C. M., *The Great Household in Late Medieval England* (New Haven and London, 1999)
Wright, Edmund, 'Henry IV, the Commons and the Recovery of Royal Finance in 1407', in *Rulers and Ruled in Late Medieval England: Essays Presented to Gerald Harriss*, ed. Rowena Archer and Simon Walker (London, 1995), pp. 65–81
Wylie, J. H., *History of England under Henry the Fourth* (4 vols, London, 1884–98)
Wylie, J. H. and W. Waugh, *The Reign of Henry V* (3 vols, Cambridge, 1914–29)
Yeager, R. F., 'Gower's "Epistle to Archbishop Arundel": The Evidence of Oxford, All Souls College, MS 98', in *Manuscript and Print in Late Medieval and Early Modern Britain: Essays in Honour of Professor Julia Boffey*, ed. Tamara Atkin and Jaclyn Rajsic (Cambridge, 2019), pp. 13–34

Index